CW01099375

LIBYA: THE STRUGGLE FOR SURVIVAL

Libya: The Struggle for Survival

Geoff Simons

Foreword by

Tam Dalyell, MP

MACMILLAN

First published 1993 by
THE MACMILLAN PRESS LTD
Houndmills, Basingstoke, Hampshire RG21 2XS
and London
Companies and representatives
throughout the world

ISBN 0–333–58886–X hardcover

A catalogue record for this book is available
from the British Library

Printed in Great Britain by
Mackays of Chatham PLC
Chatham, Kent

What more can they do? They have imposed some kind of embargo on Libya for 15 years. They have already bombed us, killed women and children. All that is left for them now is to test their nuclear weapons on Libya.

Colonel Muammar al-Gaddafi, 1992

Third World countries such as Libya and Pakistan could become targets of American strategic nuclear missiles under secret plans being drawn up by the Pentagon.

The Sunday Times, 9 February 1992

Contents

Foreword

by Tam Dalyell, MP

Leptis Magna, an hour's drive from Tripoli, surpasses any set of monuments in the Roman Empire, including Imperial Rome herself. Libya was the breadbasket of that empire, and today's Libyans pointed out to me and other British Members of the House of Commons visiting Libya in 1991 that their ancestors provided many of the best artists and craftsmen of Ancient Rome.

It is one of the many strengths of Geoff Simons's scholarly and revealing book that he shows that no Westerner can understand the present Libya without understanding the past. He illuminates Italian colonialism and Libya for those whose interest and knowledge have hitherto been confined to El Alamein, the battles of the Eighth Army, Rommel and Montgomery.

For most of the first half of the twentieth century, the Libyan people had been forced to wage war against successive colonial invaders – Turks, Italians, Germans, French and British – with all the consequences for the human lives and communities that this implies. Towns and cities, like Tobruk, were razed to the ground: whole communities were deported for incarceration in concentration camps; civilians and combatants alike were tortured and bombed; their livestock slaughtered; the survivors were racially abused, exploited as forced labour, and reduced to penury.

How many people in Britain or America realise that for years after the end of the Second World War Libya was littered with landmines and other anti-personnel devices, making farming in Cyrenaica a hazardous enterprise? Simons points out that a paper presented by the Institute of Diplomatic Studies to a Geneva-based seminar on 'War Remnants in Libya' (May 1981) emphasises that no less than sixty-eight per cent of all agricultural land was mined. When I went to Libya in 1991, I met serious and cultivated men who argued that the Second World War combatants – Germany, Italy and Britain – should pay reparations for the hundreds of Libyans killed and injured since the war by bombs and mines.

Nor have relations with the United States been any happier in recent times. Geoff Simons displays an insight into the indifference among the powerful men of Washington towards law when they wish to pursue their own strategic interests. He sets out – in what Washington perceived as propitious international circumstances – how the United States decided to target the Libyan regime of Colonel Gaddafi. The widely suspected complicity of Syria, a Gulf-War ally, and Iran in the Lockerbie bombing was to be ignored. Libya, for *raisons d'état*, was to be the sole publicly branded culprit. For months the United States made no attempt whatever to observe its obligations under the 1971 Montreal Convention: an agreement specifically designed to combat terrorist attacks on civilian aircraft. I agree with Simons that all efforts at mediation and compromise – by Dr Boutros Ghali, President Mubarak, the Arab League, the Maltese government, the Libyan authorities themselves and others – have been routinely rejected by Washington and London, interested more in targeting Colonel Muammar Gaddafi than in bringing the two accused men to court.

Lockerbie certainly was the biggest crime against Western civilians since 1945. It was horrendous to visit Lockerbie. The police from the area which I represent in the British House of Commons, and where I live, had to take an active part, day after day, in the dreadful task of clearing up the debris, human and material. On the other hand, I was no less shocked by visiting the bedroom in Tripoli, where Colonel Gaddafi's sixteen-month-old daughter, her pathetic toys scattered round the room, had been killed by American bombers, flying from British bases in 1986. I was equally horrified by the results of the 1986 attack by American, British-based, bombers on working-class housing areas of Benghazi.

Simons exposes the extent to which double-standards have been allowed to prevail. Libya was a convenient, relatively weak, unpopular target, in circumstances where similar criteria might have been applied to Jordanians and Palestinians, Iranians and Syrians. Particularly, since it has been no longer restrained by the power of the Soviet Union on the Security Council, I believe the Americans have manipulated the United Nations to the point of gross abuse, by making promises of financial help to malleable small countries, rotating in their membership of the Security Council, thus obtaining a majority for US policy.

The cause of justice should not be sacrificed on the altar of diplomatic convenience. Simons shows how the United States has succeeded in defining for its own purposes the parameters of the Lockerbie question. There was no longer any debate about who was responsible for the outrage: whether the evidence, as formerly believed over a lengthy period, pointed to Syrian and Iranian – as well as Libyan – involvement. The only issue was how the US-dominated Security Council could be induced to tighten further the noose around Libya.

Simons recognises the extent to which Libya itself has evolved, not least in its attitude towards terrorism. Economic policy has discernibly shifted in the direction of liberalisation. There is an evident movement away from the moral and practical help for dissident groups throughout the world, and constructive steps have been taken through discussion and real initiatives to improve relations with many other countries.

Allow me, finally, an unpopular opinion, which many ecologists would dispute. I believe that in the twenty-first century, Colonel Gaddafi's government will come to be seen as one of the most effective 'ecologically imaginative' governments of the twentieth century. The Great Man-made River Project might well turn out to be one of the soundest schemes ever devised. I can only say that I was convinced by the engineers and scientists, in the desert south of Benghazi, whom I saw working on the project in 1991.

Geoff Simons has performed a service to the English-speaking world by writing the first serious and comprehensive assessment of the late twentieth-century Libya available in the English language.

Preface

I came to write this book on Libya out of a growing interest in the countries of the region, following the 1991 Gulf war. It seemed to me, and still does, that a principal reason for the Gulf conflict was the requirement of the United States that Gulf oil remain in compliant hands. In the event the US was able to deploy massive military forces far from the United States without any significant political constraint. This circumstance, at a time when the Soviet Union was obligingly dissolving itself, was bound to influence Washington's perception of the extent to which it could move against recalcitrant states.

The world did not have to wait long. Apart from the unfinished business of Saddam Hussein it soon became clear that Colonel Muammar Gaddafi's Libya was high on the agenda for US attention, a priority much stimulated by the needs of an unpopular President Bush in an election year. So 1991/92 saw a rapid escalation of the pressure applied by the West to Colonel Gaddafi.

We do not have to agree with any or all of the policies of the Libyan government to question the amorality and political cynicism of the Western consensus framed by Washington. It is useful on occasions to explore in an independent spirit such matters as how the mass media work to manufacture public political perceptions and how powerful nation-states might subvert nominally supra-national institutions. More than one observer has remarked that double standards are the principal currency of the New World Order. There are issues here that relate to law, human rights, and the security of small states that presume to disagree with powerful nations.

Libya is a vast country with a sparse population. Its land area is 1,759,540 sq. km. (679,180 sq. miles), much larger than Britain, France and Germany combined; its population, at around 4.5 million, is less than half that of London. Away from the coastal areas much of the land is desert and there are few national resources – apart from some of the largest oil reserves in the world.

It is oil, coupled with radical political leadership, that has enabled Libya to work a social transformation and also to have a regional influence – for good or ill – out of all proportion to the size of its population (Libya's two main North African neighbours, Algeria and Egypt, have populations of 22 million and 50 million respectively). It is also oil that makes Libya of continual interest to energy-hungry nations, especially the United States.

With the growth of national economies and the corresponding depletion of energy resources this interest is bound to increase in the years to come.

GEOFF SIMONS

Acknowledgements

A few individuals have been very helpful and supportive during the time I wrote this book. I am particularly grateful to Tam Dalyell (Labour MP for Linlithgow, a tenacious man who works hard to expose the truth behind political façades), for writing the Foreword and for making available his personal material on Libya; and to Harold Pinter for his enthusiastic support for this book. I am also grateful to Martin Wattam (Librarian at the United Nations Information Centre, London) for finding time to send me relevant items; and to the staff of Manchester Central Library who, though having to cope with severe and debilitating cut-backs, were always pleasant and industrious in helping with research requests.

I am pleased to acknowledge permission to use two items of copyright material: Figure 5.1 from *Libya: The Experience of Oil* by J. A. Allan (published by Croom Helm, 1981); and Figure 6.1 from *Libyan Politics, Tribe and Revolution* by John Davis (published by I. B. Tauris, 1987).

I appreciate also the efforts of Colette Simons for acquiring relevant texts. Cornel Simons also helped in various ways.

As always I am grateful to my wife Chris for her various suggestions and contributions, for her critical readings of the entire text, and for tolerating my insistent arguments, often into the early hours when we should both have been asleep.

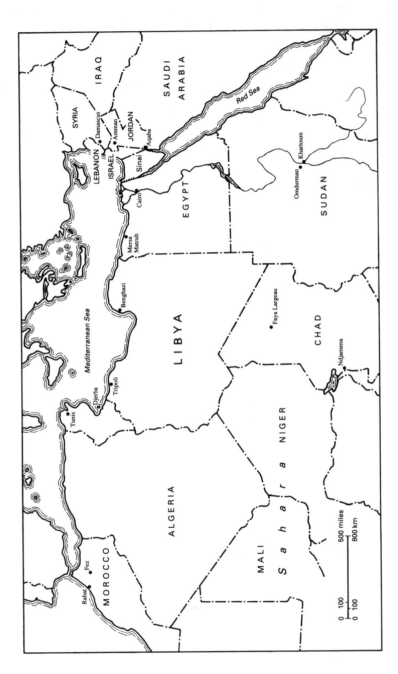

Map 1   North Africa

Map 2   Libya

Introduction

Libya is widely perceived as a terrorist state, harbouring terrorists within its borders and supporting terrorist groups around the world. The Libyan leadership, headed by Colonel Muammar al-Gaddafi since 1969, has also frequently sought to exploit political tensions in the region, to the point of military intervention and encouraging attempted *coups d'état*, in the interests of wider political objectives. For more than two decades Libya has coexisted uneasily with its neighbours and in the wider world community, unwilling to observe what most other nations claim to recognise as the proper protocols of international behaviour. In such a context it has been easy to dub Libya a 'pariah nation', led by a maverick trouble-maker, a madman even, intent only on the use of violence to further his personal political ambitions.

There is also another Libya, a vulnerable Third-World state, rich in oil but without a broad-based economic infrastructure, a sparsely populated nation that watches with trepidation the hostile moves of powerful countries in a shrinking and energy-hungry world. Throughout most of its history Libya has suffered as a conquered nation, as wave upon wave of invaders swept across the deserts of North Africa. The Phoenicians, Greeks, Romans, Turks, Italians, British – all for a time occupied the coastal towns and the more accessible areas of the vast Libyan hinterland. All, except the Arabs, departed but all left indelible marks on the national culture. For most of the twentieth century Libya was a colony, forced to suffer the humiliations and depradations wrought by foreigners. Even when independent, under a fiercely nationalist leadership, it was helpless to resist military attacks.

What may be termed the 'Libyan Question' can only be fully appreciated by considering how the two Libyas have evolved over time: how on the one hand a weak Third-World nation, with perceptions shaped by remembered pains brought by foreigners, continues to struggle for dignity and self-sufficiency in a hostile world; and how, on the other, this particular oil-rich state can be branded as responsible for violent outrages around the world. A key consideration is the nature of the conflict between Libya (population: 4.5 million) and the United States (population: 240 million) in circumstances where the Soviet Union has collapsed and where the US, through prodigious military power rather than secure economic strength, is uniquely placed to influence the global political climate.

This book considers the position of Libya in the 'New World Order'; in particular, in the context of the Lockerbie bombing and of how through the 1980s there was a progressive worsening of US/Libyan relations. These recent developments are set against a history of Libya: to indicate how the temper of today's Libyan leadership is itself conditioned by such factors as historical circumstance, Islamic conviction, pan-Arabic aspiration, and sensitivity to the pressure of external colonial and neo-colonial ambitions. One aim is to encourage an understanding of the Libyan Question that goes beyond the facile ploys designed by powerful states to disguise their hidden political agendas.

Part I (Chapter 1) suggests that analysis of the Lockerbie and UTA terrorist outrages should be considered in the context of other relevant events and developments. Thus the Lockerbie and UTA bombings are set against the US bombing of Libya in 1986 and the shooting down of the Iranian civil airliner by the USS *Vincennes* in 1988. Key aspects of the Lockerbie enquiry are highlighted. The relevance of the recent Gulf wars to the emergence of the US-defined New World Order is then considered, followed by evidence of Washington's indifference to the requirements of international law when perceived US interests are at stake.

The events leading to the decision to label Libya as the sole culprit for the Lockerbie and UTA bombings are charted, contrasting this decision with the earlier official statements that there was clear evidence of Syrian, Iranian and Palestinian complicity. This chronology clearly suggests the possibility of a US-inspired cover-up[1] designed to deflect accusations away from states with whom the US now wanted pragmatic political accommodations. The possibility of a multilayered cover-up gained further publicity when the Pan Am insurers claimed that the US government was being 'deliberately evasive, if not deliberately untruthful' when it claimed to have no information on how the bomb came to be on the aircraft.[2] A profile is also given of the events leading to the passing of the first UN sanctions resolution (Resolution 748, see Appendix 6) on Libya, with emphasis on how Washington pressured Security Council members to delivery the necessary vote. Such events have led many observers to suggest that the United Nations is today being divided and subverted in the interests of international power politics.[3]

The limited sanctions had little impact. Libya's diplomatic connections with several countries were reduced, with their airspace closed to Libyan aircraft. Planes sent to Egypt, Tunisia, Malta and Switzerland were refused permission to land and were turned back. Libya began ordering the expulsion of foreign diplomats in clear retaliation, notifying the mission heads of France, Italy, Germany, Belgium, Japan, Sweden and Czechoslovakia that 'within the framework of reciprocity' the numbers of their diplomats would have to be reduced. Increasingly it became clear that 'the US and Britain intend to maintain sanctions even if the Lockerbie suspects are surrendered'.[4] There was at the same time increasing speculation that the initial, relatively mild sanctions were a prelude to an embargo on Libyan oil sales and the launching of a unilateral US military strike.

Syria was soon indicating that it intended to defy the UN embargo on flights to Libya, with Iraq also declaring that it would ignore the measures stipulated by the UN Security Council. Syria's attempt to fly a plane to Tripoli was blocked by other states refusing to grant overflying permission,[5] but President Hafez al-Assad of Syria began a tour of the Gulf to muster support for Libya. Said one diplomat in the Gulf, 'Assad's view is – today Libya, tomorrow Syria.'[6] In the Israeli-occupied Gaza strip and West Bank at least twenty-eight Palestinians backing Colonel Gaddafi were shot and wounded by Israeli troops, and the Palestinian leader Ahmed Jibril, at one time himself accused by the West of involvement in the Lockerbie bombing, declared that his men were ready 'to champion the Libyan people'.

Russia, keen to support the US-inspired sanctions resolution, began withdrawing some of its 3000 nationals in Libya, but most nationals – including 10,000 Europeans – from other countries continued to work as usual. The 5000 British nationals, according to reports, stayed cool in Libya.[7] Tiny Rowland, the Lonrho chief, felt obliged to defend his business dealings with Libya ('I saw Colonel Gaddafi for several hours last week. His views weren't unreasonable . . .'),[8] and Paul Spicer, Lonrho joint deputy chairman, strongly dismissed speculation that the company's assets might be frozen in the United States because of Lonrho trade with Libya.[9] Kate Adie, the BBC reporter, was expelled from Libya for allegedly insulting officials, and the leading British legal firm Peter Carter-Ruck and Partners, having agreed to defend the two accused Libyans, wondered how in the light of travel restrictions it would now be able to send specialists to Tripoli.

In his first interview since the passing of UN Resolution 748 and the consequent implementation of sanctions Colonel Gaddafi appeared to be hardening his attitude.[10] He would not now, contrary to earlier assurances, give information about his dealings with the IRA: 'If I give them such a history of our connections, then they would use this information to accuse me of specific crimes. It would create another problem such as the Lockerbie accusations.' More importantly, given the supposed purpose of 748, he reiterated his refusal to hand over the two Libyans accused of the Lockerbie bombing. One problem is that one of the accused belongs to the Magaref tribe of Major Abdel Salem Jalloud, Gaddafi's fiery second-in-command. According to the Libyans, to surrender the two men would not remove sanctions but would be more likely to stimulate further Western demands.

The impasse, with various veiled threats continuing to be made by Britain and the United States, was easy to comprehend. The US, having mobilised the necessary Security Council majority (but not a consensus), was obliged to stand firm, while Colonel Gaddafi saw no advantage in surrendering the two men (the West was on record as saying that this alone would not allow sanctions to be removed). The scene was set for a temporary stalemate prior to an escalation, in one form or another, of the conflict. Libya, with much experience of foreign encroachments on its land and of foreign erosions of its natural sovereignty, thought it knew what to expect. There were many lessons in history . . . .

Part II (Chapters 2–6) presents a history of Libya from the earliest times to the present. The Italian depiction of Libya as Italy's 'Fourth Shore', and the subsequent conquest (Chapter 3), signalled how Libya (and other Third-World nations) were traditionally viewed by European colonial powers. The struggle to independence and to republican status (Chapters 4 and 5) have to be understood in the context of this history of oppression. Chapter 6 profiles some key aspects of the Libyan revolution, a multifaceted and important phenomenon, however in the comfortable West we may choose to criticise it for its limitations, its brutalities or its inherent contradictions.

In **Part III** a profile is given of another important outgrowth of the Libyan revolution, foreign adventures including terrorism (Chapter 7), and the US response (Chapter 8). Here there are immense difficulties in establishing exactly what terrorist outrages Libya has supported and what terrorist groups, despite its assurances to the contrary, it still supports. We cannot rely on accusations from Washington: the US has been wrong in the past (Chapter 8) and its disinformation campaigns have been exposed.[11] Nor can we rely on the copious accusations issuing from such interested organisations as the Israeli Mossad, itself well aware of how propaganda can be used to effect. However, we do not need to rely on the CIA and Israel to tell us that Libya has supported terrorism. In recent interviews, Colonel Gaddafi has admitted as much.[12]

The ethical problem for the West – distinct from its *realpolitik* successes – is that the United States, manifestly keen to establish itself as a ubiquitous judge and jury, has itself supported terrorists, death squads and violent insurrections.[13] This is one of the hard facts, uncongenial to the West, that has to be faced before the nature of the Libyan Question can be more fully comprehended. One purpose of the present book is to encourage this deeper understanding.

1. The likelihood of a cover-up over Lockerbie will surprise no one who considers how Washington withheld and misrepresented information about the bombing of Cambodia, Operation Phoenix (for mass assassinations in Vietnam), Operations Mongoose and AM/LASH (for the assassination of Fidel Castro and the destruction of the Cuban regime), the assassinations of the Kennedys, Watergate, Irangate, BCCI, the 'friendly fire' deaths of nine British soldiers in the 1991 Gulf war (104 inconsistencies in submitted evidence, according to the legal representations at the Oxford, England, hearings on 11 May 1992), and many other instances. We have now learned from US congressman Henry Gonzalez how President Bush and his most senior advisers ordered a cover-up to conceal their illegal support for Saddam Hussein right up to the start of the Gulf war. This involved lying to Congress, withholding information, and falsifying Commerce Department records (see Simon Tisdall, 'Saddamgate and Mr Bush', *The Guardian* (London), 2–3 May 1992).

2. John Merritt, 'Bomb Victims Accuse Pan Am of Dirty Tricks', *The Observer* (London), 26 April 1992; Leonard Doyle, 'US Intelligence Agencies to be Criticised in Lockerbie Trial', *The Independent* (London), 27 April 1992; Leonard Doyle, 'Lockerbie Trial Ruling Fuels US Cover-up Theory', *The Independent* (London), 28 April 1992. It was also reported (*The Sunday Times*, London, 10 May 1992) that the journalist David Leppard was being taken to court by Pan Am to try to force him to hand over confidential Lockerbie documents, but that 'British ministers want to prevent this because Leppard's inquiries throw doubt on the view of Western governments that the bombing was the work of Libya alone'.

3. David Hirst, 'How to Inflate a Demagogue', *The Guardian* (London), 15 April 1992; Leonard Doyle, 'Libyan Embargo Shatters the UN Consensus', *The Independent* (London), 18 April 1992; Hameed Moolla, 'International Law's Limits' (letter), *The Guardian* (London), 18 April 1992; William F. Pepper, 'Libya Ruling Undermines World Law' (letter), *The Independent* (London), 18 April 1992; Adrian Hamilton, 'West Misuses UN in Crusade Against Libya', *The Observer* (London), 19 April 1992.

4. David Hirst and Hella Pick, 'Libya Expels Diplomats as US and Britain Turn Up Heat', *The Guardian* (London), 17 April 1992.

5. 'Syria Blocked in Attempt to Flout UN Sanctions', *The Guardian* (London), 21 April 1992.

6. 'Syrians Seek Aid for Libya on Sanctions', *The Independent* (London), 21 April 1992.

7. Phil Davison, 'Britons Stay Cool in Libya', *Independent on Sunday* (London), 19 April 1992; David Hirst, 'Expatriates Remain Cool Amid the Libyan Heat', *The Guardian* (London), 16 April 1992.

8. Tiny Rowland, 'Why I'm Doing Business with Gaddafi', *The Observer* (London), 3 May 1992.

9. 'Lonrho Denies Blacklist Claim', *The Observer* (London), 3 May 1992.

10. Marle Colvin, 'Gadaffi Goes Back on his Promise to Reveal IRA Deals', *The Sunday Times* (London), 10 May 1992.

11. Bob Woodward, *Veil: The Secret Wars of the CIA, 1981–1987* (London: Simon and Schuster, 1987).

12. Donald Trelford, interview with Muammar al-Gaddafi, *The Observer*

(London), 26 January 1992; Marle Colvin, interview with Muammar al-Gaddafi, *The Observer* (London), 10 May 1992.

13.   An exhaustive listing of the cases that have reached the public domain would be lengthy and tedious. Here we need cite only the US support for, or tolerance of: the military coups in Vietnam, Chile and Iran; the Indonesian invasion of East Timor, the Israeli invasion of Lebanon, and the South African invasion of Namibia; the death squads of Guatemala and El Salvador; and the terrorists in Nicaragua, southern Africa and Afghanistan.

Part I

Libya in the
New World Order

1 Lockerbie, Libya and the West

. . . the central lesson of World Order . . . we [the US] are the masters, and you shine our shoes

Noam Chomsky, 1991

In 1991 the noose again began to tighten on Libya. The noose had been there for almost two decades, the tension varying over the years according to American whim and the vagaries of Libyan politics. Libya, under the radical leadership of Muammar al-Gaddafi, had long been available for US attention. In 1991 circumstances again conspired to bring Libya from the back burner to the front, a transition that again concentrated independent minds on the nature of international terrorism, the rule of law, and the political pressures than can be exercised by powerful states.

With the dissolution of the Warsaw Pact, the 'democratisation' of Eastern Europe and the collapse of the Soviet Union, the United States rushed to proclaim itself winner of the Cold War. The second recent war in the Gulf had demonstrated not only American military power but also how the United Nations – created in 1945 *'to save succeeding generations from the scourge of war'* – could be induced to underwrite a massive military conflict. The end of the Cold War did not herald a new age of peace and tranquillity. The United States, seemingly still beset by sin on all sides, resolved to chastise the enemies of virtue, from upstart Third World nations to an alarmingly threatening superpower in the East. There were fresh confrontations to endure, possibly new wars to fight.[1] In such a scenario it was inevitable that Libya's Colonel Gaddafi would soon be given the attention Washington knew he deserved. His likely involvement in at least two recent terrorist outrages was the the pretext, the excuse, or the just cause.

OUTRAGES

At about 7.00 p.m. on 21 December 1988 a Pan American World Airways jumbo jet, Flight PA 103, was flying six miles high over the Scottish

3

borders. The Boeing 747-121, *Maid of the Seas*, was travelling from London's Heathrow airport to John F. Kennedy airport in New York. The pilot, James MacQuarrie, and his co-pilot, Raymond Wagner, had switched on the autopilot for what was intended to be a routine overnight flight. At 7.03 p.m. a small terrorist bomb exploded in the cargo hold, punching a hole in the fuselage, and sending fragments of suitcase, clothing and other debris into the void. The blast severed the plane's electrical power supply and there was no chance to send even the start of a distress call. The early reports, before the bomb explosion had been confirmed, could only note that the Boeing had broken up so suddenly that no message could be sent, and so dramatically that wreckage and human victims were scattered over large areas of Lockerbie and the surrounding countryside. It was a secondary shock wave that was to cause the deaths of MacQuarrie, Wagner, the other crew members and the 243 passengers. This secondary shock wave burst a large jagged hole in the side of the aircraft, probably injuring some passengers and signalling to others that the plane was starting to disintegrate. Fractures from the starburst hole spread rapidly in various directions, one fracture running for more than 40 feet along the fuselage. Within seconds the skin panels were peeling backwards and the entire nose section had fallen away. As the shattered aircraft plunged into a vertical dive the engines were torn off and baggage and passengers were disgorged into the freezing atmosphere. The wings, carrying more than 200,000 pounds of aviation fuel, crashed at a speed of more than 200 miles per hour into Sherwood Crescent, a small street adjoining the main A74 Glasgow-England road. The blast registered 1.6 at a nearby seismic monitoring station and the fireball was visible more than six miles away. Several houses were vaporised by the explosion and others were gutted by fire.[2]

Most of the passengers on the *Maid of the Seas* were Americans, flying home for Christmas reunions with their families. They included servicemen and thirty-eight students from Syracuse University in New York state. It soon emerged that US embassies had received a warning that a Pan American flight would be a terrorist target for a bomb. British MPs expressed concern that the Heathrow authorities had not been told of the threat that was known to US officials.

At 8.45 a.m. on 19 September 1989 a French DC-10 airliner, UTA 772, left Brazzaville in the Congo; after a brief stopover in Chad, the plane flew north across the Sahara. About forty-five minutes later, at just after one o'clock, a terrorist bomb exploded, ripping the aircraft apart and killing all the passengers and crew. Parts of the aircraft, fragments of the bomb and the mutilated passengers were spewed over an area of 640 square kilometres in the Niger Ténéré desert. The cockpit was found more than five kilometres from the fuselage. In the weeks that followed, French paratroops, working in temperatures approaching 60 degrees Centigrade, were to collect more than 85,000 pieces of aircraft debris for reassembly in an aircraft hanger outside Paris. It was subsequently found that the bomb had been placed on the aircraft at Brazzaville. The blowing up of UTA 772 was the worst terrorist outrage that France had suffered. In an ITN television broadcast in December 1991 it was declared that the French authorities still did not know who had planted the bomb. At the same time efforts were being made to convince the world that the Libyan government had sole responsibility for the outrage.

The terrorist attacks on PA 103 and UTA 772 can be viewed as discrete outrages unrelated to prior political events, horrendous onslaughts on innocent human beings. However, such events do not occur in a political vacuum, divorced from a range of other grievances. We do not need to excuse gross acts of terrorism to remember that there are precedents to such outrages, events that can well serve to motivate those with a thirst for vengeance. Here we need only recall two such events: the 1986 bombing of Libya and the shooting down in 1988 of the Iranian airbus.

BOMBING LIBYA*

On 15 April 1986 American aircraft, flying from bases in Britain and carriers in the Mediterranean, bombed Tripoli and Benghazi. This was a much heralded air attack: the previous evening an American television correspondent had been informed by his Washington office that 'something would happen that night or the next morning'.[3] Similarly an American reporter at the El Khebir Hotel in Tripoli was told by the foreign desk of his newspaper that an air strike was imminent. Shortly before 2 a.m. thirteen F-111 fighter bombers, having flown from the UK, and three radar jamming aircraft roared over Tripoli; bombs and missiles hit the airport, the Aziziya Barracks, and various civilian targets. Most of the air defence radar had

---

*The circumstances of the 1986 bombing of Tripoli and Benghazi are considered in Chapter Eight. Particular attention is given to 'La Belle justification' to show how the United States is sometimes prone to take drastic action on the basis of only slender evidence.

been rendered useless but a gunner at the Aziziya Barracks managed to hit an F-111 that subsequently crashed in flames in the Mediterranean. Aircraft from the Sixth Fleet – Hornet and Tomcat fighters, Corsair jets, Hawkeye command planes and anti-radar prowlers – had already hit a number of targets in Benghazi.

Washington had assured the British cabinet that only military and terrorist targets would be hit. Each aircraft weapons officer was to have a 'double lock-on' – fixing the target with both infra-red night sight and Pave Track radar – before he would release his bombs, but such precautions proved to be inadequate. Soon journalists were being taken to see where bombs had fallen in residential areas of Tripoli: private villas had suffered direct hits and the front had been blasted out of an apartment building. The French embassy had been badly damaged and the building next to it completely destroyed. The journalists were shown civilian houses destroyed and bodies in the ruins; a child's foot was seen sticking out of the rubble.[4] Wounded people were shown in the central hospital, and bodies in the central mortuary; a bucket contained the skin of two people.[5]

At first Washington, alarmed at the graphic television pictures that were coming out of Libya, denied that the human carnage and damage to buildings had been caused by US bombs and missiles. Perhaps Libyan shells had fallen back on the residential areas. Perhaps bombs had fallen off the wings of American aircraft by accident. Perhaps the Libyans had deliberately destroyed buildings and then blamed the Americans. Washington need not have worried: its principal constituency, the American people, approved the specific air strike and the general strategy. Polls showed a 77% approval rating, and President Reagan's foreign policy rating shot up in less than a week from 51% to 76%. The White House switchboard was flooded with congratulatory calls, and many Americans rang the British embassy to thank Prime Minister Thatcher for her complicity. There was regret that Colonel Gaddafi had not been killed. Thus Daniel Pipes, of the Foreign Research Institute in Philadelphia, commented that the next attack on Libya 'should use massive force, anything in between is not effective'.[6] Ted Kennedy opined that he was sure 'that all Americans will stand with the President'; and *The New York Times* declared that 'even the most scrupulous citizen can only approve and applaud the American attacks on Libya . . . if there were such a thing as due process in the court of world opinion, the United States has prosecuted and punished [Gaddafi] carefully, proportionately – and justly'.[7] President Reagan was merely reflecting the American consensus, fashioned by pliant media, when he declared that Colonel Gaddafi was a 'flaky barbarian' and a 'mad dog'. Many Americans hoped that there would be a chance to strike at Libya again.

THE *VINCENNES* DISASTER

On 3 July 1988 the US guided missile cruiser *Vincennes* mistakenly shot down an Iranian airliner on a regular flight over the Gulf. A Standard missile achieved a direct hit on the airbus, killing all 286 people on board. The *Vincennes* had been engaged in a skirmish involving one of its helicopters and Iranian armed speedboats, and at first it was claimed that the ship had shot down an attacking F-14 Tomcat aircraft. Only later did the *Vincennes* Captain Will Rogers admit what had happened whereupon President Reagan, though 'saddened by this terrible tragedy' stated that the *Vincennes* had taken the 'proper defensive action'. The Iranian Prime Minister Mousavi declared that the United States would not be 'exempt from the consequences'.

This was the first direct evidence that the high-technology Aegis missile system was unable to distinguish between a Tomcat with a 64-fleet wing-span and an airliner almost three times as big. Moreover, as Iran Air Flight IR 655 approached the *Vincennes* the plane did not switch on the fire control radar that would have confirmed its hostile intent. Captain Will Rogers was confident that he was following standard procedure, as indeed was Iran Air captain Mohsen Rezaeian. It has been suggested that IR 655's rate of ascent was normal: in his last message to the Bandar Abbas control tower Rezaeian said he was climbing to 14,000 feet. Yet the Americans gave a conflicting version and repeatedly changed their story.[7]

The Americans first denied everything; then Admiral William Crowe, a chairman of the Joint Chiefs of Staff, admitted that the *Vincennes* had shot down an Iranian airbus, claiming that it had been spotted at 7000 feet descending towards the ship. This is now taken to be an absurd suggestion, though it remains odd that an Iran Air captain should have been prepared to fly a civilian airbus over a military confrontation. One suggestion is that the Bandar Abbas control tower received warnings from the US ship but failed to pass on the warnings to IR 655. Here an Iranian source has been quoted: 'The Americans issue warnings all the time. The Iranians think to themselves, "What right do the Americans have to give warnings to us in our own territory? What right do they have to be there anyway?"'[8]

There was ambiguity about the information obtained by the Americans and the actual messages that they claimed to have sent. At first they said that they had received no information from the airbus, but then changed their story to say that two messages had been received, one suggesting that the plane was civilian and one suggesting it was military. Iran claimed that this was impossible, an assertion supported by a Dubai source confirming that Iran Air had recently ordered two replacement transponders for the airbus.

Significantly enough, another American warship in the Gulf, the *John H Sides*, stated that it had picked up only the civilian signal. Captain Will Rogers had the option of warning the airbus by radio. In fact both the *Vincennes* and the *John H Sides* did this: seven times, in one version of the American story; twelve times in another. Whatever the facts, the upshot was that a $1 billion ship with an air defence system costing $500 million had failed to detect a large civilian airliner at close range. A journalist in *The Observer* noted that there had been 'no contrition from Washington. Not one major newspaper or any television network has expressed outright criticism of the Administration.'[9] Opinion polls in the US showed an indifference 'bordering on the callous and American allies have displayed a restraint close to complicity'.[10]

Two years after the incident it emerged that the US case was even weaker than originally thought, that in fact the USS *Vincennes* was in Iranian territorial waters at the time.[11] A British officer on board an Omani navy vessel is on record as twice warning the American cruiser by radio that it was within twelve miles of the Iranian coast. The soundtrack of a video recorded on the morning of 3 July includes the words: 'Your actions are not in accordance with the rights of passage. Please leave Iran's territorial waters immediately.'[12] The radio message, later repeated over the loud speaker on the bridge of the *Vincennes*, was discovered by David Evans, a former US Marine Lieutenant-Colonel and now the chief military correspondent of *The Chicago Tribune*. The message helps to explain why the American ship came under attack from Iranian gunboats and why the US authorities have consistently refused to release detailed information about the course and position of the *Vincennes* on the day in question. At the time there were frenzied calls within Iran for reprisals against American targets, one of a number of reasons why the West has until recently assumed a degree of Iranian complicity in the bombing of Pan Am 103 over Lockerbie.

On 21 July 1992 Admiral William J. Crowe, Chairman of the Joint Chiefs of Staff at the time of the *Vincennes* disaster, testified before the House Armed Services committee in Washington that the *Vincennes* was in Iranian waters when she shot down the airliner (*New York Times*, 22 July 1992). He also admitted that this information had been deliberately withheld from the public.

LOCKERBIE INVESTIGATION

On 14 November 1991 the sister of one of the Pan Am 103 victims responded to the synchronised statements by the US Justice Department and the Lord Advocate for Scotland that two Libyan intelligence agents were responsible for the Lockerbie bombing: Bonnie O'Connor of Long Island asked, 'Does George Bush take us for fools?' Some press comment was similarly sceptical.[13] It is useful to recall, first in outline, some of the pertinent post-Lockerbie events.

In March 1989 Paul Channon, then transport minister, lunched in the Garrick Club with political correspondents from *The Guardian, The Mirror, Today, The Times*, and *The Glasgow Herald*. Channon announced off the record that the Lockerbie bombers had been identified, following extensive investigations by the Lockerbie police, and that there would soon be arrests. When the news duly appeared in the press there were careful denials that the bombers had been tracked down, after which it was leaked that Channon himself had been the source of the apparently false information. Channon responded by denying this, 'was exposed as a liar and, after a decent interval, sacked'.[14] In the House of Commons Channon, questioned by Neil Kinnock, made an effort to summarise the then current state of the investigations.[15] He stated that 'the evidence which had been secured so far had not yet led to the identification of the person or persons responsible for placing the bomb in baggage on Pam Am flight 103'. Soon *The Sunday Times* was running a detailed series of articles setting out what were deemed to be the 'full facts' about the bombing (see below). Here it was claimed that the bomb had been devised by the Iranians in revenge for the shooting down of the Iran Air flight IR 655 by USS *Vincennes*. The Iranian government had employed a gang of Palestinians who enjoyed the support of the Syrian government. The bomb resembling a Toshiba cassette recorder, was planted in a suitcase in Malta and thereby on a plane which went through Frankfurt where the Pan Am flight began. The gang of Palestinian extremists was led by Ahmed Jibril, a notorious terrorist who at the time was co-operating with the Syrian-backed Abu Nidal. The man 'identified' as travelling to Malta to purchase clothes to put in the bomb suitcase was named as Mohammed Abu Talb, a Palestinian terrorist then incarcerated in a Swedish jail.

The volume of detailed information in the *Sunday Times* articles could not have been accumulated without assistance from the Scottish police or from Western intelligence sources. This suggested that Western governments had an interest in giving publicity to the then current findings of the Lockerbie enquiry: these, in essence, implicated a group of extremist Palestinians and the governments of two acknowledged 'terrorist states', namely Iran and Syria. The question remained: if so much was known, why was there no sign of an arrest? Today, in the light of the demands being made on Libya, we may ask: why was there no pressure, possibly via the Security Council, for Iran and Syria to extradite the named terrorists for trial in

Scotland or the United States? One possible answer emerged in *The Washington Post* where it was revealed that Margaret Thatcher and George Bush, speaking on the telephone in mid-March 1989, had agreed to play down the Lockerbie disaster even though their intelligence services had established the Jibril/Nidal/Talb responsibility for the outrage.[16] One possible reason for this low-key approach was that the CIA, long connected with drug trafficking,[17] was at the time organising a drugs run through Frankfurt airport in exchange for an Iranian commitment to free hostages, a deal related to the Irangate arms-for-hostages agreement. It is also possible that the West had an eye on the shifting political scene in the Middle East: it would not be long before a pliant Syria and a quiescent Iran would be useful to Washington in its onslaught on Iraq. Today in 1992 few independent observers doubt that Syria and Iran have been eased out of the Lockerbie picture because of their acquiescence in the 1991 Gulf war.

It is useful to remind ourselves of how sure the West was of Syrian, Palestinian and Iranian complicity in the bombing of Pan Am 103 – in the days before Lord Fraser, the Lord Advocate of Scotland, was required to read out the 'results' of the police enquiry, results – now naming Libya as sole culprit – that were totally at variance with the equally categorical findings publicised only a short time before. In the House of Commons Douglas Hurd, sensitive to the *realpolitik* of a post-Gulf-war Middle East, went to some lengths to exculpate Iran and Syria, the acknowledged terrorist states that Paul Channon had so roundly condemned in March 1989. *The Sunday Times*, having not long before revealed the full truth behind Lockerbie, could not quite muster the energy for a full somersault: 'The position of Iran and Syria remains obscure', it demurred.[18]

In November 1989 it was reported that fresh evidence had emerged linking two Palestinian terrorists – Abu Talb, a member of the Popular Front for the Liberation of Palestine-General Command (PFLP-GC), and Marten Imandi – to the plot devised in Malta to plant the bomb on Pam Am 103.[19] Talb, a known terrorist, was in Malta at the right time and 'surveillance records' showed that he owned a brown Samsonite suitcase of the same type that contained the bomb; he also visited premises in Frankfurt where the bomb was almost certainly made. It was reported that the Scottish police believed that a PFLP-GC member smuggled the bomb from West Germany to Malta where it was placed in a suitcase and so conveyed onto Pan Am 103. Imandi, like Talb, was linked to the bomb flat in Frankfurt. In December two detectives from Lockerbie flew to Belgrade to question friends and relatives of Mobdi Goben, a Palestinian with alleged bomb-making expertise and a known member of the FPLP-GC, 'the group believed to have been paid millions of dollars by Iran to carry out the bombing in revenge for the shooting down of an Iranian airliner over the Gulf in July 1988'.[20] Goben was believed 'to have supplied material for the Lockerbie bomb to Hafez Dalkamoni, 44, who leads the PFLP-GC's European network'.[21] (There was by now no discussion of possible US incompetence in failing to alert the public to the bomb threat. In December 1988, before the Lockerbie bombing, the US had been warned of a bomb threat to the Pan American airline: 'One warning clearly specified that the terrorist plot would involve a flight this month to the United States from Frankfurt, where the doomed Pan Am Flight 103 originated. Both warnings were phoned to US embassies and the Americans claimed that they told all the necessary security organisations.'[22] Officials at Heathrow and Frankfurt denied that they were ever told, and no warnings were given to the public.)

In November 1989, claiming access to inside information, *The Sunday Times* proudly published the 'full story' of the Lockerbie plot.[23] This account of the plot, 'based on information pieced together by Western intelligence and security sources':

names the principal bombers;

identifies who paid them;

exposes how they planted the bomb on board flight PA 103;

uncovers the extent to which the West German authorities bungled the investigation.

The report declares (p. 1) that it is 'now known that seven key conspirators, all members of . . . the Popular Front for the Liberation of Palestine–General Command (PFLP–GC), are likely to be named in a Scottish police report to Lord Fraser of Carmyllie, the Scottish Lord Advocate.' We are told that:

Western intelligence is convinced that Iran paid millions of dollars to Ahmed Jibril, the Damascus-based leader of the Palestinian faction, to carry out the bombing . . . Jibril is thought to have ordered Hafez Kassem Dalkamoni, the leader of the PFLP–GC's European terror network, to set up the bombing team . . . Dalkamoni then recruited Marwan Khreesat, a 44-year-old Jordanian terrorist to make the bomb.

The report continues in this vein. We learn what the Lockerbie investigators 'now believe'; and what the significance is of 'new evidence'. In the detailed reported (p. A15)[24] we are told how suspicion first began to focus on Ali Akbar Mohtashemi, an Iranian hard-liner thought to have paid $2 million to the PFLP–GC to carry out the bombing (a photograph insert, carrying the word 'Mastermind', depicts Ahmed Jibril, 'the man who, for $2 million, ordered the bombing'). We also find that the terrorists might have used the CIA-protected drugs channel to smuggle the bomb onto Pan Am 103: a Pan Am report leaked to a congressman 'claimed that the bomb was put on board Pan Am 103 in Frankfurt with the unwitting connivance of CIA agents who were running a secret drugs-for-hostages operation.' The investigators from Lockerbie further believed that the Jordanian terrorist Marwan Khreesat had made five Semtex bombs, 'including the one that blew up Flight 103, and that he and the PFLP–GC had intended to bomb five Western aircraft as part of the Iranian-sponsored revenge attacks'.

Khreesat's bomb, according to the Lockerbie investigators, was smuggled out of the Frankfurt flat by the known PFLP–GC terrorist Ramzi Diab, carried in a radio cassette player to Vienna, and then smuggled into Malta for subsequent handling by a PFLP–GC cell operating in a bakery. West German intelligence had established that Talb and Dalkamoni had gone to Malta to instruct the cell to place the bomb on board an Air Malta flight. Baggage lists later showed that a bag had been transferred to Pan Am 103 from an Air Malta flight: '. . . an unaccompanied bag, originating in Malta, was in the cargo hold of Pan Am 103 when it exploded over Lockerbie'.

On 17 December 1989 it was reported that the Lockerbie police were closing in 'on Lockerbie killers'.[25] Officers leading the investigation had informed their counterparts abroad that under Scottish law 'charges are now possible against certain persons'. At the same time it was emphasised that because of extradition difficulties, some of the suspects would have to be tried abroad. Lord Fraser, the Lord Advocate of Scotland, was quoted:

> While the ultimate purpose is the criminal prosecution of the individuals who were responsible for it, the criminal prosecution need not necessarily take place in this country. It could take place elsewhere. There could be several trials in several countries.

Again the familiar list of suspects was rehearsed: the Palestinian Abu Talb was a key suspect; the Jordanian Marwan Khreesat was thought to have made the bomb; the Iranian interior minister Mohtashemi paid a vast sum – this time $10 million(!) – for the bombing; and there was no doubt about the involvement of the PFLP–GC. In the detailed accompanying report (pp. A14–15), photographs of Khreesat, Dalkamoni, Jibril and Mohtashemi are shown, and we are again informed about the beliefs of the Lockerbie investigators: 'A detailed examination of the PFLP–GC cell in Germany and its links to a cell in Malta and the suspected Palestinian terrorists in Sweden has convinced the Scottish police that *the conspirators will be found among those groups'* (my italics).

The possibility of Libyan involvement in the Lockerbie outrage has been considered for some years. Clothing thought to be contained in the bomb suitcase was purchased in a boutique in Sliema, Malta; the owner, Anthony Gauci, described the buyer as a 'Libyan', a man who conversed in the 'Libyan' language.[26] It may also be significant that the Libyan People's Bureau in Malta was situated just a few hundred yards from Gauci's boutique in Tower Road. The mysterious customer, whether Libyan or not, was never identified; until, that is, the West decided to declare Libya's sole involvement in the Lockerbie bombing.

Early in 1988 two men arrested in Senegal, West Africa, were found to be carrying arms and explosives, including several blocks of TNT and nine kilos of Semtex, and also nine time-delay detonators of a type later thought to be used in the Lockerbie bomb. Vincent Cannistraro, the head of the CIA's counter-terrorism centre who led the American investigation into the bombing, suspected that the men were Libyan intelligence agents. They had Lebanese passports but were thought to be Libyan nationals; in any event they had been temporarily attached to the Libyan People's Bureau in Benin. On 16 June 1988 they were released without charge, despite American protests and suggestions that they were linked to the Abu Nidal group. One suggestion for their release without charge was the rapprochement between Senegal and Libya: American officials stated that, in order to secure the release of the two men, Libyan agents had 'suborned' unnamed Senegalese bureaucrats.[27]

Cannistraro has also claimed that when the German BKA (*Bundesmat für Verfassungsschutz*) managed to close down Ahmed Jibril's European network, Jibril sent a man to Libya to persuade Colonel Gaddafi to take over the task of carrying out the bombing. The CIA claim to have corroboration of the meeting held at the headquarters of the Libyan Intelligence Service outside Tripoli; the meeting was supposedly attended by Major Abdel Salem Jalloud, the former Libyan Prime Minister and for many years Gaddafi's official second-in-command. This is taken to explain how the known terrorist, the Damascus-based Ahmed Jibril, was able to carry out the Lockerbie bombing even after his West German cell had been put out of action. Cannistraro speculated on why Gaddafi may have had a motive for helping Jibril carry out the terrorist act: 'He may have had the American bombing of Tripoli in the back of his mind . . .'; but at the same time Cannistraro was unwilling to rule out the complicity of other states apart from Libya. He concluded: 'From an intelligence point of view this case has been solved. There is a lot of evidence which puts this at the doorstep of the Iranian government.'[28] Various individuals and states were involved in the Lockerbie bombing but 'The commissioning and the inspiration for the bombing came from the Iranians. They commissioned an operation against an American civilian airliner in revenge for the shooting down of the Iranian airbus . . .'[29]

David Leppard, deputy-editor of the *Sunday Times* 'Insight' team that investigated the Lockerbie bombing, has himself drawn attention to the CIA claim that it has evidence indicating that Ali Akbar Hashemi Rafsanjani, the president of Iran, knew of the decision to bomb the American airliner, 'and supported it'.[30] Cannistraro has commented that it was not 'a rogue decision', and has pointed out that Akbar Rafsanjani was commander-in-chief of the Iranian military at the time – in the summer of 1988 – when the bombing was supposedly commissioned through the Iranian Revolutionary Guard. The CIA has claimed also that soon after the Lockerbie bombing Ahmed Jibril celebrated with champagne at his office in Damascus.

It is hard to avoid the conclusion that individuals and/or governments of various states – Iran, Syria, Jordan and Libya – were involved in the Lockerbie bombing. It is likely also that stateless Palestinians, associated with various extremist groups enjoying the protection of particular countries, had some complicity in the plot. The West, for reasons that can be conjectured, is now seeking to attribute the blame solely to Libya.

A batch of documents lodged with the United Nations – documents that include the 'requests' made to the Libyan authorities by France, the United Kingdom and the United States – record specific charges against Libyan nationals, and 'request' that the Libyan authorities take specified actions.[31] These documents, referenced in Security Council Resolution 731 (adopted unanimously on 21 January 1992), are considered below (under 'Attributing Guilt'). First it is useful to draw attention to aspects of the supposed New World Order, and to consider the relationship between international law and the current US military hegemony.

GULF WARS TO NEW WORLD ORDER

The first (recent) Gulf war, the one between Iran and Iraq, lasted from September 1980 to August 1988; it prepared the way for the 1991 Gulf war, the one in which an anti-Iraq coalition of nations acted supposedly under the auspices of the United Nations. The 1991 war – its prelude, perpetration and immediate aftermath – coincided with the crumbling of the Soviet Union, a circumstance which gave the United States immense power on a Security Council that had witnessed one of its most formidable members, a former friend of Iraq, virtually disappear. Colonel Gaddafi involved Libya in both Gulf wars but only on the periphery, with little influence and with little consequence.

From the earliest days of the first Gulf war Iran, like Iraq, was assisted by a number of foreign states. While the Soviet Union, the United States and other Western nations were happy to witness the escalating military power of President Saddam Hussein as a bulwark against Iranian Islamic fundamentalism, other states perceived the direct or tacit support for Iraq as clear evidence of Soviet or Western imperialism in the region. In late-1980 arms and ammunition began to flow to Iran from such countries as Syria, Libya and North Korea, a pattern that was to be sporadically maintained in the years ahead. Many of the arms and much of the associated equipment reached Iran, via Syria and Libya, from the Soviet Union, the Kremlin having given permission for the onward shipment of Soviet-supplied arms and ammunition.[32] A Soviet army publication made it clear where Soviet sympathies lay, despite Moscow's intermittent support for Saddam Hussein: 'The declared aims of the [Iraqi] military actions are being changed. At first Iraq claimed the comparatively small area of 508 sq. km. . . . But now the Iraqi press is publishing maps in which the whole province of Khuzistan, called Arabistan in the Iraqi capital, is marked as Iraqi territory.'[33] This implied, at least to Moscow, that Iraq was enlarging its expansionist designs with the encouragement of the United States. In such circumstances Libya was quick to identify with what might be seen as the victim of American imperialism.

In February 1981 the Riyadh-based Gulf Co-operation Council was formed to co-ordinate internal security, arms procurement and the national economies of the member states. A year later, Washington obtained Saudi agreement for the formation of a joint Saudi/American Military Committee, a deal which some GCC members had formerly resisted but which now went through because of the perceived threat from Iran. The growing US involvement in the area was signalled also by a Pentagon directive, issued in March 1982, which declared that: 'Whatever the circumstances, we should be prepared to introduce American forces into the region should it appear [that our] security of access to the Persian Gulf oil is threatened.'[34] Here, still confronted with an evidently strong Soviet Union, Washington had little interest in piloting enabling resolutions through the UN Security Council.

Iraq was excluded from the GCC. This incensed Saddam and he quickly found other reasons why various Arab states should be condemned for their

failure to acknowledge the importance of his struggle against Iranian fundamentalism: 'Had it not been for Iraq and its army the Iranians would have
seized the entire Gulf . . .'[35] Saddam considered that the aid he was receiving from Kuwait and Saudi Arabia was less than duty dictated, and he was
so infuriated by the 'traitor' and 'opportunist' states of Syria and Libya that
he severed diplomatic links with them in October 1980. At the same time
Colonel Gaddafi, admiring the Islamic revolution in Iran and believing with
some reason that Washington was supporting the Iraqi invasion, was urging
members of the Arab League to defend Iran against Western imperialism:
'Islamic duty dictates that we ally ourselves with the Muslims in Iran in this
crusade instead of fighting them on behalf of America.'[36] With Syria and
Libya ranged against him, the Iraqi president found it difficult to argue
that he was fighting the Iranians on behalf of the entire Arab world.

Iran itself had made some effort to avoid undue dependence on either
the West or the Soviet bloc for its arms and ammunition. While it continued
to acquire military hardware from its Arab allies, Syria and Libya, and also
from such states as Cuba, North Korea and East Germany, it also had an
interest in obtaining equipment in the open market. The Iranian foreign
minister confirmed in February 1982 that Iran had made some purchases of
arms and ammunition from the Soviet Union, but Moscow was also keen to
maintain its links with Baghdad. It soon emerged that Iran's arms policy
was bearing fruit: in early 1984 Iraq lost the Majnoon Islands to Iran and
appeared to be at a disadvantage. GCC members attending an Arab League
meeting of foreign ministers called for all states to stop providing Iran with
arms and other equipment: Syria and Libya boycotted the conference,
resolving to continue observing their earlier (January 1983) joint communiqué
in which they condemned Iraq for its invasion of Iran and pledged support
for Iran against 'hostile forces'. It was clear at this time that Washington
was supporting Iraq. The American Secretary of State George Shultz met
Tariq Aziz, the Iraqi foreign minister, in October 1982 and in May 1983.
The US State Department still regarded Iraq – along with Libya, Cuba,
Syria and South Yemen – as one of the 'nations that support international
terrorism' but the Reagan administration was still prepared to sell sixty
helicopters to Iraq for 'agricultural use'. Washington also offered $460
million credit for the sale of 147,000 tonnes of American rice to Baghdad.
This was an important gesture to an Iraq beset by a severe economic crisis,
and it served to reassure many Arab and European governments of the
viability of the Iraqi regime.[37]

The US involvement in the first Gulf war continued to escalate through
the 1980s. This development was conditioned in part by the failure of Iraq
to achieve a decisive victory. An Iranian triumph was unthinkable to Wash-

ington and before long the Reagan administration was exploring ways of helping Baghdad, short of a massive US military presence in the region. The US National Security Council concluded in the autumn of 1983 that an Iraqi defeat would be seen as a direct blow to American interests, whereupon the National Security Adviser issued a directive outlining the diplomatic and military steps that Washington could take to support Saddam Hussein. The Pentagon drew up plans for A-10 warplanes to strike at Iranian tanks inside Iraq, for the use of fragmentation bombs on Iranian troops, and for the supply of air-defence weapons to enable Iraq to retain control of its airspace.[38] It was also decided that Iraq was no longer a terrorist state, a move that opened the way for the supply of further US military equipment. An American delegation visited six Gulf capitals to inform their rulers that an Iraqi defeat would be against American interests. With Iraq no longer a 'terrorist state', Iran was added to the list. The US also passed on satellite and other reconnaissance information on Iranian troop movements to Riyadh for transfer on to Baghdad.

The increased US involvement in the Gulf through the 1980s was one of the main reasons why Saddam Hussein was able to claim victory over Iran in August 1988. An inconclusive 'war of the cities' (involving the use of Scud missiles) and an equally unproductive 'war of the tankers' (leading to Kuwaiti ships flying protective American flags) had been waged; there had been a profligate waste of treasure and human life. The scene was set for the Iraqi invasion of Kuwait in August 1990 and for the ensuing Gulf war of 1991.

Saddam Hussein emerged from the first Gulf war with a host of grievances against his erstwhile Arab allies, Kuwait in particular. He claimed that overproduction of OPEC quotas, leading to a loss of $1 billion a year for Iraq, was an 'act of war'. War, Saddam pointed out, could be waged by military means, by 'sending armies across frontiers, by acts of sabotage, by killing people and by supporting coups d'états, but war can also be waged by economic means . . . and what is happening is war against Iraq.' Six weeks after the important Jidda conference, held just prior to the August invasion of Kuwait, Tariq Aziz issued a thirty-seven-page memorandum to the secretary-general of the Arab League, specifically naming Kuwait and the United Arab Emirates (UAE) as the two 'culprits' in the overproduction of oil. Other Iraqi grievances concerned the Iraqi debt to Kuwait (since Iraq had defended Kuwait the debt should be cancelled), oil pumped in excess by Kuwait from the shared Rumeila field ('tantamount to an act of war'), Kuwait's complicity with foreign powers (together conspiring to weaken Iraq as a pro-Israeli policy), and Kuwait's refusal to negotiate with Iraq on these and other matters.[39]

The subsequent invasion of Kuwait led to a prompt US response in defence of Saudi Arabia, US mobilisation of 'consensus' in the United Nations, the organisation of the anti-Iraq coalition of Arab and other states, and to the 1991 Gulf war. The countries outside the anti-Iraq coalition included Jordan, the Yemen, the Sudan, Tunisia, Algeria, Mauritania, and Libya. All these states, with the exception of Libya, are desperately short of foreign exchange and have gained nothing from so antagonising the United States. In fact a number have been punished already: for example, aid to Jordan has been blocked, ex-patriot Yemenis have been expelled in their thousands from Saudi Arabia, and Libya – along with the surviving Saddam Hussein – was soon singled out for special attention.

On the day of the invasion, 2 August, the Security Council condemned the Iraqi action and within days US forces were arriving in the region. The first Council resolution (660) called for Iraq's 'complete, immediate and unconditional withdrawal'; later sanctions imposed a number of conditions and obligations on UN member states, including comprehensive sanctions on Iraq. The speedy Security Council response was matched by prompt discussions between the Arab states, though they were unable to reach a consensus: it was fortuitous that the Iraqi invasion had happened at a time when the foreign ministers of the 45-member Islamic Conference Organisation were meeting in Cairo. As soon as news arrived about the Iraqi invasion the twenty-one Arab League ministers convened a special session, with the Iraqi Sadoun Hamadi adopting an uncompromising stand. On 3 August the ministers passed a resolution by 14 to one (Iraq), but there were five abstentions and the Libyan representative walked out. The resolution – supported by Algeria, Bahrein, Egypt, Djibouti, Kuwait, Lebanon, Morocco, Oman, Qatar, Somalia, Syria, Tunisia, United Arab Emirates, and Saudi Arabia – included the words: 'We condemn the bloodshed and the destruction of buildings [in Kuwait], and we call upon Iraq to immediately and unconditionally withdraw its troops.[40] The abstainers were Jordan, Sudan, Yemen, Mauritania, and the Palestine Liberation Organisation. On later resolutions Algeria and Tunisia joined the earlier dissenters; and Jordan, Sudan and Mauritania expressed strong reservations. Algeria and Yemen formally abstained, and Tunisia absented itself; Libya – joined by Iraq and the PLO – voted against. Already there was Arab resentment at the influx of foreign troops into the area. The position of Libya on the Arab League resolutions was one of the first signs of how Colonel Gaddafi was thinking in the early stages of the 1990/91 Gulf crisis.

The seeming paradox of his support for Iraq – when earlier he had supported Iran in the first Gulf war – was easy to comprehend. The Americans, arch-imperialists, were now hostile to Iraq: Saddam was the defender of Islam and Arab land, and the course for the true believer was clear. Even before the arrival of the foreign-troop contingents in Saudi Arabia there were many pro-Saddam popular demonstrations in the region. Gaddafi, with a populist touch and his own convictions, saw himself on the side of the Arab masses against their corrupt US-backed rulers. He did not however contemplate doing much about it.

In August there were many large demonstrations in support of Iraq and Saddam Hussein – in the West Bank, Gaza, Jordan, Yemen, Sudan, Algeria, Mauritania, Morocco, Tunisia, and Libya. Such protests were to continue through the months ahead, to achieve a crescendo just before the start of the land war in January 1991. President Gorbachev declared on Soviet television on 17 January that military operations were about to begin, adding that the Soviet Union would do everything in its power to limit the scale of the conflict: 'We appealed to a number of influential countries, including France, Britain, Germany, Italy and India [then a non-permanent member of the Security Council] and most Arab states, to take steps to localise the conflict and prevent it spreading.'[41] Immediately anti-US demonstrations took place in Algeria, Morocco, Mauritania, Tunisia, and Libya. A million people staged demonstrations in Libya, a country with a population of 4.5 million: Gaddafi himself took part in the marches, at the same time appealing to the UN secretary-general to ensure that the military operations did not go beyond the expelling of Iraq from Kuwait. The Yemeni government called on the Security Council to 'put an end to the bloodshed and destruction'; and a statement from Amman declared that 'The Jordanian leadership, government and people denounce the brutal aggression against an Arab, Muslim country and people, who have always defended their Arab brethren without hesitation.'[42] Much of the Arab anger derived from the fact that there had long been an Arab insistence in some quarters that an 'Arab solution' be found to the Gulf crisis: Arab efforts to this end had been brushed aside by the Western powers. As early as 1 September 1990 Libya had unveiled a seven-point peace plan after consultation with Iraq, Jordan and Sudan. The scheme, intended for implementation under joint UN–Arab League supervision, included the following provisions:

1 Iraqi troops should withdraw from Kuwait and be replaced by UN forces;
2 US and other international forces should pull out of Saudi Arabia and be replaced by Arab and Muslim troops;
3 The UN embargo against Iraq should be lifted;

4 The disputed part of the Rumeila oilfield as well as Bubiyan and
Warba Islands should be ceded to Iraq;

5 The Kuwaiti people should be allowed to decide 'their own system';

6 Iraq and Kuwait should negotiate on matters of debt and compensation;

7 To prevent future transgressions against OPEC quotas there should be
a 'unified Arab oil policy' to be implemented 'forcibly'.[43]

It is obvious that the Libyan plan could have provided a basis for negotiation, but in fact it was immediately rejected by Kuwait and Saudi Arabia and criticised by the Western powers. The Kuwaiti Crown Prince Saad al Sabah was particularly hostile to the idea of a plebiscite in Kuwait to determine the type of government. The second Gulf war was destined to run its brief but dreadful course.

Colonel Gaddafi had refused to join the anti-Iraq coalition but had also criticised Saddam's poor judgement in thinking he would be able to annex Kuwait without provoking a concerted Western response. The war had exposed divisions in the Arab world, most of which had long been evident, and demonstrated yet again that developed Western powers would always be able to crush Third World upstarts, whatever the scale of their military procurements. The Iraqis had hoped that the Cairo summit in August 1990 could be used to undermine Arab support for the Western machinations at the UN. To some extent they were able to rely on the radical instincts of Libya, Algeria and the PLO. But when Colonel Gaddafi, sitting with Libyan and Palestinian officials in the lounge of the conference building, commented that the conference was part of an 'imperialist conspiracy against the Arab nation', President Mubarak responded with the words: 'Muammar, if you think I would be party to such a conspiracy, as you say, then I would long ago have sent a couple of armoured divisions to occupy Libya. I had a hundred and one pretexts for doing so, as you know.' The Egyptian leader then approached a speechless Gaddafi, placed a hand on his shoulder and said, 'Come, I will buy you lunch.'[44] The Libyan position was always a minority one among the Arab states: the Iraqis could never rely on Gaddafi to deliver a united Arab nation into their camp.

The United States emerged from the 1991 Gulf war in a triumphalist spirit, having kicked the 'Vietnam syndrome' (Bush announced) and with much talk of the New World Order.[45] The manic phase soon passed: it was discovered that the Kurds in the north of Iraq and the Shiites in the south had been abandoned to persecution by a Saddam Hussein who was still in power; the Kuwaiti regime was torturing innocent Palestinians and, though re-installed at great cost, was no nearer to establishing the sorts of democratic structures that would have appealed to its Western protectors. There was some movement on the Palestinian question though Israel, blithely able to ignore the sorts of UN resolutions that had been so binding on Iraq, still seemed prepared to thumb its nose at the United States: in February 1992 the Israelis went so far as to arrest members of the Palestinian delegation to the peace talks, and to launch a tank invasion of the Lebanon, smashing through UN barricades in the process. The New World Order was characterised by a Middle East ravaged by war, a vast new lexicon of 'double standards', and a United States increasingly perplexed about whether in fact it had won either the Cold War or the Gulf War.

A central problem for the US was that Japan, long sheltering under the US nuclear umbrella, had been able to devote its resources to industrial development. Perhaps Japan, set to overtake the United States in the economic stakes by the turn of the century, was the real winner of the Cold War. So there was talk of the CIA girding itself to repulse the 'yellow peril';[46] of how a 'crippled Uncle Sam' was driven to shaking its fist 'at an ungrateful world';[47] and how perhaps the 'supercop USA is more tired than Europe knows'.[48] In such circumstances, confronted by an election year, it was inevitable that there would be immense pressure on an American president desperate to raise American morale and his own flagging ratings in the opinion polls. Military action was a good bet – it had always revived presidential fortunes in the past and it could be relied upon again – and here there were several options. In late-1991 the campaign against Colonel Gaddafi was systematically escalated (see below), and in early-1992 fresh plans for bombing Iraq were reported.[49]

In the run-up to the American presidential election of 1992 it appeared that Saddam Hussein and Muammar al-Gaddafi were receiving broadly similar attention by American officials, pliant Western politicians, and helpful media organisations. In March 1992 it was not yet clear whether the plans would move fast enough to aid a troubled John Major seeking election, but the Labour MP Bernie Grant had been sufficiently alarmed at the possibility of a military attack to launch on 24 February his No Intervention in Libya (NIL) campaign. The crucial task for the West was to go through the proper diplomatic and legal motions: in particular, to involve the United Nations and to thus demonstrate a commitment to due process. This had worked – had it not? – with the Gulf crisis, and the game could be played again.

UNITED STATES AND LAW

The depiction of the United States as a world 'policemen' (even one perplexed and weary) is of immense propaganda significance. A policeman, by definition, has a legitimate role: he is licensed to use force, to kill if necessary. A punitive action against Gaddafi or Saddam Hussein[50] by a 'policeman' would clearly be justified, part of a disinterested quest for justice. It is useful to remember that in principle a policeman's licence is issued by a superior legal authority that enjoys legitimacy through account-ability and due process: if a policeman is *self*-appointed then he may be indistinguishable from a bandit or a mercenary. In considering the relation-ship of the United States to the UN in particular and to international law in general, we need to consider the extent to which the United Nations pro-vides legitimate sanction for the actions of the US beyond its shores. This says something about how the United States has used the UN to organise sanctions against Libya.

In fact it is hard to avoid the conclusion that Washington has tended to regard treaty obligations and international law with indifference, useful only if they could by cynically exploited. Noam Chomsky, the world-famous academic and dissident, has commented that the US has always regarded diplomacy and international law 'as an annoying encumbrance, unless they can be used to advantage against an enemy'.[51] It is also useful to record that the United States was manifestly antipathetic to the UN until the time of the Iraqi invasion of Kuwait, at which time it was assumed by Washington that a UN mandate would be useful in sanctioning a range of actions that were in effect unilateral US initiatives. During the 1980s Washington had characteristically cultivated a relative political isolation in the United Nations, concerned mainly with a perceived self-interest that often involved the protection of repressive client states. Thus in the thirty-sixth UN session (1981–2) of the General Assembly, involving 134 resolu-tions and decisions, the US voted with the majority only twenty-two times; in the 1982–3 session it sided with the majority twenty-four times out of 158 votes; and in 1984–5 the US voted with the ninety-nine nations of the non-aligned movement only thirteen per cent of the time. The pattern was maintained in subsequent years. Since 1970 Washington has voted to block nearly seventy Security Council resolutions drafted to condemn, for example: Israel's bombing of Lebanon, Israel's annexation of Arab lands, the South African occupation of Namibia, the South African invasion of Angola, the US mining of Nicaraguan ports, the US invasion of Grenada, and the US invasion of Panama. For our purposes it is interesting to recall that the United States was forced to use its veto to block a UN condemnation of the American bombing of Libya in 1986.

In 1987, at a time when President Reagan was being applauded in the US for negotiations with the Soviet Union, Washington felt obliged to oppose disarmament resolutions in the UN General Assembly. A UN vote (154–1) condemning the build-up of weapons in outer space saw no abstentions and only the United States voting against. A similar vote of 135–1 against developing weapons of mass destruction was opposed only by the US. The UN General Assembly voted 143–2 for a comprehensive test ban, and 137–3 for a halt to all nuclear test explosions (here the US was supported by Britain in one case and by France in two). At the same time the US was alone in boycotting a UN disarmament conference in New York convened to discuss how reductions in armaments might release funds to aid the Third World. This followed Washington's sole opposition in a General Assembly vote (124–1) urging the creation of a South Atlantic 'zone of peace'.

The enduring US antipathy to the culture of the United Nations is also shown by Washington's failure to pay its legally binding fees for membership. Thus at the time of the onset of the 1991 Gulf war the US owed the United Nations no less than $451 million, $296 million for the general fund and $155 million for approved peace-keeping operations. In September 1992 Washington owed the UN $757 million. Such debts, outstanding since the time of President Reagan, suggest that Washington is less than wholly committed to the smooth operation of the United Nations.

US manipulation and violation of the UN Charter and other international agreements are well illustrated throughout the entire history of the United Nations. The American involvement in the Korean war, nominally sanctioned by the Security Council (claimed by the Soviet Union to be acting illegally in its absence), in fact violated several provisions in the UN Charter (in a nice rehearsal of the violations that were to occur during the 1991 Gulf war): in particular, the clear provisions of Article 47 that specifies the establishment of a Military Staff Committee comprising the Chiefs of Staff of the permanent members of the Security Council (see below). The conduct of the Vietnam war further illustrates the predictable US indifference to international law when Washington perceives that its interests are under threat.

The US citing of UN Charter Article 51 to justify military intervention in Vietnam was bogus (as were subsequent citings when Grenada and Panama were invaded). The article specifies the inherent right of self-defence if an armed attack occurs 'against a Member of the United Nations'. Yet even if an armed attack against South Vietnam had been proved, Article 51 could not be invoked since South Vietnam, not even in law an independent state, was not a member of the UN. It is important to remember that the partition of Vietnam defined in the 1954 Geneva Accords was not intended to establish independent political entities (Article 6 of the Declaration emphasises that 'the military demarcation line is provisional and shall not in any way be interpreted as constituting a political or territorial boundary').

Nor could the SEATO Treaty be cited to justify US intervention in Vietnam. In fact, faced with the threat of a French veto, Washington did not press for a formal SEATO commitment (even if this has been achieved it would have been invalid since the SEATO Treaty was subordinate to the UN Charter). In 1965, in a Memorandum of Law inserted into the Congressional Record by Senators Wayne Morse and Ernest Gruening, the US Lawyers Committee on American Policy Towards Vietnam concluded that 'the United States Government is in violation of its treaty obligations under the United Nations Charter'.[52] The Memorandum ends with a quotation from President Franklin D Roosevelt, making his last address to the Congress and urging an end to 'the system of unilateral action . . . that has been tried for centuries – and has always failed'.

The traditional attitude of Washington to the United Nations was further illustrated by the efforts of Daniel Patrick Moynihan while he was UN ambassador. In January 1976 he boasted to Henry Kissinger of how progress had been made at the UN towards 'a basic policy goal, that of breaking up the massive blocs of nations, mostly new nations, which for so long have been arrayed against us in international forums and in diplomatic encounters generally'. In his memoirs Moynihan is happy to record his success in undermining the UN reaction to the Indonesian invasion of East Timor and to the Moroccan aggression in the Sahara, both aggressions supported by the United States. In East Timor 60,000 people were killed within a few weeks, a slaughter that was to rise to more than 200,000 – amounting to a third of the indigenous population – through the 1980s; a 1991 massacre at which Western journalists happened to be present exposed the plight of the indigenous people and gave fresh publicity to the East Timor question. Moynihan rejoices in his role of helping Washington to frustrate the UN efforts: 'The United States wished things to turn out as they did, and worked to bring this about. The Department of State desired that the United Nations prove utterly ineffective in whatever measures it undertook. This task was given to me, and I carried it forward with no inconsiderable success.'[53]

The Washington policy on East Timor was paralleled by the US funding of terrorism in Central America. In 1986 the International Court of Justice at the Hague adjudicated that the United States had breached its obligations under international law, and demanded that it make reparations – for example, for the mining of Nicaraguan harbours – and refrain from similar actions in the future. The Nicaraguan Sandinista government claimed total reparations of $17 billion for the destruction wrought by the United States on one of the poorest countries in the world. The US response was to ignore the legal ruling, declaring that the World Court was not entitled to rule on American actions.* In September 1991, under pressure from Washington, the pliant Chamorro government – itself installed through US-inspired terror – dropped the World Court suit against the United States.

The US is sometimes overt in its manipulation of articles in the UN Charter: thus UN ambassador Thomas Pickering on one occasion declared that Article 51 could be invoked 'to defend our interests'[55] – a significant rewriting of the UN Charter. It is also important to note that Washington's various bombings and invasions have not been referred by the US to the Security Council for settlement, as required by Article 37 (1) of the Charter. Instead the United States had always preferred the option of unilateral action (see the discussion of Resolution 678 below). It is significant that when unilateral US actions are taken against Charter provisions this often leads to the violation of other treaty obligations. Thus the 1989 invasion of Panama was a violation of the Charter of the Organisation of American States (OAS), the Rio Treaty (Inter-American Treaty of Reciprocal Assistance) of 1947, the Declaration of Montevideo (1933), and the Panama Canal treaties (1977–78). The US invasion violated a dozen articles of the OAS Charter (most notably, Articles 18–21): Article 18, for example, forbids intervention by any 'State or group of States . . . for any reason whatever, in the internal or external affairs of any other State'. The Rio Treaty and the Panama Canal treaties contain similar prohibitions. In any event, all such treaties are subordinate to the UN Charter, with Article 2 (4) prohibiting 'the threat or use of force against the territorial integrity or the political independence of any state'.

The 1991 Gulf war has been advertised in the West as the supreme example of the United Nations acting in the way that its founders intended, moving resolutely and in concert to confront naked aggression. In fact Washington, with the support of pliant Security Council permanent members, manipulated the UN on the Gulf question through 1990–1, as it has subsequently manipulated the Security Council on the Libyan question through 1991–2.

---

*Of course, when in April 1992 the World Court gave a ruling that appeared to favour the US, Washington was quick to applaud the verdict.

Soon after the Iraqi invasion of Kuwait on 2 August 1990 the United States moved to organise an effective UN consensus, not in the General Assembly, which was largely ignored, but in the all-important Security Council. At the same time, inducements were offered to regional states — Syria, Turkey, Israel, etc. – to encourage acceptance of the American position: Syria was offered a free hand to extend its invasion of Lebanon; Turkey, as a NATO member, was reassured on territorial and financial matters; Israel was told there would be no 'linkage' of a settlement of the Palestinian question with a solution to the Gulf problem; financial inducements were offered to a crippled Soviet Union; and Egypt's $15 billion debt to the US was waived. Thus by the use of threat and bribery in unprecedented levels of politicking Bush, by telephone, and Baker, by foreign travel, browbeat enough of a troubled world to achieve what could be represented as an international consensus.

There followed a spate of more than a dozen UN resolutions on Iraq, beginning with the initial response (Resolution 660) on 2 August 1990. These resolutions merit scrutiny, not least because they illustrate how nominal declarations can be selectively applied and interpreted according to the whims and interests of powerful member states, especially the United States. This is particularly important in considering Resolution 731 on Libya, unanimously adopted on 21 January 1992. Three examples, taken from the resolutions on Iraq, suffice to illustrate the point.

It is stipulated in UN Resolution 660 (3) that Iraq and Kuwait should begin 'immediate intensive negotiations for the resolution of their differences'; and in Resolution 661 it is recorded that the Government of Kuwait 'has expressed its willingness to comply with 660'. Yet after the liberation of Kuwait its reinstated government refused to contemplate discussions with Iraq. No pressure was exercised by Washington on Kuwait to force compliance with 660 (3). Instead the UN boundary commission, with US agreement, was authorised to look at the disputed border between Kuwait and Iraq – one of the questions that Kuwait and Iraq should have been made to discuss under 660 (3) – with a view to stripping Iraq of part of its only workable port at Umm Qasr and giving Kuwait several oil wells in the disputed Rumeila field.[55] This is a violation of Resolution 660 which could only have occurred with US approval.

The violation was confirmed in August 1992 when the UN boundary commission, under instruction from Washington, concluded its redrawing of the frontiers between Iraq and Kuwait. This unilateral action, taken without the legally stipulated reference to the Iraqi government, gave Kuwait oil wells and land that were formerly Iraqi possessions, including the southern portion of the city of Umm Qasr. (The confirmation of the

redrawn borders is also a violation of UN Resolution 687 (3) which specifies that arrangements should be made with Iraq as well as with Kuwait in
demarcating the border.)

Resolution 661 (3c) nominally allowed Iraq to import medical supplies
and foodstuffs, yet throughout 1992 a *de facto* embargo on such materials
was maintained. The governments of the US and Britain, when pressed,
declared that there was no ban on the Iraqi importation of medicines and
food, but at the same time Iraqi overseas assets were frozen and oil sales
(despite one token offer) were massively restricted: Iraq is still denied the
revenues essential for the purchase of food and medical supplies in adequate quantities. As long ago as 14 May 1991 Iraq declared that it was
desperate for access to its foreign assets to buy foods for the following
months, but despite appeals from UNICEF and the World Health Organisation the United States blocked this and all subsequent requests. CIA chief
Robert Gates stated that any easing of sanctions 'will be considered only
when there is a new government in Iraq'; in the same vein Douglas Hurd,
UK Foreign Secretary, has insisted that a tight ring will be maintained
around Iraq until Saddam Hussein is overthrown. In these circumstances,
quite apart from the *de facto* ban on food and medicine, Iraq was massively
hampered in its efforts to rebuild its shattered infrastructure: the ruined
sewage treatment plants, hospitals and power stations. On 22 May 1991 a
health team from Harvard reported after a visit to Iraq that some 170,000
children under the age of five would die by 1992 as a result of sanctions.

In this way Washington has contrived a means of violating Resolution
661 (3c) while at the same time broadcasting an entirely different message.
It is also significant that other international agreements (for example, the
Geneva Convention) prohibit the denial of food to civilian populations in
time of war.

Resolution 678 (29 November 1990) deserves particular attention: this
was the so-called 'use of force' resolution. Here Member States were
authorised 'to use all necessary means to uphold and implement 660'
(which demands the withdrawal of Iraq from Kuwait). Even as it stands this
resolution was not unanimously supported by members of the UN Security
Council: China, as a permanent member, abstained, and Yemen and Cuba
– non-permanent members without a veto – voted against.

The first draft of 678 that Secretary James Baker submitted to Soviet
foreign minister Eduard Shevardnadze included the words 'use of force'.
Shevardnadze balked at this, saying that the Soviet Union could not accept
it; 'all necessary means' was accepted as a compromise despite Baker's
concern that these words were ambiguous.[56] At one stage Baker backed
off from the compromise phrase, considering it too indefinite: 'the Bush

administration did not want a domestic debate on the meaning of a UN resolution'.[57]

Thus it is clear that Baker did not regard 'force' as *synonymous* with 'all necessary means'. He declared to Shevardnadze that he (Baker) would speak to the Security Council to indicate that the US would interpret 'all necessary means' to mean 'force'; and Shevardnadze concurred. But the wording of the resolution still admitted the possibility of further interpretation: force could only be justified if it could be shown to be necessary, and who was to decide? Resolution 678 was drafted specifically to give no guidance on this. There was no reference to the role of the UN sanctions committee, no requirement that the Security Council should meet again on 15 January (1991), the stipulated deadline, to decide what further action was necessary.

This meant in effect that member states – in particular, the US – could do whatever they wanted, whenever they wanted, after the deadline date for Iraqi withdrawal; everyone was free to interpret 'necessary' as they chose. In such a fashion, Washington, while professing commitment to the UN, had thrown off all UN constraints. There was no longer any role for the Security Council; the Secretary-General Perez de Cuellar no longer had any part to play. The United States was free to take a unilateral decision on war.

It is even arguable that Resolution 678 was in direct violation of the UN Charter. The Charter does not authorise member states to take unilateral military action once the Security Council has resolved to use force. Instead, according to Article 47(1), a Military Staff Committee comprising the Chiefs of Staff of the permanent members of the Security Council is required to advise and assist the Security Council 'on all questions relating to the Security Council's military requirements'. Article 47(3) declares that the Military Staff Committee shall be responsible under the Security Council 'for the strategic direction of any armed forces'.

Such provisions clearly rule out any unilateral decision to use armed forces, once the Security Council has been apprised of a crisis and issued relevant resolutions. In particular, Resolution 678 cannot be interpreted as authorising the United States to unilaterally resort to war whenever it felt like it. On 14 January 1991 Lord Gifford and other lawyers issued a statement emphasising that Resolution 678 'is not a blank cheque for the United States to pursue its own ends by its own means . . . the ostensible reason for it [this appalling military adventure] is itself a grave breach of the international legal order'. Perez de Cuellar himself expressed distaste at the deadline specified in 678 and was frequently irritated by statements from President Bush. When Perez de Cuellar met Saddam Hussein on 13 January 1991 he urged the Iraqi president to 'deny the warmongers their opportunity'. When Saddam commented that: 'These are American resolutions. This is an American age. What the United States want at present is the thing that is passed [678] and not what the Security Council wants', Perez de Cuellar replied: 'I agree with you as much as the matter involves me.'[58] The 1991 Gulf war was contrived, initiated and run by the United States, exploiting the United Nations as a 'flag of convenience'.

There is also evidence that the US violated international law in its prosecution of the Gulf war. Article 57 of the first Protocol of the Geneva Convention stipulates that military targets in areas normally full of civilians should not be attacked by day. Yet in Nasiriya, in southern Iraq, 100 people crossing a bridge in the middle of one afternoon died when bombs were dropped and cars, lorries and people fell into the Euphrates; similarly, at Falluja, west of Baghdad, two bombs fell into the middle of a busy market place, injuring hundreds, when two aircraft missed a nearby bridge. Five months after the end of the war the Red Cross had obtained access to the graves of only twenty-one Iraqis: in contravention of Article 17 of the Geneva Convention, Washington had failed to provide even rough statistics of the Iraqi death toll.[59] The American military authorities refused to provide to the International Committee of the Red Cross information on the scale of the Iraqi dead or on the location of the mass graves in which they were buried. The Geneva Convention states that: 'parties to [a] conflict shall ensure that burial or cremation of the dead, carried out individually as far as circumstances permit, is preceded by a careful examination . . . of the bodies, with a view to confirming death, establishing identity and enabling a report to be made . . . they shall further ensure that the dead are honourably interred . . . that their graves are respected . . . properly maintained and marked so that they may always be found.' The Convention requires that graves be registered and lists compiled, with the exact locations of the graves specified 'together with particulars of the dead interred therein'. The US military leadership ignored all these basic provisions: General Norman Schwarzkopf himself declared that he was 'not in the business of body counts', yet this is just what the Geneva Convention demands.

The allied bombing of food, agricultural and water-treatment facilities were a violation of Article 54 of Protocol 1 (Geneva Convention) prohibiting starvation as a means of warfare. The targeting of civilians, as with the attack on the Ameriyya air raid shelter in which 300 to 400 people were killed, was a similar violation of Protocol 1. Even if the shelter had been used partly by military personnel the Convention requires that a warning should have been given to allow the civilians to evacuate the building. A report issued by the human rights group Middle East Watch, based in New York, found that despite the much-vaunted technology available to the allies the laws intended to govern the conduct of war were violated 'in several respects, both in the selection of targets and in the means and methods of attack'.[60]

This section has illustrated the US attitude to the United Nations in particular and to international law in general. There is no intention here to demonstrate a unique derogation of legal responsibility on the part of successive American administrations: it would be easy to present a similar catalogue of violations for other members of the United Nations, for other permanent members of the Security Council. At the same time it should be acknowledged that US derogations, deriving from the scale of American military power, have often had global consequences: this is the perverse *de facto* (but not *de jure*) privilege of a vast hegemonic power able to set itself above international organisations. *This should be borne in mind when considering the orchestrated US campaign, through late 1991 and 1992, to mobilise the UN Security Council against Libya.*

ATTRIBUTING GUILT

At the end of the 1991 Gulf war the United States began to frame the lineaments of the New World Order in general and the New Middle East Order in particular. As always, countries were *grata* or *non grata*, sheep or goats. But the categories altered in the light of the new considerations. George Bush and James Baker had been prepared, in the interest of defeating Iraq, to converse with President Assad in Syria and even to agree a new accord with the Iranian ayatollahs. The prosecution of the Gulf war, the subsequent (largely abortive) Middle East peace conference and the steady flow of released hostages from Beirut would have been impossible without a relaxation of tensions between the US and Syria, and between the US and Iran. It had well suited Washington to slide at least a couple of states from the *non grata* to *grata* categories. The new situation was signalled in various ways.

In March 1992 Sir John Moberly and the Royal Institute of International Affairs held a two-day conference – partly financed by British Petroleum and approved by the Foreign Offices of London and Tehran – entitled 'Britain and Iran in a Changing World'. The aim, it seems, is to improve relations between the West and Iran with a view to expanded trade and other contacts. The addresses at the conference said nothing about Iran's appalling human rights record, nothing about Iran's massive recent arms procurements, nothing about the 'death sentence' on Salman Rushdie, and nothing whatever about possible Iranian complicity in the Lockerbie outrage. The demand of the 'New Orders' – both regional and global – require that little attention be given to such embarrassing topics.

Syria too, though still classified by the US as a 'terrorist state',[61] evidently deserves the protection of the United States because of President Assad's compliance in the Gulf war. Thus Syria has been allowed to import Scud-C surface-to-surface missiles from North Korea, weapons that one day might be used against Israel. On the eve of the visit by US Secretary of State James Baker in October 1991 to the Middle East to arrange the peace conference, Washington warned Israel not to attack a North Korean ship carrying missiles to Syria. The possibility of an Israeli strike against the cargo ship *Mopu* had been discussed by President Assad and President Mubarak, with Assad declaring that if an attack took place he would immediately withdraw from the peace talks. North Korea, to the discomfiture of Israel, has sold a number of Scud-C missiles (improved versions of the Soviet Scud-B), with a range of up to 600 miles, to both Syria and Iran. Again, Washington is prepared to allow such arms build-ups in the light of the new political situation.

In September 1991 it emerged that the West was keen to label Libya as the sole perpetrator of the Lockerbie and UTA DC-10 outrages, despite many earlier claims that there was evidence also of Syrian and Iranian involvement. It was reported in France that the investigating Judge Jean Louis Bruguière had concluded after two years of painstaking work that the attack on the UTA plane, en route from Brazzaville to Paris, had been instigated and paid for by Libya.[62] It was announced that the judge would bring charges against Libya's deputy foreign minister Musa Kusa, the deputy head of the Libyan secret service Abdallah Sanussi, and Abdallah Elazrang, the then first counsellor of the Libyan embassy in Brazzaville. One crucial claim was that the fuses used to blow up the UTA plane were of exactly the same type as those used to explode the bomb on Pan Am 103 over Lockerbie.

The French enquiry had formerly found evidence to suggest Syria complicity in the UTA bombing, with Libya at that time not regarded as a leading suspect. There were clear signs that the Damascus-based Ahmed Jibril, enjoying Syrian protection, had been involved in the bomb plot; and when the French investigators received instructions from the presidential palace to abandon the leads pointing to Syria, Patrick Quentin, a former lawyer for the UTA relatives, resigned in disgust from the case. In an interview broadcast on ITN in December 1991 he declared that the decision was 'inexplicable and shocking', commenting on how the investigators had now 'completely ceased all investigations tracing the route of the suitcase

[bomb] in question. Nevertheless there are still unanswered questions about this . . . There are political pressures which are self-evident . . . even a judge as strong and honest as Bruguière cannot remain completely indifferent to those pressures.' Bruguière himself had suggested earlier that it had been a struggle to obtain the co-operation of the French government in his investigation, and that he had not ruled out the involvement of countries apart from Libya in the UTA bombing. Similarly, one of Bruguière's colleagues, Xaviet Raufer of the French Institute of Criminology, had commented that there could well be 'other groups and other countries'. There were clear signs that Judge Bruguière, a much respected investigator,[63] was to some extent in conflict with Paris and London who wanted to establish sole Libyan involvement.

On 14 November 1991 Washington announced that two Libyan nationals were to be charged with complicity in the bombing of Pan Am 103 over Lockerbie, a move that followed an assertion by CIA chief William Webster that Syria was not involved and that proxies employed by the Iranian government had carried out the plot.[64] The report commented that 'there have been suggestions, not least by Lockerbie relatives, that the United States was covering up Syrian complicity to foster good relations with Damascus'. The US acting Attorney-General had earlier commented that he was very satisfied with the progress of the Lockerbie investigation. On 15 November there was public speculation about steps that might be taken to make Libya yield up the two suspects, Abdelbaset Ali Mohmed al-Megrahi and al Amin Khalifa Fhimah. The previous night President Bush had declared that 'This is very serious business' and that he would be contacting Prime Minister John Major and other leaders to co-ordinate action. The White House spokesman Marlin Fitzwater stated: 'We are considering international responses. We won't discuss the options.' He refused to rule out the possibility of military action against Libya. (In May 1990 a presidential commission recommended that the US take military action against proven terrorists and the states that protect them. US legislation empowers American officers to capture terrorist suspects and bring them back to the US for trial.)

The UK Foreign Secretary Douglas Hurd called in the Commons for Libya to surrender the two men for trial in the United Kingdom or the United States for 'mass murder', commenting that 'the interests of justice require no less. This fiendish act of wickedness cannot be passed over or ignored.' Later, on BBC television, Libya's ambassador to France, Saeeb Mujber, declared: 'Nobody surrenders his own nationals and this way surrenders his sovereignty . . . This is a political thing. This is a lynching to bring Libya to its knees.' And Lord Fraser, the Scottish Lord Advocate, announced: 'In consultation with the United States Attorney-General, I have come to the conclusion that there is sufficient evidence to justify application to court for a warrant for the arrests of the named individuals'; the Procurator Fiscal in Dumfries at the same time lodged charges of conspiracy, murder, and contravention of the Aviation Security Act of 1982.

The investigation, we were assured, had been most thorough. The Chief Constable of Dumfries, George Esson, stated that enquiries had been carried out in seventy countries; no less than 15,000 statements had been taken; and more than 20,000 names recorded on computer. The investigation had so far cost more than £17 million. The conclusion was that al-Megrahi was director of the Centre for Strategic Studies in Tripoli at the time of the Lockerbie bombing, having also been a chief of airline security. Fhimah had been a station officer with Libyan Arab Airlines in Malta. The two men are accused of placing a suitcase containing a bomb on board an aircraft at Malta's Luqa airport on 21 December 1988; the case was then allegedly carried to Frankfurt and placed on a Pan Am flight for London Heathrow for transfer to Pan Am flight 103 for New York. The Libyans – and the Libyans alone – were held to be responsible. The White House national security advisor Brent Scowcroft had spoken to John Major, and Washington and London were in full agreement. Douglas Hurd stated that neither Syria nor the PFLP–GC had been involved, and President Bush remarked: 'A lot of people thought it was Syrians. The Syrians took a bum rap on this.'[65] There was no mention of the Iranians.

It was also reported that the Israeli secret service, Mossad, had been informed of the Western plans a month before the public statements, to prepare the ground for a co-ordinated political and diplomatic action against Libya. Ruling out Syrian and Iranian complicity in the bombing was widely regarded as a signal that could help in the release of Western hostages, including Terry Waite, and encourage the holding of the US-sponsored peace talks on the Middle East.[66] It was also reported that 'even within the past few weeks, security services had been claiming that Iran had "commissioned" the bombing from the Syrian-backed terror group, the PFLP–GC . . . but that, after West German police had "blown" the PFLP–GC cell, its leader, Ahmed Jibril, had been forced to subcontract the bombing to Libya.'[67] Dr Jim Swire, whose daughter Flora died in the Lockerbie bombing, commented that 'a couple of Libyans are only likely to be small minnows in a very large pond. What we want to know is why they did it and who put them up to it.'[68] In a similar vein the American Susan Cohen, whose daughter Theodora died, declared: 'A lot more is needed than to simply indict a couple of Libyans . . . I don't think this is adequate after almost three years. They have only done this for political expediency. I think that any involvement by Syria and Iran would not be brought to light because all you have to do is look at George Bush's foreign policy.' Bonnie O'Connor, of Long Island, whose brother John Ahern was killed, commented that 'Indicting Libyans is only a convenience for George Bush's Mid-east peace policy. Does George Bush take us for fools?' And Tom Currie, whose aunt Jean Murray was killed in Sherwood Crescent, doubted that 'only two men were responsible for the bombing'.[69]

On 16 November, it was revealed that Britain and the United States were planning to call a worldwide trade embargo on Libya if Colonel Gaddafi refused to forswear terrorism and to hand over the two suspect Libyans for trial. There was talk of asking the European Community to back sanctions and seeking support from the Group of Seven (G7) leading industrial countries. It was suggested that an approach to the United Nations was possible to secure the widest possible support for a trade embargo against Libya: there was some speculation that China might use its veto on the Security Council. The signs were that Washington would seek to impose international sanctions on Libya, and then move to tougher action if these did not work. The Americans were still refusing to rule out the possibility of military action, though they refused to speculate in public as to what form this might take. According to one quoted senior source, the US and Britain had decided against the use of military force 'in the medium term', and that the economic sanctions would begin with a ban on air flights to Libya.[70] The same source suggested that if a military strike *were* to be launched the new available technology would prevent such an attack being bungled, like the 1986 air strike that failed to assassinate Colonel Gaddafi. The Pentagon was already developing contingency plans for a raid on Libya – with the aim, no doubt, of killing its leader. Marlin Fitzwater was quoted: 'We're talking about the full range of matters that are available to countries in terms of their authorities – diplomatic, civilian, military – across the whole gamut.'[71]

The two accused Libyans, according to one report, boasted of their plan to 'destroy America' just days before the Lockerbie bombing; they added for good measure that Ronald Reagan was 'a stupid cowboy with no brains'.[72] A British businessman in Malta, a former military policeman, described his encounter with the two Libyans to police investigating the bombing. It was now being suggested that a ban on Libyan Arab Airlines flights world wide would be quickly followed by the freezing of Libyan assets. A State Department source declared: 'This man has got away with too much for too long and this time we are determined to make him pay.' The CIA was still prepared to state its conviction that both Syria and Iran had a hand in the bombing but the White House was clearly determined to focus the issue on Gaddafi and on him alone. In November 1991 a senior Israeli official, Yigal Carmon, advisor on counterterrorism to Prime Minister Yitzhak Shamir, reaffirmed the Israeli belief that Ahmed Jibril's PFLP–GC, backed by Syria, was implicated in the bombing of Pan Am 103. Carmon commented that the Israelis never claimed to know the last link in the chain but still insisted that Jibril had complicity in the crime. Another Israeli official commented at the time that if Dalkamoni, working with the Damascus-based PFLP–GC, was not involved 'and the two Libyans were really the perpetrators, then this must be the coincidence of the century'.[73]

The Arab world, already sensitised to the slaughter of Moslems by the Americans in the Gulf war, began to express doubts about the wisdom of a further US attack on an Arab state. Washington, it appeared, was increasingly eager to use a big stick against recalcitrant Arab states but was prepared to tolerate for an indefinite period Israel's contempt for UN resolutions aimed at curtailing its own territorial ambitions. President Mubarak of Egypt expressed his anxieties at the escalating campaign against Libya, reflecting the growing opinion that Libya had been selected for attack because it was a small and 'safe' target: the Bush administration could be seen to be acting decisively without incurring significant risks. The London-based *al-Quds al-Arabi* newspaper contended that after all the fingers of suspicion had so firmly pointed at Syria and Iran, to suddenly point them at Libya as sole perpetrator was tantamount to 'hurling allegations at will'.[74] And again there was the possibility that the West was deciding to deny Syrian and Iranian culpability as a way of securing the release of Terry Waite and Thomas Sutherland: Libyan television commented that 'Libya was meant to be the scapegoat in the deal to release Western hostages'; and many Arab commentators were prepared to agree that the release of the hostages was a 'reward' for Syria and Iran being so conclusively cleared of the Lockerbie plot.

President Mubarak twice phoned President Bush to declare that any military strike against Colonel Gaddafi would smash the peace process and drastically damage the standing of the United States in the region. Mahfouz al-Ansari, editor of the Cairo-based publication *al-Gomhuriya* and close to Mubarak's chief political advisor Osama al-Baz, commented that any shots fired at Gaddafi would ricochet against America's allies: 'You delivered your blow [in the Gulf war], liberated Kuwait, and maintained legitimacy. Everyone stood behind you and with you, although the punishment was directed against a dear and brotherly country . . . this time around, if you try to strike a blow or hand out punishment to another brother, to Libya, believe me, you will then be punishing friends, more than you will be punishing the colonel.'[75] On the same newspaper the overtly pro-American chairman

Samir Ragab declared to President Bush that 'we can never accept that Washington should be transformed into the heavy-handed policeman who misuses his powers to the greatest extent'.[76] Similarly the staunchly pro-American Saudi newspaper *al-Sharq al-Awsat* chose to rebuke both Britain and the US for hinting at military action before allowing due legal process; and it supported Libya's call for the whole matter to be laid before the International Court of Justice in the Hague. Hopefully, the United States would see the issue as a legal and not a political matter, or one had better 'pray to God to help the good-natured Libyan people, who may find themselves paying yet again for something of which they are completely innocent'.[77]

At the end of November 1991, long before any 'enabling' resolution had been agreed in the Security Council, the West was putting the finishing touches to a package of sanctions to be used against Libya if Colonel Gaddafi refused to hand over the two suspect nationals. Again there was press speculation about the likelihood of 'all necessary means' being used against Libya to ensure compliance with Western demands.[78] A British diplomat hinted that sanctions might even begin before the issue had been brought to the United Nations, that the UN might be invoked if a spate of unilateral actions by the West failed to achieve the desired results. An initial step would be for the UN to approve any sanctions already introduced by Britain, the US and other states: this would have the effect of extending the sanctions policy on a worldwide basis. Later a Security Council resolution akin to 678 (on Iraq) might be introduced – and agreed in a pliant Security Council – to authorise 'all necessary means' to be use to punish Libya for failure to accede to Western demands. This schedule, according to the British diplomat, was 'not only possible but even likely if the Libyans do not conform . . . Still, we want to avoid a naked threat at this stage. Every Arab government knows that Gaddafi has been nothing but trouble since he took over; but Libya is also part of the Arab nation so it is difficult to cut it out from the rest.'[79]

On 27 November Britain and the United States demanded that Colonel Gaddafi accept full criminal and financial liability for the Lockerbie bombing. If he failed to do so he would face unspecified economic sanctions within a matter of weeks, and the possibility of military action had not been ruled out. At the same time France issued similar warnings over the bombing of the UTA airliner. Now the US, Britain and France were urging Libya to purge itself of terrorist crimes and 'promptly, by concrete actions, prove its renunciation of terrorism'. Libya was required to take 'complete responsibility for the actions of Libyan officials' and to surrender the accused men, to 'disclose all it knows of the crime . . . and allow full access to all witnesses, documents and material evidence, including the remaining timers, and that it pay appropriate compensation.' With no sign that Libya would accede to such demands, the West continued to threaten unspecified sanctions and refused to rule out the possibility of harsher measures. By now the Libyan authorities had appointed a judge to investigate the Western allegations. On 28 November Colonel Gaddafi made a surprise visit to President Mubarak for talks, a day after the US, Britain and France had demanded the surrender of the two accused Libyans. It was also significant that over the previous week Libya sent envoys to Egypt, Syria, Iran and Lebanon in an apparent effort to generate opposition to the gradually escalating Western campaign. It was reported that Egypt was working to prevent a military attack against its neighbour, an official declaring that 'We are trying to find a way to allow the Americans to be satisfied and for the Libyans not to suffer.'[80] A British official was quoted as saying that Libya would be required to comply within weeks, while a statement by the Libyan foreign ministry said that Judge Ahmed Taher al-Zawi, charged to investigate the Lockerbie accusations, had asked Britain and the US to let him see relevant documents. The statement, carried by the Libyan news agency Jana, reiterated Libya's rejection of 'all forms of terrorism and terrorist attacks that target civilians. Libya . . . has not and will not be linked to any group . . . that carries out such an inhuman act, because Libya itself was a victim of terrorism', referring to the US bombing of Tripoli and Benghazi in 1986.

In early December 1991 reports appeared that US aircraft were already carrying out practice bombing exercises ready for an attack on Libya.[81] The exercises were said to involve F-111 fighter-bombers engaged in 'live' attacks on Garbh, an uninhabited island off Cleit Dhubh, four miles from the north-west tip of Scotland. The island, near Cape Wrath, was used for bombing practice shortly before the 1986 strike against Libya. James Tytler, keeper of the Cape Wrath lighthouse, observed: 'They have been practising bombing up here all week. The weather has been foul, with the occasional gale force winds. But not even that has stopped the planes.' The US planes flew to Garbh from the US Air Force base at Lakenheath, Suffolk, being refuelled in mid-air by KC10 tankers based at nearby RAF Mildenhall. The headquarters of the US Air Force at Mildenhall refused to confirm or deny the exercises, with an official at the Pentagon stating that any plans would be purely on a 'contingency basis'. (Britain has no formal powers to prevent any command from President Bush urging the planes into action, but no doubt there would be 'consultations' with the British government.) By December a Washington poll was putting approval for President Bush at 46 per cent, the lowest since he took office.

On 4 December the Libyan authorities arrested the two accused men, declaring that a Libyan investigation would be carried out into the Lockerbie allegations. (At the same time the UK Foreign Office minister Douglas Hogg acknowledged that Gaddafi had agreed to disclose his earlier connections with the IRA.) Libya's intelligence chief Colonel Youssef Abdel-Qadir al-Dabari was still maintaining the innocence of the two men: 'The two Libyan persons linked by the American and British judiciary to the Pan American plane bombing in 1988 are in custody. The real criminal is now free.' Colonel al-Dabari confirmed that the two would not be extradited to face charges in Britain or the United States. The Saudi newspaper *al-Sharq al-Awsat* quoted al-Dabari as saying that there is no legal basis 'for saying that the investigation has to take place where the incident happened'. It was also confirmed that the four Libyans wanted by the French authorities for the bombing of the UTA airliner had also been arrested. Douglas Hogg, visiting North Africa to whip up anti-Libyan sentiment, was quoted as saying: 'It does seem as if the intelligence services of Libya were responsible for what happened . . . and if it is a form of state crime you cannot really expect the victims to accept that the state responsible should be playing a significant part in investigating or in trying those that are charged with the events.'[82] He added that he was anxious to persuade our friends to persuade Colonel Gaddafi, 'a worried man', what must happen.

By now it was clear that some sort of stalemate was developing. Colonel Gaddafi, seeking to adopt a conciliatory pose, had refrained from calling mass demonstrations in the streets of Tripoli or from resorting to revolutionary rhetoric, as he might have done in earlier years. Instead he promised to investigate the allegations, again renounced terrorism, and made an offer – quickly and predictably dismissed by Douglas Hogg – to disclose what he knew of the IRA and to close down the terrorist training camps in Libya. He had moreover communicated extensively in North Africa and beyond, seeking to win suitable friends and protectors. The Libyan ambassador to France repeated that there would be no extradition of the accused Libyans but promised that Libya would grant 'full co-operation and assistance' to any investigators from London or Washington who wished to travel to Libya: 'That we have appointed a judge and arrested some men does not represent a retreat, but a step forward'; if the men were proved guilty, they would be punished 'twice, since they would have also betrayed Libya as well as committing a criminal act'.[83]

The West was unimpressed. The US, Britain and France continued to threaten sanctions, and to hint at the possibility of military action. The French foreign minister Roland Dumas commented in an interview published on 6 December that there would be 'no limits' to the retaliation that would be meted out to the Libyan government if it was found responsible for the UTA bombing. Colonel Gaddafi had promised to break off relations with organisations 'described in the past as movements of liberation but have turned into terrorist movements', and had even claimed that he had intervened at one point to stop Terry Waite being killed by his Lebanese kidnappers. None of this did anything to alter the resolution of the West; Douglas Hogg's contribution was to declare that 'what has been made plain is that we are determined.'

The two accused men were soon denying their complicity in the Lockerbie bombing: Pierre Salinger reported his conversations* with the two men and with Colonel Gaddafi.[84] The Libyan foreign minister Ibrahim Beshari also invited Salinger to visit Rabta, the plant which the CIA had identified as a chemical warfare site, and the Al Qalah camp, claimed by the Americans to be the terrorist training base for Abu Nidal. Megrahi, one of the accused, produced his passport which supposedly showed that he had arrived in Malta on the day the indictment stated he had bought the clothes that were subsequently put in the suitcase bomb; but he denied any involvement in the bombing, saying that he could not have gone to Malta with a false passport and under a false name as he was too well known there (Salinger: 'Megrahi's answers . . . were not always convincing'). Fhimah, the second suspect, also denied any connection with Libyan intelligence, claiming that in fact his family had been seen as belonging to an anti-Gaddafi movement so he would never have been allowed into any intelligence organisations. He admitted being in Malta on the critical days but denied all involvement in the bomb plot (Salinger: 'I found Mr Fhimah a simple man, and it was hard to believe that he had been involved in a terrorist case'). Both the accused declared that they would be happy to talk to Scottish or American invest-igators, just as Ibrahim Beshari stated that Western investigators would be welcome in Libya and that the Libyan judge would like to have sight of the US and Scottish evidence so that he could conduct a solid interrogation of the two men. Beshari emphasised that the Libyan judicial system had been set up by the British in the 1950s and was independent of the government. Salinger then visited Rabta ('One of the company executives walking with us said it would be impossible to produce poisonous gas in the plant . . . there were no glass-enclosed areas or any de-contamination sections') and Al Qalah ('clearly not a terrorist camp, but a Palestinian refugee camp').

---

*In March 1992 Scotland Yard, spurning all Gaddafi's invitations to visit Libya, issued a subpoena against Pierre Salinger, demanding that he hand over all his interview records. The Western authorities could have interviewed the men themselves.

Pierre Salinger met Gaddafi in a tent surrounded by camels and security men. The Colonel started in anger when the question of the Pan Am bombing was raised, and he commented that 'our country has become a victim of terror – particularly from the United States. Libya is becoming a bottle of Pepsi Cola. They shake it, shake it, until it explodes.' He added that he was angry about the Lockerbie accusations, 'but I am satisfied that things are moving according to law. I am satisfied that there is a legal way to deal with this'; and he contrasted Reagan's attack on Libya with Bush's handling of the Gulf war ('Bush went to the world. He got UN resolutions. He got allies. Reagan did not say he was going to take his own decision').

On 6 December the UK government expressed dismay at the emerging Arab League support for Colonel Gaddafi on the Lockerbie question. In Cairo the League had called on the United Nations to join Libya in studying the Western charges of Libyan complicity in the outrage, a move which prompted the British foreign secretary Douglas Hurd to write to the League Secretary-General Esmat Abdel Maguid: 'I cannot understand how, in these circumstances, the Arab League thinks it right to express its solidarity with Libya.'[85] A day later Ahmed al-Taher al-Zawi, the investigating judge appointed by the Libyans, declared that the two men would face the death penalty if they were convicted in a Libyan court, and he reiterated the Libyan position that the accused Libyans could not be tried elsewhere. Beshari, visiting Dakar for an Islamic summit, told journalists that it would be an infringement of Libyan sovereignty to hand over the two men: 'The Libyan judicial authorities will try them. If they are guilty they will be punished. If they are not guilty they will be found innocent.' London was quick to reject Beshari's comments.

The Libyan judge continued his investigations, despite Western hostility to his efforts, and on 9 December suggested that his enquiries could widen to include other individuals. In an interview at his Tripoli office Zawi stated that the investigation was proceeding step by step and it could not be said how long the enquiries would take ('If they prove guilty, investigation will extend to other quarters and people if necessary. But so far we cannot say they are guilty'). Zawi had asked the British and US authorities to issue an order allowing him to study the findings that led to the accusations but all suggestions were rejected, with a repeat of the demand that the two men be handed over without delay. On 12 December Dr James Swire, whose daughter Flora died at Lockerbie, handed a sealed letter to the Scottish Lord Advocate from Libyan judges, following his (Swire's) five-day visit to Tripoli: Swire had met Gaddafi, Muhammed Aljadi, the head of the Libyan supreme court, and Ahmed Zawi, the investigating judge (Swire, on his meeting with Colonel Gaddafi: 'We talked about our daughters. I lost Flora and he had lost his 16-month old daughter Hannah in the American bombing raids in 1986. Both of the deaths were caused by indiscriminate violence. He accepted a photograph of Flora to put in the room where Hannah died'). There was American anger at the Swire visit. Bert Ammerman, the president of the American families group, accused Dr Swire of 'shotgun behaviour' and declared that the visit would damage relations between the British and American families. Ammerman had been pleased that the Lockerbie issue had been raised from a criminal matter onto the political stage, and he claimed that the Libyans were doing no more than manipulating a private individual 'who is hardly astute in the ways of the world'.[86] There can be little doubt that Colonel Gaddafi welcomed the Swire visit, if only to give him a communication route to the Lord Advocate, the man who had issued warrants for the two accused men. Gaddafi was obviously seeking to create an impression of compliance, without being prepared to agree the West's main demand. He had already instructed the Libyan people not to demonstrate over the Lockerbie charges, Libyan television declaring that he 'appealed to the masses to stay put and carry out their normal daily life, affirming that he was close to them if necessary'.[87]

On 14 December it was reported that the Libyan authorities intended to send investigators to Malta to search for evidence implicating the two accused men.[88] It was suggested that, in the absence of British co-operation, the Libyans would have to carry out their own investigations. A spokesman for the Crown Office in Edinburgh dismissed the Libyan intention to try the men in their own country as a 'calculated absurdity', noting that nothing less than the handing over of the two men would suffice. The West knew that Gaddafi would be unwilling to do this, as would any state, particularly in the absence of an extradition treaty. It can only be presumed that Britain and America, clearly liaising carefully at every stage of the escalation, had a schedule mapped out, a coherent set of steps designed to increase the pressure of Libya and to inflate the issue to massive international proportions.

The next step was to involve the United Nations. It was disclosed on 19 December that the United States, Britain and France were planning to ask the Security Council to impose a ban on all air traffic and to and from Libya. Senior diplomatic sources confirmed that suitable action would be taken as soon as Britain took over the presidency of the Security Council on 1 January.[89] It was conceded that firm action against a 'terrorist state' would help both George Bush and John Major in an election year, and that such a move would be facilitated by the fact that both Cuba and Yemen, both perceived as anti-Western, would be off the Security Council in the New Year. At the same time there was still some anxiety about the possibility of a Chinese veto on mandatory sanctions. A series of documents (Appendix 1), which would come to form the basis of the subsequent UN resolution, were then lodged with the UN Secretary-General. In essence these recorded the charges against the identified Libyan nationals and drew attention to the demands made on Libya on 27 November 1991, in particular that the Government of Libya must:

> surrender for trial all those charged with the crime; and accept responsibility for the actions of Libyan officials;

> disclose all it knows of this crime, including the names of all those responsible, and allow full access to all witnesses, documents and other material evidence, including all the remaining timers;

> pay appropriate compensation.

The document (referenced S/23308) concluded: 'We expect Libya to comply promptly and in full.'

On 27 December Colonel Gaddafi declared, in an interview broadcast on ITN, that Britain and the US could send independent judges to Tripoli to handle the case of the two accused men, but again refused to hand the two men over. In a separate interview the foreign minister Beshari declared that Libya was willing to send judges to Washington, London and Paris to discuss the case. Gaddafi suggested that the two Libyans would not get a fair trial abroad but expressed doubts that Bush and Major would launch further air strikes against Libya: 'They are different from both Reagan and Thatcher, and I don't think they would commit such injustices.' Commenting on his previous support for the IRA, Gaddafi remarked that they were committing acts of terrorism 'which we reject. We do not want a war between the Protestants and Catholics.' Beshari also revealed that judges of the Tripoli high court had sent messages to their counterparts in Scotland, France and the United States, and he urged that the Western judges should study the transcripts of the Libyan investigation of the two men. He observed that the case 'does not threaten international peace and security', so there was no reason to involve the Security Council ('It is a political and legal case that can be solved peacefully'); and Beshari added that the foreign ministers of the five-nation Arab Maghreb Union – Libya, Algeria, Tunisia, Morocco and Mauritania – intended to meet in January to agree 'the broad lines of an initiative aimed at solving the Lockerbie crisis'.[90]

The West rejected all the offers of co-operation made by Gaddafi and Beshari. Joe Snyder, a US State Department spokesman, told a regular press briefing: 'Libya must surrender for trial all those charged with the crime related to Pan Am 103. The United States and the United Kingdom have jurisdiction in this case. We expect Libya to comply promptly and in full.' He also remarked that the US, Britain and France were discussing how best to retaliate against Libya, though no decision had yet been reached.

On 1 January 1992 the UK Foreign Secretary Douglas Hurd outlined the issues that he expected would dominate Britain's foreign policy agenda in the months ahead.[91] In this account he stated:

> We are taking the Lockerbie bombing before the Security Council. We cannot have confidence in Libyan promises to try the alleged perpetrators, since they are alleged to be Libyan intelligence officers. We consider it entirely reasonable to insist on our demands that Libya should hand over the accused men for trial, accept responsibility for the attacks on the Pan Am flight and a French airliner, and provide information on all aid provided to terrorist groups.*

Two days later the Libyan authorities announced that they might not be able to pay foreign companies or workers, or to contribute to international organisations, because of US financial sanctions on the country. At the same time Britain, France and the United States told the new UN Secretary-General Boutros Boutros Ghali of their plans to force Libyan co-operation over the terrorist accusations. It was declared that there would be a Security Council resolution requiring Libya to comply with the Western demands for extradition; and that if Libya failed to comply the Security Council would be asked to impose sanctions. However, there were some signs that the Western parties to the dispute would not have things all their own way: France had already objected to using the G7 machinery for punitive purposes, Japan and expressed doubts about the use of further sanctions against Libya, and other countries – for example, Italy – were worried at the possible loss of trade. Moreover, there were doubts that Arab and African countries would observe UN sanctions, even if they were demanded in a Security Council resolution; it was noted that the Arab League had already expressed support for the Libyan position.

---

*The prejudging of Libyan guilt was never more clearly signalled. Libya is expected to accept responsibility for the Lockerbie bombing before a trial has even taken place. It is not difficult to see how the Libyan government might be inclined to doubt the objectivity – in this matter – of the Western courts.

Colonel Gaddafi, in an evident attempt to forestall sanctions, then launched an appeal to the international community, writing to the United Nations to urge the convening of a General Assembly session to find a way to eliminate 'terrorism, acts of violence and other grave issues of concern to all nations'. This letter, seeming to Western eyes an eccentric document, was presented to the Secretary-General by foreign minister Beshari: it urged the elimination of all the world's naval fleets, the liquidation of all the world's overseas military bases, and compensation to be paid to all people who were ever colonised. This was not all. The document also recommended an 'international irrigation system to prevent the flow of rivers, rain, snow and ice into the seas and oceans and their diversion to the land'. Moreover, the General Assembly should adopt 'a resolute approach' to curing cancer, AIDS, malaria and polio; and world attention must be directed to the problems of Northern Ireland, Palestine, Kurdistan, Kashmir and Cyprus. This Libyan initiative was widely seen as a rather clumsy attempt to divert attention from the Lockerbie issue. At the same time Libya was complaining to the International Air Transport Association about an alleged intrusion by planes from the US Sixth Fleet in the Mediterranean into the Tripoli flight information area, with the Libyan news agency Jana calling the incident 'a clear violation of the Civil Aviation Convention signed in Chicago in 1944': officials speaking for the US Navy denied the allegation. A few days later, on 13 January, Douglas Hurd was again demanding international support in dealing with the Libyan question: 'Since Libya has still not responded we will work for a Security Council resolution calling on Libya to comply with our demands. Further action may be needed if Libya does not then respond . . . The Libyan response has been totally inadequate.'[92]

On 20 January the Labour MPs Tam Dalyell (Linlithgow) and Bernie Grant (Tottenham), speaking in an adjournment debate in the Commons, managed to highlight crucial aspects of the Lockerbie investigation. Dalyell drew attention to part of a report submitted by the Lockerbie police to the Scottish Lord Advocate, Lord Fraser. This report is cited to suggest that the Lockerbie police suspected a Syrian involvement in the outrage, and it concludes with the words:

There can be little doubt that Marwan Abdel Razzaq Mufti Khreesat is the bomb-maker for the PFLP–GC, that he was brought to West Germany for that express purpose and there is a possibility that he prepared the IED [Improvised Explosive Device] which destroyed PA103. As such he should not be at liberty but should be closely questioned regarding his activities with a view to tracing his associates in the attack.

Douglas Hurd had commented on 14 November that 'there was no evidence about the involvement of other Governments'. Had the Foreign Secretary, Dalyell asked, been shown that document by the Scottish police? And what of the 'substantial information, still relevant, pointing to the involvement of an Iranian and Syrian-based organisation'? Why had the Foreign Secretary 'been so categorical in ruling out the involvement of other parties when Lord Fraser, the Lord Advocate, had gone out of his way not to rule out the involvement of other states?' Dalyell then quoted from David Leppard's book *On the Trail of Terror,* already cited, to indicate CIA knowledge of Iranian complicity; commented that 'Libya is being used as a sole whipping boy when there was an alliance of elements from Iran, Syria and Libya'; and quoted from a powerful editorial in *The Sunday Times* (24 November 1991):

Maybe it has been necessary to be nice to Iran and Syria to secure the release of the remaining hostages in Beirut. It must be more than coincidence that both countries were officially cleared of any Lockerbie involvement just a few days before Terry Waite and Thomas Sutherland were at last released. Our joy at their freedom should be tempered by the shame of the cost: the relatives of the victims of the Lockerbie bomb must now come to terms with the fact that most of those behind the murder of their loved ones are going to get away with it. The cause of justice is being sacrificed on the altar of diplomatic convenience. We will live to regret it.

Tam Dalyell also highlighted a lead article in *Tribune* (17 January 1992) in which Ian Williams, the paper's UN correspondent, comments on speculation 'in the United Nations that John Major and George Bush are looking to fight their 1992 election campaigns on the back of military action against Libya'.[94] Here it is suggested that even pro-Western Arab diplomats are worried by what they perceive as the 'Iraq syndrome' developing in the Security Council – 'in which support for one seemingly unexceptionable resolution is then used to conscript support for another'. For those who remember that Syria was prime suspect in the Lockerbie bombing, Libya's protestations are seen to 'have some merit'.[95] Ian Williams comments: 'One can imagine the reaction of the White House if Nicaragua had tried to extradite Oliver North for his admitted terrorist actions against the Sandinista Government. It is not necessary to be an admirer of the Gaddafi regime to suspect that double standards are rapidly becoming the accepted reserve currency of the New World Order.'[96]

Bernie Grant, speaking in the adjournment debate, focused on the legal aspects of the Lockerbie accusations, emphasising President Bush's insistence on the need for legality, international law and respect for a nation's sovereignty. 'Under which international convention or agreement' is the minister [Douglas Hogg] acting? Grant emphasised that under the 1971 Montreal Convention, the convention for the suppression of unlawful acts against the safety of civil aviation, unless there is an extradition treaty in force, Libya 'is entitled, indeed obliged, to try the offenders under her own domestic law'. Since there is no extradition treaty between Britain and Libya, Article 7 of the Montreal Convention applies:

> The Contracting State in the territory of which the alleged offender is found shall, if it does not extradite him, be obliged, without exception whatsoever and whether or not the offence was committed in its territory, to submit the case to its competent authorities for the purpose of prosecution. Those authorities shall take their decision in the same manner as in the case of any ordinary offence of a serious nature under the law of that State.

It is also significant that Article 14 of the Convention states that:

> Any dispute between two or more Contracting States concerning the interpretation or application of this Convention which cannot be settled through negotiation, shall, at the request of one of them, be submitted to arbitration. If within six months from the date of the request for arbitration the Parties are unable to agree on the organisation of the arbitration, any one of those Parties may refer the dispute to the International Court of Justice by request in conformity with the Statute of the Court.

Both Britain and Libya are signatories to the Montreal Convention. For Britain, in these circumstances, to demand extradition of suspects from Libya would be a violation of the Convention; if, moreover, Britain disputes this interpretation of the Convention then Article 14 stipulates a course of action. Britain has not chosen to observe the Convention, preferring to threaten sanctions and to hint at the possibility of military action. Libya, by contrast, 'has acted in accordance with its own domestic law and with international law by appointing a High Court judge who is carrying out an investigation into the charges levelled against the two Libyan citizens'. Why is the British government not permitting police officers or other officials to work with the Libyans in their efforts to deal with the matter, 'as international law both permits and demands that they do, especially as the articles in the Libyan criminal procedure code, which prohibits the handing over of the men without proper evidence, were set up by the British in 1973'?

Grant also emphasised the little-publicised fact that the Maltese government, working alongside the Scottish police and the FBI, have come to very different conclusions. The Maltese authorities have suggested that the evidence to support a Maltese connection 'is, at best, very feeble': there is no evidence to support the UK/US assertion that the bomb originated in Malta, and without such evidence the entire case against the accused Libyans collapses (Grant: 'The Maltese government's views could not be reconciled with the views of the United States and the United Kingdom governments, despite visits to Malta by the Minister of State, the deputy Attorney-General of the United States and the Lord Advocate'). It is suggested that the Maltese government is satisfied that the Libyan authorities are acting properly under international law 'by investigating the charges laid against the two Libyans and by refusing to extradite them'. Finally Bernie Grant emphasised the appalling consequences that would flow from further military action against Libya.

Douglas Hogg, replying to Dalyell and Grant in the adjournment debate, had no stomach for presenting a defence of the UK/US case. Of the contributions made by the hon. Members for Linlithgow and Tottenham, Hogg commented: 'Both went into the events in considerable detail. I have no intention of doing so.'

Tam Dalyell had succeeded in gaining publicity for the likelihood of a Syrian involvement in the Lockerbie bombing,[97] and Bernie Grant had highlighted the importance of current legal provisions, being ignored by the British and the Americans in their approach to the Lockerbie case. It was not difficult to find support for the legal interpretation that suggested that the Libyan authorities were acting properly in the face of threats, and a nice disregard for legal procedure, on the part of London and Washington. Thus a correspondent to *The Guardian* (21 December 1991) commented that in the absence of an extradition treaty with Libya, 'it is hard to fathom why the US and Britain should have entertained the expectation that Libya would hand over its citizens on the basis of evidence whose provenance can only have been from (not disinterested) intelligence agencies and against what now seems to be a pretty empty threat'. The same point is made by Marc Weller, research fellow in international law at St Catherine's College, Cambridge, in an article on the legal aspects of Lockerbie.[98] Here it is stated that the US and British demands for the surrender of the two Libyan nationals 'appear to violate international procedures on extradition . . . In the absence of an extradition treaty, the 1971 Montreal Convention applies . . . So far, Libya has followed the procedure to the letter . . . even if the two alleged offenders are handed over, the episode will smack of the application of power politics in disregard of legal procedure.'

On 20 January the UN Security Council unanimously adopted a resolution (Appendix 2) calling on Libya to observe the earlier demands made by the United States, the United Kingdom and France. It was reported that the US, Britain and France were considering 'how much of a role to give the UN Secretary-General, Boutros Boutros Ghali, as the events unfold'.[99] Again, a supposed UN initiative was to be run by the Western powers. Weller commented that the legal defect in the US/UK approach had 'not been healed by the UN Security Council's support for the demands'; moreover, the Security Council 'is not the right forum to make retrospective decisions of a legal nature'.[100] The passing of the new resolution (731) represented a further step in the escalation of pressure on Libya. The US ambassador to the United Nations, Thomas Pickering, commented: 'If further action should be necessary, we are convinced that the Council is ready to face up to its full responsibilities.'[101] Western diplomats declared that selective sanctions against Libya would be sought in 'a matter of weeks' if Libya still refused to hand over the two men.

A few days later Colonel Gaddafi again declared that he was willing to renounce international terrorism and to consider outside inspection of Libya's alleged chemical and nuclear weapons sites. To an emissary sent from the UN Secretary-General he said that he was under no legal obligation to surrender the two Libyan suspects and he challenged the British and the Americans to produce the evidence, adding: 'The truth is they don't have it.' Gaddafi had invited British and US lawyers to attend the Libyan enquiry and to interrogate the accused, and he had welcomed representatives of the victims' families. The possibility of transferring the enquiry to a 'neutral forum' such as the International Court of Justice in the Hague was being considered, and it was suggested that Libya might be prepared to put substantial funds into escrow in an overseas account to pay compensation and damages if any Libyan liability over Lockerbie was established in the courts. At the same time Iranian President Rafsanjani was reported as supporting Libya's recommendation that an international tribunal be allowed to investigate the bombings of the US and French airliners.[102] Gaddafi himself continued to advertise his willingness to co-operate with international organisations. On 3 February the International Atomic Energy Agency (IAEA) announced that Libya would allow inspection of any sites rumoured to be involved in the development of nuclear weapons. When the IAEA director Hans Blix visited the only site already declared under Libya's safeguards agreement with the agency, the Soviet-built Tajura research reactor outside Tripoli was found to be lying idle. It had been shut down since June last year, with spare parts no longer available and most of the Soviet scientists gone home.

On 11 February the Libyan authorities moved quickly to deny a report that the two accused Libyans had disappeared and may have been executed. *The Washington Post* had quoted Vincent Cannistraro, the former CIA counter-terrorist chief, as saying that Libya had planned to announce the disappearance of the two men to suggest that they might have been kidnapped. Some sources suggested that the statement might have been part of a US disinformation campaign against Colonel Gaddafi: 'the execution claim was bound to cause sufficient dismay among Libyan agents for them to defect'.[103] The investigating judge Ahmed al-Zawi denied the *Post* report and invited anyone to visit Libya to see the two men, and even a Libyan opposition source said that the *Post* story appeared to be 'yet another part of the psychological warfare against Gaddafi by the Americans'.[104] Stephen Mitchell, a British lawyer advising the Libyans' lawyer Ibrahim Legwell on the extradition aspects of the case confirmed that the men were alive and well: 'I saw them in the office of their lawyer . . . The two accused were brought pursuant to an order of the . . . investigating judge of the Libyan Supreme Court . . . I am absolutely satisfied . . . they are the people who are the accused.'[105] In London the visiting US Vice-President Dan Quayle continued to make threats, saying that 'Gaddafi had better realise we are serious' and adding that 'you just have to look in the past to see that we have the political will to make these kinds of requests happen'.[106]

A sudden move by Libya on 12 February seemed to take the Western powers by surprise: the Libyan authorities announced that France would be allowed to question the four senior intelligence officials accused of bombing the UTA airliner. France, Britain and the United States held urgent consultations in New York to agree a common response. The next day there were even suggestions that Colonel Gaddafi might surrender the two accused men if the necessary safeguards could be guaranteed. Lord Trefgarne, after discussing the Lockerbie issue with Colonel Gaddafi, said that the Libyan authorities had wanted talks with the Scottish legal authorities to request assurances about a fair trial if the two men were handed over. Trefgarne, a former Foreign Office minister, declared: 'They are prepared in principle to hand them over but they need proper assurances about the safeguards these men will enjoy when the time comes. What they want to do . . . is have a dialogue with the Scottish legal authorities to try and ascertain whether these safeguards exist.'[107] He suggested that the matter would not be resolved by 'megaphone diplomacy' and declared that the Libyans expected the UN Security Council to move to sanctions, 'maybe even worse'. Douglas Hurd moved speedily to veto the Libyan suggestions, insisting that the issue could only be handled under the terms of the existing Security Council resolution (731).

On 15 February the official Libyan news agency Jana announced that the two accused Libyans would appear at a public hearing before Judge Ahmed al-Zawi, while the UK Foreign Office issued a statement saying that Britain, the US and France would be consulting other members of the Security Council about the steps to be taken to force Libyan compliance. A Foreign Office spokesman insisted that nothing had been ruled out, again encouraging speculation that 'even military action' was being considered.[108] US officials declared that the US, Britain and France would push for a mandatory sanctions resolution by the end of the month. On 18 February, following the earlier Libyan promises, the two accused men appeared in a courtroom in Tripoli amid tight security. The men arrived in a convoy of five police cars and were escorted up the steps of the court building by men armed with Kalashnikovs. Once in the courtroom the men were not given the opportunity to answer questions but Megrahi told the assembled foreign Press: 'I just want to say we are not guilty.' Zawi emphasised that judicial proceedings could only begin if the West co-operated with Libya in providing evidence to support the accusations. The authorities in Scotland and the United States had refused to offer any evidence but Zawi did not rule out the possibility in the right circumstances of a trial of the accused by a neutral international court. Again he declared that if the men were tried in Libya and found guilty they would face the death penalty. However, the main point was the lack of help from the Scottish and US authorities: Zawi insisted he had requested evidence from witnesses, the plane's black box and other sources but had been denied any assistance in his enquiries.

The United States quickly dismissed the proceedings as a travesty of justice, the State Department spokesman Richard Boucher announcing: 'We don't put much faith or credence in what a Libyan judge might say. We think that a Libyan investigation or a hearing is a travesty of justice, amounts to nothing more than another attempt by Libya to delay and to evade its responsibility.'[109] The next day it was announced that UN envoy Vasily Safronchuk would convey a letter, a 'kind of ultimatum', from the UN Secretary-General Boutros Boutros Ghali to the Libyan government. The scene was set for a further escalation of the pressure on the Gaddafi regime.

All the signs were that the Western campaign was doing no more than consolidating Colonel Gaddafi's hold on power. Senior diplomats in Tripoli were commenting that the West's failure to produce evidence of the guilt of the two accused men was convincing ordinary Libyans that the Lockerbie bombing was being used as an excuse to target the country as a whole. One diplomat said: 'Up to November and December, people were very critical of the government, but now their mood has changed. Now they think that the Americans want to get rid of Gaddafi and gain control of Libyan oil.'[110] The ordinary Libyans feel 'that the campaign against them is unjust', but the atmosphere in Tripoli was more relaxed than three months earlier when many felt that a US air strike was imminent. In November and December some Tripoli residents moved out into the desert to avoid the expected American bombing, those that remained stockpiling food at home, 'so there was a sudden shortage of flour and sugar in the shops'.[111] American press reports suggested that the Libyans were preparing to withstand economic blockade or military attack, but diplomats in Tripoli have said that they are mystified by such reports. In February 1992 there was little sign in Libya of such preparations.

The situation was that the two accused men were still in custody. Judge Ahmed el-Tahir al-Zawi had declared that he would quit the case because of the West's failure to produce requested evidence and because there were signs that Colonel Gaddafi was trying to sidestep the Libyan judiciary to do a deal with the US, the UK and France. In February 1992 a report from the Palestine Liberation Organisation (PLO) provided fresh evidence of Iranian involvement in the Lockerbie bombing, deepening *'the controversy of why the Scottish police and the American FBI changed their minds after claiming for 18 months that the bombing was committed by members of Ahmed Jibril's group, the Popular Front for the Liberation of Palestine–General Command, under the umbrella of Iran and Syria'*.[112] Abu Sharif, the political adviser to PLO chairman Yasser Arafat, claimed that the PLO had 'gathered very accurate and sensitive information related to the Lockerbie affair', and that this information 'points clearly to the involvement of Middle East parties, not Libya, in this crime'.[113] The 80-page report details the meetings between Jibril, Ali Akbar Mohtashemi, the former Iranian interior minister, and other Iranians to discuss the planned outrage. The report 'includes the most specific evidence yet of Iran's role in the bombing'.[114]

The West, interested above all in its hidden agenda, moved to secure its mandatory sanctions resolution from the UN Security Council. Again Libya – and Libya alone – was to be held solely responsible.

IMPOSING SANCTIONS

The United States had succeeded in defining for its own purposes the parameters of the Lockerbie question. There was no longer any debate about who was responsible for the outrage; whether the evidence, as formerly believed over a lengthy period, pointed to Syrian and Iranian – as well as Libyan – involvement. The only issue was how the US-dominated Security Council could be induced to tighten further the noose around Libya. The overt purpose was to force the Libyan authorities to yield up the two Libyan suspects for fair trial in Scotland or the United States, but the West was already assuming their guilt and in any case the surrender of the two men was not the only demand stipulated in Resolution 731 (see Appendix 2). It was already clear that if Washington achieved a mandatory sanctions resolution in the Security Council this would afford a permanent pressure on Libya: even if the two Libyan suspects were surrendered to the West for trial Washington would be free to veto any attempts to terminate the sanctions resolution until Libya had complied with any or all of further US demands.

On 25 February the Egyptian president, Hosni Mubarak, arrived in Paris to discuss the Lockerbie issue with President Mitterrand. Colonel Gaddafi had already declared that he wanted the United Nations to create a mechanism to allow the two suspects to be tried by a neutral body if the evidence against them was provided to Libya. There was speculation that the Mubarak initiative was intended to enable the two men to be tried in such a neutral country, though it is hard to imagine that Colonel Gaddafi would have seen France, one of the sponsors of Resolution 731, as a suitable candidate. At the same time it was obvious that Gaddafi feared a further US military attack and was keen to conciliate Washington, if this could be achieved without totally abnegating Libyan rights. Thus in an interview in a French daily newspaper he declared: 'We immediately protested and proclaimed our innocence. But very quickly we understood that we were confronted by virtual state terrorism and that the Americans wouldn't hesitate to launch a massive military operation. An armed confrontation would crush us. We are aware of the danger. That's why we prefer to play the card of conciliation and justice, rather than of defiance.'[115] The Libyan minister of justice, Ibrahim Mohammed Bakkar, had visited Cairo prior to Mubarak's talks with Mitterrand and it was reported that Paris and Tripoli had made some progress in working out a judicial compromise.[116] Mubarak denied that he was mediating but commented, after his talks with Mitterrand, that he was involved in steps 'with the hope of reaching a just and positive solution which would be welcome'.[117]

At the end of February American and British government sources released a story that Colonel Gaddafi had ordered his agents to kill a 'supergrass' defector, Abdu Maged Jiacha, said to have information that would incriminate the two Libyan suspects. It was declared that a senior Libyan intelligence officer had travelled to the Netherlands in an effort to locate

Jiacha but that the defector had been taken into the federal witness protection programme and was living on the US west coast. One unnamed source commented: 'There are very senior people in Tripoli who are hell bent on getting him. If they can get him back from America they'll be able to shut him up.'[118] As with any information from interested sources it is difficult to know what to make of this story. What is clear is that Washington was keen to bolster its case following criticism that it had conveniently ignored evidence of Syrian and Iranian complicity in the Lockerbie outrage.[119] And the view was also emerging that US intransigence was unhelpful to Western interests. Some diplomats in Tripoli have insisted that Washington and London are deliberately ignoring the changes in Libya in order to target Gaddafi but that this policy risks fostering hardline Islamic fundamentalists instead of the Western-oriented pragmatists that may be preferred.[120] President Mubarak would hardly welcome a fundamentalist resurgence in an adjoining state; and the Russians have suggested that a fundamentalist Libya might give a fresh impetus to Iran's efforts to subvert the 15 million Muslims in the southern republics of the Commonwealth of Independent States.

On 1 March the Libyan foreign minister, Ibrahim Beshari, announced after a meeting with the Russian foreign minister, Andrei Kozyrev, in Cairo that Libya was willing to hand over the two Libyan suspects to a neutral country for trial: 'Libya is ready to hand over the two suspects for trial in front of a neutral court in any neutral country and hopes that the UN Security Council will not make any resolutions against Libya.'[121] Kozyrev commented that 'the best thing would be to hand over the suspects to the UN Secretary-General without any conditions and for him to take further action himself'. At the same time the Libyan Supreme Court judge, Ahmed al-Zawi, asked to be removed from his role in leading the investigation into the Western charges. According to Libya's official news agency Jana he gave nine reasons why he was unable to conduct a proper investigation, including 'lack of co-operation by the authorities in the US, the United Kingdom and Scotland'.

The Secretary to the Libyan Arab People's Bureau in Paris, Saad Muhber, reported in the Western press and elsewhere, gave reasons why Libya could not extradite its own nationals and made various suggestions 'to get out of this impasse'.[122] He commented that the relevant law dated to 1953 and was British-inspired as the then colonial power; that the two accused Libyans could not expect a fair trial in the US or the UK as they had already been judged guilty by the media and government authorities; that there were other saddening 'cases of prejudgment' (the Birmingham Six, the Tottenham Three and others); and that the accused might be subjected to 'torturous methods'* in order 'to force them to accept responsibility of whatever the two countries wish to throw at our door'. Muhber then proposed that the Montreal Convention of 1971 should be implemented, 'otherwise why did we all adopt it?'; that perhaps an independent commission could carry out an independent investigation, the results of which would be binding on all the concerned countries; that if strong evidence of guilt is established then the Libyan authorities would bring the accused to an open trial 'in the presence of lawyers of the concerned governments, families of the victims, UN representatives and human rights groups'; and that the independent commission could have access to the accused in a neutral country provided that their 'accommodation, safety and their availability only to the commission' could be guaranteed. It is then remarked that if the West refuses all the compromises and alternatives that are offered it is clearly seeking not justice 'but a pretext for the repetition of the earlier 1986 Anglo-American aggression . . .'. In fact the West was now making it clear that no compromises or discussions would be tolerated, that the Western demands must be fully implemented without delay.

In early March the terms of the draft UN resolution imposing sanctions on Libya became clear: a package of economic, military and diplomatic measures were being drawn up by the US, Britain and France to mark, according to one Arab commentator, 'the beginning of the siege of Libya'. The draft resolution, not yet enacted, included a ban on civil air links, a banning of arms sales and the scaling down of diplomatic representation. Colonel Gaddafi continued to adopt a conciliatory posture to discourage the passing of the mandatory resolution in the Security Council. Having already proclaimed Libyan innocence in the Lockerbie outrage he told the General People's Congress in Tripoli that 'any relationship with the IRA must be severed' (in any case the Provisional IRA had been supported only because of the Western bombing raids on Tripoli and Benghazi). There were signs also that Gaddafi had agreed in discussion with the UN Under-Secretary-General, Vasily Safronchuk, that he would hand over the two suspects to the United States if Washington promised to normalise relations with Libya (which clearly would be unacceptable to the US); and it was even reported that Gaddafi was prepared to hand over the two men to the Islamic Development Bank.[123] There were also some signs in the international community that the Western policy on Libya was beginning to arouse disquiet. King

---

*I myself confess to a knee-jerk reaction against the idea of 'torturous methods' being used in Britain but then recalled the pictures of the beaten faces of the Birmingham Six when they were brought before an English court.

Hassan of Morocco, for example, the only Arab member of the Security Council, declared that he would find it difficult to vote for the projected sanctions resolution or to apply sanctions unless there was proof of Libyan involvement in the Lockerbie bombing. And the West continued to show great reluctance to offer such proof. It was becoming increasingly clear that Washington was experiencing unexpected difficulties in mobilising the international community for a prolonged siege of Libya ('The UK and US have both become alarmed by the success of Col Gaddafi's conciliatory tactics'[124]).

The UN Secretary-General, Boutros Boutros Ghali, in a report (see Appendix 4) that 'irritated London and Washington',[125] conceded that there had been 'a certain evolution' in Libya's position and that this should be acknowledged before punitive measures were adopted against Tripoli. This suggested that Gaddafi had made some concessions when visited by UN Under-Secretary-General Safronchuk, and that this would make it more difficult for Washington to muster enough support in the Security Council for a tough resolution. Colonel Gaddafi was also hoping that his appeal to the International Court of Justice would put a further brake on US plans for the targeting of Libya, but at the same time was taking what measures he could to protect the Libyan economy. On 5 March it was reported that Libya had shifted between \$2 billion and \$3 billion of its overseas assets from Europe to banks in the Middle East.[126] Between March and September 1991 Libya had already halved its deposits in British banks, to £781 million, and substantial liquid assets were also removed from other European centres. A London banker commented that Libya 'feels it has some sympathy among other Arab countries and the obvious place to put the money is with banks in the Gulf region'. In a parallel move to protect its assets Libya was now demanding payment for its oil exports, wherever possible, in Swiss francs rather than dollars, so reducing the number of transactions that must be cleared through US banks. The US authorities have traditionally exploited the clearance procedures to block dealings that they regard as undesirable, and the Libyans no doubt well remember how \$2 billion of Libyan assets were frozen in the US in 1986 in retaliation for Libya's alleged terrorist attacks in Rome and Vienna.

The suspicion continued to grow that President Bush was considering a fresh military strike against Iraq or Libya to boost his popularity in an election year.[127] It was acknowledged that the planned sanctions resolution would have only limited effect: it would be unlikely to achieve the hand-over of the two suspects and even less likely to topple Gaddafi. An option for a further resolution, beyond the immediate projected sanctions, would be for an international ban on Libyan oil. There could be no doubt that such a ban would cripple the Libyan economy and probably destabilise the regime. Thus Mehdi Varzi, an oil specialist at Kleinwort Benson, has been quoted: 'If Libyan oil is excluded from Europe then they are in deep trouble.' Libya uses oil revenues to pay for food imports which amount to as much as a fifth of all imports; and the regime uses its oil wealth to purchase the loyalty of clan and tribal leaders without whose support Gaddafi, operating in a traditional tribal society, could not survive. However, an oil ban would also hit various Western importers who may in consequence be reluctant to support such extreme measures. In such circumstances Washington may again be tempted to take military action.

On 6 March the International Court of Justice scheduled hearings for 26 March on Libya's request for an emergency ruling to halt any possible American or British military action. There were many signs that Gaddafi was increasingly worried by the possibility of Western military strikes against Libya, not least because he himself would be a principal target. Mohammed Heikal, a distinguished Arab commentator and for years a confidant of President Nasser, has observed: 'See what Gaddafi is doing. He is acting like a threatened mouse. The lesson of the devastation of Iraq is there for everybody to see. I have many responsible Libyans coming to see me in Cairo, saying: "What can we do to appease them?" They were even ready to take the two men to the UN, to give them to poor Boutros Ghali and Boutros Ghali would not touch them.' According to Heikal, Colonel Gaddafi sent a message to Mubarak in February, saying: 'I am going to leave it [Libya] all to you and I am coming to Egypt as a private citizen.'[128] It was now increasingly obvious that the projected sanctions resolution would be passed in the Security Council within a matter of days and that, once passed, the United States would be able to veto any move to rescind it. Soon a further step towards the siege of Libya would be taken.

As the UN Security Council moved inexorably towards the imposition of mandatory sanctions, Britain and the US advised their nationals to leave Libya. On 17 March Britain advised its nationals in Libya to 'consider carefully whether they need to remain in the country'. Such nationals were urged to leave while it was still possible, since many Libyan entry and exit visas are endorsed for travel 'by air only' – and there was about to be a ban on all civil air flights. The British Foreign Office also set about discouraging people from travelling to Libya. It was now being announced that Britain, France and the United States had finally achieved formal agreement with the other Security Council members (Russia and China) on the wording of the draft resolution (it was soon to emerge that China, unenthusiastic about mandatory sanctions, had been threatened by Washington with dire economic consequences if it vetoed the resolution). The resolution had been drafted under Chapter VII of the UN Charter, which demands observance by all UN members, but again it was clear that not all members were in favour of the draft resolution. It was surmised that neighbouring countries, such as Morocco and Egypt, might be reluctant to cut air links or to withdraw their diplomats from Tripoli. At this stage the idea of imposing a ban on Libyan oil exports had already been floated at the United Nations but Italy and Germany, both dependent on Libyan oil, had resisted the idea.[129] It was still the case that an eventual military strike was a possibility. Prime Minister John Major, in an interview for *The Times* in London, commented that the sanctions resolution would precede the use of force.[130] It was clear that the military option was still open.

Now other countries (Germany, Austria, Switzerland and Denmark) were joining the US, France and Britain in urging their nationals to leave Libya before being stranded there. Libya itself, while seemingly posing no threat to foreign nationals, remained keen to publicise what it perceived as the injustice of a Security Council run by a few Western nations. Jana, the official Libyan press agency, even went so far as to declare that the Islamic states were considering a mass withdrawal from the United Nations.[131] The Jana editor for Islamic affairs accused the West of monopolising the UN and turning it into an anti-Islamic Christian organisation: 'The Islamic states are considering withdrawing en bloc from the United Nations to form a new United Nations, especially when injustice reached an unbearable level. The Islamic countries and the Muslim peoples cannot tolerate any more the Western countries' insults to Islam and Muslims and their arrogance towards Libya, the small Muslim country.' This statement, from a transparently interested source, can be viewed with scepticism, but it signalled what was becoming increasingly obvious, that Colonel Gaddafi could look to a measure of support in the Arab world and in the wider Muslim community.

On 20 March there were fresh signs of a possible breakthrough: North African diplomats claimed that Gaddafi, under pressure from Tunisia and Morocco, might be moving to hand over the two men to the UN Secretary-General, Boutros Boutros Ghali, a possibility that had been discussed and discounted on earlier occasions. It was reported that the Arab states were working on such a solution and that the Libyan leader had already agreed in principle to hand over the two suspects to allow Dr Boutros Ghali to decide what to do next. No reaction from the UN was reported and the Western powers were predictably sceptical. A British Foreign Office spokesman commented that 'the US and Britain are not interested in principles, but only in facts', suggesting that this was yet another attempt by Gaddafi to ignore the legitimate UN demands. However, a few days later a Reuter report in Cairo stated that the UN Secretary-General had told the Arab League Secretary-General, Esmet Abdel Maguid, that Libya could hand the two men over to Maguid, after which they could be handed over to 'the proper authorities'.[132] It was further reported that if the Libyan authorities were prepared to agree to such an arrangement Dr Boutros Ghali would ask the Security Council to issue a formal proposal along these lines. At the same time the Arab League issued a resolution calling on the Security Council to 'avoid adopting economic, military or diplomatic measures against Libya' and to 'resolve the conflict between that country and the United States, Britain and France by negotiation and mediation' (see Appendix 5). This important resolution, agreed by the 21-member body, also called on the Security Council to 'wait until the International Court of Justice rules upon the issue'. Again it was clear that support for Gaddafi was growing in the Arab world and that this manifest fact would serve as an irritation to the Western powers.

Libya then announced that it would give up the two men to the Arab League. The Libyan ambassador to the United Nations, Ahmed al-Houderi, declared that he was able 'to confirm that the decision had been taken to hand the men over to the Arab League', emphasising that this 'was not just rumour' but that he could not say what would happen to the two men afterwards ('That is up to the Arab League').[133] Even now the position was unclear. Some reports suggested that the Arab League was reluctant to take charge of the two men and there was pressure on Gaddafi to deliver them directly to the United Nations. It was clear that Boutros Ghali had an interest in preventing the imposition of sanctions on Libya but equally clear that Britain and the United States would tolerate no compromise on the demands laid out in Resolution 731. Thus a British official was prepared to express 'full confidence' in Dr Boutros Ghali, at the same time emphasising that he 'was at no stage empowered to negotiate for the extradition of the two Libyans'. The French ambassador to the UN, Jean Bernard Merimée, declared that the Libyan willingness to hand over the two suspects to the Arab League 'is a sign of progress', though the three Western powers were still pressing Libya to hand over the men within a matter of days. On 24 March it was reported that China had announced publicly that it would not support the projected sanctions resolution.[135]

It soon became clear that, whatever Libyan officials had said, it was unlikely that the two suspects would be handed over to the Arab League or to the United Nations. According to the British ambassador to the UN, Sir David Hannay, the UN Secretary-General had asked Libya to confirm in writing its willingness to deliver the two men, but there were no signs that the Libyan authorities were prepared to put their offer in writing. Again

Libyan procrastination was feeding the general mood of disbelief among Western diplomats. Diego Arria of Venezuela, the President of the Security Council during March, commented to reporters: 'Today is an important day ... we got information that they would be delivered today from the Arab League representative.' However, whatever the expectations nothing transpired and an early passing of the mandatory sanctions resolution seemed likely. At the same time there was growing unease about the stringency of the proposed sanctions: in one report, China, Morocco, India and Zimbabwe were 'expressing quiet fury' at the prospect'.[136] That some of Libya's neighbours had already stated that they would not observe sanctions would moreover have the consequence that UN authority would be damaged.

On 25 March Libya declared that it would only hand over the two suspects on condition that they were not then delivered to Britain or the United States. It was now stated by Gaddafi's second-in-command, Abdel Salem Jalloud, that announcements by the Libyan UN ambassador had been 'inaccurate', a statement that hardened Western suspicions that Gaddafi was simply playing for time.[137] Now Britain, the US and France were renewing their efforts to secure the sanctions resolution, convinced by the new developments that there had never been any real prospect that Gaddafi would comply with the demands expressed in Resolution 731. On 26 March a Libyan representative, pressing the Libyan case before the International Court of Justice, declared that Libya would never give in to 'illegal and arbitrary blackmail' by Britain and the United States, and urged the sixteen judges on the World Court to rule that Britain and the US be barred from taking military action against Libya.* Britain, who took the trouble to send Alan Rodger QC for the British delegation, commented that the World Court had no jurisdiction in the case and that there was no way that Libya could be trusted to try the suspects in its own courts. Rodger had commented that Libya is wriggling and twisting the law and that Tripoli would 'say anything, however inconsistent, which may help postpone the day when it will have to accept responsibilities for its actions. That I fear is the true purpose of this court hearing.' Against this view the Libyan representative, Mohammed Sharaf al-Faitouri, declared that Libya was not responsible 'directly or indirectly for the hideous crime in which it is alleged to be implicated'. There was, he claimed, no reason to surrender the suspects because 'the accusers have at no time agreed to supply copies of evidence

---

*Pamela Dix, of the UK Families Flight 103 Group representing relatives of Lockerbie victims and a supporter of the UK 'No Intervention in Libya' campaign, stated: 'We do not want to see any military action against Libya' (*The Socialist*, 11–24 March 1992).

they claim to possess.' Faitouri also reminded the court that in 1986 force was used against Libya 'without the slightest justification', subsequent investigations having absolved Libya of any responsibility for the alleged involvement in the attacks in Europe.[138] Tripoli argues that the World Court had jurisdiction because Britain and the US are in breach of the 1971 Montreal Convention, an agreement signed by all parties to counter terrorist acts against civil aircraft. It was now clear however that whatever the court findings London and Washington were resolved to achieve the sanctions resolution.

It was now emerging that, as a nice rerun of the US threats and inducements designed to achieve 'international consensus' at the time of the 1990/91 Gulf crisis, Washington was threatening any nations inclined to oppose the passing of the sanctions resolution. In these circumstances China was a key player. Of the five permanent Security Council members three were the architects of the draft resolution, Russia – desperate for US support to prevent internal economic collapse – could be relied upon, and China had declared publicly that it would not support the new mandatory resolution. The United States responded by telling China that if it vetoed the resolution it would risk losing its Most Favoured Nation status, a move that would deprive China of billions of dollars in trade with the US.* Other countries on the Security Council (such as Morocco, Zimbabwe, Venezuela, Hungary, India, Ecuador and Cape Verde), all without the power of veto, were openly said by diplomats to be frightened of upsetting the United States.[139]

By the end of March it was clear that the sanctions resolution would be passed in the Security Council. On 29 March the Arab League called on the United Nations to delay the plans for imposing sanctions on Libya, with mediators from seven Arab countries agreeing to send a message to Dr Boutros Ghali requesting that the Security Council defer its action. Now it was widely recognised that the efforts of the Arab League and of the UN Secretary-General himself would not be able to delay further the passing of the mandatory resolution. In the event the resolution – Resolution 748 (1992) – was passed on 31 March, giving Colonel Gaddafi until the end of Ramadan on 15 April to hand over the two accused men (see Appendix 6). The resolution was passed by a vote of ten in favour with none against and five abstentions (China, Cape Verde, India, Morocco and Zimbabwe). Ahmed al-Houderi, the Libyan ambassador, noted that Libya had reaffirmed its readiness to cooperate with the Council in a manner that would not

---

*This UN version of jury tampering is what passes for 'skilful diplomacy' in today's Security Council.

damage Libyan sovereignty or violate international law. The current impasse, he claimed, was due to a rejection of all attempts to achieve a neutral and fair investigation; and he expressed concern that the ground was being prepared for further action against Libya.

Now it emerged that Libya was apparently delaying the issue of exit visas to foreign nationals wishing to leave the country, and soon the idea was being floated in the Western media that a new 'human shield' situation, akin to that orchestrated by Saddam Hussein in Iraq, was being created in Libya. However, the Libyan authorities, no doubt disappointing some of the more voracious Western journalists, stated that it had no intention of preventing anyone leaving Libya if they wished: Colonel Gaddafi, it appeared, was not in the business of hostage taking. Prime Minister John Major was said to have reacted angrily to the possibility that exist visas might be refused, declaring that this was 'intolerable . . . We shall watch the situation and make sure the security of our people is absolute and they can get out.' The matter soon dropped out of the news, suggesting that it was a non-issue; but perhaps it has been enough to tar Gaddafi, albeit briefly, with the Saddam brush. The important measure was the passing of the new UN resolution, and again there were reports of how China had been pressured not to veto the move: 'the US is understood to have leaned heavily on Peking by threatening to withdraw its most-favoured trading partner status . . . Other Third World countries on the Council had their arms twisted in similar fashion.'[140]

The Libyan authorities continued to take measures to help the country ride out the sanctions that would be imposed on 15 April. Funds continued to be transferred from West European banks to Geneva and Gulf states, and there was evidence that the central Libyan bank was withholding letters of credit, except for key imports such as food, and that this was having an impact on local business. Bankers stated that Libya was spending money stockpiling food and medicine, though there appeared to be little extra traffic through the port of Tripoli. Again it was felt unlikely that Egypt would try to close its lengthy land border with Libya, and more than one observer noted that it would be easier to feed Libya than it had been to feed Iraq, again encouraging the perception that Gaddafi and Saddam Hussein were being viewed by the West in similar terms. It was also clear that foreign nationals, despite advice from their governments, were not rushing to leave Libya. The South Korean authorities, with some 10,000 workers in Libya, had not even suggested that Koreans return home. The sanctions specified in Resolution 748 were increasingly seen as largely symbolic, unlikely to topple Gaddafi but signalling Western hostility and the possibility of sterner measures in the future.

On 1 April Colonel Gaddafi threatened to halt oil sales and to sever business ties with all countries that imposed UN sanctions against Libya. Speaking to the Italian periodical *Europeo* he declared: 'The embargo does not frighten us. Whoever does not support the cause of my people will have nothing: no oil and no business.' It was easy to discount such rhetoric: nothing, short of military action, would damage Libya more than a curtailment of its oil sales. Gaddafi's statement followed a speedy US refusal to allow the Libyan leader to visit President Bush to discuss the Lockerbie issue, and the UN decision to send Vladimir Petrovsky, UN Under-Secretary-General for Political Affairs, to Tripoli for talks. On 2 April Colonel Gaddafi broadcast a message on Tripoli radio, warning that 'warplanes will come to us from beyond the seas'; hours later Libyan protesters launched attacks on various foreign embassies in Tripoli.

In one attack about two hundred protesters forced their way into the Venezuelan embassy, destroying equipment, files and living quarters; vehicles outside were set on fire. At the UN the Libyan ambassador, Ahmed al-Houderi, commented that the violence was directed not at Venezuela but at the Security Council, an observation that was unlikely to win friends. The Council commented predictably that any attempt to link the attacks with actions taken by the Council was 'extremely serious and totally unacceptable', and it demanded that Libya make full compensation to Venezuela. The protesters had also burned US and British flags outside the Belgian and Italian embassies, broken windows at the Austrian embassy, and attacked the Russian and French embassies. Protestors at the Indian and Moroccan embassies came armed with flowers, a reward for countries that had refused to vote for the crucial Resolution 748. A Western diplomat remarked that 'in Libya it is sometimes very difficult to tell what is a spontaneous demonstration and what is orchestrated by the government, though not necessarily by Gaddafi himself'. In an interview with *The Independent* newspaper the Libyan UN ambassador, in a marked shift of emphasis from his earlier statements, declared that the protests were 'the work of an angry mob and it's now under control . . . We used tear gas to break up the demonstrations, which we normally never use. It's just unfortunate that things got out of hand, but it's under control now.'

There were growing signs that Western intransigence, the refusal to present relevant evidence or to discuss the matter with Tripoli, was stimulating Libyan militancy. A senior European ambassador in Tripoli observed that 'if Gaddafi decides the Americans want his head – and there is no room for compromise – then he will fight it out . . . In November and December people were at first very critical of the government . . . After the UN resolution on sanctions, the mood changed. They feel they are all now under pressure. They think the Americans want to get rid of Muammar Gaddafi and impose control on Libyan oil.'[141] It seemed that Colonel Gaddafi could rely on more Arab support than Saddam Hussein was able to muster over the Gulf crisis: there was still the persistent suspicion that Iran was implicated in the Lockerbie outrage, and there was growing Arab unease about a new Middle East order that seemed to be nothing more than a fresh wave of American imperialism. Thus Atef al-Ghomari, writing in the semi-official Egyptian daily *al-Ahram*, remarked that the current 'anti-terrorist campaign by the US is aimed less at combating terrorism than redrawing the map of the region'. When, on 4 April, Vladimir Petrovsky arrived in Tripoli to discuss the escalating crisis it is likely that the Libyan authorities had few illusions about the course of events that the United States had set in train. Armed troops and police were deployed around the threatened embassy buildings, and a Western diplomat observed that 'everything is back to normal and is quiet. The police are being very co-operative.' It was also reported that a small exodus of Britons and other nationalities had begun and that there were no problems in obtaining exit visas. At the same time the Imam of the Moulay Mohammad mosque in Tripoli declared in a sermon broadcast live on television that the lives of diplomats representing countries that voted for sanctions were in danger: 'We demand that their embassies be closed, their companies nationalised and all the citizens belonging to these states be evacuated. We warn them that their lives are in danger.'[142] Colonel Gaddafi himself was quite content to characterise the crisis in religious terms. He noted that the accused men could be tried in an Arab country or in a friendly country: 'that would be fine. But they want them tried in a Christian country. After finishing with Communism, the Christian crusaders have turned against the Muslims . . . The Crusader enemy is coming to each Libyan home.'[143] Even Arab states, he declared, who supported the West against Saddam Hussein, are uneasy at the aggressive posture adopted by the United States, arguing that 'America is playing policeman, gang leader, judge and prison warder all at once.'[144]

In early April Yasser Arafat, with some advisors, rushed to Libya to discuss how resistance to the pressure being put on Gaddafi might be organised. Unfortunately the Libyan leader had a prior engagement: Arafat was told that Gaddafi had 'gone to the desert to talk to his God and take direction from Him'. On 7 April Arafat, suffering his own desert storm, disappeared over the Libyan desert, his plane forced to crashland. The PLO leader was found relatively unscathed some hours later, and the story was put about that the US had provided satellite data to enable the crashed plane to be found; however Margaret Tutwiler, a spokeswoman for the US State Department, commented that 'we did absolutely nothing. Nothing.'[145] Captain Adnan Beleidy of the Palestine Liberation Army, the PLO's military wing, declared that a Libyan air force plane had spotted the survivors – some crew members were killed – at dawn. Subsequent television pictures showed Colonel Gaddafi talked to Yasser Arafat in a hospital bed, and there was talk of a new bond between Libya and the PLO: again, observers noted, Arafat was choosing to back a loser. Western commentators were habitually keen to depict Colonel Gaddafi as a loser or as unstable and reckless. Soon also it was being strongly implied that the Libyan leader was a dangerous force – the 'mad dog' signalled by President Reagan in 1986 – that had to be dealt with. Thus at this timely moment it was claimed that Colonel Gaddafi, like Saddam Hussein, had a thirst for weapons of mass destruction that had to be countered: for example, the *Sunday Times* Insight team was soon on the job telling how Gaddafi was building a 'huge poison gas arsenal'[146] – as if Britain and the US righteously refrained from developing and deploying weapons of awesome destructive power.

On 7 April the UN envoy, Vladimir Petrovsky, arrived in Tripoli to be confronted by demonstrators that blocked his motorcade and chanted 'to hell with America and Britain', and by some three hundred angry youths pushing to get into his hotel. Tear gas was used to break up the demonstrations and Petrovsky later began 'frank, serious and businesslike' talks with officials at the Libyan foreign ministry. There was no sign of a breakthrough. Petrovsky then travelled to Geneva to brief Dr Boutros Ghali. It now seemed that nothing could prevent the implementation of Resolution 748, demanding the imposition of sanctions, on 15 April. However, the World Court still had to adjudicate, its decision scheduled for 14 April, and Colonel Gaddafi was about to offer a further compromise solution to the crisis.

The Maltese government then issued a statement saying that: 'Malta has acceded to a request for the two suspects to be tried in Malta, provided that all parties to the dispute are in agreement and consistent with Malta's obligations under the UN Charter.' It was announced that the Maltese foreign minister, Professor Guido de Marco, had received a letter from his Libyan counterpart informing him that the two men had asked to be tried in Malta. The Maltese Prime Minister, Dr Edward Fenech-Adami, commented that Malta had a judicial system 'of which we have been extremely proud ... Our laws will give all the guarantees one can think of for any democratic country.'[147] Washington quickly dismissed the offer as unacceptable.

On 14 April the International Court of Justice in The Hague ruled by eleven votes to five against granting Libya a temporary restraining order against Britain and America, declaring that it had no power to prevent the UN Security Council enacting sanctions against Libya. Mr Shigeru Oda, the vice-president of the International Court, declared that the vote ruled on the competence of the court to issue the protective injunction. It was also emphasised that the five judges in the minority did not necessarily endorse Libya's claim to international protection, but believed that the court was underestimating its powers in this particular case.[148] The United States had resisted all efforts to delay the passing of Resolution 748 until after the World Court had ruled, so putting the court in an immensely difficult position. Whatever the justice of the Libyan case it was hard to imagine that the court, a UN body, would rule against the UN Security Council. We can speculate that if the sanctions resolution was scheduled for a vote but not yet passed then the court ruling might have been different. By pushing for an early vote on the resolution, and by threatening China with dire consequences if it used its veto, Washington had put the World Court under immense pressure. In such circumstances the court was bound to rule, observing Article 103 of the UN Charter, that the demands of a Security Council resolution should take precedence over the requirements of the Montreal Convention. However, such speculations are largely academic: Washington had already declared, before the court adjudication, that whatever the judges ruled the sanctions would be implemented on 15 April. The United States was quite prepared to ignore the ruling of the World Court, as it did when ruled against over its treatment of Nicaragua; but when the court seemingly supported the US against Libya Washington was quick to applaud the verdict. This is the grim Catch 22 confronting any Third World country in conflict with a hegemonic United States.

The unexpectedly moderate stand of Colonel Gaddafi on the Lockerbie issue, his evident search for a legal solution and his declared willingness to hand over the two accused men to a neutral state had clearly caused the West some problems. Many observers saw Britain and the United States, rather than Libya, as the intransigent parties to the disputes. Thus in Cairo the normally pro-American newspaper *Al-Ahram* commented that the harassment and punishment of a small country like Libya on the strength of unsubstantiated charges put America's 'allies and friends in the region' in an extremely 'embarrassing' position. It was reported that Egypt would help Libya cope with the effects of UN sanctions, while at the same time Cairo would officially support the new resolution.[149] Libyan Arab Airlines organised extra flights between Cairo and Tripoli before Libya's official day of mourning on 14 April for the victims of the US bombing raids on Libya in 1986, and the Egyptian authorities began reviewing measures to provide increased land transport between Libya and Egypt. The national carrier, EgyptAir, and Libyan Arab Airlines agreed to co-ordinate air flights with a bus shuttle service over the border.

It was widely assumed that the sanctions, as specified in Resolution 748, would not achieve their objectives. A ban on civilian air travel would act as an irritation rather than a serious impediment; a ban on arms sales would have little effect on a trade that was in any case often clandestine or on a country that was already massively armed; and a scaling down of diplomatic activity would represent only a degree of political isolation rather than a mechanism for forcing Colonel Gaddafi's compliance with UN demands. The main significance of 748 was that it represented the first stage of what many observers thought would be an escalating process, a planned strategy that was intended to lead to the crippling of the Libyan economy and the toppling of the Libyan leader.

On 15 April 1992, as expected, the mandatory sanctions came into effect. Italian fighter aircraft were scrambled to turn back a Libyan passenger aircraft, and Tunisia and Egypt refused to grant permission for Libyan planes to land. The US informed the Libyan mission at the United Nations that it would have to reduce its staff from twelve diplomats to nine, the Libyan deputy chief of mission being one of the expelled staff members. France, Japan, Sweden and Belgium announced that they would expel a number of diplomats, and Switzerland declared that it would curb arms sales. Russia, with an eye on much-needed American aid, said that it would withdraw hundreds of its military experts training the Libyan armed forces, providing the UN would agree to special exit flights. Libya immediately threatened to take 'reciprocal measures' against any countries that expelled its diplomats, with Libyan radio attacking the sanctions as 'the continuation of a war by the imperialist states against other peoples and an attempt to force them to submit to hegemony'; Libyans, an official statement declared, would 'kneel to no one but Allah'. The scene was set for a protracted – and escalating – struggle: Article 13 of Resolution 748 stipulates that 'the Security Council shall every 120 days, or sooner should the situation so require, review the measures imposed'.

The situation was that – in what Washington perceived as propitious international circumstances – the United States had again decided to target the Libyan regime of Colonel Gaddafi. The widely suspected complicity of Syria and Iran in the Lockerbie bombing was to be ignored, Libya to be the sole publicly branded culprit. For months the US had made no attempt whatever to observe its obligations under the 1971 Montreal Convention, an agreement specifically designed to combat terrorist attacks on civilian aircraft. All efforts at mediation and compromise – by Dr Boutros Ghali, President Mubarak, the Arab League, the Maltese government, the Libyan authorities themselves and others – had been routinely rejected by Washington and London, interested more in targeting Colonel Muammar Gaddafi than in bringing the two accused men to justice.

Few observers believed that the two Libyans could have had a fair trial in America or Britain. Thus the English lawyer Geoffrey Robertson commented that a trial by jury in Scotland or the United States would be 'objectionable', and that the prosecution case was 'almost as convincing as the original cases against the Birmingham Six and the Guildford Four'.[150] Similarly Dr Marc Weller, a legal research fellow at the University of Cambridge, a lecturer in the law of the United Nations, castigated what he saw as the 'double standards' being perpetrated at the UN by the British and US authorities.[151] Moreover the guilt of the two accused men, and of Colonel Gaddafi himself, has been assumed and frequently proclaimed in the Western media – for example, *The Independent* said of Colonel Gaddafi: 'Clearly he played a role in the Lockerbie bombing'[152] – rendering any trial of the men in Britain or the US a travesty of justice. The US-orchestrated campaign against Libya has little to do with fair trials for accused men, more to do with a programmed hidden agenda that is not hard to fathom.

On 16 April 1992 the US State Department declared that the United States would not end sanctions, even if the two men were surrendered for trial. It also announced that the US would maintain a worldwide economic offensive against Libya.

NEW WORLD ORDER?

The imposition of sanctions on Libya, with frequent threats of worse to come, graphically illustrated the character of the post-Cold War World. Throughout 1992 it became increasingly clear that Washington, supported by at least one supine ally, would act through the United Nations only if the requisite pressures could be brought to bear on other members of the Security Council. If not, then the United States would not shrink from taking unilateral action: British foreign secretary Douglas Hurd was quite happy to admit that the air exclusion zone on southern Iraq, for example, was not sanctioned by UN resolutions.[153] Unilateral US action was widely perceived as particularly likely if the cynical calculations of presidential advisors in an election year judged such action to be useful.

The pressure on Libya was maintained despite accumulating evidence that the US posture was factually flawed and legally indefensible. Worse, it was increasingly clear that Washington, in its cavalier pursuit of a favourite *bête noire*, had gravely damaged the integrity of the United Nations. In June 1992 the Spanish police arrested a Syrian national, Monzer al-Kassar, suspected of involvement in the Lockerbie bombing – highlighting yet again the possible complicity of states other than Libya in the 1988 outrage.[154] At the same time the German public prosecutor Volker Rath announced, in a statement that received little publicity, that Germany would be suspending its legal proceedings against the two Libyan suspects as there was insufficient evidence of their involvement.[155]

The Libyan authorities themselves were making efforts, short of surrendering the two men, to meet the Western demands. In May 1992 the Libyan news agency Jana stated that links with terrorist groups were being terminated and that any UN committee was free to visit Libya to ascertain that there were no terrorist camps on Libyan territory (an offer repeated in July). In June Libyan officials provided information to the British authorities about earlier Libyan support for IRA terrorists; British officials commented that Libya did provide 'most of the answers they promised.'[156] Such developments failed to impress Washington; and, this being so, the British government carefully refrained from applauding Libya's obvious efforts to improve relations (the information supplied was 'incomplete and unsatisfactory', decided Prime Minister John Major).

While these events were in progress the United States was taking steps to circumvent the inconvenient terms of extradition law. How insolent of weaker nations, in the absence of an extradition treaty, to refuse to surrender people whom Washington may wish to bring to court! Why not abolish extradition controls at a stroke? On 15 June 1992 the Supreme Court in Washington ruled that US agents were legally entitled to kidnap foreign nationals abroad and return them to the United States for prosecution.[157] Dissenting judge, Justice John Paul Stevens, called this 'a monstrous decision.' However, he should not have been surprised at the Supreme Court ruling: the policy on Libya, if nothing else, has provided ample evidence of Washington's contempt for international law when it is perceived to threaten US interests.

In April 1992 Professor Francis A. Boyle, professor of International Law at the University of Illinois, Urbana-Champaign, prepared a Memorandum of Law on the US/Libyan dispute over the Lockerbie bombing allegations.[158] He examines Libya's liabilities under the terms of the 1971 Montreal Convention, the pertinent legal framework for confronting terrorist acts against civil aircraft. It is enough to quote briefly from the detailed document:

> . . . Libya has fully discharged its obligations . . . there is no obligation whatever for Libya to extradite its two nationals to either the United States or the United Kingdom . . .

. . . both the United States and the United Kingdom have effectively violated most of the provisions of the Montreal Convention.

. . . the United States government has admitted that it will pay no attention whatsoever to its obligations mandating the peaceful resolution of international disputes as required by UN Charter articles 2(3) and 33(*).

The United States government has purposely and illegally made it impossible for there to be a pacific settlement of this dispute . . .

In the same vein, Marc Weller, Research Fellow in International Law at St Catharine's College, Cambridge, England, has written a detailed analysis of the US/Libya dispute.[159] He concludes that at the levels of both Libyan state responsibility and the responsibility of two individuals, Libya has responded 'in accordance with international legal requirements.' To secure the UN resolutions the claimant states 'had to expend considerable political capital and goodwill in the Security Council, bullying fellow members to obtain the necessary votes, and enraging many non-members of the Council who keenly observed this spectacle . . .' The US and UK governments 'may well have contributed to, or brought about, an abuse of rights by the Security Council.'

It may now be necessary, in Weller's judgement, for the International Court to seek a judicial review of decisions of the Security Council 'if the constitutional system of the UN Charter is to recover from the blow it has suffered in this episode.'

On 20 June 1992 Jana reported from Assawani in Libya that a depot storing fireworks and explosives had accidentally blown up. A health ministry official was quoted as saying that the wounded could not be flown abroad for treatment because of the UN-imposed air embargo and 'this led to an increase in the number of dead'. Two months later, on 12 August, the UN Security Council decided to retain the sanctions imposed on Libya; and the following week a senior UN envoy threatened harsher measures to come.

On 2 September 1992 Colonel Muammar Gaddafi appealed to the United States to begin direct talks to resolve their differences. Washington made no response. On 15 October Douglas Hurd, addressing the Council for the Advancement of Arab–British understanding in London, declared that unless the Libyan government agreed to hand over the suspects, 'there is nothing really to talk about'. The sanctions would remain in place.

Part II

The History of Libya

2 The Libyan Past

PREHISTORY

A vague area known as Libya existed long before the Arab incursions and long before the birth of Islam: the Arabs, only one of many invading groups, were to bring the word of the Prophet to an ancient and recalcitrant people. The term 'Libya', of Egyptian origin and derived from the Berber tribes known as the Lebu, was used in antiquity to denote all of North Africa west of Egypt. The ancient Greeks referred to *Libye*, and in A.D. 300 the Roman emperor Diocletian created the provinces of Libya Superior and Libya Inferior in northern Cyrenaica. The earliest signs of human life on the Libyan coastal plain, and in the Saharan wastes to the south, are dated to around 8000 B.C. In some areas of Fezzan – with Tripolitania and Cyrenaica, one of the three great regions of historical (and modern) Libya – there is a profusion of prehistoric rock art, with paintings and carvings of animals today only found in tropical Africa but once sought by Libyan hunters.

Thousands of primitive pictures can today still be seen at around two dozen sites: most in Fezzan, to the north in Brak, in the Brak/Murzuk/Sebha triangle, and in the Acacus and Tibesi mountains. There is one rock-art site in Cyrenaica, near to the borders of Egypt and Sudan, and at least four in the Gebel of Tripolitania. In 1850 the German explorer Heinrich Barth first drew attention to the significance of the ancient rock art, though it was not extensively studied until the twentieth century: Professor Fabrizio Mori, for instance, spent more than ten years (1950s/1960s) studying the paintings and carvings in the Acacus. The ancient artists used sharpened flints to work on smooth rock surfaces: in what was to become the largest desert in the world they drew clear pictures of elephants, giraffes, crocodiles, rhinoceroses and many other creatures. There was water in abundance for the hippopotami and for the trees whose fossils have been found in parts of the desert where trees no longer grow. The findings suggest that by the end of the Old Stone Age, about 10,000 years ago, the Libyans were a brown-skinned, black-haired race, one group among many ancestors of the modern inhabitants of North Africa. One anthropological authority, Gustave Glotz, writing early in the twentieth century, comments that in prehistoric times there was 'a Mediterranean race, with a long head, an oval face, short stature, dark skin, and wavy black hair. In Europe the Iberians and the Ligurians belonged to this type, and in Africa the Libyans and the Egyptians.'[1]

The region became increasingly dry and barren as a result of climatic changes at the end of the last Ice Age. Many of the animals retreated to the south, or were marooned in the shrinking islands of vegetation in the desert. A few species today cluster around the oases but these too face extinction. The ostrich survived for many centuries after other species had disappeared: it flourished as late as Roman times but it is not since 1914 that the last wild ostrich was seen in Libya. And it was inevitable that the shifting climatic changes would also affect human populations. The artists no longer drew pictures of cattle as the herds disappeared, as the hardier goat and camel eventually replaced the cow. And there were also frequent human incursions that disrupted established patterns and added to the gene pool.

The region of Libya served in antiquity as a convenient crossroads between Europe, Africa and the Middle East. Before the twelfth century B.C. the wide-ranging Phoenicians had established links with many of the coastal towns of North Africa, including the settlements that were to become Tripoli: for many centuries slaves and other forms of merchandise were fed from Central Africa through Libya to the sea. The Berbers, often seen as the original Libyans, probably came from Southwest Asia around 3000 B.C. and were in their turn pushed back by the Phoenicians who increasingly dominated coastal trade and sought to establish colonies of their own. One invasion included fair-haired, blue-eyed people and it has been suggested that these 'white Caucasians', living in North Africa, were the race that the Greeks called 'Libyans'.[2] Early documentation of Libyan history can be dated to the time of the Egyptian Old Kingdom (2700–2200 B.C.) when Berber tribes (the 'Lebu' or 'Rebu' in Egyptian inscriptions) raided east of the Nile Valley. The repeated skirmishes eventually led to the subjugation of the Lebu by the Egyptians during the time of the Middle Kingdom (2200–1700 B.C.) but in 950 B.C. a Berber officer in the Egyptian forces seized power in a palace coup and thereafter ruled Egypt as Pharoah Shishonk I. It is likely that Libyan Berbers served as his successors during the twenty-second and twenty-third dynasties of Egypt (950–720 B.C.).

THE PHOENICIANS

The Phoenicians, great merchants and sailors, cautiously journeyed across the Mediterranean, never willingly losing sight of land. Reluctant to travel at night, they often beached their craft at convenient points on the North African coast, and so became one of the first peoples to establish settlements in Libya. They originally came from the region of what is today the Lebanon: by 1000 B.C. they had established extensive trading networks throughout the eastern Mediterranean. In due course they sailed westwards to the Balearics and Spain, keen to trade in ores, spices and other produce. The early North African settlements, like the many Phoenician outposts elsewhere, were often little more than useful provisioning stations, strong bases overlooking a safe anchorage.

Carthage, which was to become the centre of a line of Phoenician trading posts and colonies that spread across North Africa, was originally established as an ancient city-state in 814 B.C. by emigrants from Tyre. It rose to prominence in the sixth century B.C. and established an effective hegemony over Sardinia, Malta, the Balearic Islands and much of North Africa. Trading posts were built at the Phoenician Ui'at (later Tripoli) and at the Phoenician Lpqy (later Leptis Magna), and it is suggested that the town of Sirte, about two hundred miles to the east, may have been established by the Phoenicians.[3] The Tripolitanian town of Sabratha was originally a Phoenician trading post and here as elsewhere the primitive Berber tribesmen were significantly influenced by the incursions of a more sophisticated culture. The Phoenicians had developed an intensive agriculture on the terraced hills of the Lebanon, and their knowledge had impressive application on the broad coastal plains of North Africa: they are said to have introduced the olive, the vine, the peach and the fig to the region.

The city of Tyre, whose people had helped to found Carthage, was sacked by Alexander the Great in 332 B.C. Carthage, which by then had developed a vast Phoenician hinterland, continued the traditions of the original Phoenicia for a further two centuries, until in due course it was sacked by the Romans. When Carthage collapsed in 146 B.C., Tripoli (from the Greek *tripolis*, meaning the three ancient cities of Sabratha, Oea and Leptis Magna) became a Roman colony.

THE GREEKS

Cyrenaica had been colonised by the Greek states from the time of the seventh century B.C.: over a period of two centuries Cyrene and four other cities (the Pentopolis) had been established. One of these, Berenice, later became known as Benghazi. But like many invaders the Greeks never managed to establish total control over the broad area today known as Libya. For example, the region of Fezzan, away from the coastal towns, was loosely controlled by the Garamantes tribe from about 1000 B.C. The early

Greeks were enthusiastic travellers, and Cyrenaica was a convenient option for settlement and colonisation. It was only 250 miles from the Peloponnese and 200 miles from Crete, and its fertile highlands rose in tiers from the coast, beckoning the traveller in search of a pleasant land. By the end of the sixth century the cities of Cyrenaica had developed into important trading centres, linked to other Greek cities on the Mediterranean. The trade routes ran southwest to Murzuk and southeast to the Siwa Oasis, with the bulk of Cyrene's wealth coming from the fertile highlands of northern Cyrenaica: within a century the Greeks had made the region famous for its agricultural produce, having introduced new crops and developed a thriving trade in barley, corn, olive oil, apples, saffron and essence of roses. Great herds of sheep and cattle were supported and Cyrenaica was said by the ancients to be 'abounding in fleeces' and 'a breeder of flocks'. One product, the Silphion plant, was of particular value: it served as an excellent cattle fodder and also as a medicine, used to treat the ailments of people, animals and trees. This mysterious plant is now extinct.

Eight Greek kings ruled the province around Cyrene until it became a republic in 400 B.C., but there were frequent incursions by other military powers. The whole of Cyrenaica had been subjugated by the Persian Cambyses in 525 B.C. after he had conquered the Greeks in Egypt. Alexander the Great reached Cyrene in 331 B.C. and the Greek population of the city was said to have cheered and presented him with war-horses. When Alexander died in Babylon in 323 B.C. his vast empire was divided between his Macedonian generals. Ptolemy was given Egypt and Cyrenaica. The whole area had seen, and continued to witness, a procession of conquerors, infusing many disparate cultural elements and rendering Cyrene a supreme artistic and intellectual focus of the ancient world.

The Greek historian Herodotus, born around 480 B.C. at Halicarnassus on the south-west coast of Asia Minor, visited Egypt, Mesopotamia, Palestine, Russia and North Africa. In *The Histories* he describes how the Carthaginians, on their account, traded with a race of men 'who live in a part of Libya beyond the Pillars of Heracles'.[4] They arrange their goods along the beach and raise a smoke, whereupon the Libyans come down to the beach, place gold on the ground, and then move off to a distance. The Carthaginians inspect the gold and, if satisfied, collect it and go away; but if they think the offering to be inadequate they go back aboard their ships and wait. The Libyans are then expected to offer more until there is agreement ('There is perfect honesty on both sides; the Carthaginians never touch the gold until it equals in value what they have offered for sale, and the natives never touch the goods until the gold has been taken away').

Herodotus describes the geography of the area ('On the Libyan side of Egypt there is another range of hills where the pyramids stand'), noting how the soil of Libya is reddish and sandy, 'while in Arabia and Syria it has a larger proportion of stone and clay'. He remarks on how the frontiers of Egypt form the 'true boundary' between Asia and Libya, and describes the attitudes and behaviour of the people. We learn that the inhabitants of Marea and Apis, on the Libyan frontier, objected to certain religious observances, especially the prohibition against eating the flesh of cows. They presented their case at the shrine of Ammon, saying that they were in no way bound by Egyptian custom as they were not Egyptians at all, but Libyans; but the oracle ruled against their plea. And Herodotus also observes that there are not many wild animals in Egypt, 'in spite of the fact that it borders on Libya' – so supporting what the ancient rock art has already told us, that there was once a prolific Libyan fauna. Such animals as do exist in Egypt – whether they are wild or tame – are held to be sacred.

We also learn that the Egyptians, for health's sake, purged themselves on a regular basis – every month for three successive days – with emetics and clysters, in the belief that all diseases come from the food we eat. The policy, it seems, was sound: 'next to the Libyans they are the healthiest people in the world'. Herodotus also records the tribute paid during the Persian occupation: Egypt, together with the Libyans on the border and the towns of Cyrene and Barca, were required to pay 700 talents, in addition to the revenue from the fish in Lake Moeris and 120,000 bushels of corn for the Persian troops and their auxiliaries stationed at Memphis. And it is suggested that the hot climate of Libya is liable to affect the growth of cattle. Thus a line in Homer's Odyssey – *Libya, where horns grow quickly on the foreheads of lambs* – is deemed 'a sensible remark, indicating that a hot climate favours the rapid growth of horns; whereas in severe cold cattle do not grow them at all, or hardly at all'.

The Phoenicians, Herodotus observes (Book Four of *The Histories*), sailing from the Arabian gulf, are apt to put in at some convenient place on the Libyan coast, to sow a patch of ground, and to wait for next year's harvest. Then they put to sea again and after various travels arrive at Egypt. We are surprised to find that such travels provided evidence that Libya 'is washed on all sides by the sea except where it joins Asia', a circumstance first suggested by the Phoenician sailors and later by the Carthaginians. Another tale concerns the Greek Polymnestus and his mistress Phronima who gave birth to a son who lisped and stammered. It is said that the son was called 'Battus' (meaning 'king' in the Libyan language of the day) by the priestess at Delphi since she knew that he was to become a king in

Libya. When he consulted the oracle about his defective speech he was
answered, according to Herodotus, by the lines:

> O Battus, for a voice you come; but the lord Apollo
> Sends you to Libya, nurse of flocks, to build a city.

When Battus failed to heed this invocation he experienced various dis-
tresses on the island of Thera. His compatriots also encountered nothing but
ill luck and when they journeyed to Delphi for advice were told that their
fortunes would only improve if they joined with Battus to found a settlement at Cyrene in Libya.

Thus a party of men in due course sailed for Libya in two fifty-oared
galleys. They reached the Libyan coast but, uncertain how to proceed,
returned to Thera, whereupon the islanders threw missiles at them in the
harbour to force them to try again. The men returned to Libya but settled on
the island of Platea off the coast, but when their fortunes had not improved
after two years they again asked the Delphic oracle for advice, whereupon
they were urged to found a settlement on the mainland. They then journeyed
via Platea to the mainland to settle at Aziris where they lived for six years
until the native Libyans urged them to establish a settlement in a better
place. The Libyans timed the subsequent travel so that Battus and his men
would pass through the fine region of Irasa in the dark, so that the interlopers would not see it. In such a fashion Battus came to the site of what
was to be Cyrene, the place where the Libyan guides urged him to settle,
'for here there is a hole in the sky'.

Battus ruled Cyrene for forty years, during which time the population of
the town did not increase. However, during the rule of its third king, Battus
the Fortunate, the Delphic oracle urged native Greeks to join the settlement.
Land grants were offered to new settlers, and the oracle declared that
'whosoever came to delightful Libya after the land was parcelled out,
should one day rue it'. The population of Cyrene increased dramatically,
leading in due course to conflict with the surrounding territories. The
Libyan king Adicran, resenting his loss of land and the domineering attitudes of the Cyreneans, asked for the help of the Egyptian king Apries who
sent a force against Cyrene. Unaccustomed to the methods of Greek fighting, the Egyptians were defeated, and in consequence Apries had to face a
rebellion amongst his own people.

Arcesilaus, a son of Battus the Fortunate, quarrelled with his brothers
and forced them to move to another part of the country where they founded
Barca as a new settlement. In a subsequent battle between the Libyans and

the Cyreneans, the Libyans won a great victory slaughtering as many as seven thousand heavily armed men. Arcesilaus, perhaps in consequence, fell ill and was duly strangled by his brother Learchus who in turn was killed by Erixo, the wife of Arcesilaus. A son of Arcesilaus, a new Battus, assumed the lordship of Cyrene, whereupon the troubled Cyreneans again sought advice from the oracle. They were advised to seek help from a man in Mantinea in Arcadia. In due course a certain Demonax, with a high reputation amongst the citizens of Mantinea, was invited to suggest how the disordered situation in Cyrene could be improved. Demonax proceeded to Cyrene and introduced various measures: the population was divided into three sections or tribes, one comprising the emigrants from Thera, one the people from the Peloponnese and Crete, and the third of people from the islands. He assigned Battus certain lands and priestly offices but also assigned unprecedented powers to the people in general. The arrangements were maintained through the lifetime of Battus but his son, a new Arcesilaus, came to demand the restoration of his full ancestral rights, causing further civil strife.

The new Arcesilaus was defeated and fled to Samos, his mother seeking refuge in Salamis on Cyprus. Arcesilaus set about creating a fresh army in Samos, and then journeyed to Delphi to tap the wisdom of the oracle. The priestess declared that Apollo would grant him power over Cyrene 'over a period of eight generations under four rulers named Battus and four named Arcesilaus; but he advises you to make no attempt to keep your power beyond that period. As for yourself, when you return to your country, be gentle. If you find the oven full of jars, do not bake them but send them away down-wind. But if you do heat the oven, enter not the land surrounded by water, for otherwise you will die, and the best of the bulls with you.' Whatever was to be made of this, Arcesilaus was sufficiently encouraged to return to Cyrene and to regain supreme power. Alas, contrary to the words of the oracle he drove his political opponents into exile; those that fell into his hands he sent to their deaths in Cyprus. Some shut themselves in a high tower, whereupon Arcesilaus stacked wood around the base and burnt them alive. Too late, he realised that this was what the oracle had warned him against. When he was seen walking in Barca some of the local people, in concert with exiles from Cyrene, killed him and also his father-in-law Alazir. When his mother Pheretima heard of her son's death she fled to Egypt and threw herself on the mercy of Aryandes. He put all the forces of Egypt at her disposal and, when the inhabitants of Cyrene claimed that they were all equally responsible for the death of Arcesilaus, the Egyptian forces marched to subjugate all of Libya.

Herodotus also describes the many tribes of Libya: for example, the Adyrmachidae who live like the Egyptians but dress like the rest of the Libyans. The long-haired women wear a bronze ring on each leg and when they catch a bug on their bodies they bite it before throwing it away. The Giligamae are conspicuous among the Libyans for their use of four-horse chariots, just as the Nasamones are known for catching locusts which they dry in the sun and then grind up fine. As with the Massagetae, wives are used in common: when a man wants to lie with a woman, he erects a symbolic pole to indicate his intentions. In taking an oath they lay their hands on the tombs of their countrymen with a good reputation for integrity and valour; to achieve accurate divinations they sleep, after praying, on the graves of their ancestors; and in making a compact, each drinks from the other's hand or licks up dust from the ground.

The Garamantes of Fezzan are said to possess no weapons of war, and do not know how to defend themselves; here, where wild beasts live, the people seek no contact with other tribes. The Macae wear their hair in a crest, shaving each side of the head and growing the hair long in the middle. Part of their land is the densely-wooded Hill of the Graces. Unlike the Garamantes they are equipped for war; ostrich skins are used for shields. The women of the Gindanes wear leather bands around their ankles to signal the number of their lovers, and the women with the greatest number of bands enjoy the highest reputations. Within the territory of the Gindanes live the Lotophagi, a tribe that lives on the fruit of the lotus, eating it as an essential food and also making wine from it.

The Machlyes and the Auses live on the shores of a lagoon, with the river Triton forming the boundary between them. The Machlyes grow their hair on the back of their heads, the Auses on the front. At an annual festival in honour of Athene the girls divide themselves into two groups and fight with sticks and stones, an immemorial rite by which they pay due obeisance to their native deity: if a girl dies it is proof she was not a virgin. The best looking girl, in a suit of Greek armour and a Corinthian helmet, is driven round the lagoon as a prelude to the conflict. As with other Libyan tribes, the women are held as common property: there are no married couples and sexual congress is a casual matter. A fully grown child is deemed to belong to the man it most resembles.

To the west of the river Triton live the Maxyes tribe, where the hair is allowed to grow on the right side of the head and shaved on the left. The Maxyes stain their bodies red and claim descent from the men of Troy. Again we find evidence of abundant fauna. Eastern Libya 'abounds with forest and animal life': there are huge snakes, lions, elephants, bears, asps and horned assess, 'not to mention dog-headed men, headless men with eyes in their breasts (I don't vouch for this, but merely repeat what the Libyans say), wild men and wild women, and a great many other creatures by no means of a fabulous kind' (Herodotus). In the country of the nomads there are white-rump antelopes, gazelles, deer, asses that can do without water ('they do not drink') and a huge antelope as big as an ox whose horns are used to make the curved sides of lyres. And the territory of the nomads also contains foxes, hyaenas, hedgehogs, rams, jackals, panthers, crocodiles, ostriches and small snakes equipped with a horn; there are weasels and three kinds of mice. So much for the abundant Libyan fauna: Herodotus has made his account 'as full and accurate as my extensive inquiries permit'.

The Zaueces, like the Machlyes, favour the idea of the warrior woman: the drivers of the war-chariots are invariably female. Their neighbours, the Gyzantes, enjoy honey, paint themselves red, and eat from their abundant supply of monkeys. And on the near-by island of Cyrauis the girls dip feathers smeared with pitch into the mud to bring up gold dust ('I merely record the current story, without guaranteeing the truth of it'). Herodotus himself has seen how pitch is retrieved from the water of a lake: thus in Zacynthus myrtle is tied to the end of a pole which is then thrust to the bottom of the water to bring up the pitch. This is then poured into a trench and finally into jars ('In view of all this, the account of what happens in the island of Libya may quite possibly be true').

Herodotus suggests that Libya is inhabited by four races, two indigenous and two not. The Libyans in the north and the Ethiopians in the south are the true indigenous peoples, the immigrants being the Phoenicians and the Greeks. He also acknowledges the impact of the Persians, about whom the Libyans 'cared nothing'. The waves of colonial incursion are a perennial theme in Libyan history.

THE ROMANS

The Romans conquered much of the region in 74 B.C. and ruled it as a province. The Greek influence persisted however and Cyrene remained a centre of Hellenic culture, producing wine, wool, grain and herbs, and also such scholars as the geographer Eratosthenes and the epigrammatist Callimachus (remembered not least for his remark, 'A big book is a big bore'). Much of Cyrenaica was dominated by the Greeks for some 1200 years, from 600 B.C. to A.D. 600. The Romans were forced to fight periodic battles with the Fezzan Garamantes, already encountered, who proved themselves a redoubtable foe. They had developed a form of mechanised warfare with their battle chariots, and had commanded a vast desert kingdom from as early as 1000 B.C. There remains little evidence of their rule apart from the extant inscriptions in *tifinagh*, a geometrical alphabet still used by the Tuaregs of the Sahara. Herodotus remarked that the Garamantes were 'an exceedingly great nation who sow the earth they have laid on the salt. The sparse archeological sites suggest that the Garamantes had a Neolithic culture dating to the first millenium B.C.[5]

Some researchers have argued that the Garamantes had kinship with the Tuaregs, while others have proposed Berber connections. Their control of Fezzan gave them influence over the ancient trade routes: from their capital at Gerama they were able to control the desert caravans moving from Ghadames to the Niger River, eastwards to Egypt and beyond, and westward to the region that is today Mauritania.[6] The Romans were never able to subjugate totally the kingdom of the Garamantes and elements of their rule were encountered by the invading Arabs as late as the seventh century A.D.[7] And the impact of Rome on northern Africa was, to some degree, reciprocated, not least by the emergence of a Libyan emperor.

Septimus Severus, a native of Leptis Magna, rose to rule as Roman emperor from 193 to 211 during the 400-year period when both Cyrenaica and Tripolitania were governed as Roman provinces. He and his wife Julia Domna were heads of the state pagan religion. When Emperor Constantine converted to Christianity his head appeared on coins in Sabratha, and thus a Christian impact was felt for a time in Libya and other parts of North Africa. But the hold of the new religion on this area was never secure and it was further weakened by its decisive split from Judaism. During the first Roman pogrom against the Jews in Palestine (63 B.C. to A.D. 135) many Jews had fled to settle in North Africa. In Cyrene the king-messiah Lukus Andreas led a revolt in A.D. 115 that spread into Egypt, which was soon followed by a revolt led by the Jewish Simon Bar Kochba against the Roman Emperor Hadrian. In neither case did Christianity offer support to the rebels, and the two faiths drifted further apart. Jewish scholars brought Talmudic texts to North Africa, weakening further the isolated Christian communities that were in any case increasingly infected by heresies that eroded the security of the dogma. One of the most significant blows against Christianity in Cyrenaica was the turbulent Monophysite heresy, a bloody conflict over whether Christ was human or divine. And when in A.D. 395 the Roman Empire was divided into eastern and western halves a fresh chasm was created between Greek Cyrenaica and Latin Tripolitania, diluting further the weakened integrity of the Christian faith.

To the Romans the Mediterranean was *Mare Nostrum* ('Our Sea') and on the southern shore Roman Tripolitania developed over two centuries until the collapse of the empire. Augustus put Africa under the rule of a pro-consul sited in the rebuilt city of Carthage; and a new military force, the *Legio III Augusta*, was created to police the region. For nearly three centuries this legion, generally comprising around five thousand men, was the manifest sign of Roman power from the Sirtica to the Atlantic. Various expeditions were launched against recalcitrant tribes. For example, when the Spanish-born proconsul of Africa L Cornelius Balbus marched first to Ghadames, an important Garamantean trade centre 250 miles from the coast, and then to the Garamantean capital of Gerama, the expedition was hailed as a great victory and Balbus was granted a triumph. But the Garamantes were not completely subdued and further campaigns against them were launched. They were a mysterious race and little is known about them beyond what is recorded in Herodotus and Pliny: the first-century geographer Strabo comments that 'For the most part the nations of Libya are unknown.' One Roman expedition reached 'the land of the Ethiopians', and another marched south until it reached 'Agysimba' in the Sudan. The Roman conquest of Northern Libya was completed in A.D. 85–6 when they overcame the Nasamonians, a great Tripolitanian tribe that was driven into the desert. After this event the emperor Domitian declared that the Nasamonians no longer existed.

The Romans had developed a successful agricultural economy, helped by Saharan trade, throughout Tripolitania. In the early days of the empire Berber peasants worked smallholdings but eventually they were forced off the land by the large landowners and state-controlled organisations.[8] An urban élite, including Romanised Afro-Phoenicians and other elements, had evolved but following the dissolution of the empire were unable to consolidate their hold. In 429 the Vandals entered North Africa from Spain and established a kingdom with its capital at the site of Carthage, but the new order was overthrown by the Byzantine general Belisarius in 533, an event which led to a brief period of Byzantine rule. For a time the indigenous Berber tribes were relatively free of the weight of colonial conquest: they reverted to their traditional nomadic pastoralism, and in the fifth and sixth centuries formed the great Berber confederation of the Zenata, a group not averse to augmenting its economy resources by systematic pillage.[9] However, the Berbers were not to enjoy their independence for long. The most influential incursion of them all, the Arab conquest, began in the seventh century.

THE ARABS

In 642 Omar Ibn al-As led Arab Muslims to conquer Cyrenaica and the sweep continued across North Africa. Gerama, the long-secure capital of the Garamantes, fell to the Arabs in 663. The Berbers struggled to maintain areas of rebellion but in due course accepted Islam though remaining hostile to the Arabs. There was a certain appeal about the clear certainties of monotheistic Islam, in contrast to all the confusing mix of sects and deities brought to North Africa by the Phoenicians, the Greeks and the Romans. Here, it seemed, was a direct route to God that the North Africans had rarely encountered in the competing faiths of Christianity and Judaism.[10] The seventh-century invasion was a herald of what was to follow: the first incursion established a colonial base and had an indelible impact on the whole of North Africa, but larger Arab invasions of the region were to follow.

The Egyptian Fatimid dynasty, established in 910, extended its control over the whole area of Tripolitania, but in 1049 the Berbers revolted against the Shia Fatimids in order to reinstate Sunni orthodoxy. In a dramatic move that was to transform the character of North Africa the Fatimid caliph sent two Arab tribes, the Beni Hilal and the Beni Salim who had both settled in the Nile Valley, into North Africa to crush the rebellion. This great incursion comprised not only warriors but entire social groups: no less than 200,000 families moved into the region of Tripolitania over the period of only a few months, and in this fashion was the eventual character of Libya as an Arab nation determined. The radical change in the culture of North Africa was one of the most important historical transformations.

Before the time of the Arab conquests of the seventh century there was a sense in which Egypt, Syria and North Africa were 'Western' countries.[11] In all these areas, and in Greece and Italy, the same official languages had been used; there was a common currency and unrestricted travel across national borders was largely guaranteed. When Rome under Constantine adopted Christianity there were strenuous efforts, albeit unsuccessful, to spread the new religion throughout the empire. Thus North Africa and many other regions had been shaped by the predominant influence of a thousand years of Graeco-Roman culture. But as Islam evolved from roots that were contiguous to Christianity the whole region became split between the pressures of competing ideologies. The Mediterranean, well controlled by the Romans, had been free of naval battles for centuries; following the Arab conquest the Mediterranean was split horizontally into two halves, with Syria and North Africa together forming a front facing France, Italy and Greece.

The rival Berber dynasties of the Almoravids and the Almohads rose to power in the eleventh and twelfth centuries. In 1160 the Almohads extended their control to Tripolitania, with Cyrenaica continuing to maintain its ties with Egypt for several centuries. The Beni Hilal and the Beni Salim tribes had continued to consolidate their influence in the whole of Libya, though their fortunes varied from one region to another. The Beni Hilal had journeyed westward into Tripolitania while the Beni Salim had settled in Cyrenaica. The Arab penetration was slowest in the southern Fezzan, and for a while trade continued to be controlled by the Berber tribes. Fezzan prospered through Saharan trade, with large cities supporting baths, mosques, markets and scholarship; attracting poets, lawyers and holy men; and inviting caravans from every region. The states of Kanem and Bornu exploited the trade route from Lake Chad to the coastal towns of Libya.[12] Thus Tripoli, inviting the traffic from the African interior through Fezzan, became one of the great mediaeval Mediterranean ports. This complex trade system was to be disrupted by the French and British penetration of the region when, for reasons of imperialist requirement, commerce was diverted from the Sahara to the Atlantic.

Saladin conquered much of the region in the twelfth century: by the time he made his triumphal entry into Damascus in 1192 he was ruler of an empire stretching from Barca in North Africa to Mosul and Erbil in Kurdistan. At that time he was said by the contemporary Arab historian Ibn al Athir to be contemplating expanding into Iraq and Persia, but he died, aged fifty-seven, in Damascus in 1193. The Mamluks continued to rule the area until the Turks conquered Egypt in 1510, at which time Cyrenaica too came under Ottoman control. At the same time Spain captured Tripoli and eventually handed it over for administration by the Knights of St John of Malta. It was not until 1551 when the Turks drove out the Knights and brought Tripoli, to join most of the rest of Libya, under Ottoman control. The Turkish control of Libya was to be maintained, through many vagaries, until the time of the Italian conquest in 1911.

THE TURKS

Sicilian Normans captured Tripoli in 1146, nearly half a century after the fall of Jerusalem to the Crusaders. The Arabs had taken Sicily in the ninth century but by 1087 the Normans had conquered it, and for a brief period the island saw a unique Norman/Arab culture. In 1158 the Norman garrison at Tripoli was massacred with the rise of anti-Christian feeling throughout the region. Further incursions, by the Portuguese the Spanish and others, occurred in various parts of Cyrenaica and Tripolitania until a large part of the area was brought under the rough control of the Turks.

The Ottoman Turks gained power in Anatolia in the fourteenth and fifteenth centuries, taking Constantinople in 1453. They had conquered Egypt by 1517 and corsair captains were seizing other parts of North Africa for the Sultan. In 1513 the corsair Khair al-Din, one of the two brothers known to Europe as Barbarossa, conquered the island of Jerba and four years later took Algiers. It was clear that the growing Turkish power would soon dominate the whole region. Tripoli still gave some protection to Christian shopping in the Mediterranean but its position was becoming increasingly fragile. The Knights of St John inspected the defences of Tripoli in 1524, and six years later the city was handed over to the Order, by now under pressure from Pope Clement VII to defend a city regarded by the emperor Charles V as 'one of the two eyes of Christendom'. All efforts were futile and in 1551 Tripoli, seen as 'a Christian oasis in a barbaric desert', fell to the Turks.

From the middle of the sixteenth century Libya, as a province of the Ottoman empire, was ruled by a Turkish Bey supported by officials and Janissaries, the Turkish mercenary military caste. However, the Turkish rule in North Africa was often far from complete and practical authority was frequently exercised by military leaders and pirate captains rather than by the Sultan's officials. Thus in 1711 power was seized by the Karamanli, a grouping founded from a mix of Berber, Arab and Janissary, and effective authority was exercised by this faction for 125 years. The Karamanli dynasty extended its control to much of Cyrenaica and Fezzan, so establishing the shape of the Libyan state which in modern times the Western powers were to claim as their own invention. The traditional trade routes were maintained under the Karamanli, where Bedouin and other tribes controlled the traffic and supplied logistic support for the caravans.

The Ottomans maintained large garrisons in the provincial cities of Libya and the other regions under their nominal control. Within twenty or thirty miles of the major cities the farmers were heavily taxed, and in consequence often encouraged to move into other areas: far from the cities the distant tribes could not be effectively taxed, though tolls may be demanded by local tribal chiefs. Every few years the Turks, with their mercenary support, would march into the tribal territories to demonstrate the hegemony of the Sultan. If the troops avoided ambush they would destroy villages, slaughter the local people, and seize crops and livestock. On occasions a local chief would act as a mediator and bribes would often be placed to placate military leaders and provincial governors. Alternatively tribe would be set against tribe or junior members of ruling families would be 'recognised' by the Turkish officials to sow the seeds of internal tribal discord. Terror was another frequent means of intimidation: a local tribal leader would be captured, loaded with chains, and despatched to Istanbul for summary execution. Such methods, not uncommon among later colonial administrations around the world, had their predictable effects. The tribes resisted, by guile and by force, wherever they could; the Ottomons were constantly faced by hostile and recalcitrant populace, inevitably uncooperative and always ready to exact a price, in both men and treasure, on the colonial authorities. There were, however, few dreams of Arab nationhood in the occupied territories.

The Turks used two separate security forces – the city police and the rural gendarmerie – in their efforts to maintain order. The gendarmerie accompanied the tax collectors and dealt with rural disorders; the officers were often Arabs who had found it convenient to absorb aspects of Turkish culture. This again represented the familiar colonial ploy of employing natives to police difficult indigenous peoples. The approach was simple and direct: as soon as members of the gendarmerie entered a village (for example, to investigate a local crime), they would seize people at random and beat them into providing information. At the same time it was assumed that the villagers would prepare a feast for their new guests. In such circumstances it was the police sergeant rather than the distant sultan who was the effective ruler of the local villages.

The Arabs in the cities were more susceptible to the impact of Turkish culture: the state schools taught in Turkish, causing many Arabs to be more fluent in the imposed language than in their own. Moreover successful Arabs, merchants and scholars, had a pragmatic interest in law and order; so they came to regard the lawless rural Arabs as an alien element, outsiders with whom they could no longer identify. Again, the familiar colonial stratagem: weakening a nation by dividing it against itself. At the same time it has been pointed out that until the time of the seventeenth century the Ottomans were better administrators than were the colonial Europeans: thus Christian villagers in southern Greece chose Turkish rule against that of the Venetians, and some Christian villages in Hungary preferred Turkish government to that of their own countrymen.[13]

The Ottoman empire became increasingly ineffectual throughout the nineteenth century. There were growing tensions within the Turkish administration, making it difficult to retain the qualified loyalty of conquered lands. In 1835, following the fall of Algiers to the French and the revolt by Mohammed Ali in Egypt, the Turks found it necessary to secure Tripoli to prevent further losses of land that was nominally part of the Empire. A religious revival, under the threat of the French guns, was taking hold in Algeria and was to radically shape the course of Libyan history. At the heart of the revival was Sheikh Muhammad Ibn Ali al-Sanussi, born in the Berber region of Mazouma in western Algeria and one of the key founders of the Sanussiya religious order. To strengthen Islam against the encroachments of the Christian Europeans he founded a series of religious lodges (*zawiyas*) designed to provide accommodation for travellers, religious instruction and even trading facilities. The first lodge, a veritable monastery, was established in Mecca, with others soon following across North Africa; the first zawiya in Libya was built at Beyda.

The founder of the order, known as the Grand Sanussi, was born in the 1780s of a family with impeccable religious credentials: descent was claimed from the Prophet's daughter, Fatima. He first studied in Fez where he came into contact with the religious fraternities of Morocco, after which he travelled with his disciples through the Sahara, Tunisia, Tripolitania and Cyrenaica, preaching a return to the true religion of the Prophet. One of the earliest zawiyas was built in 1843 at Gebel Akhdar in Cyrenaica, a well chosen location. In contrast to other parts of the region, Cyrenaica was a political vacuum; Tunisia was experiencing internal turmoil and Algeria was being taken over by the French. Furthermore, it was evident that Cyrenaica 'provided an outlet to Central Africa, an area which the Grand Sanussi must have thought of as a possible field of expansion'.[14] The grandson of the Grand Sanussi, Sayyid Amir Mohammed Idris became leader of the order in 1916 and later became King of Libya.

The Sanussi, as Sunni or orthodox Moslems, are one of the principle orders of Islam. They insist of conformity to what are taken to be the original teachings of the Prophet, a stern approach to faith and morals that is as well suited to the traditional Bedouin of Cyrenaica as it was to the Arabian Bedouins of the seventh century. The Sanussi are also part of Sufism, a creed which 'appealed to the popular imagination because it supplied men with spiritual satisfaction and vitality as against the rigidity of the law and its teaching'.[15] At the same time it was now unknown for tribesmen to exploit the Sanussi name, undertaking kidnappings or theft in the name of the religious order. Thus European travellers in Libya and elsewhere became acquainted with what they perceived as Sanussi fanatics. But the true Sanussi, though devout, were far from fanatical: they were not supposed to beg or to practise asceticism but to work for a living. There was a general prohibition on the extreme aspects of Sufi mysticism – self-flagellation, dancing to distraction, dervish-type whirling and such like. Instead the Sanussi were expected to live simple lives, showing charity to their neighbours and practising an uncomplicated piety at all times.

The Order impressed the nomadic Bedouin more than it did the relatively sophisticated townspeople. The anthropologist Evans-Pritchard remarks that 'The Order poured its vitality southwards along the trade routes to the interior of Africa, into the Fezzan and the various regions (then) called the French Sahara and French Equatorial Africa.'[16] The focus of the Order and the seat of its Islamic University were established at Jahgub, an oasis on one of the trade routes from the coast to the Sahara. The oasis zawiyas attracted scholars, the prophets and holy men, the cultivators of the land, and the traders who, in addition to their other activities, exploited the slave traffic. The inhabitants of the zawiyas often worked as guides to the slave holders, providing transport and escorting the caravans along sections of the trade routes. Many of the pious Sanussi were themselves slave traders, seeing their devoutness as no barrier to the traffic in human bodies; indeed the reverse was true – 'the holier the person, the more he charges'.[17] The Sanussi also benefited from the customs dues paid by the caravans at the various centres on the trade routes.

There was often conflict between the Sanussi organisation and the French as they expanded their colonial ambitions: at the beginning of the twentieth century the Sanussi, in alliance with other African groups, were fighting a *jihad* against the invading French armies. The second master of the Sanussi Order, Muhammed el-Mahdi, led a further Islamic revival and soon found himself in conflict with the French incursions. By 1867 as many as fifty zawiyas had been established on the Barca plateau in Cyrenaica; and by 1897 a lodge had been built in the north of Chad, near to the Libyan border. When this region, Bir Allali, was conquered by the French, Muhammed el-Mahdi was killed. In 1902 a certain French officer Gentil Lamotte, an Arabist, was constrained to observe: 'Islam had brought immense progress to all of the Central African populations, but it is a serous danger for us: never will a Muslim accept, without serious reservation, Christian domination, and this truth appears more certain because, in the center of Africa, the influence of the Sheikh al-Mahdi ibn Sanussi is considerable.'[18] Many of the townsmen of Cyrenaica found it helpful to their advancement to belong to the Order, and thus in much of urban Libya could be found rich and successful citizens who were pleased to see themselves as part of the Sanussi organisation. The Sanussi were astute enough to exploit the Turkish presence when it was convenient, and to resist it at other times. The British had gathered intelligence reports suggesting that a Sanussi revolt against Turkish rule was developing in the years before the Italian invasion.

The Turks had for long been struggling to retain their grip on the Empire. By the middle of the nineteenth century they had deposed the last of the Karamanlis and reestablished direct rule by the sultan. But as well as the

French threat from Algeria there was growing Arab resistance to the Turkish occupation. In the interior of Libya the Arabs were led by Abdel Jalil Seif al-Nasr, chief of the Awlad Slaiman tribe, who had gradually assumed control over Fezzan during the time of the Karamanli war with the US Navy (Chapter Eight). Then Abdel Jalil moved to organise the tribes of Tripolitania and Sirte against the Turks: one of these tribes was the al-Gaddafa which was to produce the parents of Muammar al-Gaddafi. However, the Arabs were eventually subdued by the Turkish general Ahmed Pasha who, in time-honoured fashion, destroyed the villages, killed the inhabitants and stole produce and animals. The Libyan Arabs were not yet in control of their own land: in fact they would be forced to suffer a further colonial occupation, the most devastating of them all, before Libya could succeed in emerging as an independent nation.

In summary, a region known in antiquity as Libya (the land of the Libu, *Libye* to the Greeks) was populated by numerous peoples and was at the heart of pivotal historical events. Libyans contested land with the ancient Egyptians and with the warriors of many other nations: the Pharoah Ramases III of the twentieth dynasty (twelfth century B.C.) even used Libyan mercenaries, with Greeks and Nubians, to form the backbone of his army.[19] Wave after wave of invaders were variously accommodated, resisted, and made to pay a heavy price in men and treasure. Over all the tumultuous centuries the Libyans were never totally subjugated: whether the invades came from the sea or marched on Libya from the North African deserts they always encountered a resourceful stiff-necked people, favoured by a difficult terrain and a stubborn nature that made secure conquest an impractical ambition.

The Greek historian Herodotus of Halicarnassus travelled widely in the area and talked to many others who had ventured into the reaches of Fezzan, Cyrenaica and Tripolitania. For a time he lived in Athens or on Athenian territory as one of the original colonists to Thurioi in 444 B.C. We have seen how, with his lively Ionian mind, he was keen to record details of geography, local fauna and flora, the appearance and habits of native peoples. His aim, as he explained, was 'to save that which has occurred from passing out of men's memory by lapse of time, and from oblivion the great and marvellous deeds of Greeks and barbarians alike, and especially the reason for their going to war with one another'.

He is not always reliable: sometimes what he relates is manifestly untrue ('It is my business to tell what was told to me, but not necessarily to believe it'), but still he conveys a wealth of impressions and beliefs, a rich web of what could be deemed credible to the ancient mind. There is reason to think that on the whole he was, while not infallible, a reliable witness. Thus the celebrated historian H. J. Rose observes of Herodotus, the 'Father of History': 'No historian is freer from the guilt of deception, or from concealment of his own ignorance or uncertainty.'[20] It is from Herodotus that we learn most of what it was like to be a Libyan in antiquity.

The Libyan tribes encountered in Herodotus and in the works of later writers together represent a rich cultural soil that was further mulched by the endless invasions that chased each other over the centuries – Phoenicians, Egyptians, Greeks, Romans, Turks, French, Italians, Germans, British. The Americans bombarded the coastal towns in the nineteenth century; the Axis powers and the Allied forces ravaged Cyrenaica and Tripolitania in the twentieth. The history of Libya is in part a bloody chronicle of slaughter and destruction at the hand of the foreigner. But the frequent depradations were in due course to serve as midwife to an independent nation: the tough and durable Libyans had been pregnant with independence over all the troubled centuries. First they had to survive the most oppressive colonialism of them all.

3 The Fourth Shore

Italy, sensing the growing colonial impotence of the Ottomans, invaded Libya in 1911 and thus consigned it to Italian occupation for three decades. Had Italy been content, had it not been seduced by the illusion of further rich pickings in the Second World War, Libya would probably have remained an Italian territory for longer than it did. As it was, Italy's ambition hastened the colonial collapse: after a brief neocolonial interregnum, Libya became independent.

PRELUDE TO INVASION

In 1838 Giuseppe Mazzini, the Italian revolutionary and political writer, who worked for a united Italy under a republican government, declared that 'North Africa must belong to Italy.' Tunisia was the tip of Africa nearest to Sicily and this was the region that had been Rome's first African colony. Again, in the second half of the nineteenth century, Italians moved to settle in Tunisia until, by 1881, they had built a community of some 25,000 immigrants. In August 1863 the Turin publication *Opinione* observed: 'If Egypt, and with it the Suez Canal, falls to the British, if Tunis falls to the French, and if Austria expands from Dalmatia into Albania, etc, we will soon find ourselves without a breathing space in the dead centre of the Mediterranean.' Already Italy felt squeezed by the competing pressures of the colonial powers and when, despite a twenty-year agreement signed by Italy in 1868, the Bey recognised the protectorate of France in Tunisia, Italy felt impelled to join the colonial 'scramble' for Africa. In the 1880s the Italian Prime Minister Francesco Crispi, who had aided Garibaldi in the conquest of Sicily, was talking of converting the sea between Sicily and the two Sirtic Gulfs into 'almost an Italian strait'. Crispi proclaimed the strategic importance of Libya and emphasised how Italian interests would be threatened if it fell into the hands of any of the other European powers. When the French began talking of the Mediterranean as a 'French Lake', there was fresh talk in Italy of 'Mare Nostrum': in due course the Italians would attempt to justify their invasion of Libya as an effort to counter the colonial ambitions of France and other powers in the Mediterranean. Mussolini was to reflect the view of most Italians when he said: 'for others the Mediterranean is just a route, for us it is life itself'.

In the 1880s Italy began a policy of 'peaceful penetration': the required breathing space was to be obtained through purchase rather than through naked conquest. Italian trade had extended to all the main Libyan ports by the end of the 1880s and schools were opened in Libya to spread Italian language and culture; the great Banco di Roma was urged in 1905 to begin an 'economic penetration' of the land. The bank opened the first branch in Tripoli in 1907 and then others in Benghazi and other Libyan towns. New businesses were financed and controlling interests were acquired in shipping and in many sectors of the export trade: cereals, wool, ivory, sponges and ostrich feathers. Expeditions to prospect for minerals in Tripolitania were funded, and within a few years the Banco di Roma controlled much of the domestic and foreign trade of Libya: all this, despite the hostility of the Turkish authorities. But there were restrictions on the Italian acquisition of land, the key to effective settlement. The Italians had long known the value of Libyan land and pressures were mounting for a more effective colonisation of the North African territories. The German explorer Rohlfs had observed in 1879 that land in Cyrenaica was so green that it reminded him of Italy: 'To me the possession of Tunis is not worth one-tenth that of Tripoli.' And in 1884 the Italian explorer Manfredo Camperio had proposed that Cyrenaica was well suited for the settling of Italian farming colonies.[1]

The British were securely established in Egypt, as were the French in Algeria, Tunisia and extensive tracts south of Libya. Moreover the diplomatic stage had been prepared by various agreements and understandings with the other colonial powers: for example, an Anglo-French convention in 1899 recognised that Italy had a legitimate sphere of influence in Tripolitania; and in 1909 Czar Nicholas of Russia resolved not to oppose Italian expansionist plans. Popular songs were written in Italy to celebrate *Tripoli, bel suolo di amore* ('Tripoli, fair land of love') and romantic paintings conveyed the seductive charm of the shore across the seas. At the same time there was academic and political opposition to the growing prospect of a full-blooded invasion of the Libyan mainland. Leone Caetani, a distinguished Italian scholar on Islam, declared himself opposed to a military expedition,[2] as did Gaetano Salvemini, conscious of 'the harm that this wave of nationalism might cause Italy'.[3] Such doubts however had little impact against Italian nationalism and colonialism strongly supported by a virtually unanimous press campaign.[4] And the Roman Catholic Church was not averse to bolstering the 'missionary' and 'crusading' spirit.[5] Italians were being told, with increasing fervour, that emigration was servile, 'but to conquer colonies is a worthy task for a free and noble people.'[16]

Giovanni Giolitti (1841–1928), prime minister of three Italian governments between 1903 and 1914, had a paramount influence during this period. Seen as one of the 'parliamentary dictators', he maintained a majority in parliament by bribing deputies from the south. He refused to use traditional violence to quell industrial strikes and made a number of other concessions to groups of workers whose support he needed, but at the same time he abandoned the peasants to the great landowners whose interests he favoured. It is easy to see Giolitti as an arch pragmatist. When he leaned to the political Left it was a calculated ploy, often designed to balance one faction against another; and when he launched the Libyan war to satisfy the nationalist Right he also perceived that this move would help to unite the country under a common banner.

When Giolitti first took power the development of the Italian economy largely depended upon foreign capital. Universal manhood suffrage was not to be applied until 1913, and early in the twentieth century parliamentary politics was mainly a matter of deals and accommodations between ministers, prefects, individual deputies and grand electors. Local notables were able to exert pressure in various ways to control political affairs, a circumstance that is far from dead in the practical *realpolitik* of modern Italy. Giolitti himself manipulated Catholic, socialist and other factions to maintain a viable political machine but he constantly underrated the nationalists, the forerunners of the future Italian fascists, who were already agitating for colonial adventurism. There were currently various stimuli to Italian nationalism.

There was a nostalgic upsurge in irredentism, in recollection of the Italian party formed in 1878 to capture or recapture for Italy various territories claimed on language or other grounds; a new philosophy of nationalistic violence, developed by *Action Française*, was being imported; and there were international developments that were affecting Italian sensitivities. The other European powers were pressing for land and influence: France and Britain threatened to thwart Italian ambitions in the Mediterranean, and in 1908 Austria had formally annexed the Turkish region of Bosnia-Hercegovina without reference to other interested nations. The Austrian move suggested to Italy that it should be paid compensation in view of the doctrine invented by the Italian historian Cesare Balbo to the effect that the Hapsburg empire should expand into the Balkans to enable Italy to move into Lombardy and Venetia. The Italian nationalists, though a minority on the Right, had powerful and wealthy friends. Their propaganda was extensive in the press and not unrelated in impact to the patriotic works of such artists as the poet Carducci and the composer Verdi. It could be calculated that a foreign war – to gain a territory long viewed as well within the legitimate sphere of Italian influence – would serve to secure a government under threat from both Left and Right. Giolitti, with little taste for colonial adventures, planned the Libyan war as a purely political move, designed – like many wars – to divert attention from domestic troubles.

There were suspicions that the French would move towards Tripoli. The Italians had acquiesced in the British exercise of control over Egypt, and expected Britain to show a similar restraint when Italy flexed its colonialist muscles. Italian anxieties about France were exacerbated by the French attack on Morocco since it was assumed that once France had secured its control over Morocco she would be hostile to any Italian attempt to grab Libya. Turkey had predictably complained about the Anglo-French agreements on zones of influence south of Tripoli, and the Italian government was quick to voice similar objections. In 1902 the Italians managed to gain a promise of French indifference to any Italian adventure in Libya in exchange for recognition of the French position in Morocco; and in the same year Italy won a guarantee from Austria and Germany that it would be allowed freedom of action in Tripoli. The ground was being prepared for invasion.

In April 1902 a left-wing deputy in the Italian parliament noted that Tripoli was 'necessary to the existence of Italy', and another deputy argued that a military occupation would enhance the value of Italian-controlled Eritrea by facilitating a new trade route between the Mediterranean and the Red Sea.[7] Italy obtained yet more guarantees at the 1906 Algeciras Conference, by which time it was emerging that even the United States had an interest in Libya. The Jewish Territorial Organisation despatched a commission to Cyrenaica in 1908 to consider the possibility of establishing a Jewish homeland under Turkish protection: some thought at that time that Israel would be planted in North Africa. In May 1910 agreement was reached between Turkish and Franco/Tunisian commissions on a new frontier that seemingly expanded Tunisia at the expense of Libya, while in 1911 France placated the Germans by surrendering a slice of its Congo territory to the German colony of Kamerun.

These developments, plus the requirement for a diversion from domestic problems, convinced the Italian government that it was time to act. Despite their economic penetration of North Africa effective Italian control had been limited for some time to the dry and infertile coastline of Eritrea and Somalia. It was time to assert a more effective Italian colonial presence in the region: if Italy failed to act now the chance would be lost. It has been argued that Italy's Libyan war produced a series of upheavals 'that were to lead to Sarajevo'.[8]

1911 INVASION AND AFTERMATH

The plans for the invasion of Libya, drawn up by Giolitti and the Chief of the General Staff, General Pollio, were completed by the end of August 1911. Early in September Ibrahim Pasha, the Turkish governor of Tripoli, returned to Constantinople to report on the Italian preparations for war. Turkey could do little since troops had been recently sent from Tripoli to quell a revolt in Yemen, but a cargo ship, the *Derna* – carrying 20,000 rifles, two million rounds of ammunition, and a quantity of mountain guns for trustworthy Libyans – was sent from Turkey. While the ship was still in transit the Italian government declared that it would regard the sending of war material to Tripoli a serious threat to the *status quo* in the region. On 28 September Italy issued an ultimatum, announcing that the shipping of arms to Tripoli was a 'manifestly hostile act' and that the Italian community in Tripoli was in danger. It further declared that Italy intended to extend Italian jurisdiction over the Ottoman provinces in North Africa: the stated intention was the military occupation of Tripolitania and Cyrenaica, and Turkey was told to state, within twenty-four hours, that there would be no objection to the Italian plan. If the Ottoman Porte refused to relinquish sovereignty then Italy would have no option but to use force. The Ottoman authorities protested but offered what was intended as a conciliatory reply. This was deemed by Italy to be unsatisfactory and Giolitti announced that the nation was about to fulfil *una fatalita storica*, a historic destiny.

The Italians launched a sea-borne invasion on 3 October. Italian troops landed at Tripoli, Benghazi, Derna, Tobruk and Khums; and there was immediate fighting with Ottoman forces. The Turkish garrison in Tripolitania was unwilling to capitulate but resolved instead to wage a war of resistance. The commanders, including General Ishaq Pasha, withdrew south and established a camp from which they hoped to launch a counter-attack. Turkey itself also took what steps it could to organise resistance to the Italian invasion. Two senior Turkish generals, Enver Pasha and Ali Fethi Bey, were given responsibilities in the new situation, as was Mustafa Kemal — already a member of the revolutionary faction 'Committee of Union and Progress' – who later emerged as Mustafa Kemal Ataturk, the influential leader of modern Turkey. Mustafa Kemal journeyed to Libya from the east, only to find that the British had closed the Egyptian frontier. He then took the train westward from Alexandria and, aided by Bedouin garb, was allowed to pass by an Egyptian officer who hated all the Christian imperialists, Italian as well as British. Kemal was soon promoted to major and given a command. *Jihad* was declared and the Arab tribes rallied to support their Turkish masters, now seen as warriors of the same faith, fighting to resist the Christian invasion. The Italians tried to bolster their own forces by employing Muslim troops from their territory in Eritrea, but these were seen as traitors to Islam, stimulating still further the joint Turkish/Libyan resistance to the alien incursion.

At first the Italians made little progress inland. A fresh sea-borne landing was attempted at Misrata, but the results were indecisive and the Italians were beaten at Rumeila. Despite their setbacks, the Italians proclaimed a great victory and formally announced the annexation of Tripolitania and Cyrenaica: 'If any nation of Europe has the right of possession or protectorate in this land, that nation is Italy.'⁹ Some local leaderships on the coast favoured collaboration with the Italian invaders: thus the merchant families, such as the Muntassers of Misrata and the Ben Zikris of Tripoli, calculated that conciliation would allow the continuation of normal trade. But other important leaders – for instance, Farhat Bey, a judge from Zawiyah, and Suleyman al-Baruni of the Ibadi Berbers, both in the Ottoman parliament – appealed for volunteers to join the Turkish forces. The Italian advance was slow but soon it was aided by Turkish reverses in the Balkans: after defeat in the Balkan war Turkey signed a peace in 1912 with its European opponents, including Italy. One of the key provisions was that the Turkish sultan relinquish all rights in Libya, though there was no requirement for a recognition of Italian sovereignty in the region. The Libyan Arabs were granted 'administrative autonomy', though this was never implemented. After the signing of the peace in November in Lausanne, Switzerland, the Ottoman forces were withdrawn and the Libyans were left to resist the Italian incursions as best they could. The Turks continued to supply their Libyan allies with guns, ammunition and other provisions but most of the Arab resistance factions in Tripolitania were subjugated by the time the First World War began in 1914. In Cyrenaica the Sanussi leader Ahmed al-Sharif assumed command of surviving Sanussi cells in Tripolitania and Fezzan, and a Libyan counter-attack drove the Italians back to their coastal garrisons in Tripoli, Homs, Zuara and the Cyrenaican ports.

Soon after the 1911 invasion the Italians began to establish agricultural settlements, many of which were later abandoned following Libyan resistance. The Italian governors prepared reports to specify the forms of land settlement that should be adopted: for example, the 1912 Bertolini Commission proposed privated (*libertist*) land settlement, whereas the 1913 Franchetti Commission favoured a state scheme of land settlement (*statalisti*), where peasant families would be granted small landholdings. The *libertisti* option predominated but in July 1914 colonists from Tripoli and Tunis were allowed to establish forty-three smallholdings on some of the land around Tripoli previously held by the Turkish authorities. A scheme of *colonizazzione associata* was proposed, whereby local Arab labour could be exploited on subsistence wages. Such plans gained little local support from the indigenous peoples: Libyan compliance could not be relied upon and the Italian settlers were facing increasing uncertainties. In April 1915 Libyan troops under Italian command mutinied at Qasr Bu Hadi, stimulating further revolts throughout the region. The leader of the initial revolt, Ramadan al-Suwayhili, invited the support of Ottoman and German military advisors, and his home town, Misrata, became a German base, sheltering submarines, recruiting mercenaries and raising taxes.

Italy formally entered the war in 1915, allying itself with the British in Egypt; the Germans, in collaboration with the Turks, worked to increase the flow of arms and other supplies to the Libyan resistance. A number of prestigious Muslim leaders, including Nuri Pasha from Turkey and Abdel Rahman Azzam from Egypt, journeyed to join with Ahmed al-Sharif in Cyrenaica. When the Libyans were badly defeated by the British army in the Egyptian desert, Ahmed al-Sharif surrendered the Sanussi command to Sayyid Muhammad al-Idris who became Grand Master of the Sanussi Order in 1918 and King Idris I, with the support of the Western powers, in 1952. The Libyans had committed *mujaheddin* forces of around 30,000 to support the Ottomans against the Italians, a move which had isolated Ahmed al-Sharif among the Sanussi leadership. Forced to transfer all authority to his cousin Idris, who had already made contact with the British in Cairo, he fled to Constantinople aboard a German submarine. In 1916 Idris sent a *mujaheddin* force under Safi al-Din, another cousin, to impose Sanussi control over the pro-Ottoman administration in Misrata, but he was defeated by Ramadan al-Suwayhili at Bani Walid. However, the British, already impressed with Idris's credentials, interceded with the Italians, and in the Akramah accord of April 1917 the Sanussi were granted a nominal autonomy in the region of Cyrenaica. At that time the Italians declared their willingness to regard Idris as the hereditary Emir of the interior. Limited self-government was also granted to Tripolitania, with provincial Libyan councils expected to assist the Italian administration. However, though Idris was now Emir ('prince') there was growing conflict between the Italians and the Sanussi Libyans.

Britain made efforts to end the Libyan/Italian conflict, not least by enlisting the support of the Khedive in Egypt and the Emir of Arabia.[10] When a truce was eventually signed in 1916 Britain recorded that Idris 'had been made to understand thoroughly that he was to be recognised only as the religious leader of his sect and not as chief of a political entity, and second, that he must make peace with both powers (Britain and Italy) or with neither'.[11] The truce specified that the Sanussi were to recognise the

Italian administration in the towns, while the Italians were to recognise the *de facto* Sanussi rule in the country. Idris had declared 'the unification of the fatherland' as a political goal,[12] but his health was poor and he was little more than a nominal leader: soon after his promotion to Emir he travelled to Egypt, not to return until installed back in Libya by the British in 1943. Idris had, it is recorded, 'long made financial preparations for this eventuality out of the Italian subsidies'.[13]

By the end of the First World War the colonial grip on Libya had been severely weakened. The collapse of the Ottomans, the weariness of the Italians, the intercession of the British with an interest in peace in the region – these and other factors had combined to boost the hopes of those Libyans who continued to strive for national independence. But the Libyans themselves were divided: decades of conflict had produced many contending factions. Some were rooted in Islamic fundamentalism, others in the perceived need to adjust to the dramatically changing features of a post-war twentieth century; some factions, apolitical and cosmopolitan, had no interest beyond trade; while others, sensitive to the upheavals wrought by Bolshevism, saw revolution as the only route to national pride. Some groups sought to protect their trading interests by collaborating with the Italian merchants and administrators, and some speculated on whether a defeat of the Italian colonists would simply return Libya to Turkish control. There were also, as in any political environment, the competing leadership claims, whether favouring a continued colonial tutelage, the imagined virtues of republicanism, the eternal verities of messianic religion, or whatever. The disruptions brought by the competing European powers fuelled Arab nationalism and further stimulated efforts to bring a final end to colonial occupation. In much of Libya Italy was able only to claim a nominal control, but it succeeded nonetheless in exploiting the discordant strife, in exacerbating racial tensions: for example, between Arabs and Berbers. The Italians remained in a state of virtual siege in their coastal enclaves but the Libyans, disunited and poorly led, were in no position to evict them from all Libyan land. Moreover, the ending of the European war was already suggesting to the Italians that a more effective conquest of Libya might be a realistic option.

In 1918 a rebel government managed to establish itself in Tripolitania, despite the bombing of Misrata by Italian and Malta-based British aircraft. Italy then despatched General Garioni with troop contingents to Tripoli to prepare for the possibility of reconquest. By March 1919 some 70,000 soldiers had landed and ships were delivering flame-throwers, heavy artillery, tanks and aeroplanes. Garioni declared that the reconquest would be completed 'within two months'.[14] But the Italians, perhaps for domestic

reasons, were reluctant to embark upon a fresh colonial adventure. Major-
General Giuseppe Tarditi talked to the tribal leaders, instructing them to
submit to Italian rule or to face military action. The Arab leaders – who
included Ramadan Shutaywi, Sulaiman Baruni and the Egyptian Abdel
Rahman Azzam – refused to heed the Italian threats, even threatening to
intensify the guerrilla struggle if the talks broke down. Italy would be
allowed to maintain garrisons in some of the coastal towns, but the tribes
would not disarm and Italy would recognise the Tripolitanian republic. The
resolute Arab stand resulted in a partial climb-down by the Italians: a statute
was issued in October 1919 giving Tripolitanians the right to a parliament
and all the benefits of Italian citizenship. At the same time the Italians
thought that they would be able to maintain an element of control, in
collaboration with local leaders, through governing and local councils. The
70,000 troops were sent home, never having ventured beyond Tripoli, and
little seemed to have changed. The Italians maintained their coastal strongholds and the Libyans mounted guerrilla raids while continuing to fight
among themselves.

Conflict between Ramadan Shutaywi and the Orfella tribe, early in 1920,
resulted in Shutaywi's death. The Italians had worried that Shutaywi would
overrun the country and governor Menzinger, having failed to prevent the
crisis, was replaced by governor Mercatelli. He was however prevented by
the Italian government from taking any military initiatives, being told that
'"every warlike act, even an insignificant one, would have unfortunate
repercussions" – in Italy, not Tripolitania.'[15] Signs of fresh political turmoil
in Italy suggested that potentially hazardous military adventures would be
avoided, at least in the short term. In the early 1920s Italy was on the verge
of dramatic social changes and was reluctant to pursue a further aggressive
war in North Africa. The declaration of a republic in Tripolitania was
followed by Cyrenaica establishing its own parliament, a body that lacked
full autonomy but which for a time suffered only indirect control from Italy.
In such circumstances the pressures mounted for true Libyan independence.
A delegation from the Tripolitanian republic visited Rome to lobby left-
wing deputies to declare their total repudiation of any form of Italian
sovereignty over Libya. Such developments made the Italian government
increasingly unhappy with its compromise rule in North Africa and the
scene was set for a radical change of policy. One option was for Italy to
withdraw from its 'fourth shore', to acknowledge at last that its position in
North Africa was untenable. However, such a course was unacceptable:
Italy was not about to give up its strongholds on Libyan territory.

The Tripolitanian delegation had achieved nothing: Mercatalli's refusal
to issue passports had not stopped Mohammad Khalid al-Gargani from

travelling with the delegates to Rome (Gargani was later to attend the Muslim Revolutionary Congress in Moscow), but the delegation was discredited by another Libyan group headed by Hassuna Pasha Karamanli, the mayor of Tripoli and long a friend of Italy. The group denounced Gargani as a revolutionary troublemaker and the Italians withdrew recognition from his delegation on the ground that it did not represent all Tripolitania. This led to further military tensions in Libya, whereupon Mercatelli moved to exploit Arab/Berber differences, urging Sulaiman Baruni to organise his Berber followers in an 'anti-rebel' front. The orthodox Muslims moved to crush the Berber resistance and Yefren, a Berber centre, fell in 1921. Mercatelli made what efforts he could to help the Berbers, despatching a relief column that did not manage to reach Yefren (a shortage of water halted the column thirty miles short). Governor Mercatelli, increasingly frustrated by the Libyan impasse, took the decision to resign. He was duly replaced by Count Giuseppe Volpi.

The Italian government had been pressured into making many concessions to the Libyan nationalists. Before Idris sought refuge in Egypt he and his family had been paid monthly allowances; and the Italians met other expenses, subsidising the Emir's army and police, tribal sheikhs, officials and others. Idris was allowed freedom of movement, and he was consulted on the appointment of Italian officials to his territory. Similarly the Italians gave increasing latitude to the Cyrenaican parliament, which convened in Benghazi in April 1921 for the first time. Most of the sixty parliamentary members were elected tribal sheikhs, with the Italian community being allowed only three representatives. Contrary to Idris's agreement with the Italians he had failed to disarm the tribal guerrillas or to break up the armed camps. A further accord, designed to put the camps under joint Italian/ Libyan control until they could be disbanded, was signed at Bu Mariam on 11 November 1921. For a time the 'mixed camps' were jointly policed but the scheme was not judged a success: the Italians tried to make the camps subversive centres of Italian influence deep in the country, further exacerbating the tensions between the Italian administrators and the Arab leaders.

The time for radical decisions had been reached. The compromises made by Italy over its Libyan territories were increasingly seen as expensive and unworkable. It was time to withdraw totally from North Africa or to embark upon a fresh conquest of Libya. In August 1921 Giuseppe Volpi, the eleventh governor in ten years, arrived in Tripoli; on 28 October 1922 Benito Mussolini marched on Rome to initiate a twenty-year period of fascist dictatorship in Italy. The early 1920s was not the time for Italians to contemplate an abject surrender of their North African possessions.

RECONQUEST

Prelude

In 1919 Mussolini had written in *Popolo d'Italia*: 'As for Libya, it is obvious that we cannot withdraw the garrisons that are needed for our security',[16] and soon afterwards he organised the meeting at which the *fasci di combattimento* were created. As always, the press could be largely relied upon to suggest the romantic appeal of colonial adventure, to stimulate the nationalist imaginations of ordinary citizen and politician alike. Gaspare Colosimo, for example, responsible for the Italian colonies from 1916 to 1919 in a secondary government position, was influenced by nationalist declarations celebrating the 'solidity – in terms both of territory and population – of Italian rule with that of other colonial empires'.[17] Even supposed Liberal opinion deemed it necessary 'to consolidate our rule wherever present-day circumstances have rendered it somewhat insecure', though it was recognised – at least by Senator Scialoja, president of the Royal Commission for the post-war period – that 'in Libya, particularly, the religious question is of fundamental importance', and that 'we shall not be able to get a just, sound settlement of our relations with the inhabitants of the colonies unless we first take account of their moral requirements'.[18]

When the fascist Giuseppe Volpi arrived in Tripoli in August 1921 the situation was worse than he had imagined: the Italians held a number of the coastal towns but little else. Beyond the barbed-wire defences the Reform Committee of the Tripolitanian republic issued its own edicts, imposed taxes, and raised its own levies; and sometimes the Committee pursued its activities in the urban areas under nominal Italian control. Volpi's instinct was to go on to the offensive, but he was constrained by Rome and abandoned plans for an incursion into Misrata Marina. The Italian government was alarmed by a report that the region would be resolutely defended by 100,000 armed tribesmen. Volpi met the local chiefs, declared that he was prepared to recognise their authority over their own people – a classic colonial ploy – but emphasised that no Emir claiming to represent the whole country would be tolerated. But there were signs that the Libyans were working to develop a more united front to oppose the Italian occupation. Thus in late 1921 Volpi received reports that Idris was meeting Tripolitanian envoys and that the Tripolitanians were talking to various Sanussi factions at Sirte. Such events were seen by Volpi as further evidence that a more robust Italian policy was essential: if Rome continued to hesitate he would himself take action. By 18 January 1922 Volpi was prepared to invade Misrata and its port, and on the following day the Italian

Minister of Colonies sanctioned the scheme as an 'internal action' for which Volpi would carry sole responsibility.

A force sailed from Tripoli and accomplished a dawn landing of some 1500 troops near Misrata Marina on 26 January but the plan faltered, even though there was only a small defending force. Air and sea reinforcements had to be sent from Italy before the port could be taken, seventeen days after the launch of the campaign. The poor showing of the Italian forces did nothing to convince Volpi that military measures were ill-advised. Instead he concluded that a more vigorous military posture was the only answer to the Libyan question: 'Italy is forever destined to bathe the assertion of her rights in blood!'

The Italian invasion provoked a response from the Tripolitanians. The railway line from Tripoli to Azizia in Eritrea was cut and the garrison at Azizia was besieged. Actions were launched against most of the Italian enclaves, and by the end of February the Italians were looking for a truce. Volpi returned to Rome to discuss fresh plans with a new Minister of Colonies, Amendola. Negotiations were begun with the tribal leaders who were threatened with military action but who responded by demanding self-rule under a Muslim leader. On 1 April Ahmad Marayid sent a note to Volpi revealing that the Tripolitanian and Sanussi representatives had agreed at Sirte to a united Tripolitania and Cyrenaica under a Muslim leader with supreme powers. Volpi, increasingly impatient, decided that a policy of direct rule from Italy was the only solution: 'Neither with the chiefs, nor against the chiefs, but without the chiefs.'[19] With the ending of the cease-fire on 10 April 1922, Volpi – now with 15,000 troops under his command – was ready to 're-establish normalcy', to launch a fully fledged reconquest of Libya.

An early Italian success was achieved when Rodolfo Graziani, a young colonel working in concert with other competent officers, managed to retake the whole of the Tripoli/Zuara coastal strip. The siege of the Eritrean garrison at Azizia was lifted by Pietro Badoglio, and on 30 April Graziani was able to march into the town. Other regions were reoccupied and Graziani was given enlarged responsibilities: Volpi had now decided that further negotiations with the Arabs were a waste of time. He declared a state of martial law in areas where the rebels were active, working to crush the rebellion before effective links could be forged between the anti-Italian factions in Tripolitania and Cyrenaica. The newly assertive policies were to gain added support following the social and political changes in Italy.

Soon after Mussolini took power in October 1922, he set about the reconquest of the whole of Libya: 'Civilization in fact is what Italy is creating on the fourth shore of our sea – Western civilization in general and

Fascist civilization in particular.' Volpi himself, writing some years later, declared what the arrival of Fascism had meant to him: 'The absolute identity of policy and intention and the end for ever of the tormenting unease which up to then had increased the difficulties of action.'[20] The scene was set for a fresh onslaught by a modern well-equipped nation on the tribal peoples of Libya.

Shape of Aggression

The reconquest of the 'fourth shore' had begun in earnest in late 1922. The Italians made quick gains – northern Tripolitania was soon brought under control – but it took several years to subdue the entire region. By 1928 the Sirtica desert had been conquered, and in 1930 the Fezzan was pacified. There was scattered resistance in Cyrenaica until 1931 but Italy's merciless tactics eventually convinced the tribes that there was no point in further conflict. One of the principal guerrilla leaders, Omar al-Mukhtar (see below), was captured, tried and executed in 1931; and in January 1932 the total subjugation of Libya was finally announced. In 1937 Mussolini had himself ceremonially proclaimed the 'Protector of Islam', two years before Libya was officially integrated into metropolitan Italy.

This bare chronology does nothing to convey what the indigenous people suffered through this period. The Libyan authorities have stated that some 750,000 people were killed during the Italian conquest, and though this may be an exaggeration there is no doubt that many Libyan communities were displaced, slaughtered and driven into concentration camps. The researcher John Wright has claimed that the Italians were executing 12,000 Libyans annually.[21] A German visitor to Tripoli, Von Gotberg, commented that 'No army meted out such vile and inhumane treatment as the Italian army in Tripoli. General Kanaiva has shown contempt for every international law, regarding lives as worthless.'[22]

Omar al-Mukhtar had fought the Italians since the time of the original invasion in 1911. He served under Ahmed al-Sharif until forced into a period of exile in Egypt until 1923; then he returned to Libya to command a force of up to six thousand guerrillas, mainly nomads. Leadership in Libya was provided by Reda, Idris's brother, until Reda was captured by the Italians in 1928 and banished to Sicily. Mukhtar became the effective leader of the unpacified territories by night, able to raise taxes and recruits for the guerrilla movement. An Italian/Egyptian agreement in 1925 gave Italy sovereignty over the Sanussi strongholds at the Jarabub and Kufra oases, making it easier for the Italians to cut off the Libyans' sources of supply in Egypt, but the conflict continued. The Italian supply lines, communication facilities and troop convoys came under frequent attack, with the Italians responding by blocking water wells with stones and concrete; slaughtering the herds of camels, sheep and goats that the tribes depended on; moving whole communities into desolate concentration camps in the desert; and dropping captured Libyans alive from aircraft.

In January 1923 General Luigi Bongiovanni was appointed by Mussolini as the first Fascist governor of Cyrenaica. He had been given a directive to crush the rebellion quickly, to demonstrate that the new regime in Rome was in effective control of the colonial territories. Bongiovanni first invited Reda al-Sanussi, now the head of the Sanussi Order after his brother's departure for Egypt, to disband the 'mixed camps' and all other armed bases. When this failed to happen the Italians invaded the camps and arrested the Sanussi forces; all pacts with the Sanussis were declared void, and the Italians demanded that the tribes recognise complete Italian sovereignty over the whole of Cyrenaica. The second Italian/Sanussi war, begun in 1922, was to lead to the crushing of the tribes and the stern imposition of a Fascist order. Small numbers of nomads resisted the Italian forces as best they could, but they were poorly equipped, able to muster only half a dozen machine guns, a few pieces of artillery, and no more than 6000 regular and irregular riflemen.[23] Many of the tribes fought hard to keep their independence but it was difficult to resist armoured onslaughts on their camps. More than 20,000 nomads were subjugated in the spring of 1923; eight hundred were killed between May and September and 12,000 sheep were confiscated or killed. The mechanised raids continued to crush the camps but the Libyan 'non-combatants' (*sottomessi*, those who had 'submitted') continued to support the active guerrillas where they could.

A principal guerrilla stronghold was the Gebel Akhdar, a rough region with woods, caves and ravines, ideal guerrilla country. By the end of 1924 the Italians had conquered the western end of the Gebel Akhdar, though minor skirmishes – ambushes and small engagements – still occurred. The Italians used armoured vehicles wherever they could be taken, and could often rely upon air support. The guerrillas lost around 1100 men between April and September 1927, the time that has been seen as the half-way point in the battle for the Gebel Akhdar and Cyrenaica.[24] After this time, events unfolded with a grim predictability: tribesmen equipped only with rifles were no match for the more numerous Italian troops equipped with armoured vehicles, artillery and aircraft.

When on 6 March 1923, General Bongiovanni began a surprise attack on the Sanussi forces to signal the start of the campaign to conquer Cyrenaica he was able to call on considerable forces: four Italian battalions, five Eritrean battalions, two Libyan battalions (the eleven battalions together comprising an infantry strength of more than 8000 men), two Savari (Libyan cavalry) squadrons, two mountain batteries, two gunnery companies for fortifications, two companies of engineers, a motorised unit divided into twelve sections, and two squadrons of aircraft (including four Caproni Ca 3 bombers and eight Sva spotter planes).[25] We have seen that the Sanussi had around 6000 men equipped with rifles and little else. The 'mixed camps' were broken up and fresh territory in Cyrenaica was soon occupied by the advancing Italian forces, but the invaders were not always successful: in two successive engagements in Sirtica the Mogarba severely mauled the Italians, who lost thirteen officers, forty Italian soldiers and 279 *ascari*.[26] Firm Italian rule was established over what were seen as the more stable tribes in the region of the towns, though tribal resistance continued in the Gebel and in many of the arid southern regions: the Mogarba, the southern Auaghir, the Brahasa, the Abid, the Faied, and some of the Dorsa and Abeidat.[27]

The offensive in the Gebel continued through 1924: in the spring of that year, according to official Italian figures, six hundred guerrillas and some 25,000 animals were killed, though only ninety-seven rifles were seized. The mobile rebel groups were able to avoid the fixed Italian garrisons but guerrilla losses continued to mount as the campaign wore on. In spring 1925 the Italians attacked the southern slopes of the Gebel, killing 250 men, 5000 camels and more than 10,000 sheep; only fifty rifles were collected from the battlefield, which suggests that the Italians were attacking ordinary tribespeople rather than the organised guerrilla forces. In 1926 the Italians, gaining experience in the use of trucks and aircraft in desert terrain, moved further into the Gebel. At that time the rebels lost 500 men, 100 horses, 2300 camels and more than 30,000 sheep; the Italian losses were three officers, twenty-five troops and twenty-four *ascari*.[28] In four years of fighting the Gebel tribes had suffered losses of some 1500 men and as many as 100,000 domestic animals, but they still managed to retain control of parts of the Gebel. Moreover they achieved some significant victories: on the 28 March 1927 the Italian-led Seventh Libyan Battalion of 750 troops was ambushed at er-Raheiba with nearly half the force wiped out. General Mezzetti acknowledged this 'notable military success against us' and provided a description of the engagement.[29] In November 1926 Attilio Teruzzi, an influential member of the Fascist party, took over from General Mombelli as governor of Cyrenaica. The Italian forces were quickly built up with the aim of establishing complete control of the Gebel, and again the contrast between the sizes of the contending forces was manifest. The Italians now had massive mobile forces: nine Eritrean battalions, two Libyan battalions, four Savari squadrons, one *meharist* squadron, a squadron of armoured cars, and various bands of irregulars – all totally more than 10,000 men well equipped to move fast through desert terrain. In addition there were the fixed garrisons in the towns and the increasing number of rural pacified areas, and a supporting force of twenty aircraft. Against this array of men and hardware, Omar al-Mukhtar commanded fewer than two thousand men. Now the war was moving decisively to a conclusion. Mukhtar's forces were dispersed, though they often managed to escape with their light weapons intact, the supposedly impregnable Kuf stronghold was finally overrun, and Mezzetti launched repeated attacks on the Gebel from July to September 1927. The rebels lost 1300 men killed, 250 women and children taken prisoner, 3000 camels killed and 850 captured, and 5000 sheep killed with 18,000 captured. Throughout the whole of the summer campaign the Italians lost two officers, five airmen and sixty-one *ascari*.

It seemed in 1927 that the Italians had finally defeated all serious resistance in the Gebel, perhaps the most significant rebel region in the whole of Libya; but even General Mezzetti, while rejoicing in the Italian victory, acknowledged that there may be further rebel offensives. He recognised the strengths of the rebel resistance, noting the solidarity of the *sottomessi*, and the leadership qualities of the Sanussis. However, there was still an unwillingness to recognise that the tribes were involved in a legitimate struggle for national independence: 'Mezzetti and other exponents of Italian colonialism were compelled to fall back on racist ravings in order to explain the innate belligerence of the primitive peoples of Libya.'[30]

To consolidate Italian control of the Gebel, Mezzetti built a network of fortified points to hamper the movement of any surviving rebel groups and to provide effective logistic support for the Italian forces. New forts were established and an effort was made to draw clear dividing lines between the sites of the pacified population and the regions in which the rebels still had a toe-hold: this meant that any animal or person south of the principal demarcation line could be attacked by mechanised units on the ground or bombed from the air. In fact it came to be realised that the 'non-combatants' could not be effectively separated from the rebels: the garrisons multiplied, the Italian forces became thinly spread, and the Sanussi leaders were able to restart the rebellion.

In October 1927 Governor Teruzzi and Mezzetti called a meeting in Benghazi of all the officials responsible for the administrative districts of Cyrenaica: the officials were asked to estimate the number of armed rebels still active in the territory. Mezzetti later wrote that the officials claimed that there were not more than 'a hundred or so' armed rebels in the whole of Cyrenaica. Again this statement has been taken as indicating that the Italians did not really understand the dimensions of the national struggle.

The 'non-combatants' were still solid in their hostility to Italian rule, and the armed factions were struggling to reorganise their forces. Thus in November a fresh offensive was launched with a raid in the area of Slonta and attacks on the Italian communication lines.[31] Omar al-Mukhtar had realised that frontal assaults on the Italian forces would be suicidal, and so resorted to classical guerrilla tactics: there was still talk of Mukhtar's 'night government'.

The resistance suffered a fresh set-back when Reda, Idris's brother, gave himself up to the Italian authorities, highlighting internal disagreements among the Sanussi. Reda's eldest son Hassan took over the Sanussi leadership, and tactical moves by the Italians had the effect of stimulating further rebellion in Cyrenaica. Perhaps misled by their own scanty information the Italians decided to concentrate their forces in Tripolitania, and in conquest of the Sirtic region and certain oases south of the Gebel. This encouraged guerrilla activities in the Gebel, but the fresh Italian moves – supported by radio, armoured cars, trucks and aircraft – achieved considerable successes in their new operations. In particular, the pro-Italian Libyan mounted *mehara* units were as mobile as the rebels' *mehalle* and with much superior equipment: a 400-strong *mehalla*, intending to attack the Italian forces in Sirtica, was spotted and bombed by aircraft, then attacked and destroyed by Italian mobile units. In this engagement the rebels lost 226 men and 173 rifles.[32] Rebel attacks continued in the Gebel, despite widespread and largely indiscriminate Italian bombing. The Italian publication *Notiziario* noted that while the air force had not failed to bomb any camps and groups that it sighted, 'recent reports indicate that such attacks have not been very effective in view of the fact that the soldiers have easily managed to withdraw, hiding in the caves of the high *wadis*'.[33] At the same time bomb fragments 'caused heavy losses among livestock'.

Mezzetti then withdrew forces from Sirtica to mount a further offensive in the Gebel: on 31 March a large caravan was destroyed at Baltet-es-Zalgh, leaving 200 dead and 1500 camels killed.[34] Again, in the face of the new onslaught, the rebel groups dispersed among the people, mingling with the *sottomessi*, and the Italians were reminded how impossible it was to separate the active guerrillas from the supposed non-combatants in the tribes. *Notiziario* observed how the rebels had infiltrated the ranks of the Abeidat *sottomessi*: 'So-called dissidents, moreover, have sent all their livestock into Abeidat territory, where it has mingled with the animals of the *sottomessi*; they have also done the same with their families and much of their chattels.'[35] In December 1928 Mezzetti gave an optimistic account of his two years of command, but conceded that absolute control could only be achieved by the destruction of the rebels as a politico-military organisation, and that this would be accomplished by the politico-military organisation of the country. At the end of 1928 the Italians were forced to admit that, despite massive offensives with considerable support, the Sanussi were still able to control parts of the country and to operate at night in many of the occupied regions.

In the first half of 1928 the Italians had occupied a further 150,000 square kilometres of territory in operations, in the words of an Italian commentator, 'worthy of entry in the most glowing pages of colonial-military history of the world'.[36] But the mobile Libyan forces always managed to avoid total annihilation: Italian thrusts had divided rebel forces from each other, but they were still able to function as self-contained units, living off the inhospitable land and continuing to rely on the support of the people. In January 1929 Pietro Badoglio, the marshal of Italy, was made governor of Tripolitania and Cyrenaica, an indication of the importance the Italians attached to their Libyan territories. He quickly issued a proclamation offering 'peace, clemency and generosity' to all those who were prepared to submit to Italian rule. The proclamation was printed in thousands of copies and dropped by aircraft over wide areas. One hope was that it would forestall a planned rebel offensive by Hassan and Ahmad Saif al-Nasr. At the same time the military pressure on the tribes was maintained within the context of an infrastructure that the Italians had developed over many years. Graziani, now a general, had built a network of garrisons, largely disarmed many of the tribes, and had locked and poisoned wells to restrict the mobility of the rebels. Hassan, despite his ambition to drive back the Italians, was forced to retreat south across barren country; and Ahmad Saif al-Nasr was defeated at Al-Shuwayrif (Graziani: 'Thus, in miserable fashion, the rebel plan failed once again').

The Badoglio proclamation promising peace (and also declaring: 'If obliged, I will wage war with powerful systems and means, which they will long remember. No rebel will be left in peace, neither he nor his family nor his herds nor his heirs. I will destroy everything, men and things') met with little response. Instead new Italian offensives were launched: at the end of 1929 Graziani's forces reached the area of Fezzan, quelling the last pockets of rebel resistance, but guerrillas still managed to remain active in some parts of Cyrenaica. Badoglio brought Reda back from exile and began secret negotiations, after which there was a reduction in hostilities leading to a truce.

However, the truce – of which there are various interpretations – was short-lived. Badoglio informed Mussolini that the truce represented an unconditional surrender on the part of Mukhtar and the other Libyan leaders, but Mukhtar saw the truce as a temporary arrangement to allow the continuation of negotiations: in fact when Mukhtar went to meet Badoglio, the Arab leader was accompanied by a strong retinue of warriors, a circumstance which does not suggest abject surrender. Elements of the Libyan forces remained intact, and the hoped-for disarmament predicted by the Italian authorities had not been achieved. The Italians tried to prolong the negotiations but when it was clear that no progress was being made Mukhtar announced that no further adjournments would be accepted and that hostilities would be resumed from 24 October 1929. The scene was set for the final crushing of the Libyan forces.

It was left to Rodolfo Graziani to put down the final efforts of the weakened Cyrenaican rebellion. He had recently conquered southern Tripolitania and Fezzan, and, a general at forty-two and now vice-governor of Cyrenaica, he was regarded in some Italian circles as a national hero. He was also known in Cyrenaica as 'Butcher Graziani'. On 5 April 1930 he wrote to Badoglio: 'I see the situation in Cyrenaica as comparable to a poisoned organism which produces, in one part of the body, a festering bubo. The bubo in this instance is the *dor* of Omar al-Mukhtar, which is the result of a wholly infected situation. To heal this sick body it is necessary to destroy the origin of the malady rather than its effects.'[37] Many saw him as waging a personal vendetta against Mukhtar.

Repression

In 1930 General Graziani began his final task in Cyrenaica by building a two-hundred-mile-long barbed-wire fence along the Egyptian border – from the Bardia oasis near the coast to just north of the Jarabub oasis – to block all guerrilla supplies coming from Egypt's Western Desert.[38] The fence, ten yards wide and five feet high, was patrolled by armoured vehicles and aircraft; anyone trying to penetrate it was shot. Graziani himself compared the fence to the Great Wall of China, though the actual effectiveness of the wire entanglements was debatable. In addition, Graziani disbanded his pro-Italian Libyan contingents, replacing them with units of Christian Eritreans, hated by the Arabs. Any contact with the guerrillas was made a capital offence, the Sanussi *zawiyas* were closed, shaikhs were arrested on thin charges and exiled, and almost the entire population of nomads in northern Cyrenaica, along with all their livestock, was forcibly moved for incarceration in bleak concentration camps on the coast and in the desert. The camps comprised rows of government tents set in straight rows, the whole area enclosed by barbed wire fences and protected by machine guns. Thus the wandering Bedouin nomads, accustomed to roaming over vast open areas, were confined to miserable wire enclosures, their traditional modes of existence shattered. Graziani declared to the press in June 1931 that 'no radical change in life has been imposed on the people'. Now the proud *sottomessi* were only allowed to subsist as 'caged beggars . . . ashamed at having submitted while others were still fighting'.[39] Wright quotes Knud Holmboe, an Arabic-speaking Danish Muslim, who travelled from Morocco to Derna in 1930, and who later described in his book *Desert Encounter* a camp he encountered near Barce:

> It was fenced in with barbed wire, and there were guards with machine guns at every entrance . . . children came running towards us. They were in rags and hungry, half-starved, but evidently they were accustomed to getting money from the Commandant on his visits, for they stretched out their hands and shouted in Italian: *'Un soldo, Signore, un soldo!'* The Bedouins gathered around us. They looked incredibly ragged. On their feet were hides tied with string; their burnouses were a patchwork of all kinds of multi-coloured pieces. Many of them seemed ill and wretched, limping along with crooked backs, or with arms and legs that were terribly deformed.[40]

There is a lengthy catalogue of war crimes perpetrated by General Graziani, for which he was never called to account. It is suggested that the Italians deliberately bombed civilians, killing vast numbers of women, children and old people; that they raped and disembowelled women, threw prisoners alive from aeroplanes, and ran over others with tanks. Suspects were hanged or shot in the back, tribal villages – according to Holmboe – were being bombed with mustard gas by the spring of 1930. As with all atrocity tales, there is probably an element of exaggeration, but Holmboe noted that during the time he was in Cyrenaica 'thirty executions took place daily . . . The land swam in blood!'[41] Few Libyan families survived this period without loss: Muammar Gaddafi himself lost a grandfather, and three hundred members of his tribe were forced by the Italians to seek refuge in Chad. Graziani was well aware that the alleged atrocities, under his command, were tarnishing his military reputation: he noted the 'clamour of unpopularity and slander and disparagement which was spread everywhere against me', but recorded in his book, *The Agony of the Rebellion*, that his conscience was 'tranquil and undaunted to see Cyrenaica saved, by pure Fascism, from that invading Levantism which sought to escape from the civilising Latin force'. The means to 'save' Cyrenaica, with the rest of Libya, had been much discussed and carefully planned.

The people of the Gebel were deported in order to isolate the few pockets of guerrilla resistance still under the control of Omar al-Mukhtar. Badoglio, in protracted discussion and exchange of letters with Graziani, noted that it was essential to create a well-defined territorial gap between the guerrillas and the 'subject population'. He observed in a letter to Graziani on 20 June 1930: 'I do not conceal from myself the significance and gravity of this action, which may well spell the ruin of the so-called subject population.'[42] Moreover, it was essential that this path be followed *'even if the entire population of Cyrenaica has to perish'* (my italics). In fact the deportation plan was already well under way in May 1930, with some tribes having been moved near to Italian bases where the Arabs could more easily be controlled: Graziani himself recorded that 1400 Dorsa tents had been established around Tolmeta, with 900 Abid tents on the Barce plain, and 3600 Abeidat tents in the area of Derna. But now the scheme was dramatically expanded as Graziani ordered 'the total clearance of the Gebel by moving the entire population, under its first phase, from Tolmeta to the sea'. Soon there were signs of the scale of the operation: plans were set in motion for 7000 Abeidat tents to be conveyed to an approved area, and Badoglio noted one of the advantages of the concentration camps that were being established ('we shall go on . . . to carry out a strict census of people and livestock'). Badoglio also suggested that the *sottomessi* were now thoroughly cowed, understanding that the Italian government would carry out 'any form of extreme measure'[43] to ensure that all orders were completely obeyed. There was to be no ambiguity in the prevailing policy regarding the concentration camps. Thus Graziani declared that 'the government is calmly determined to reduce the people to most miserable starvation if they do not fully obey orders. The same severity will be meted out to all those outside who act on their behalf.'[44]

Little publicity was being given in Italy to the events on the North African mainland, and the other European powers had little interest in what was happening in Libya (it is worth recalling that the French, English, Belgians and Spanish had carried out similar policies in their own colonial territories). In such circumstances Mussolini felt free to authorise Badoglio and Graziani to adopt whatever repressive measures they chose, without fear of consequences for his own regime. Thus the region of the Gebel became an empty land, without livestock or animals: 80,000 inhabitants and hundreds of thousands of animals were deported into severe camps and other areas that could be mercilessly policed. The *sottomessi* had been reduced to beggars, forced labourers – demoralised victims of a colonial power. Details provided by Graziani indicate the character of the concentration camps: ten of thousands of people huddled together, with the bare means of subsistence, scant health facilities (in one region two doctors were each responsible for two camps and more than 30,000 people), and little hope for the future.

The rebellion was now virtually over. Successive Italian offensives had divided the tribes from each other, making it easier to deport the conquered peoples. The outside world, with its own preoccupations, had no concern with what might be happening in Italy's North African lands. It had taken Italy more than two decades to subjugate an underdeveloped tribal people, but now the task was largely complete – most graphically signalled by the capture and trial of Omar al-Mukhtar; and by his execution, before a silent gathering of 20,000 tribesmen.

Capture of Mukhtar

In a battle in October 1930 Omar al-Mukhtar, then over seventy, lost his gold spectacles and their silver chain; when they were found and identified by an Italian patrol, Graziani declared: 'Now we have the spectacles; the head will follow one day.'[45] In early September 1931 the Italians in the Gebel received news that the rebel Brahasa-Dorsa *dor* (a hundred or so horsemen), reinforced by Mukhtar's Abeidat *dor*, was concentrating to the south of el-Beda in preparation for a raid around Cyrene. The alarm was raised and scouts were sent into the region. On 9 September rebels were sighted near Slonta, not far from an Italian garrison, and on the following day Colonel Giuseppe Malta moved three Eritrean battalions and a group of Savari squadrons into the zone. At dawn on 11 September the detected *dor* was attacked in the Wadi Bu Taga, but the horsemen were already on the move and as they dispersed they managed to move through the Italian lines. One of the small groups of horsemen was sighted by aircraft and a signal was sent to the closest Savari squadron which quickly set off in pursuit of the rebels. Hampered by the poor state of their horses and with the guerrillas themselves suffering from lack of food and sleep, eleven rebels were gradually overtaken and killed. The horse of the twelfth was shot from under him, and as the aged rebel, wounded in the arm, lay trapped under his dead mount he was recognised by his pursuers as Omar al-Mukhtar.

On 12 September Mukhtar was put on board a destroyer and taken to Benghazi where he was formally identified by Italian officials; at no time did he try to conceal his identity or his position as leader of the rebels. His capture was quickly announced in Tripoli and, in a letter to General De Bono, Badoglio declared that Mukhtar would soon be executed: 'Should the captured man really be Omar al-Mukhtar, I think it would be opportune to hold the trial and carry out the sentence, which will undoubtedly be the death penalty, in one of the big native concentration camps.'[46] De Bono wrote to Graziani on 14 September: 'Good. We shall hold a trial and then unfailingly a sensational execution.'[47] Badoglio then instructed Graziani to hold a criminal trial 'which can only end with the death sentence according to local customs', declaring also that it was necessary for the sentence to be carried out in the most important concentration camp.

Mukhtar had been initially interrogated on board the Italian destroyer, the Orsini; and later on the premises of the Investigative Office of the Benghazi Regional Prison. The prisoner, testifying before judge Giuseppe Franceschino and military lawyer Giuseppe Bedendo, admitted the numerous guerrilla attacks that had taken place under his command; as was to be expected, he blamed the Italians for the Libyan rebellion ('I never submitted to the Italian government. I only had conversation with it'). The trial was held later the same day, on 15 September 1931, at the Palazzo del Littorio; there were elements of farce, and the result was entirely predictable. An extempore contribution was made by Public Prosecutor Giuseppe Bedendo who remarked that the Prince of Piedmont had a birthday on that very day, which gave him the chance to appoint himself spokesman 'for the feeling of the people'.[48] This has been depicted as an 'absurd interlude' (Rainero), though faithfully recorded in the trial proceedings. Bendendo, the mouthpiece of Graziani, later wrote a tribute to the General in a poem which celebrated the fate of Omar al-Mukhtar.[49]

The Italians had assembled soldiers and local *sottomessi* in the hall of the court to witness what was essentially a propaganda exercise, to demonstrate that 'Omar al-Mukhtar's fate should point the direction of this new imperial change of course'. The prosecutor used constant sarcasm and vituperation against Mukhtar and no-one doubted that a death sentence would be demanded and given. Thus Bedendo declared that the trial would put an end to 'the fame of a legendary hero who always takes flight in times of danger . . . you are not a soldier but a bandit who has always lived underground . . . you have said God has this time abandoned you, but if he has failed you, human justice has caught up with you'. The character of the trial was further revealed by the Fascist treatment meted out to the defending council: Captain Roberto Lontano was punished with ten days of close arrest for having argued 'the defence in an apologetic tone, in contrast to the guilty man and the special conditions of the place and surroundings' in which the case was held'.[50]

The trial lasted for half an hour, after which the death sentence was pronounced. Mukhtar reacted with seeming indifference ('From God we have come and to God we must return'), disappointing the Fascist regime who wanted to use the episode as a symbol for the crushing of all resistance.

At 9 o'clock on 16 September 1931 Omar al-Mukhtar was hanged in front of the 20,000 inmates of the Soluk concentration camp, all from the Gebel; even Graziani was forced to record that Mukhtar faced his death with 'a composed, firm and decisive bearing'. The trial had been a mockery, rushed through in haste to its predictable end.[51]

An Italian commentator observed that Omar al-Mukhtar was 'the faithful and intelligent servant of Idris and the mind and heart of the Cyrenaican rebellion', with Idris himself declaring Mukhtar 'a supreme example of chivalry and godliness'.[52] Today main streets in many Libyan towns and cities – including Tripoli, Benghazi and Baida – are named after him. A Western feature film, *Lion of the Desert*, starring Anthony Quinn as Mukhtar and Oliver Reed as Graziani, has been dubbed into Arabic and is shown regularly on Libyan television. Omar al-Mukhtar is one of Muammar Gaddafi's great national heroes and is frequently mentioned in his speeches.

AFTERMATH

After the death of Mukhtar desultory efforts were made to keep rebellion alive, but without success. It had taken a relatively powerful Italy two decades to subjugate the Libyan people, and it would only be able to maintain its colonial hold for a further decade: the First World War, with the defeat of the Ottomans, had facilitated Italy's incursions into North Africa whereas the Second, with the defeat of Benito Mussolini, was to extirpate Italian colonialism in the region.

The final crushing of the Libyan rebellion did not succeed in establishing political harmony in Rome. Tensions grew between Badoglio and Graziani when both claimed the main credit for the ending of the Mukhtar affair. Thus the correspondence of the Italian ambassador in Egypt, Roberto Cantalupo, highlights Graziani's repeated claims for exclusive credit and his criticism of the diplomatic attempts to end the rebellion. Similarly the self-serving Graziani memoirs omit any mention of what Badoglio or the Tripoli authorities had done to combat the Libyan rebels. In contrast, Badoglio emphasised that Graziani had merely 'followed the instructions I have given him'; and there was disputation about the effectiveness of particular policies and actions – for example, the efforts to close the frontier with Egypt. However, such wranglings did not inhibit Rome's facile depiction of recent events in North Africa. The 'bandit Omar al-Mukhtar' had been eliminated, and the other two major colonial powers in the region – France and Britain – were not keen to stir up disputes that might endanger their own rule in the North African territories. There was predictable protest from Arab countries that Mukhtar's reputation had spread far beyond the frontiers of Libya – but Colonial Minister Emilio De Bono felt able to declare:

> It's time now to end it all: the Moslem world must no longer be tricked by a handful of intriguers. The name of Italy, with a civilization going back thousands of years, recognised by all the nations, blessed in mosques and schools, in *mahcamah* (courts of the Cadi) and hospitals by more than a million Moslems who for years have benefited from generous government and wise justice as embodied in laws and decrees, known and available to all – the name of Italy cannot be defamed by a group of a few hundred marauders, rebels against all forms of order, against every human and divine law, who, in the name of God, are trying to prolong indefinitely an uncertain situation merely for their own selfish purpose of plundering, exploiting others and committing all manner of violent actions and crimes.[53]

The rebellion in Libya against Italian occupation had been crushed but many Libyan groups – forced to flee to such countries as Tunisia, Syria, Lebanon, Turkey, Iraq and Transjordan – kept alive the dream of national independence. Chekib Arslan's obituary of Mukhtar spoke for many: 'The blood of Omar al-Mukhtar will remain for ever an infamy that will lie heavily on the Italian leader . . . The day will come when he will see the fruit of his arrogance and know that the Moslems are not dead and their rights are not lost.'[54] In fact Mussolini was to outlive Mukhtar by little more than a decade.

The final crushing of the rebellion gave a considerable boost, albeit short-lived, to the development of Italian colonisation in the North African territory, Italy's 'Fourth Shore'. Italian families were encouraged to emigrate to Libya while land was taken from the tribes and Mussolini was happy to celebrate the planting on North African soil of 'Fascist civilisation'. Two state-run settlements at Tigrinna and Suani ben Adem in Tripolitania – the *Ente di Colonizzazione per la Cirenaica* and the *Ente per la Colonizzazione della Libia* – served as models for further large state-financed and state-run schemes. Model villages and farms were developed by selected families from southern Italy, forerunners in 1933/1934 of thousands of later colonists. Italo Balbo became governor of Tripolitania and Cyrenaica in 1934 and quickly proceeded to settle Italian peasant families by the thousand; in 1938 Mussolini approved Balbo's ambitious programme and some 20,000 colonists were then scheduled to arrive in Libya the following October. As many as 30,00 Italian and Libyan labourers were organised to construct eight new colonial villages, to clear and plant the land for 1800 farms, to drill wells and dig irrigation channels, and to lay roads and tracks. Families in Italy were interviewed for 'export' to the Fourth Shore: the approved families were generally large, literate and, if not party members, at least politically sound. The 20,000 chosen people sold up, packed their belongings, and travelled by train to the fleet of waiting liners destined for Tripoli and Benghazi. Banners ('Mussolini redeems the soil and founds cities') and noisy crowds greeted their arrival and the colonists were then driven off to their designated villages. Rarely was there a more graphic illustration of Fascist order and regimentation. Martin Moore, a *Daily Telegraph* correspondent, accompanied the immigrants and later wrote: 'Twenty thousand peasants sat down at the same hours to identical meals spread on identical wooden tables in identical concrete houses.'[55] The ambitious scheme was a massively expensive enterprise, and for it to be successful the Italian investment would have to be maintained (Moore: 'everything depends upon the State continuing to pour money into Libya for many years to come . . . there is no foreseeable revenue which could balance the cost of garrisoning the coast and policing the desert'[56]). The rebels had been defeated – Badoglio had officially declared hostilities at an end in 1932 – but the colonists could not be complacent about their new holdings.

New colonists arrived in October 1939 for settlement in eight newly constructed villages; and at the same time work was begun on a 100-mile aqueduct to link Ain Mara to the western end of the Gebel. The early settlers were funded in part by a semi-governmental organisation, the *Instituto Nazionale Fascista per la Sociale*, financed from capital allocated to the unemployed, but the shift to mass migration after 1936 was supported by specific colonisation companies responsible as state agents for the settlement of newly developed lands; the state itself focused on the settlement of formerly reclaimed lands. The companies and the state awarded various types of tenancies to the migrating peasant families. By 1940 there were nearly 40,000 colonists in Libya (Table 3.1).

The programme of 'demographic colonisation' was conducted with evident discipline and commitment; had not the Second World War intervened there would have been some 100,000 settlers in Libya by 1942, with around half a million planned by the early 1960s. It is also clear that, in agricultural and financial terms, the settler farms achieved a measure of success. Thus in 1950 a United Nations report on Libya commented that: 'The Italian farms . . . represent a remarkable feat of pioneering and land reclamation which . . . has recently begun to demonstrate its full productive value.'[58]

Table 3.1 Agricultural Settler Population in Libya, 1940

Type of Colonisation by Region	Number of Farms	Colonist Population	
		Families	Number of People
Tripolitania:			
State land grants and private property	1322	1877	8213
Colonisation companies	2353	1878	15308
Total:	3675	3755	23521
Cyrenaica:			
State land grants and private property	264	466	1524
Colonisation companies	1813	1740	13490
Total:	2077	2206	15014
Total Libya	5752	5961	38535

Source: G. L. Fowler, 'The Role of Private Estates and Development Companies in the Italian Agricultural Colonisation of Libya', in Joffe and McLachlan (eds), *Social and Economic Development of Libya* (1982).

In such circumstances little attention was paid to what had been suffered by the indigenous Libyan tribes. Countless traditional villages had been razed, whole herds slaughtered, thousands of people – civilians and combatants alike – terrorised and killed. The wealth of the indigenous peoples had been decimated: in 1926 there were 800,000 sheep in Cyrenaica, in 1933 less than 100,000; out of a total of 75,000 camels, 72,000 had been killed through deliberate slaughter on the ground or by bombing from the air; and the horse population had dropped from 4000 to 1000.

According to the current Libyan authorities, the Italian forces had committed virtual genocide, with perhaps half the original Libyan population dying in the Italian conquest. The surviving Libyans were sullen and pauperised, resentful of new development schemes, indifferent to all attempts to repair the psychological damage wrought by years of war. As with much of European colonisation, schemes were implemented that brought some benefits to the indigenous peoples, but the Italian presence – despite the inevitable quota of mercenary collaboration – was never accepted by the broad mass of the Libyan people.

When Mussolini visited Libya in March 1937 – to open the 1132-mile-long *Litoranea* (or *Via Balbo*), running from Tunisia to the Egyptian frontier – he found the colony 'morally and profoundly Italian'. The Muslims of Tripoli supposedly greeted him as 'the greatest man of the century and the sincere friend of Islam'[59] – whereupon, after being presented with 'The Sword of Islam', the Duce decided as the Protector of Islam to defend the rights of Muslims in Libya and beyond. Libyans, whether Christian or Muslim, were already expected to give the Fascist salute; many wore black shirts and cheered Mussolini through the streets of Tripoli and Benghazi; and Libyan youth had been given its own Fascist group, the *Gioventu Araba*, modelled on the Italian *Balilla*. In 1939 Libyans were allowed to apply for *Cittadinanza Italian Speciale* (Special Italian Citizenship), but this new status offered only petty privileges that were not valid outside Libya. No Libyan was allowed a post or profession that would result in Italian subordinates: in 1949 there was a grand total of sixteen Libyan university graduates.

The tribes had been decimated and impoverished, their authority destroyed: in Fezzan the councils of family heads (the *Jemaa*) were abolished, with approved *Mudirs* instructing the tribespeople what to do. Italian courts had jurisdiction in most matters: courts of Summary Justice delivered speedy and harsh rulings. It was inevitable in some circumstances that Libyans would suffer racial abuse, earning less than Italians for the same work and with most routes for advancement blocked to them. The Sanussi Order, perceived as a subversive political faction, was banned, though an element of religious freedom was maintained. But the brutal imposition of Fascism did nothing to enlist the loyalties of the bulk of an embittered and recalcitrant population. Even after the colonial war and all the enthusiastic influx of Italian colonists, the Libyan Muslims still comprised well over eighty per cent of the national population: it was upon this majority that a future independent Libya would be based.

SECOND WORLD WAR

Mussolini took the decision to invade Abyssinia (Ethiopia) in 1935, partly as a simple desire to expand the empire ('not only a territorial, military and mercantile expression, but a spiritual and moral one') and partly as a desire to counter what was perceived as an alarming growth in German power. The German ascendancy was seen as aided in part by Britain's evident indifference to the terms of the Versailles Treaty, resulting in the appeasing of Hitler. Reasoning that Britain might be similarly purblind to the Covenant of the League of Nations, Mussolini launched the invasion of the ancient kingdom of Abyssinia on 3 October 1935. The League, still believing that Hitler was the greater danger, promptly voted sanctions that were, in the event, only partial and timidly enforced. Part of the problem was that Mussolini aroused much admiration in Britain (not least in Winston Churchill) and other Western countries. Thus the historian Christopher Hibbert writes of Mussolini: 'The accolades which had been so enthusiastically and gratuitously cast upon him by conservative writers and public figures . . . had been so frequent and so unequivocally phrased that he had no trouble in believing that he was indeed the greatest statesman of his time.'[60] When Addis Ababa was occupied on 5 May 1936 Mussolini declared 'Abyssinia is Italian'; and the English *Saturday Review* (which on 25 April had headed an article 'Bravo, Mussolini!') published a telegram sent to Il Duce which began 'TEN THOUSAND TIMES BRAVO BRAVISSIMO: OH! SPLENDID MAN!!' and ended with the sentiment 'ALL YOUR ENGLISH FRIENDS CONGRATULATE YOU ON YOUR GREAT VICTORY.' The telegram was sent by Lady Houston, a not unrepresentative right-wing polemicist of the 1930s.[61] Mussolini encountered little opposition to his conquest of Abyssinia, just as the other colonial powers had largely ignored his onslaught on Libya; but the friendship of Fascist Italy with Britain and France was severely damaged when these countries began to perceive that their own colonial holdings might be under threat, and the front against Germany was destroyed. The Nazi leadership was quick to see the implications. The historian William Shirer, celebrated author of *The Rise and Fall of the Third Reich* (Secker and Warburg, 1960) noted in 1941 that either Mussolini 'will stumble and get himself so heavily involved in Africa that he will be greatly weakened in Europe, whereupon Hitler can seize Austria, hitherto protected by the Duce; or he will win, defying France and Britain, and thereupon be ripe for a tie-up with Hitler against the Western democracies'.[62]

Hence step by step Mussolini inadvertently laid the ground for the collapse of the Italian empire in North Africa. His successes in Libya led him into Ethiopia, and thence into his ill-fated alliance with Nazi Germany. The defeat of the Axis hastened the day of Libyan independence, but not without yet more conflict and carnage throughout North Africa.

After Hitler's invasion of Poland, Libya's exiled Arab leaders met in Alexandria in October 1939 to consider Italy's likely involvement in the escalating war. Already it was seen that here was a further chance for Libyan independence. Idris was chosen as the leader of the nationalists, and the Libyan Arabs announced their support for the Allies. Italy entered the war in June 1940 and by August the first British/Libyan contacts had been made, despite the reluctance of some Libyan leaders to make common cause with a country unlikely to win the war. Sir Henry Maitland organised Libyan forces to fight under a Sanussi flag and under the command of a British officer. Libyan leaders asked for a guarantee of Libyan independence after the war; this was refused but Anthony Eden, then Foreign Secretary declared to the House of Commons that 'at the end of the war the Sanussi in Cyrenaica will in no circumstances again fall under Italian domination'.[63] Five Libyan battalions were raised, composed largely of Cyrenaicans who had fought against the Italians in the colonial wars; at the same time the Italians were creating their own Libyan contingents.

On 10 June 1940 Count Ciano informed Sir Percy Loraine, asked to attend the Italian Foreign Ministry in Rome, that the King of Italy would consider himself in a state of war with Britain as from midnight on 11 June. In North Africa, British armoured vehicles were soon moving towards the Italian positions on the border between Egypt and the enemy province of Cyrenaica.[64] On the night of 11 June British troops ambushed a column of Italian lorries near Fort Capuzzo, and the desert war had begun. It would end nearly three years later, after swaying backwards and forwards, after the opposing armies had variously advanced and retreated nearly four thousand miles. The Italians, with their locally raised contingents, soon bolstered and led by German General Erwin Rommel's Afrika Korps, fought countless engagements with the British Empire forces of Generals Wavell, Montgomery and Auchinleck. These great tank battles in the desert, with air and sea support, were the first of their kind in history: the devastation that they brought to the native peoples of the region is too rarely considered.

In the spring of 1941 Rommel's first offensive had forced the British back to Egypt, and by the time the Axis forces were again driven out of Cyrenaica towards the end of 1941 vast areas of the land were falling into ruin. Nationalist Libyans, taking advantage of the retreating Italians, attacked the farms of the unprotected Italian colonists, though Idris had condemned revenge-taking in any form. Much of the damage to the land was caused by the Allied air forces: Benghazi alone was to suffer more than one thousand air raids throughout the war; and one observer, Alan Moorehead, entering Benghazi on Christmas Day 1941, commented that it was 'no longer a city any more. The plague of high explosive had burst on the place . . . ruin succeeded ruin as we drove along . . . For nearly a year the RAF had gone on and on, night after night, and here we were looking at the scoresheet – a ravaged, ruined city.'[65] Then the British were again forced out of Cyrenaica until they managed to reoccupy the territory towards the end of 1942 for the third and final time. Some of the engagements had involved vast numbers of men and massive amounts of hardware. Thus in one early encounter a British force comprising one armoured division, two infantry brigades and a Royal Tank regiment (31,000 men in all) had driven an Italian force three times as large out of Egypt, capturing 38,000 prisoners. A subsequent British offensive, under the command of General Wavell, succeeded in routing an army under the command of Graziani, now a Marshall. The operation continued until 7 February 1941, by which time the British had pushed 500 miles across Cyrenaica, destroyed an Italian army of ten divisions in Libya, taken 130,000 prisoners, 500 tanks and 1240 guns. The British lost 500 killed, 1373 wounded and fifty-five missing. General J. F. C. Fuller reckoned this 'one of the most audacious campaigns ever fought'.[66] Hitler subsequently sent German forces, including Luftwaffe squadrons, to Libya.

By the end of 1942 two Allied armies were moving towards Tripoli; Montgomery's Eighth Army was moving rapidly from the east, while General Leclerc's Free French Brigade was heading north across the Sahara. The French in Chad had entered Fezzan from the south, capturing oases from the Italian garrisons before rushing towards Tripoli. Early on 23 January British tanks entered the city and the governor of Tripoli, Alberto Denti di Pirajno, offered a formal surrender. Later he was to comment wryly that 'The last hospital ship making for Zuara had been crammed, not with the wounded, but with gold braid and chests covered with ribbons and medals.'[67] By February the Allies had extended their occupation of the region, and Richard Casey, the British Minister of State for the Middle East, announced the various steps that would be taken against Fascists: leading Fascists in Libya faced arrest, Fascist schooling would cease, and Fascist clubs and other social organisations associated with the Italian occupation would be closed. In January 1942 Winston Churchill praised Rommel in a speech to the House of Commons ('We have a very daring and skilful opponent against us, and, may I say across the havoc of war, a great general'); now he dubbed Rommel 'the fugitive of Egypt, of Cyrenaica and of Tripoli'. Libya had been liberated from yet another colonial occupation, but national independence had not been secured.

At a second meeting of the Libyan leaders in Cairo on 9 August 1940, a Sanussi Emirate for Cyrenaica and Tripolitania was proclaimed; and it was also declared that a provisional Sanussi government-in-exile was to be created; Sayyid Idris had been empowered to make political, military and financial agreements with the British. During 1940 and 1941 Idris repeatedly raised the question of Libyan independence, though the British had made no promises. Already there were Sanussi anxieties about British intentions: would British colonialism simply supplant Italian at the end of the war? In December 1942 General Montgomery issued a proclamation stating that Tripolitania, not yet 'liberated', was under British occupation; and by January 1943 Libya came under the military administration of two colonial powers – the British in Tripolitania and Cyrenaica; and the French, following an agreement between General Alexander and General Leclerc, in Fezzan. In one view, the administrations saw themselves 'as caretakers pending the end of the war';[68] other observers – Arabs amongst them – suspected that the British and French had more permanent intentions.

For most of the first half of the twentieth century the Libyan people had been forced to wage war against successive colonial invaders – Turks, Italians, Germans, French and British – with all the consequences for human lives and communities that this implies. Towns and cities were razed to the ground; whole communities were deported for incarceration in concentration camps; civilians and combatants alike were tortured and bombed, their livestock slaughtered; the survivors were racially abused, exploited as forced labour, and reduced to penury. For years after the end of the Second World War Libya was littered with landmines and other anti-personnel devices, making farming in Cyrenaica a hazardous enterprise: in one estimate, no less than sixty-eight per cent of all agricultural land was mined.[69] To this day the Gaddafi government argues that the World War combatants – especially Italy, Germany and Britain – should pay reparations for the hundreds of Libyan dead and injured caused by unexploded bombs and minefields since 1943. Even today there are occasional casualties in remote areas.

The Second World War hastened the end of colonialism in Libya, though a fresh colonial phase endured into the post-war years. In 1952, under United Nations auspices, Libya was established as an independent kingdom – but not before more years of European wrangling, Great-Power disputation, and Libyan struggle.

4 From Idris to Gaddafi

It is often said that war is the midwife of nations: in fact the Second World War delivered many offspring, albeit sometimes after difficult and protracted labours. Japanese and French colonialism in the Far East was fatally damaged, so stimulating nationalisms and new ideologies; European colonialism in India, the Middle East and Africa was weakened, allowing the emergence not only of nationalist aspirations but also of pan-Arabist and pan-African sentiment. The War had shaken the old framework, eroding the position of the European colonial powers and giving fresh impetus to the imperial theme in the history of the United States. A ravaged Soviet Union was forced to adopt the guise of a superpower against a massively strengthened America: new regional and global hegemonies were being shaped but in the immediate post-war years many of the political patterns were unclear. This was true of Libya, just as it was true of many other peoples emerging from centuries of dominance by foreign powers.

TOWARDS INDEPENDENCE

The Cyrenaican leader Sayyid Idris* had not hesitated to raise an army to fight alongside the Allies in North Africa, despite British unwillingness to promise him eventual Libyan, or even Cyrenaican, independence. Nor was Idris himself convinced that full independence was a desirable goal: years of contact with British officials had persuaded him that it was enough for Libya to remain under UK tutelage, albeit with an element of 'internal independence'. Thus on 27 August 1940 Idris wrote to Colonel Bromilow, the British officer responsible for the Sanussi forces, proposing three minimum conditions:[1]

1 Great Britain to grant Libyans internal independence;

2 Libya to have its own government headed by a Muslim Emir acceptable to the British government;

---

*Idris, when he eventually became King of Libya, was officially known as al-Sayyid Mohammad Idris al-Mahdi al-Sanussi.

124

3 Great Britain to hold the protectorate over Libya and direct the organisation of its financial and military affairs until it reached a higher social and cultural level.

Such proposals were congenial to the British who, particularly in the uncertain early stages of the war, were keen to secure their influence in North Africa; but it was hardly surprising that many Libyan nationalists saw the Idris proposals as a means of replacing Italian control with British, a fresh colonialism that had to be opposed.

It was clear that in the early 1940s, sensing new opportunities, Idris was making a bid for leadership of the whole of Libya, though he expected it would be secured by a continued British presence in the region. However, few British pledges were given. It had been declared that Cyrenaica would never again be allowed to fall under Italian control, but no similar promise had been made about Tripolitania; and the French, with secure bases in Chad, were now entrenched in Fezzan, increasingly seen as vital for the security of French Algeria. The prospect of a unified Libya, even as a British protectorate, seemed unlikely. And as in 1943 the Free French brigade under General Leclerc was securing its position in Fezzan, the United States took over the Mellala (later Wheelus) airbase, east of Tripoli. General Montgomery had declared a cessation of hostilities in Cyrenaica in December 1942 and the exiled Sanussi leaders began to return to their country; but the defeat of the Italians in Libya had been replaced by an effective occupation by the British, French and Americans. The situation was volatile but Libyan independence seemed far off.

With the return of the exiles tensions began to emerge between the younger men, influenced by Arab nationalism in Egypt, and the older sheikhs and confederation officials. One group, led by Assad Bin Umran, founded the Omar al-Mukhtar Sporting Society, an ostensibly non-political organisation intended only for recreational purposes but one in which discussions were invited on post-war solutions for the political problems facing Libya. By April 1943 the purpose of the club was clear to all: it was renamed the Omar Mukhtar Club and became a focus for Arab nationalists, attracting the militant and politically-aware sons of the tribes in Benghazi and Derna. The Club, without as yet a fully developed nationalist programme, demanded that Idris be recognised as the Emir of Cyrenaica and that some sort of unification be formed with Egypt. In September 1946 the British administrator, E. A. V. de Candole, banned *al-Watan*, the Club's newspaper.

The various nationalist groups were divided and factionalism was rife; some pressed for radical political agendas while others did little more than seek the patronage of the local British administrators in Tripoli. The British had failed to give any nationalist leaders a place in the regional administration, and to some extent this helped to unite the various contending groups. When in 1946 it emerged that Britain, with purblind insensitivity, was contemplating reimposing Italian rule as part of a postwar settlement in parts of the region, there was a further move to nationalist unity. The United National Front was formed under the leadership of Selim Muntasser, a leading merchant, and the Mufti of Tripoli, Mohammed Abu al-Isad al-Alim. The Front proposed the unity of Libya and its total independence under Sanussi leadership: there was little confidence that Britain would not renege over its Cyrenaican pledge and a principal aim was to avoid the restoration of Italian colonialism. Idris was quick to see the Front as a useful vehicle for his own ambitions and on 9 August 1946 he declared to a gathering at Municipality Square in Benghazi: 'I have found that the leading tribal chiefs have been thinking of forming a National Front representing all the elements in the country [I have approved of] this organisation, for it will support me in achieving the country's aspirations and lighten the burden of my efforts.'[2] The inauguration of the Front was timed to influence a British War Office Working Party, under Sir Bernard Reilley, intended to report on the situation in Cyrenaica and to make recommendations on the future of the region. It was already clear that the Great Powers, including the Soviet Union, perceived the strategic importance of Libya; and that this was the context that would shape any future agreements on Libyan independence.

At the end of the War it appeared that the case *against* Libyan independence was 'overwhelming'.[3] The surviving population, around one million were politically inexperienced, poorly educated and extremely poor; the War had totally disrupted trade and stopped the few social programmes introduced by the Italians. Vast numbers of buildings had been destroyed, the rudimentary industrial base had been shattered, Italian colonists had been evicted from their successful farms, and unemployment was widespread. Not only had the developing infrastructure been ravaged (Bardia and Tobruk flattened and three-quarters of the buildings in Benghazi damaged or totally destroyed), but the land was now infested with unexploded ordnance. To many observers, Idris's 1940 proposal that Libyan independence should not be granted until the country had attained a 'higher social and cultural level' did not seem ridiculous. But the newly emerging nationalists, impatient with the self-interested views of foreigners, wanted to force the pace of change.

At the end of 1946 the British Working Party under Reilley visited Cyrenaica, and in January 1947 proposed that the region should be granted independence in three consecutive stages:

1 The British military administration to remain for a short time.

2 The establishment of an Arab state under British trusteeship. Adequate financial assistance should be given for not less than ten years, including the rendering of administrative training and promoting educational and technical development.

3 The establishment of a fully independent state. During the second and third stages, Cyrenaica might be connected with Tripolitania in a unified Libya, as the creation of such a state is consistent with the specific recommendations for Cyrenaica. A treaty of alliance with a major power is also recommended.

However, such proposals seemed too radical for the British and were received with little enthusiasm, not least because they invited dissent among the Big Four: no initiative could be taken without the unanimous approval of Britain, France, the Soviet Union and the United States. France was keen to retain control of Fezzan, and Italy – even at this stage – had not abandoned all ambitions for a colonial presence in North Africa. Rome urged British support for at least an Italian trusteeship in Tripolitania but the United States and the Soviet Union opposed any European trusteeship in the area. Subject to these conflicting pressures, Britain decided to refer the question to the newly fledged United Nations. In May 1949, the British Foreign Secretary, Ernest Bevin, sufficiently impressed by the European representations, proposed that trusteeships be granted to the British in Cyrenaica, the French in Fezzan, and the Italians in Tripolitania. Even now, the Italian demands weighed more heavily with the British than did the Arab aspirations for independence. However, the Bevin scheme, proposed jointly with the Italian Foreign Minister Count Carlo Sforza, was rejected in the UN General Assembly by one vote. Instead it was decided that Libya should become a sovereign state.

The British/Italian plan had galvanised indigenous Libyan opinion: here yet again the perfidy of the European colonial powers had been exposed, at least to the satisfaction of the nationalists. On 14 May 1949 the Libyan leaders met in Tripoli to organise their response. At this meeting the United National Front, the National Party (with 15,000 members) and the Libyan Liberation Committee decided to create the Tripolitanian National Congress headed by Bashir al-Sadawi. The Congress then embarked upon a systematic campaign of civil disobedience involving strikes, public meetings and demonstrations. The campaign was maintained until 17 May when the UN so narrowly defeated the Bevin/Sforza plan. The Libyan protests may be judged to have had some impact on the UN deliberations but it is likely that the perceived interests of the United States were a dominant factor. The US was reluctant to see any form of UN-sponsored trusteeship in the area, not least because such an arrangement would have gravely weakened its own presence at the massive Wheelus site near Tripoli. Thus Henry Villard, the State Department official then responsible for the former Italian colonies in North Africa, commented: 'It may be worth noting that if Libya had passed under any form of United Nations' trusteeship, it would have been impossible for the territory to play a part in the defence arrangements of the Free World.'[4] It was significant that under the UN trusteeship system, 'the administrator of a trust territory cannot establish military bases: only in the case of a strategic trusteeship as in the former Japanese islands of the Pacific are fortifications allowed; and a 'strategic trusteeship' is subject to veto in the Security Council.'[5] Thus the United States opposed a UN-sponsored European trusteeship because it feared a Soviet veto in the Security Council: how much better it would be for an 'independent Libya' to agree defence treaties with the Western powers as part of the global alliance against communism. It is ironic that this policy should have led to the rise of Muammar Gaddafi, and to the emergence of Libya as one of the most persistent Third-World thorns in the flesh of the United States.

DEBATE AND DIPLOMACY

The bulk of the debate over the future of Libya had little concern with the interests of the indigenous peoples. Just as the War had raged over the area as though it were nothing but empty desert so the wranglings over the future of North Africa were fuelled by no more than how the United States and the European powers perceived their own interests. At the end of the War Italy still enjoyed nominal sovereignty over the colonies of Somaliland, Eritrea, Ethiopia and Libya, still seen by Italy and other countries as important strategic outposts for the control of north-east Africa and the eastern basin of the Mediterranean. The War had well demonstrated that control of the Tripoli/Benghazi/Sicily triangle, together with dominance in the Aegean, could effectively counter any sea-power in the eastern Mediterranean. In the immediate post-war world, with the growth of the Cold War, the European powers, the United States and the Soviet Union saw clearly the strategic advantages offered by Libyan territory: here was a lengthy coast-line and vast interior spaces, ideal for the siting of bombers, other aircraft and electronic monitoring facilities.

The Big Four had agreed at Potsdam that Italy would renounce all its rights in Africa, though it is likely that at that time France and Britain perceived the benefits of a fresh Italian trusteeship as part of *quid pro quo* arrangements. It was obvious that Britain had an interest in developing a Middle East defence system close to Suez, and France was determined to hold on to its African colonies. Moreover the United States, in the business of developing a global presence, was keen to retain large bases in North Africa. It was now the case that three quarters of the world's invested capital and two thirds of the industrial capacity were concentrated inside the United States.[6] Even before the end of the War the US had spent tens of millions of dollars developing the Wheelus airfield, as the first American air base in Africa: the US was not disposed to sacrifice such a prize. At the same time the United States claimed to be exercising only 'limited diplomacy' in the Middle East, a far cry from the US posture that was to develop in later years. Already the United States perceived that its oil interests in the area gave great strategic value to a military presence within easy reach of the 'not so distant Middle East'.[7] When the Soviet Union, as one of the Big Four, proposed that it too should have a presence in the area the three Western powers were happy to condemn any 'intrusion of the Soviet camel's nose into the Libyan tent'.[8] The dynamic of the Cold War was already beginning to shape the character of the postwar settlement.

When the Soviet Union saw that there was no way it could secure a legitimate hold in North Africa it decided that no external powers had rights in the area. Thus it emphasised the 'post-war differentiating factors connected mainly with foreign interests' that represented 'an obstacle to the normal economic and social developments of Libya'. The peace treaty at which Italy renounced its territorial sovereignty paid no attention to such matters but resolved that the question should go to the United Nations if the Big Four could not agree to a solution to the Libyan problem. The Bevin/Sforza agreement, a piece of secret diplomacy, was a gross infringement of the terms of the Peace Treaty but served to demonstrate the desperate ambitions of the British and the Italians: as little as four years after the end of the War, during which Italian aggressions and atrocities had been roundly condemned, Britain was eager to agree a British/Italian compact to secure its own colonial holdings. Bevin/Sforza was defeated, in part by an equally self-interested United States; and this represented – paradoxically enough – a significant victory for Arab nationalism.

On 21 November 1949 the UN General Assembly voted on the question of independence for Libya: independence was agreed with a vote of 48 to one (Ethiopia) and with nine abstentions (including France and five Soviet bloc countries). A detailed resolution (Appendix 7) was passed, and the General Assembly voted the United Nations Assistant Secretary-General, Adrian Pelt of the Netherlands, as the UN Commissioner for Libya. In fact by the time the Fourth Session of the United Nations opened in September 1949 the scene was set: the United States, with a majority in the General Assembly, had decided to back the formula of an independent Libya. The passing of the draft resolution – proposing 'That Libya, comprising Tripolitania, Cyrenaica and the Fezzan, shall be constituted an independent and sovereign state' – was a foregone conclusion. Dr Pelt's task, of supervising the transition from the British and French provisional administration to Libyan control, was not an easy one: few Libyans had real political experience or administrative knowledge, and the country was bankrupt, with *per capita* income the lowest in the Middle East. John Lindberg, an American economist who visited the area during the period of transition, commented: 'The standard of housing is extremely low; a large part of the population lives in caves, lacking furniture and the simplest conveniences. Clothing is made out of home grown wool. The poor are clad in rags and walk barefoot, even during the fairly cold winters.'[9] In his *First Annual Report* Pelt declared that 'The Arab population of Libya stands in need of as much financial and technical assistance as the United Nations can supply.'

Within two weeks of the UN rejection of the mischievous Bevin/Sforza Plan, Idris felt able to announce the independence of Cyrenaica and the assumption of his position as Emir. The announcement was made with British approval, not least because many legal and financial matters were still under the control of British advisors. Britain also kept control of defence, foreign affairs and the disposal of Italian property; though at the same time the British government declared that 'in taking these steps . . . nothing will be done to prejudice the eventual future of Libya as a whole'.[10] In fact Britain had anticipated the UN resolution and had taken steps to protect its own interests. It declared that it 'could not continue to refuse the people of Cyrenaica its indisputable right to the greatest possible measure of self-government consistent with the international obligations of the United Kingdom Government . . . The Government has therefore given the Emir of Cyrenaica absolute powers in the internal affairs of that territory . . . the Government . . . could do no less than grant Cyrenaica that full measure of self-government.'[11] The British ploy was well practised, the familiar aim being to secure power by exploiting existing political structures. In Libya the plan was to convert the Sanussi emirate into a constitutional monarchy with which Britain could deal on congenial terms. Thus there was a clear sense in which the British action effectively pre-empted the vote in the

General Assembly. By the time Dr Adrian Pelt was charged with the task of supervising the transition, the British military administration was already deeply enmeshed in the affairs of the new Cyrenaican government. A new Cyrenaican legal system, drafted largely by British lawyers, was being prepared; and there were plans to build a Cyrenaican army on the model of Jordan's Arab Legion, itself constructed and advised by British officers.

It is hardly surprising in these circumstances that Dr Pelt saw his task as a 'race against time'.[12] The UN resolution had stipulated that Libya would gain its independence not later than 1 January 1952; if the transitional timetable were not adhered to, then the future of Libya would be uncertain. It was not out of the question that the Bevin/Sforza Plan, or some equivalent, would prevail; and Libya would again be at the mercy of European colonialism, perhaps with a US dimension thrown in, with no obvious escape route. Even after the UN vote on the resolution, France argued that independence should perhaps be indefinitely delayed; and the British government had taken what steps it could to ensure that the inexperienced Libyans would in effect still be run from Whitehall. Pelt quickly perceived that France and Britain had little interest in the UN resolution, concerned less with Libyan unity than with securing their own spheres of interest.[13] Pelt commented that the 'semi-independent status' already conferred on Cyrenaica by the British government represented a 'disquieting precedent that was in utter conflict with the General Assembly resolution'. Yet at one level it was difficult to fault the British initiative: had they not granted a people – who had suffered greatly through colonialism and war – a right to an independent future? It was only when the nature of the new independent status was scrutinised that the real picture could be discerned. The British aim was that Cyrenaica – and later the whole of Libya – would be granted a quasi-independence over which a practical British control would be maintained for an indefinite period. Even though the UN transitional timetable was observed the British grip on the newly emerging Libya, to be ruled by a pliant monarch, was not in doubt.

At the beginning of the transitional phase the British Foreign Office submitted a confidential memorandum to Dr Pelt proposing regional self-government for Tripolitania with a degree of autonomy on the Cyrenaican model. Again at this stage there was little interest in a unified Libya with genuine independence. Already Britain and other observers detected the growing split between the older traditional leaders, who may be tempted by the British scheme, and the younger nationalists sensitive to any plan that would delay Libyan independence. France, following the British example in Cyrenaica, installed in Fezzan a transitional regime that would favour a continuing French influence in the area. Saif Ahmed Seif al-Nasr, a prominent Sanussi leader who had returned to Fezzan with the French forces, was made *chef du territoire* with specified powers; but at the same time the French military administration retained control of the region. Like the British, the French were taking steps to ensure that they retained a presence in a Libya whose independence seemed increasingly inevitable. Pelt observed how the British and French tried to shape the character of a Libya approaching independence:

> In Tripolitania the British authorities used indirect tactics, carefully supporting certain political parties and opposing others, in an endeavour to promote controlled emancipation . . . the French administration, while ostensibly trying to match the British policy in Cyrènaica, went about matters in its own way . . . it held up constitutional development by repressive measures, the intensity of which varied from oasis to oasis and village to village.[15]

And he also noted that British policy was 'considerably more constructive' in the economic and social fields while also the French 'introduced economic measures which considerably improved living conditions in the territory'.

The UN Commissioner was keenly aware that the British and French moves would run against the spirit of the independence resolution. As soon as Dr Pelt arrived in Libya he began talks with Idris to emphasise the requirements of the transitional agenda, but it quickly emerged that the Sanussi Emir was already negotiating with Britain to secure British financial aid in return for a continued British military presence in Cyrenaica. Neither Idris nor the authorised British Resident were prepared to show the UN Commissioner a copy of the draft treaty. Under pressure from Pelt, but when also it had become clear that Idris would become head of an independent Libya, Britain agreed to defer the signing of the Treaty. Libya, it seemed, would become an independent state and would then sign financial/military pacts with Britain and France, so ensuring the continued presence of foreign forces in the region. Pelt feared a backlash from nationalist Arabs but emphasised in his report to the General Assembly that once Libya had been given independence his task was over.

The Libyans, perhaps unaware of the extent to which Britain had already shaped the outcome, continued to debate the features of the coming independent government. The National Congress Party of Tripolitania urged a unitary form of state with proportional territorial representation in the National Assembly; whereas Cyrenaica and Fezzan favoured a federal state and parity representation aimed at nullifying the Tripolitanian presence.

This latter proposal – because it was backed by Idris, Britain and the United States – was the inevitable outcome. All the sides agreed that the recognition of the Emir as monarch was the only workable basis for a unified state, and in December 1951 Idris was offered the throne.

The British-backed plan for a constitutional monarchy was presented to Libya as a *fait accompli*: the National Assembly, not elected but selected, was stacked with members likely to agree Britain's federal plans. The Mufti of Tripolitania had been persuaded into selecting members that would support the framework favoured by Cyrenaica and Fezzan, and by Britain. It was predictable that the contrived National Assembly would reject any all-Libyan referendum on the constitution it had prepared. Pelt expressed 'grave doubts' about whether the appointment rather than the election of the National Assembly would have 'the necessary moral and political authority to elaborate a final and definitive Constitution for Libya'. His doubts were well founded: the nationalists, largely outmanoeuvred, organised demonstrations supporting a unified and genuinely independent Libya (on one occasion more than 800 demonstrators were arrested[16]).

The nationalists were unable to prevent the implementation of the planned constitution, but the seeds of political turmoil had been sown. The undemocratic National Assembly was already pointing the way to how the post-independence government would behave, to how a group of nationalists would feel able to overthrow the constitutional monarchy. Idris had selected the representatives from Cyrenaica with those from Fezzan appointed by Ahmad Saif al-Nasr. A Preparatory Committee (the 'Committee of Twenty-One') had met under the chairmanship of the Mufti of Tripolitania to approve the composition of the National Assembly. The Mufti's own list was approved by sixteen votes of the Committee: one Tripolitanian member voted against it, one abstained, another Tripolitanian member and the appointed representative of the minorities were absent – which meant that the Mufti's nominees were approved by only three Tripolitanian members. It was becoming increasingly clear that the National Assembly had few democratic credentials: it was a largely unrepresentative body of placements, shaped by Idris in concert with foreign powers. Soon there were criticisms from outside observers. Kamil Salim, the Egyptian representative on the UN advisory council, declared that the Preparatory Committee had 'deviated' from, and 'flagrantly violated', its terms of reference.[18] Salim, significantly enough, was vigorously opposed by the representatives of Britain, the United States, Cyrenaica and Fezzan. The United Nations Political Committee, after considering Pelt's first report in October 1950, criticised the way in which the National Assembly had been constituted; and in November the Arab delegates to the General Assembly declared that the National Assembly was 'undemocratic and unconstitutional'. The Soviet Union introduced a resolution calling for Libyan unity and the withdrawal of all foreign forces from Libyan territory. Pelt expressed his 'grave doubts' about the National Assembly but when pressed by the Egyptian delegate declared that there was no time for elections for a democratic National Assembly if Libya was to become independent by the UN-specified date. On 17 November 1950 the General Assembly passed a resolution reaffirming the 1949 independence resolution and calling on the National Assembly to establish a provisional government before 1 April 1951, the intention being that the provisional administering authorities would transfer their powers to the new government before 1 January 1952. The United Nations had lent its authority to the work of the Preparatory Committee, however, flawed, and the scene was set for Libyan independence.

The National Assembly, empowered to draw up a constitution, convened for the first time in Tripoli on 25 November 1950. The Mufti of Tripolitania was elected as the president of the Assembly, and within a week it was agreed that Libya was to be established as a democratic, federal and sovereign state with a constitutional monarchy. The federal principle was strongly supported by the members from Cyrenaica and Fezzan but the powerless Tripolitanians accepted it reluctantly. Idris was formally offered the throne but decided to be known as 'king-designate' until after the formal handing over of powers by the administering authorities. The nationalists ('extremists') continued to oppose federation, seeing it as a ruse whereby the British and French could maintain their grip over Libya; and when the Assembly voted for federation there were violent protests in Tripoli on 5 December. Two weeks later there were further protests, with demonstrators shouting their support of the 'king-designate' but denouncing the federal format as a 'divide and rule' scheme of the 'colonialist' powers. It was significant that British military police were used to break up the demonstrations and that the Tripoli Newspaper *Al-Mirsad*, hostile to federation, was closed down. Bashir Sadawi and Abdel Rahman Azzam, now Secretary-General of the Arab League, continued to question the legality and competence of the Assembly.

CONSTITUTION

On 4 December 1950 the National Assembly elected a 'Committee on the Constitution', comprising six members from each territory, to prepare and submit a draft constitution: a six-member working group was formed to write the draft and to submit it chapter by chapter to the Committee for discussion and approval. The constitutions of other national federations were studied as examples, with the chapter on human freedoms drawing heavily on the constitutions of Egypt, Iraq, Jordan, Lebanon and Syria, as well as on the Universal Declaration of Human Rights. Particular areas – foreign affairs, finance, defence, communications, justice, education and health – were deemed the responsibility of the federal government; and the working party also considered such topics as Libyan nationality, language, the powers of the king, ministerial responsibility, electoral law, and the structure of the parliament. In September 1951 the completed constitutional draft was presented to the National Assembly for discussion and approval.

It soon emerged that there were several points of disagreement among the members. The Cyrenaicans insisted that Benghazi be the future capital of Libya whereas the Tripolitanians and Fezzanese favoured Tripoli, a more obvious choice: Tripoli was at the heart of the most highly developed and populous region and was nearer than Benghazi to western Europe. Tripoli was also Libya's chief port and the centre of commercial and cultural activities; it was larger than Benghazi and had been less ravaged by the War.

It also emerged that the Cyrenaicans had little faith in the democratic process, urging greater powers for the king and fewer for parliament. However here the Tripolitanians prevailed when they argued that only an effective parliamentary system would fulfil the terms of the UN resolution on independence. By the 3 October the National Assembly had agreed all the articles except one dealing with the distribution of customs revenue, the succession to the throne, and the naming of the capital. On this last an unhappy compromise was decided: Tripoli and Benghazi would be joint capitals. On 7 October 1951 the National Assembly reached final agreement on a constitution of 213 articles; Pelt commented that 'Ten months to write a constitution by people none of whom had any previous comparable experience in this field is indeed a remarkable accomplishment.' The Assembly approved the draft Electoral Law on 6 November. It remained in session until Independence Day but now its work was done.

The new constitution stated that 'Libya is a State having a hereditary monarchy, its form is federal and its system of government is representative. Its name is "The United Kingdom of Libya".' The three regions of Libya were termed 'provinces' of the kingdom, and legislative power was vested in the king and in a parliament comprising a Senate and a House of Representatives. Half of the Senate members would be appointed by the king, the other half of the twenty-four members (eight from each province) to be elected by adult male suffrage. The Prime Minister and the provincial governors were to be appointed by the king, with each governor (*Wali*) in Tripolitania and Cyrenaica able to appoint a quarter of the members of the Legislative Assemblies, the rest of the members being elected by the people. A Supreme Court, its judges appointed by the king, was created to hear disputes between the provinces and between the provinces and the federal government.

INDEPENDENCE

The independence of Libya was declared on 24 December 1951, one week before the UN deadline. The last nominal powers held by the British and French Residents were transferred to the provisional Libyan government, the foreign administrations were concluded, and the National Assembly was dissolved. A formal Declaration of Independence was made by the king-designate at a ceremony at the Manar Palace, the former residence of General Graziani in Benghazi:

> We joyfully proclaim to the noble Libyan people that . . . our beloved country has, with the help of God, attained independence . . . We formally proclaim that Libya has, from today, become an independent sovereign state and . . . we take henceforth the title of "His Majesty the King of the United Kingdom of Libya".

> We welcome also the coming into force at this moment of the Constitution of the country . . . It is our wish, as you well know, that the life of the country should conform to constitutional principles, and we intend henceforth to exercise our powers in accordance with the provisions of this Constitution . . . it is our duty one and all to preserve what we have gained at so dear a price, and to hand it down carefully and faithfully to posterity.

> At this blessed hour we call to mind our heroes of the past. We invoke God's mercy and reward upon the soul of our righteous martyrs, and we salute the sacred banner, the legacy of our fathers and the hard-earned symbol of our unity . . .

The Prime Minister of the provisional government, Mahmud Muntasser, then tendered his resignation and formally asked the king to form the first national government. Muntasser was offered the premiership and the Foreign Affairs portfolio; Omar Shannaib, formerly Defence minister, was later appointed head of the royal *Diwan*; other appointments included Ali Assad al-Jirbi (Defence) and Mohammad bin Othman (Health); Mansur bin Gadara (Finance) and Ibrahim bin Shaaban (Communications) were retained. The king also selected the governors (*Walis*) for the three provinces; and Libya applied for membership of FAO, WHO, UNESCO and the United Nations. In a letter to the president of the UN General Assembly Muntasser declared: 'Our thanks to the General Assembly must be directed above all to its agent, the United Nations Commissioner in Libya, Mr Adrian Pelt. We have come to regard him not only as our beloved friend and wise counsellor, but as one who toiled without regard for personal convenience or health for our interest.'[18] The *Lungomare*, the main sea-front thoroughfare in both Tripoli and Benghazi, is named after Adrian Pelt. In his Supplementary Report Pelt commented that 'Libya has made its entry into the family of nations without any ties which its Government will not be free to sever, modify or continue in the light of the country's interests or affinities'; and he defended the new Libyan constitution against charges that it was too advanced for the country's needs: 'When a politically adolescent people acquires its first constitutional garment, it seems wiser to allow a size permitting a degree of political growth, rather than to select one of such tight-fitting proportions as to risk congestion of the body politic.'[19] Libya had become – with Egypt, Ethiopia, Liberia and South Africa – one of the five independent African states.

However, not all Libyans rejoiced on Independence Day. Pelt himself remarked that it would be an exaggeration to pretend that all Libyans were happy about the constitutional developments. In particular, the nationalists who wanted a unitary state perceived that the country would still be dominated by the traditional forces, not least by the ever-present European powers; the three provinces had been given excessive autonomy, so eroding the solidarity of the nation; and the king, with his customary closeness to Britain, represented an unwelcome constraint on democratic development. Libya had emerged as a state 'heavily committed to the West. This was to be the fundamental cause of the coup d'état which overturned the monarchy eighteen years later.'[20]

FACE OF MONARCHY

The Libyan federal monarchy, from the beginning, had many weaknesses.

King Idris had sweeping constitutional powers that were frequently abused in what he saw as his own interests and those of his foreign supporters. He had the power to appoint half the members of the Senate (the upper house) and could dissolve House of Representatives (or Chamber of Deputies, the lower house) or veto its legislation. The Tripolitanians saw the emergence of a Cyrenaican Sanussi as king as a stumbling block to political progress, and Idris's actions soon confirmed their doubts. Libya's first general election was held in February 1952, after which all political parties were dissolved and prohibited.

Many of the tribal leaders and important urban political centres, often under the influence of the nationalist Arabs, had been opposed to Idris's installation as king and as a vehicle for continued British influence. The king was obviously a religious leader and many secular-minded intellectuals regretted that the new Libya had been shaped along religious lines. In Benghazi the Omar Mukhtar society became a focus for young nationalists who had opposed the British military administration, and who now were even flirting with republican ideas. The Society still nominally supported the monarchy but at the time of independence some of its leaders were in prison for demonstrating against the previous Cyrenaican administration. The British were keen to support the monarchy as a well-tried device in the Middle East for countering Arab nationalism, pan-Arabism, socialist agitation and other evils that would threaten British control in the region. Britain had relied upon client monarchies – in Iraq (Feisal), in Transjordan (Abdullah), and in the Trucial States – as a way of organising the potent forces of religion behind the traditional tribal leaders, The first British Ambassador to Libya had recently served in Jordan and belonged in the Foreign Office generation that had carefully cultivated a range of feudal monarchies as the bulwark of British influence in the Middle East. Ruth First notes that 'The House of Sanussi was comfortingly reminiscent of the Hashemite kingdom.'[21] What the British had learned in Jordan and elsewhere they were to implement in the new Libya. Events later proved that this was a short-sighted policy. Arabists in the British Foreign Office already detected new sociopolitical forces stirring in the Middle East and North Africa, and it would not be long before a discredited Idris regime was swept away.

The Americans too worked to protect their own perceived interests in post-independence Libya: the new Ambassador cultivated his own placements in the fresh Libyan Cabinet, including – appropriately enough – the Minister for War 'whose undisguised ambition is to be sent to the United States' and the Minister for Finance.[22] The agreement over the Wheelus air base involved a range of aid provisions designed to secure Libyan compliancy in the troubled atmosphere of the Cold War. Wheelus Field, an enormous American installation seven miles from Tripoli, had been leased from 1400 different individual owners of property. By 1955 the American investment in Wheelus was roughly estimated at between $50 million and $100 million, with the Libyans unhappy at the rent being paid. The journalist Robert C, Doty remarked in 1954 that 'The Air Force was in the position of a man who builds a mansion on a lot without buying the lot first.'[23] In September 1954, after protracted negotiations, the American government agreed to pay Libya $45 million over a period of twenty years, and to provide other economic assistance to the country. Arab nationalists continued to object to Wheelus as what they saw as a clear violation of Libyan sovereignty.

Wheelus Field served a variety of purposes. It served as a useful stop on the global routes of the United States Military Air Transport Service, offered vast areas for aircraft gunnery practice, and supported other US bases in the area, notably those in Morocco. Wheelus was the oldest US air base in Africa, and more than six hundred American children attended its school. Not far from the 11,000-foot runway was the stadium that Mussolini had built for the Tripoli automobile race-track. Supposedly the largest cantilever structure in the world, it presented the American demolition squads with many problems. The Wheelus base was only a part of US investment in the new Libya, and by the mid-1960s it stood at around $450 million. The Western grip on the constitutional monarchy seemed secure.

The King derived his power from the claim to religious legitimacy on which all the Arab monarchies were founded, and from the class structure of traditional tribal society. The Sanussi *zawiyah* (or lodges) coincided with the main power centres in Bedouin society, the sheikhs served to link the Sanussi head (at that time Idris) with the land-owning tribes. The Sanussi hierarchy reinforced the royal household (the *Diwan*) and at the same time operated an administrative system through the *zawiyah* structure. It was significant that none of this was written into the constitution, nor could it be: it necessarily functioned as a complex power system that had evolved over many generations and which was uneasily grafted onto the formal lineaments of the new constitution. These circumstances alone gave clues as to why tensions should develop between the traditional sources of Arab power and the younger nationalists looking to the wider world.

The King, through his control of the Prime Minister, encouraged the frequent shuffling of ministers: this helped to ensure, as far as the King's perceptions went, that he would represent the symbol of security and stability, with no ministerial placement or caucus able to consolidate influence and power. Idris inclined to solve problems in peremptory fashion, by dictat; or he procrastinated, in due course retiring to Tobruk, leaving power not in the constitutional Cabinet but in the *Diwan*. In 1955 King Idris was in his middle sixties, frail and thoughtful, with dominating characteristics of 'erudition, piety and suspiciousness'.[24] He knew no Western languages, but was said to be an Arabic scholar of considerable attainments. Many observers saw him as a quietist, interested more in withdrawing from problems than in confronting them (unless they admitted of a quick decision), and lacking force of character. He had been head of the Sanussi Order since 1917, and the subsequent decades of turmoil in Libya forced him into exile for twenty-one uninterrupted years. The image of Idris as 'absentee monarch' never fully disappeared, and his apparent eagerness to flee from foreign incursions contrasted unhappily with the dogged heroism of such nationalists as Omar al-Mukhtar. After an assassination attempt in Tripoli, when he was still Emir of Cyrenaica, he was reluctant to visit the region; and later demonstrations against him, as he paraded in a Rolls-Royce as 'king-designate', did little to encourage contact with the people. Idris was also heavily superstitious. In 1952 he decided that he would transfer the remains of his father (who had died in a distant oasis) to Benghazi. While the body was en route by truck a terrible storm developed whereupon Idris, seeing this as a bad omen, stopped the truck, abandoned his plans, and sent his father's remains back to their original resting place. It was inevitable that Idris should have been regarded as a symbol of the old tribal society, increasingly ill-suited to be leader of a modern state.

The tensions between the old traditionalism and the new constitutional provisions were quick to surface. Political parties contended for power in the general election of February 1952, after which they were dissolved and banned. Two opposing tendencies had come into conflict: the Istiqlal party under Salim al-Muntasser, linked to business and the British military administration; and Bashir Bey Sadawi's National Congress Party, leaning towards the Arab League. The Congress Party won all the seats in Tripoli, but lost in the rest of the country, a result that confounded its expectations and led to claims that the government had rigged the ballot. As soon as the results were announced Congress supporters invaded government buildings, cut telephone wires, and blocked transport. The government arrested scores of demonstrators, banned the Congress Party, and banished Sadawi to Egypt. The fledgling multi-party politics of independent Libya had collapsed at the first test, and it was destined not to return: factions continued to operate on a clandestine basis but healthy political contention was at an end. Idris had secured his nominal authority, though fresh undercurrents of agitation would soon become apparent. The Cabinet was now the unquestioning servant of the Palace, most candidates in subsequent elections were government nominees, and voting criteria were most characteristically tribal and nepotistic. With political parties suppressed, the Palace felt free to remove governments when it wished, so nullifying any residual claims to constitutional propriety.[25] In the seventeen years of the monarchy there were eleven governments and more than two hundred ministers in all. It was the discovery of oil in 1955 (Chapter Five) that was to transform the character of government and the shape of the future Libyan state.

The ending of party politics resulted in petty manoeuvrings for power, a host of corrupt practices, and one political crisis after another. In October 1954 a major internal crisis focused on a family quarrel involving some of the thirty-eight royal princes.[26] Various members of the royal family increasingly resented what they saw as the disproportionate power wielded by Ibrahim al-Shalhi, for some forty years the King's loyal adviser. As the King had no surviving children by his wife Fatima, Sayyid Ahmad al-Sharif's daughter, Sayyid Ahmad's descendants claimed the succession for their side of the family. Idris, supposedly advised on this question by Shalhi, preferred that his (Idris's) brother, Mohammad al-Reda, be seen as the legitimate successor to the throne. The dispute came to a climax when a grandson of Sayyid Ahmad, Al-Sharif, shot and killed Shalhi in a street in Benghazi. Family members were then put under house arrest for their own safety, seven younger members were exiled to the oasis of Hon, and many of the family members lost their titles and the right to hold government positions. Al-Sharif was convicted of murder and then executed in February 1955, his corpse exposed in public for twenty minutes at the spot where Shalhi was killed.[27]

The King, perhaps looking to his own security, then moved from Benghazi to the British garrison town of Tobruk. One crisis had been averted but there was still the unresolved question of the succession, the perennial problem of childless monarchs (and of monarchs with incompetent offspring). In 1955, with Libyan monarchy an institution well favoured by the British, the writer John Gunther was able to opine that 'King Idris has no male heir, which is a tragedy for the country.'[28] Idris was first married when he was only eight years old, and two subsequent marriages were dissolved when they produced no living offspring. In 1932 Idris married his cousin Fatima (Al Sayyida Fatima Al Shifa bint al-Sayyid Ahmad al-Sharif), and by 1954 Fatima had managed fourteen miscarriages. A pregnancy in 1952 was attended by doctors from Wheelus Field, but the son born early in 1953 died after a few hours. After Idris had temporarily resolved the family crisis over the succession he designated his brother Reda 'Deputy King', hoping to forestall any further trouble from the thirty-eight male members of the royal family: some thirty-two of the thirty-eight princes, from a different branch of the Sanussi family, had reportedly opposed Idris on occasions.[29] Gunther, as a contemporary observer, concluded: 'In the present phase Idris is the only person capable of holding Libya together, but he himself hardly seems capable of doing so.'[30] Nor was the situation helped by a fifth marriage – to Alia Abd-al-Kadr Lamlum, the daughter of an Egyptian merchant – which was dissolved in 1958 after a childless union; or by the sudden death of the Deputy King, Reda, in 1955. Idris chose Reda's second son, Emir Hasan al-Reda, as his heir. Perhaps it was the apparent fragility of the monarchy that encouraged Idris to flirt with the idea of turning Libya into a republic.[31] At the same time events outside Libya were increasingly impacting on political concerns within the country.

In 1954 there was growing hostility among Libyans to French policies in Tunisia, Morocco and Algeria; this resulted in nationalist pressures on the Libyan government to evict the residual French troops from Fezzan. France was still maintaining garrisons, totalling around four hundred men, at Sebha, Ghat and Ghadames under an agreement whereby they contributed to the Fezzanese budget. It was perceived in Libya that these troops were strategically well placed to intercept the significant flow of arms from Egypt to Algeria. Nationalist Libyans, increasingly sensitive to pan-Arabism, would accept nothing less than the total withdrawal of the French forces from the region; and here their demands were successful.

The special arrangements with France, whereby a French presence had been agreed for Fezzan, were officially ended on 31 December 1954, and in August the following year a treaty of 'friendship and good-neighbourliness' was signed. The new agreement stipulated a withdrawal of the French garrisons by 30 November 1956, with France agreed certain limited air and transit rights in exchange for contributions to Libyan development spending. As the French had feared, Fezzan soon became a direct supply line for the revolutionary forces in Algeria fighting against the harsh French occupation. The Libyan success in evicting the French from Fezzan encouraged the Tunisians and Moroccans to adopt a similar course. Such developments were clear signs that the residual colonialism in North Africa was beginning to crumble. This in turn eroded further the authority of the national factions and institutions – such as the Libyan monarchy – that had been happy to make pacts with Britain and other traditional colonialist powers.

TOWARDS THE COUP

The second general election in Libya was held in January 1956 but it had little democratic significance: political parties no longer existed and voting was on the basis of personality, tribal links and nepotism. All political clubs and associations were banned, political gatherings were prohibited, and the press was subject to licence and control. The Omar Mukhtar group had been banned as a political organisation, though its members contrived to meet clandestinely from time to time; the Libyan Communist Party had not survived the expulsion of seven of its leaders in November 1951, and the diligent attention of the Libyan police in subsequent years. Some political activities continued to take place in sports clubs, the need for 'recreation' being a suitable cover, and some trade unions encouraged an element of political debate: in 1960 there was overt political rivalry between the Libyan General Workers' Federation and the Libyan Federation of Labour and Professional Union. On 3 February 1962 eight-seven people were sentenced by a Tripoli court to imprisonment, on charges of 'forming in Libya cells of the Arab Socialist Ba'ath Party and carrying on subversive activities aimed at overthrowing the political, economic, and social system'. The sentences ranged from eight months to two years and eight months; the party cells were dissolved; funds, papers and books were confiscated; and a number of the defendants, from other Arab states, were deported.

Trade unions, seen by the authorities as inclined to socialism and subversion, were suppressed by the Libyan police; and in March 1962 the International Confederation of Free Trade Unions threatened to take 'direct action' in protest against Libya's refusal to allow a delegation to visit the country and investigate the reported repression of trade unions. Libya was now an oil producer and trade unionists agitated for its petroleum exports to be blocked. Thus L. A. Hoskins, General Secretary of the International Federation of Petroleum Workers, declared that he saw no reason why labour organisations should agree to tolerate supplies from a country 'engaged in anti-union action of a dictatorial character'. Britain continued to train and offer advice to the Libyan police forces and the military; and there was little doubt that the hostility of the Libyan government to trade union organisation was supported by the British. In November 1962 talks in London agreed the formation of a Libyan navy: the British government promised to train naval cadets in Britain and to equip Libya with a training ship and a mine-sweeper. But the British-supported federal monarchy was becoming increasingly ill-suited to running a modern economy based on oil; and in 1963, two years after the first commercial oil shipment, Idris issued a royal proclamation abolishing the federal system. The monarchy, for a long time highly congenial in British eyes, was being forced to acknowledge the impact of Nasser's Arab socialism and the increasingly restive nationalist voices in Libya itself. But efforts to shift Libya away from its traditional tribal roots provoked inevitable reactions. Some of the restrictions were lifted from the press, but moves to reduce the power of the governmental sheikhs were unsuccessful. Student demonstrations in 1964 were crushed by the British-backed security forces, and the government was replaced by one that better represented the traditional interests of the tribes.

In 1960 a celebrated scandal over the building of the Fezzan Road had exposed the characteristic 'tone for the *enrichissez-vous* activities of the ruling group'.[32] Here a Libyan construction company, with some foreign involvement, had exhausted the money provided for the whole project with only one third of the work actually completed. The parliament passed a vote of 'no confidence' in the government and the Prime Minister, Abdul Mejid Coobar, was forced to resign: this was the first time that the parliament had successfully challenged the Libyan Cabinet. The development contract had been landed through favouritism and the whole scheme was corruptly administered. Tribal notables in government worked mainly to divert government resources to their own tribal areas, and to place contracts with their own colleagues and family members. Parliament had forced the collapse of the Coobar government, but when a new cabinet emerged under Mohammed Othman al-Said it was found to contain a majority of members who had served in the old one: the parliamentary victory was hollow. And other events conspired to outrage the growing nationalist opinion.

An economic settlement had been agreed between Libya and Italy, but on terms that were not wholly to Libya's advantage. Most Italian public property was transferred to Libya, though with Italy still retaining some buildings: several schools and buildings for consular and diplomatic use. The Libyan government agreed to recognise various Italian commercial rights and the Italians were given permission to continue investing in some of the colonisation schemes: Italian colonists were to remain owners of their land, regardless of the brutal way in which it had been acquired. Colonists who wanted to return to Italy were free to sell their Libyan land and to transfer the capital to Italy. The colonial conquest of the prewar years was continuing to bring profits to foreign land-owners.

The treaty designed to clarify the position of the colonists was ratified in March 1957: it affirmed that 'all questions relative to . . . the transfer of sovereignty' had now been settled. Many of the colonists sold their land and went back to Italy but some – calculating that Libya would now have a more settled future – resolved to stay and develop the land they had inhabited so precariously for many years. This circumstance again did little to pacify the growing nationalist clamour.

In 1955, after secret negotiations, it was announced that Libya and the Soviet Union had agreed to open diplomatic relations: Soviet diplomatic missions were established in Tripoli and Benghazi but the Libyan government was unwilling to agree Soviet offers of aid, including the transport of pilgrims to Mecca. An alarmed United States responded to these developments by increasing economic aid. The Libyan Prime Minister, Mustafa bin Halim, the successor to Mohammad al-Sakisli (the former Head of the Royal *Diwan*), was quick to insist that Libya would not be exposed to communist influence. It was useful to demonstrate that Libya was not quite in the pocket of the West, and in any case Soviet support for Libya's admission to the United Nations was useful; in December 1955, four years after independence, Libya and fifteen other states were admitted to the UN, following backstairs talks between the Soviet Union and the United States.

Libyan nationalism received a further boost in July 1956 when Nasser moved to nationalise the Suez Canal (Halim declared the move a 'wise and courageous step'). The Libyan government demanded an assurance from Britain that the bases and troops in Tripolitania and Cyrenaica would not be used against Egypt; this assurance was given of 30 October – and the following day Britain, France and Israel attacked Egypt, arousing further anti-western feeling in Libya. Demonstrations were organised against British and US military installations, an explosion at the Tripoli branch of Barclays Bank wounded ten Libyans, and British families began to leave the country. Harold Macmillan had recorded in his Diaries (18 August 1956) that if Nasser 'gets away with it', Britain would be done for: 'It may well be the end of British strength and influence for ever. So, in the last resort, we must use force and defy opinion, here and overseas.' The UK socialist newspaper *Daily Herald* urged 'No more Hitlers'; just as the Labour Party leader Hugh Gaitskell commented that it was all 'very familiar. It is exactly the same that we encountered from Mussolini and Hitler.'[33] However, comparing the Arab hero Nasser to Mussolini could have been scarcely less calculated to impress Libyans with the soundness of the enduring British influence in their country.

Harold Macmillan, after a conversation with Winston Churchill, presented the government's Egypt Committee with a detailed minute urging the need to 'destroy Nasser's armies and overthrow his government'.[34] One option, despite the British government's assurances to Libya on 30 October, was to launch a land attack on Egypt using the Armoured Division based in Libya. In the event this option was not adopted, but for tactical reasons rather than for any consideration of Libyan sovereignty. The possibility of conflict between British and Egyptian forces on the Cyrenaican border continued to alarm the Libyans, and the decision was taken to move Libyan troops into eastern Cyrenaica. The sudden end to the fighting in Egypt, not least following US pressure on Britain (America at that time had some concern for the growing current of Arab nationalism), saved Libya from further crisis, though not before 'extremist' opinion in Libya had received a further boost. Libya had managed to stay out of a conflict raging so near to its territory, but on 1 June 1957 the Cairo newspaper *Al-Ahram*, an official government mouthpiece, accused bin Halim of having allowed the British to use the El Adem airfield for raids on Alexandria. The Libyan government denied the charge but Halim had already resigned, nominally over a matter of domestic policy.

At the same time Libya managed, following Tunisian independence, to establish links with the Arab Maghrib: in January 1957 bin Halim and President Habib Bourguiba had signed a twenty-year treaty of friendship and co-operation that Halim had termed 'the cornerstone of North African unity' and which was intended to establish the basis for the development of common policies, a move towards pan-Arabism but one seen by the Tunisian government as a means of countering Egyptian influence in North Africa. In March 1957 Richard Nixon, then US Vice-President, visited Libya to explain the recently declared 'Eisenhower Doctrine', an economic and military aid programme intended to counter communist influence in the Middle East; two days later James P. Richards, Eisenhower's special envoy, arrived in Tripoli to press further economic aid on the Libyans. The Libyan government expressed acceptance of the Eisenhower Doctrine, agreed $7 million in increased aid, and declared that none of this would increase Libyan commitment to the West. After bin Halim's resignation, over the question of legislation by royal fiat, Abd al-Majid Kubar, the Speaker of the House of Representatives was asked to form a government. He thereupon set about increasing Libya's dependence on the West by persuading both Britain and the US to increase their aid, while rejecting a Soviet offer of $2,800,000 for health, education and other purposes. In April 1958 Kubar went to London to discuss an Anglo-Libyan treaty that would guarantee financial aid up to 1963: $3,250,000 in British subsidies over a five-year period were agreed, as well as supplies of military equipment and training. The annual contribution of £1 million to the Public Development and Stabilisation Agency would end, but the United States agreed to pay $5,500,000 over the next five years instead.[35] In July 1960 West Germany agreed a loan of £5 million for agricultural and industrial development.

These agreements enhanced Kubar's reputation in some Libyan circles, but elsewhere the various treaties were perceived as 'unequal', attracting Western financial and military aid but consigning independent Libya to a subservient status, wholly vulnerable to Western whim in the uncertain atmosphere of the Cold War. The 1956 Accord with Italy, granting the settlers special privileges, seemed particularly humiliating. The treaty included the words: 'no claim, even on the part of individuals, can be advanced in respect of properties of Italian citizens in Libya, by reasons of acts by the government or the lapsed Italian administration of Libya, that occurred before the constitution of the Libyan state. The Libyan government consequently guarantees Italian citizens owning property in Libya, in respect of Libyan law, the free and just exercise of their rights.'[36] The Libyan government, under pressure from the West, decided that there was no alternative to legitimising the Italian land seizures. The Italians continued to dominate much of the business and commercial life of the country, and when this influence was added to the rapidly escalating levels of British and US aid it was obvious that the new Libya had little room for independent economic movement. Moreover the various aid agencies, operating under Western or UN auspices, advised 'the need to restore the settlers' confidence, or expect the continued decline of the agricultural base'.[37]

The practical limitations on Libyan sovereignty were further demonstrated when on 18 July 1958, following the overthrow of the monarchy in Iraq, British troops were landed in Cyrenaica. The British government declared that the reinforcements came under the terms of the Anglo-Libyan treaty and were justified in view of the deteriorating Middle East situation. The Idris government declined to recognise the new regime of Brigadier Abd al-Karim Kassim in Iraq, though the decision faced mounting domestic opposition and – alarmed by the effect of British troops of nationalist feeling – Idris recognised the Kassim regime on 4 August. Then the Libyan government sent a supplicatory note to Cairo, declaring for the first time that 'Libya is an integral part of the Arab nation' and that 'Libya will continue to oppose foreign intervention in the Middle East.'[38] Idris, like other traditional factions in Arab politics, were being increasingly pressured to recognise the undercurrents of nationalist feelings that had been stimulated through the colonial years and which were now being boosted by many parallel and mutually supportive developments throughout the Arab world.

Egypt had always had a considerable impact on Libyan political thinking. Idris himself, the Sanussi head, with many Libyan exiles had lived there for a lengthy period. For many years after the Second World War there were more Egyptian teachers in Libyan schools than there were Libyan; and after independence the majority of Libyan university students attended Egyptian universities. Libya's first army officers were trained both in the Baghdad academy and in Cairo, as well as by the British. Literate Libyans read newspapers produced in Cairo and Beirut, and Cairo radio was a constant source of information and opinion to politically conscious Libyans. Libyan political groupings were increasingly influenced by the republican sentiments associated with Nasser and with the Ba'athists: Nasser had led a successful revolution and now organised powerful diplomacy against Western influence in the area. The Ba'athists, like Nasser relying on the army for power, had a secular focus that pulled against traditional tribal attitudes. The late 1950s saw a brief marriage between the two tendencies when Nasser's Egypt and Ba'athist Syria formed the United Arab Republic. Syria seceded three years later, and Libyan politics inherited the divisions. The Ba'ath Party was influenced in Libya in the early 1960s but a trial against the illegal grouping resulted in the dissolution of Ba'athist cells, the confiscation of funds, and the exile of non-Libyans among the accused. Cairo Radio encouraged the anti-Ba'athist feeling in Libya, the Ba'athist Party declined, and Nasserite factions became increasingly influential. The Libyan monarchy continued to be hostile to independent political parties and was increasingly forced to take action against them. Students, defying the police, protested in 1964, and there were sympathy protests by Libyan students in Britain and West Germany. In 1966 the first conference of the Libyan Students' Union opted for the Leftist tendency within the Arab Nationalist Movement, pledged support to the Vietnamese resisting Western aggression, demanded a radical approach to the Palestine question, criticised the government's oil policy, and demanded the ending of Western bases on Libyan territory. During the Six-Day War Libyan students forged links with the trade-union movement, and oil and dock-workers struck, refusing to allow the pumping of oil and the loading of tankers.[39] In 1967 the government resorted to a mass trial to discredit the student movement and to remove the militant trade union leaders. It also made cosmetic concessions to Arab nationalism designed to weaken internal dissent and discourage criticism from Egypt. Idris began negotiations for the withdrawal of the foreign bases, but only continued the talks until the furore had died down. Idris succeeded in nullifying political opposition, using the rapidly expanding oil revenues for material concessions. In addition to the flow of foreign aid, as a Cold War ploy, Libya itself was increasingly able to invest in schools and industrial development. Prosperity helped to discourage dissent, helped to counter the nationalist voices. But Idris misjudged the increasingly turbulent political undercurrents. His time was running out.

One problem was the growing social stratification in the country: there had always been a class hierarchy in Libyan society, as in all other cultures, but now this was being exacerbated by a number of economic developments, not least the rapid growth in oil wealth that was encouraging urbanisation. It was inevitable that any large drift of population from the rural areas to the towns would produce massive congestion and overcrowding. Shanty-towns grew up around Benghazi and Tripoli: one 1967 estimate suggested that the shanty-town population of Tripoli was at least 40,000.[40] The author Hadi Bulugma described one of the shanty-towns, Sabri, on the edge of Benghazi:

> The shanty-town of Sabri . . . gives a clear picture of a primitive and miserable society living on the lowest margins of human subsistence. In winter, the people suffer from dirt, mud and rain. Summer conditions were better . . . but millions of flies live on the dirt and sewage found all over the place . . . Neither modern dwellings nor medical services, sanitation, hygiene, pipe water or electricity, are yet known, despite the fact that the eastern part of the area lies along the main northern entrance to the city.[41]

As much as a quarter of Benghazi's total population, around 35,000 people, were estimated to live in Sabri. Nor was the problem helped by the government's agrarian policy. The regime decided in 1961 that agricultural credits should be provided to enable Libyan nationals to buy land. The plan, prompted by World Bank recommendations in 1960, was intended to encourage the buy-out of Italian settlers.[42] In fact the scheme simply facilitated the purchase of land by the wealthy urban traders, so encouraging a drift of population from the urban areas. Efforts to organise a trade-union response to the increased polarisation of commercial wealth led to predictable responses from the government and the increasingly powerful commercial class.

The Sanussi leadership, beginning to benefit from oil revenues, agreed with the wealthy merchants that the trade union movement should be suppressed. A strike had occurred in Tripoli as early as 1959, with hotel workers demanding shorter hours and a fair distribution of tips, and later the same year 350 airport workers (porters, firemen, refuellers and radio operators) followed their example. In another protest Libya's largest press, the Italian-owned Poligrafico Maggi, was brought to a halt by a union strike for improved pay. The federal government, though opposed to union activities, relied on the provincial authorities in the various regions to take action against worker militancy. Thus in a confrontation with the Libyan General Labour Union (LGLU), the provincial governor of Tripolitania Ali Dhili drew on the large numbers of urban unemployed to serve as 'blackleg' labour in a concerted strike-breaking plan. The strikers at Idris airport were quickly replaced, and a fresh labour law was quickly enacted. Trade union offices were taken over by the police, and the LGLU General Secretary, Selim Shita, along with other union leaders, was arrested and subsequently tried on state security charges. All the leaders, including Shita, were eventually acquitted but the union had been destroyed. Power was increasingly concentrated in the state apparatus, the Sanussi leadership and the wealthy merchant/capitalist class able to secure their hold on oil revenues and other sources of wealth, but only temporarily – the war in June 1967 was to exacerbate the social tensions that together were making the Idris monarchy increasingly insecure.

The Israeli attack on Egypt on 5 June stimulated the Libyan trade union and student movements, both already antipathetic to the Idris monarchy and the other traditional elements within the country. Students stirred the urban poor into a rampage against foreign-owned property in Tripoli and elsewhere: Jewish property was destroyed and a number of people were killed. Then the anger turned against the regime's support for British and American bases in Libya. The Libyan trade movement, dormant since 1961 but now resurgent, decided to begin an oil boycott ahead of the formal decision by the scheduled meeting of the Arab oil producers in Baghdad. The oil workers struck on 7 June, refusing to handle oil company vessels in the Port of Tripoli; and the government, fearing it would lose control, ordered the tankers to remain outside territorial waters. An oil company memorandum, issued on 14 June, declared that Libya was 'on the verge of revolt'.[43] Some leading families had already fled the country. When it became clear that the Arabs had suffered a serious defeat by the Israelis, much of the Libyan turmoil subsided. The state then embarked upon another bout of repression to secure the Sanussi leadership. Trade union and student leaders were arrested, and seven union leaders were sentenced to terms of imprisonment. By August much of the opposition to the monarchy had been crushed, but the weakness of the traditional power structure had been exposed.

In October 1961 King Idris had been able to declare that 'The coming years will be years of abundance, owing to the wealth God had given us from our soil'; but it had soon become clear that, despite a significant volume of social investment, the Libyans with access to capital were the ones who had benefited most from the discovery of oil. The contrast between the smart new villas in Tripoli and Benghazi and the surrounding shanty-towns were obvious to everyone; wealthy Libyans and foreigners were often living only a few hundred yards from tent-cities and shanty-towns built of wooden remnants and discarded tin sheets. The writer and journalist Ronald Segal noted in 1962 that there were countries 'not far from Libya' where oil had enriched only a small group, making the surrounding poverty even more desperate, and he proposed that 'Libya would do well to learn from their example, or its government may find the discovery of oil something more than a sudden stroke of luck.'[44]

The foreign bases were still in place, and had been there for many years. Wheelus Field, originally built by the Italians, was acquired by the British who passed it on to the Americans, who developed it further. The pressures of the Cold War had rendered it important to the United States that it retain a complex of bases in the Middle East. As early as January 1951 President Truman had obtained emergency powers from Congress for war mobilisation, had reintroduced selective service, had sent two more divisions to Europe, had doubled the number of air groups, had increased the Army by fifty per cent (to 3.5 million men), had stepped up aid to the French in Vietnam, had offered aid to Fascist Spain in return for military bases, and had obtained new bases in Morocco, Libya and Saudi Arabia.[45] Aid, in one form or another, was generally offered in return for the use of foreign land for aircraft or troop concentrations. Figures collated by the British Overseas Development Institute show that during the period 1945 to 1963 Libya received no less than seventeen per cent of the total bilateral aid which Britain provided to all foreign countries outside the Commonwealth for that period. The Institute noted that 'although these payments to Libya are counted as "aid" there is no doubt that they are in essence straightforward payments to the Libyan government in return for the use of bases'.[46]

The US Strategic Air Command in 1955 had a considerable global strength. In the UK alone more than 11,000 US servicemen worked for SAC, and the command had bases in Libya and Morocco, with agreements to move bomber groups into Iceland, Cyprus and Turkey in time of military need. In the early 1960s the USAF Aerospace Communications Complex (AIRCOM) maintained key automated communications centres in various countries, including Britain, Germany, Iceland, Spain and Libya. The complex Ringstead-Gorramendi link provided the UK atomic Joint Co-ordination Centre at High Wycombe with a direct connection to the US nuclear forces in Spain and Morocco and at Wheelus Field in Libya. In the 1950s and 1960s the West developed a massive war-making capacity that straddled the globe; the Mediterranean bases, including those in Libya, were a part of this global scheme. Nothing short of a revolution would shake Libya out of a world order designed to protect the defined interests (real or imagined) of the Great Powers.

The social and political tensions in Libya were characteristic of many societies, some of which managed to make the necessary evolutionary adaptations in a changing world and some of which did not. Ostentatious wealth side-by-side with poverty, trade union and political aspirations with no useful outlet, the tensions sustained by a residual Italian colonial presence, the collapse of the monarchies in Egypt and Iraq, the constant nationalist resentment sustained by the presence of European and American bases on Libyan land – all these combined to threaten the traditional political structure. Astute observers at the time had little doubt that the days of the Idris monarchy were numbered. The English politician Denis Healey remarked with hindsight that 'It was obvious that the monarchy was likely to fall at any moment to an army coup'; and he tried to guess who would lead it. He got it wrong ('but not very wrong'): 'In the end I decided it would probably be Colonel Shelhi, an intelligent young man who was said to be influenced by Nasser.'[47] The rank was wrong and the name was wrong: the coup against King Idris on 1 September 1969 was led by Signals Captain Muammar al-Gaddafi. The event was, according to two English journalists, 'a last minute panic with a lot of chaos and just a touch of farce'.[48] In any event, an era was at an end. Yet another Middle East monarchy had fallen and there would be far-reaching consequences, not only in the region but in Europe, the United States, and elsewhere.

MUAMMAR AL-GADDAFI

Gaddafi's parents – Mohammed Abdul Salam bin Hamed bin Mohammed (known as Abu Meniar, 'father of the knife') and Aissha al-Gaddafi – produced two daughters and a son, all born in a tent twenty miles south of the coastal town of Sirte. His father belonged to a small tribe, the Gaddafa (literally 'those who spit out or vomit'), a basically Bedouin group that showed strains of the many other peoples – Berbers, Circassians, Turks, Jews and others – who had inhabited Libya over the years.[49] His parents were poor and illiterate, but they told stories, in the tradition of the Bedouin, about their tribe and its history, about ancient battles and foreign enemies. Aissha died in 1978; and Abu Meniar, well over ninety, in 1985. Their son, Muammar, was born around 1940 (the date is uncertain).

The Gaddafa, though a small and humble tribe, knew the value of education; and so Muammar's parents pooled their meagre savings to send their son first to a Koranic elementary school and later to high school at Sebha in Fezzan. At around the time of independence Gaddafi enrolled at the primary school in Sirte and so became the first member of his family to read and write. At school during the day, he slept in a mosque at night, trekking home through the desert every Thursday, at the start of the Muslim weekend, and returning late on Friday. He was the oldest boy in his class and, as a rural Bedouin, viewed by his classmates as something of a country bumpkin. His father saw him as a serious and pious student. When Gaddafi was fourteen his family moved to Sebha whereupon he enrolled at the local secondary school – to attract a group of friends who remained with him until he took power in 1969. These were exciting times in Libya: the country was newly independent, the weak King Idris was unable to suppress the growing political agitation, and young students were stimulated by new ideas and foreign examples of political initiative and nationalist success.

The young had unprecedented opportunities for education; they read newspapers and books; and listened to the radio, particularly to the powerful rhetoric of the Egyptian leader Gamal Abdul Nasser. Committed Nasserites were teaching in Libyan schools and serving in the Libyan bureaucracy, helping to create an atmosphere in which political upheaval was an increasingly realistic option. Nasser's *Philosophy of the Revolution*, describing how he formed an 'army officers' club' and overthrew the Egyptian monarchy in 1952, was one of the most important books that Gaddafi encountered during that period. It was inevitable that such a work, with a narrative that reads like a thriller, would have gripped the imaginations of the young Libyan students at Sebba and elsewhere. 'Our life [wrote Nasser] was like a thrilling detective story. We had dark secret and passwords. We lurked in the shadows; we had caches of pistols and hand-grenades, and firing bullets was our cherished hope . . . I can still remember our emotions and feelings as we dashed along that melodramatic path.' Nasser's first 'glimmer of Arab awareness' came when, like Gaddafi, he was a student in secondary school; he used to strike every December to protest against the Balfour Declaration which Britain had made on behalf of the Jews. In all this Gaddafi saw a supreme example, the model for the forthcoming Libyan revolution.

Already Gaddafi was a charismatic figure, attracting followers and eager to convince his fellow students (his friends carried a stool around that he could use when he wanted to make a speech). One of his Sebba teachers, the Egyptian Mahmoud Efay, related how Gaddafi had handed him a note which had three questions: 'What is a pyramid organisation and which is the best manner to organise such a structure? Does the possibility of organising a revolution in Libya exist? If a revolution were to be carried out in Libya would Egypt come to the assistance of the Libyan people?'[50] Efay was sympathetic and answered the questions as well as he could; in particular, he emphasised that a successful revolution would need the support of the army.

In October 1961 Gaddafi demonstrated against Syria's decision to break its unity agreement with Egypt (already he was sensitive to pan-Arabist aspirations). This was, declares Frederick Muscat (a flattering biographer of Gaddafi), the first test of his organisation of followers. On 5 October he led a protest into Sebba town centre, brandishing Egyptian flags and pictures of Nasser; Gaddafi stood on his stool and railed against the continued presence of foreign bases on Libyan territory, after which he collected money to send cables of support to Nasser. Twenty students were arrested, and the next day Gaddafi was told by Seif al Nasser Mohammed, a local pillar of the town, that he would be expelled from the Sebba school. (This followed another incident in which Gaddafi and some friends had broken windows in a hotel where, against Islamic teaching, alcohol was available.) A month later the expulsion order, duly signed by the Minister of Education, was received by the school's headmaster ('I convey to you the penalties which we deemed necessary to be applied against the following students who perpetrated acts contrary to their duties as students: 1) Muammar Abu Meniar al Gaddafi discharged from the school and prevented from studying at the schools of the state . . .'). The ruling ('oppressive' and 'cruel' according to Gaddafi and Muscat; 'distinctly mild', according to Blundy and Lycett, *op. cit.*) may be judged to have further alienated Gaddafi from the sociopolitical system in Libya and to have further fuelled his revolutionary ambitions.

Gaddafi's father appealed for his son to be found a place at another school, and in fact the appeal was successful. Since Gaddafi at nineteen was now too old to begin at a fresh secondary school a sympathetic official provided a false birth certificate; Gaddafi's political agitations thus continued at another secondary school, this time one at Misrata. He soon became famous for his frank speaking and attracted more followers: on one occasion he publicly denounced the English-language inspector, a certain Mr Johnson, for being no more than an agent of imperialism, an act that impressed his fellow students. Omar Meheshi, a fellow revolutionary in Misrata, declared: 'When I heard this I was so struck by his audacity that I wanted to meet him, to get to know him.'[51] The group had resolved to follow Nasser 'and Nasser alone. Our line was to support Arab nationalism.' The rules were laid down by Gaddafi: the group members must not drink, play card games, or fool around with women; they must pray and study, and always attend the necessary political meetings. Then, remembering the advice of his Egyptian teacher Mahmoud Efay, Gaddafi decided to join the Libyan armed forces.

In 1963 Gaddafi enrolled in the Royal Libyan Military Academy in Benghazi, set up in 1957 to serve, under British guidance, as the Libyan equivalent of Sandhurst. It is a sad reflection on Libyan security that someone like Gaddafi was allowed to enroll in the academy and join the Cyrenaican Defence Force, an elite group charged with the special task of protecting the King. Gaddafi was already known to the police and the security forces, though no effort seems to have been made to block his entry into the armed forces. The academy was headed by Colonel Ted Lough from 1960 to 1966, and he remembers Gaddafi well: 'He was our most backward cadet . . . 98 per cent of the cadets passed their exams, 2 per cent failed, and he was one of them. He was probably not as stupid as I thought at the time. Part of his problem was that he wouldn't learn English. I didn't like him and he made life difficult for my officers and men because he went out of his way to be rude to them.'[52] Gaddafi was often reported for insubordination but little action was ever taken. Lough has said that Gaddafi 'was inherently cruel'; and there is some evidence that he, with some fellow officers, was involved in a summary execution of a man accused of 'some sexual offence, possibly homosexuality'. The killing was reported to the Libyan chief of staff but nothing was done. However, it seems that Gaddafi did not always avoid punishment.

A Major Jalal Dalgeli, in charge when the commander of the academy was away, has observed that he had 'no time for Gaddafi' and could remember him being forced to crawl in the gravel on his hands and knees, with a weighted rucksack on his back, until the skin came off his knees. It is hardly surprising that Gaddafi was not a good cadet: his purpose was altogether different. He set about subverting the officers in various ways. They were encouraged to collect information on other staff, about stocks of arms and other matters; the first meeting of his Free Officers' Movement was held in 1964. Gaddafi later commented on Egyptian television: 'we were faced with many difficulties; we had to meet during vacations and often late at night . . . sometimes we had to travel hundreds of miles and put up with long sessions in atrocious weather. We would often sleep in the open . . . all members of the committee had to buy private cars and to put them at the disposal of the Movement.' It is obvious that Gaddafi's industry and application paid dividends: he quickly developed a revolutionary group among officers who were more committed to Arab nationalism than to residual European colonialism, and in any case the British seems increasingly uncertain about their role. An unnamed British NCO has been quoted: 'We were there not really to train the army but to keep an eye on it, to find out what was going on. We made regular reports about it to the British embassy people. I felt for a long time that something pretty drastic was going to happen.'[53]

Many observers perceived that the situation was ripe for revolution, a circumstance that encouraged the British not to arm the Libyan army too heavily (Lough: 'our policy was not to arm them too well'). It was well perceived that many of the Libyan officers were interested in politics and much influenced by talk of Arab nationalism. Lough, seeing Gaddafi as the most likely revolutionary focus, made frequent reports to British intelligence in Libya; and has expressed anger that the Foreign Office paid such scant attention to the information he provided. One such report was made in 1964 when Gaddafi joined the Libyan army's signals unit in Benghazi and proceeded to order elaborate radio equipment that could cover the whole of Libya. Lough himself was unable to gain access to the radio equipment: it was held in a secure area of the compound in Benghazi ('Gaddafi had got himself into a strong position with a weak commanding officer'). Gaddafi was known to be a major security risk five years before he launched his successful coup.

Gaddafi then applied for a four-month military training mission to the United States. Herman Eilts, the deputy head of mission at the US embassy in Tripoli, interviewed Gaddafi (and five of his colleagues) and was impressed with his leadership qualities. Gaddafi was not granted permission to go to the United States, but for reasons that are unclear: Eilts himself did not suggest a ban ('Maybe the Libyan authorities were on to Gaddafi at that time'). (Years later Gaddafi was to plan the assassination of Eilts in Cairo.) Gaddafi did however manage to win a place on a four-month training course in Britain (Lough: 'I can't understand it. He must have slipped through the net'). He first went to Beaconsfield to study English, and then to the Royal Armoured Corps headquarters in Bovington, Dorset, to learn about signals, driving maintenance, and gunnery on armoured vehicles. It is suggested by Muscat that Gaddafi did not enjoy his visit to Britain: offended by racism and other endemic features of English society, he always wore his traditional Bedouin robes in London. By the time he returned to Libya it was becoming increasingly clear to many observers that a weak Idris would not be able to retain power much longer. Lough commented that Idris feared his own army ('We got him six Centurion tanks but he was so anxious about an army revolt that he locked them away'). In this situation events would quickly move to a head.

The new oil wealth in Libya, far from securing the monarchy, had simply led to fresh levels of graft and corruption. A memorandum to President Kennedy on 16 October 1962 reported the 'sheer financial chaos' in Libyan, the 'uncontrolled spending (and grafting)' that had produced a cash shortage. The foreign oil companies allowed money to flow into the pockets of a privileged Libyan elite but the mass of the Libyan people were receiving disproportionately few benefits. The US National Security Council issued a report, 'US Policy Towards Libya', on 15 March 1960 which included reference to the 'little loyalty' to the King 'among the younger urban elements who do not now have significant political power but who will have such power in the future'; moreover 'there are a number of loose political factions and interest groups and pan-Arab nationalism has considerable appeal, particularly to the younger urban elements'. The report also suggested that the British would probably intervene 'to maintain a regime favourable to their interests'. Already a post-Idris regime was being contemplated by the West, with speculation about what actions such a scenario would demand. President Kennedy approved NSC guidelines demanding that contact be maintained with groups in Libya 'likely to play a significant role in the event of the King's death'; that contingency plans be developed for action 'in the event of a violent upheaval in Libya'; and that a suitable response be made 'to a Libyan request for armed assistance under the American doctrine for the Middle East'. Such provisions and preparations, had they been known at the time, would have left no one in doubt that the 'imperialist' powers still had far-reaching designs on parts of the world that were deemed of strategic or economic importance.

The Israeli war against Egypt and other Arab states in 1967 was another serious blow against the security of the Libyan monarchy. Arab nationalists perceived that Idris had little commitment to the Arab cause; there were demonstrations in Tripoli and attacks on British and American property. After the sudden ending of the war the protests continued. The British embassy in Benghazi was attacked and the consulate next door was burned down. Americans were given refuge in the British Royal Inniskilling Fusiliers' camp, where they stayed until the authorities had regained control. But now the situation was unmanageable: in the words of the former Libyan Prime Minister Bakoush, 'The country was up for grabs in 1969.' There were already signs that Idris wanted to abdicate: he had gone so far as to offer a letter of abdication to the parliamentary heads in Greece, where he was – equipped with 400 suitcases – on holiday. Peter Wakefield, then counsellor and consul-general at the British embassy in Benghazi, knew about the abdication plans but suggested that the reports were vague ('We were wondering who the hell would take over').

There is still debate about the extent to which the British and Americans knew that a coup was imminent; some observers have even suggested that the Americans help Gaddafi into power. While this last possibility may be reckoned unlikely it is difficult to imagine that the Western powers knew nothing about Gaddafi's intentions. A detailed dossier on Gaddafi had been available to the British as early as 1966, and it is likely that they would have shared their information with the King and with the Americans. Colonel Shelhi, Denis Healey's candidate for coup leader, was supposed by Gaddafi to know about the coup plans and it is possible that he handed on his information; moreover it was also likely that there would be leaks from Gaddafi's own organisation. Colonel Aziz Shenib, number three in the

Libyan army, has said that senior officers knew about Gaddafi's plot but did not take it seriously. They thought it best to send the young officers on courses outside the country and to place them 'here and there' in the army on their return.

At Beaconsfield, Gaddafi had benefited from the British signal corps training that was to stand him in such good stead: the British instructors had been happy to tell him that the control of communications is a direct channel to power. As soon as he returned to Libya he used radio and a simple cryptosystem (of his own creation) to keep in touch with the various ('first' and 'second') cells, in a two-level hierarchy, that he had established. After the Arab defeat in June 1967 there was a fervent desire among Arab nationalists for revenge, for a reason to be able again to hold up their heads. A Radio Cairo 'Voice of the Arabs' broadcast was heard all over Libya:

Dear Arab brothers, raise your heads from the imperialist boots, for the era of Tyranny is past! Raise the heads that are bowed in Iraq, in Jordan, and on the frontiers of Palestine. Raise your head, my brother in North Africa. The sun of freedom is rising over Egypt and the whole of the Nile Valley will soon be flooded by its rays. Raise your heads to the skies.[54]

Such words caught the mood. The plans had been laid over many years. Gaddafi, with some helpful training by British technicians and officers, was the best-placed revolutionary leader to take advantage of the increased political instability in the country. The coup was imminent.

COUP

In early January 1969 Gaddafi sent a four-line 'first alert' to his fellow conspirators, urging them to check the control of soldiers, transport, arms and ammunition. Once they confirmed that this task had been done, Gaddafi set 12 March as the day for the coup against the monarchy. However, it transpired that the Egyptian singer Oum Kalthoum – able to improvise ballads about Palestine, Nasser and the Arab heroes – had scheduled a concert in Benghazi for that very night. Moreover the concert was intended as a benefit for al-Fatah, the Palestinian guerrilla group: it would be very bad form to interrupt such proceedings. And many of the regime's senior figures would be at the performance, making it much more difficult to arrest them without raising a general alarm. Therefore Gaddafi decided to call off the coup for that night, and he visited his parents in Sirte instead. On his way back to the Gar Yunis camp at midnight, he and his two friends had a car crash: a tyre burst, the car overturned and was badly damaged. When the wrecking crew arrived they found, not the coup plans buried under the mangled vehicle but a bottle of water which they mistook for gin. Gaddafi found himself upbraided for the sinful use of alcohol which he never touched.

He then decided that the new day for the coup would be 24 March, but alarm spread amongst the plotters when it seemed the army was being alerted. Armoured units were brought together in the central barracks at Bab al Aziziya, and trucks from some Tripoli units were concentrated in a camp near Benghazi. Other units had their ammunition recalled while military intelligence officers kept watch at barracks and ammunition stores. Gaddafi himself later observed: 'They were taking counteraction as though they knew about our plans. That was a bad time for us.' Some of the Free Officers contacted Gaddafi, urging him to come to Tripoli at once. He was still resolved to take power on the night of 24 March but on 19 March Idris was flown from Tripoli to Tobruk, near to the protection of the British forces. The plan was again cancelled, with June 5 the next proposed date.

However, Colonel Shelhi, with his brother planning a coup of his own, sensed that plans were afoot and managed to arrange for some of the Free Officers to be transferred to new posts and abroad for training. Idris, having spent part of the summer in Greece where he delivered his abdication message, then journeyed to Turkey for medical attention; from Turkey he announced on 4 August that he had made a firm resolution to step down. Gaddafi, knowing that the Shelhi brothers intended to act no later than 4 September, realised that he could delay no longer: he set 1 September as the date for the coup. A batch of young officers was due to be posted to Britain on 2 September, and the Free Officers knew that the postings would seriously erode their committed manpower. And there was a further reason why the Gaddafi coup had to take place on 1 September: the plot was about to be exposed inside the army, and if Gaddafi did not act he would probably lose his chance for ever. Power would fall into fresh military hands, and all his years of careful planning would have been in vain.

The date of 1 September 1969 was finalised in a series of meetings that took place over the previous week in the office of Signals Captain Gaddafi at the Gar Yunis camp, just outside Benghazi. The coup, named 'Operation Jerusalem', required that specified military and governmental installations in Benghazi and Tripoli be taken over simultaneously. The Free Officers were not ideally distributed, from Gaddafi's point of view, in Tripoli and Benghazi but he concluded nonetheless that the coup had to take place on the specified date.[55] In any case he remained aware that some of his officer colleagues were scheduled to depart for Britain for training in connection with Libya's purchase of the *Thunderbird* and *Rapier* missile systems. Gaddafi sent Lieutenant Omar al-Meheshi to Tripoli to tell the fellow conspirators that Operation Jerusalem would proceed as planned; Gaddafi himself was to handle the Benghazi end of the operation.

The plan had been refined over many months despite, or because of, the many delays and interruptions to the schedule. An uprising in Gar Yunis Barracks would be followed by an advance of a motorised column on Benghazi whose task was to seize the radio stations, the police station and the post office, as well as senior military and government officials. Members of the royal family and the clutch of advisors around the throne were a key priority; it was useful that Idris was still in Turkey. The Free Officers in Tripoli – Khweildi Hamidi, Abdul Munim al-Houni, Abu Bakr Yunis Jaber and Abdel Salem Jalloud – would capture the Crown Prince, with troops from the Tarhouna Barracks moving to the town centre in armoured cars to capture the key installations. A key task would be to incapacitate the Cyrenaica Defence Force (CYDEF), an important defence ring around the monarchy.

The coup went off smoothly. In less than two hours from the onset of operations (at 2.30 am) most of the key installations in Tripoli and Benghazi had been secured. The Crown Prince and other senior military and government men were captured with little difficulty. The Chief of Staff, Abdul Aziz Shelhi, frustrated in his own ambitions, was found by mid-morning after spending the night in a swimming pool. There were some gun battles but these were short-lived and in Tripoli the plan was ahead of schedule. Considering the scale of the social and political upheaval there was little bloodshed. In one of the most important battles of the night, the CYDEF unit in Gurnada suffered one fatality and fifteen wounded.

Gaddafi arrived at the Benghazi radio station at 6 am, martial music was playing on the radio from Tripoli, and Libya had effectively changed hands. At 6.30 am Gaddafi went on the air to deliver 'Communiqué One', partly ad-libbed and partly based on hurriedly scribbled notes (for security reasons this first broadcast of the new regime was anonymous):

> People of Libya. In response to your own will, fulfilling your most heartfelt wishes, answering your incessant demands for change and regeneration and your longing to strive towards these ends, listening to your incitement to rebel, your armed forces have undertaken the overthrow of the reactionary and corrupt regime, the stench of which has sickened and horrified us all. At a single blow your gallant army has

toppled these idols and has destroyed their images. By a single stroke it has lightened the long dark night in which the Turkish domination was followed first by Italian rule, then by this reactionary and decadent regime, which was no more than a hotbed of extortion, faction, treachery and treason.

Finally Gaddafi took steps to reassure Libya's foreign allies:

On this occasion I have pleasure in assuring all our foreign friends that they need have no fears either for their property or for their safety. They are under the protection of our armed forces. And I would add, moreover, that our enterprise is in no sense directed against any state whatever, nor against international agreements or recognised international law. This is purely an internal affair.

Now Libya was to be a free self-governing republic, The Libyan Arab Republic: 'She will advance on the road to freedom, the path of unity and social justice, guaranteeing equality to all her citizens and throwing wide in front of them the gate of honest employment, where injustice and exploitation are banished, where no-one will count himself master and servant, and where all will be free, brothers within a society in which, with God's help, prosperity and equality will be seen to rule us all.'[56]

It was not until 8 September, when Gaddafi was promoted to Colonel and made commander-in-chief of the armed forces, that it became clear who the main coup leader was. Until that time public statements had been made by Colonel Saad al-Din Bushwairib, a temporary figurehead leader of the new regime. It would be another four months before the other eleven members of the Revolutionary Command Council were announced.

AFTERMATH

On the afternoon of 1 September 1969 the Crown Prince broadcast a message renouncing his claim to the throne and urging co-operation with the new regime. The local commanders of the police force gradually accepted that the coup had been successful, though remnants of CYDEF continued to resist in the east of the country. Within three days the last CYDEF unit was forced to surrender, the CYDEF commander Brigadier Sanussi al-Fezzani having been arrested on the morning of the coup, and the

British base at Tobruk unwilling to give sanctuary to CYDEF troops. Idris, paradoxically enough in view of his earlier talk of abdication, seemed unwilling to accept the finality of the coup. From Bursa, the Turkish holiday resort where he was convalescing, he despatched Omar Shelhi to London to ask Britain to help reinstate the monarchy: in theory Idris could invoke the 1953 Anglo-Libyan Treaty, pledging Britain to protect the Libyan state from external aggression. However, the Labour government, under Harold Wilson, was not prepared to act. The Foreign Secretary Michael Stewart agreed to see the King's envoy but only out of courtesy: 'My motive in acceding to Idris's request to send an envoy to London was simply that it is not creditable in the long run to appear to cut off your old friends once they are down.' Peter Wakefield observed that 'It was too soon after Suez.'[57]

It had become clear to Britain and the United States that their hold on Libya was being eroded. On 30 November 1963 a secret memorandum for the US President noted that: 'We need Wheelus base for quick deployments to the Middle East and India, but a weak Libyan government is letting our title be eroded'; and on 8 June 1967, at the time of the Six Day War which stimulated widespread anti-US protests in Libya, the then US ambassador David Newsom commented on the 'numerous reports of possible demonstrations against embassy and Wheelus . . . Feeling obviously running high. Accordingly we are reducing embassy staff to minimum tomorrow and removing last of classified files to Wheelus. Marine guards will remain on duty for final destruct crypto gear if necessary.'[58] The United States had decided to end its Wheelus tenure in 1970, with the British also deciding to evacuate their forces by 1971. In the event Britain, pushed by Gaddafi, evacuated their bases by March 1970 and the Americans agreed a June deadline. A primary requirement for the Western powers was to find a way of co-operating with the new regime to protect their developing oil interests.

The more radical Arab states moved quickly to recognise the new Libyan government: Egypt, Iraq, Syria and Sudan offered immediate recognition, even before the character of the new regime had emerged. Once it was clear that Britain was abandoning its Sanussi clients after a long relationship, Shelhi flew on to the United States to enlist the support of the Nixon government, but he received a cool reception: Shelhi was not invited to official interviews in Washington or even offered the normal protocol for diplomatic emissaries of foreign governments. He left the United States having accomplished nothing.

Idris now recognised that the coup could not be reversed. In a *Daily Express* interview (5 September 1969) he disassociated himself from the

Shelhi mission and publicly acknowledged the coup as a *fait accompli*. He said he had not enjoyed being King 'very much' and had already tried to abdicate the previous month. Later he went into exile in Egypt to live out his retirement in the Cairo residential area of Dokki. He died on 25 May 1983, aged 93 years.

5 The Oil Factor

Libya, a little more than a generation ago, was a poverty-stricken country, a hapless pawn of Great Powers with strategic matters on their mind. In 1955 the author John Gunther, with monumental Western condescension, was able to depict Libya as 'a child learning to walk', with a future dependent on 'how well it is brought up'. Or perhaps Libya was only weak and enfeebled: 'If it is frail, give it a brace.'[1] And of course Libya was not viable, 'unless it manages to stay united and continues to receive foreign aid' – Western aid, that was, to avoid 'surrendering' the country 'to Communism'. Gunther and his ilk did not reckon with the seismic change that Muammar al-Gaddafi was to bring to Libyan politics; perhaps more importantly they did not reckon with the oil factor. In the decade after independence Libya was the poorest nation state in the world, its main exports being esparto grass, used in paper making, and the scrap metal salvaged from the detritus of the Second World War.[2] All this was to change.

LIBYAN ECONOMY

Today Libya has few natural resources apart from oil. Efforts to develop agriculture took place, historically, in settler enclaves often disrupted by national resistance to colonialism or by the ravages of the Second World War. The desert battles of the early 1940s were reported and celebrated by the Allies as though such massive conflicts occurred in a featureless terrain bereft of local people: in fact, the battles totally disrupted what little agricultural progress had been made in the region, bringing famine and desolation to tribes that had already been made to suffer greatly by the many foreign incursions throughout the twentieth century.

In earlier times the Libyan economy, though frequently shaken by foreign conquest, had a more varied aspect. Herodotus gave some indication of the extent of Libyan fruit growing and livestock production, and settled agriculture was known to thrive under the Roman occupation. There was extensive trade in raw materials and manufactured goods, mostly produced outside North Africa, though most of the indigenous peoples were pastoralists or farmers. The Italian occupation in the early-twentieth century, and the subsequent bouts of war and Western colonialism, forced the collapse of the ancient trans-Saharan trade routes through Fezzan and the coastal towns. The Italians tried to introduce state-sponsored agriculture but it operated in a hostile environment and was inevitably accompanied by the destruction of tribal oases and the disruption of traditional farming practices. When oil was discovered there were further dramatic consequences for agriculture. Labour was attracted to the lucrative oil sector of the economy and the traditional problems associated with poor soil, an inadequate water supply and uncertain weather were compounded by a manpower shortage. During the colonial period there had already been a drift of labour from the rural areas to the regions of urban development funded by the Italians; but what was a labour trickle soon escalated to a torrent when serious oil prospecting began in the mid-1950s. Farmers from northern Tripolitania, shepherds from all over Cyrenaica and the Sirtica, the oasis-tenders from Fezzan – all were attracted to the oil camps and the urban areas where rapid developments promised high wages, even for unskilled or semi-skilled labourers.[3] The oasis-gardens went untended, the farms were neglected, and the desert encroached on reclaimed land.

The Idris government, sensitive to these trends and developments, launched an ambitious Five-Year Economic and Social Development Plan in 1963 with £29,300,000 allocated to forestry and agriculture out of a total budget of nearly £170 million; only public works was scheduled to receive a greater level of investment. The government perceived that it was agriculture rather than oil that would offer employment to the majority of people and at the same time help to consolidate social and economic bonds. Schemes were outlined for land reclamation, agricultural settlement, afforestation, farm renovation, irrigation, and the development of animal resources. Already non-agricultural workers were earning twice as much as workers on the land and, despite the government's efforts, the trends continued. Before the discovery of oil, in the face of all the agricultural difficulties, Libya had functioned as a net exporter of agricultural produce, but in the 1960s it became a net importer: 'the slaughterhouses had to turn to Sudan for cattle, and American corn oil went on sale in a country where the Italians had planted 3 million olive-trees'.[4] By the mid-1960s agriculture was able to meet only 40 per cent of home demand, and over a ten-year period prices had risen by nearly 70 per cent.

The government implemented various schemes to try to improve the position of agriculture in the national economy. The National Agricultural Bank, founded in 1957, offered low-interest, long-term loans to farmers, as well as offering subsidies for farm machinery and buying agricultural surpluses; in 1966 the Bank stopped charging interest altogether. The

National Agricultural Settlement Authority (NASA) was established in 1963 with a substantial budget and the responsibility for land reclamation and farm renovation; scrubland in the Gebel Akhdar was to be cultivated, and oases developed afresh in Fezzan. It was found that a mineral oil mulch could be sprayed onto dunes to hold the sand down long enough for tree seedlings to take root and grow.

A Ministry of Industry was set up in 1961 to develop private and state industries and to run the existing nationalised enterprises. A principal aim was to reduce the dependence on foreign imports through investment in Libyan manufacture and a reduction in unemployment. However, the domestic market was small and there was a shortage of skilled labour, only partly addressed by the various government-funded training schemes. Moreover it was difficult to export to a sophisticated European market, and many Libyan enterprises were forced to rely on regular foreign imports. Neighbouring African countries, with relatively underdeveloped economies, were inclined to protect their own domestic enterprises, and there were in consequence few opportunities for Libyan exporters in this direction. Efforts to broaden the base of Libyan industrial activity were largely unsuccessful, and the national economy was increasingly forced to rely upon oil production. Before the time of the Gaddafi coup Occidental was investing in oil-linked developments, Esso was building a refinery and gas liquefaction complex at Marsa Brega (and contemplating a sulphur plant with an annual capacity of 45,000 tons), and other oil-based companies were negotiating for prospecting rights in the region. Development of the Libyan oil potential continued to be the most favoured option to foreign investors. A second Five-Year Plan, which was to have been launched in 1968, was postponed because of unfinished projects in the first; by 1969 efforts to diversify the Libyan economy were meeting with little success. The oil industry was increasingly the sole engine of economic development.

Libya has been dubbed a 'hydrocarbon society', one in which the government 'is financed to a very great extent by revenues from petroleum (and natural gas)'.[5] Thus hydrocarbon societies are ones in which their governments obtain more than 90 per cent of their revenues for oil, a circumstance which makes it unnecessary for such governments to tax their citizens' productive activities but one which makes such economies very vulnerable to variations in the price of oil in international markets (with the converse: that oil-producers can use oil as a political weapon to exert pressure on oil-dependent states – see below). Libya is one such hydrocarbon society: other obvious candidates are Kuwait, Saudi Arabia, Brunei, Oman and the United Arab Emirates.

The success of oil production in this context inevitably has a debilitating effect on other sectors of domestic industrial enterprise: there is little incentive, for citizens or government, to develop other productive areas if high revenues from oil seem assured. The danger is that concerted sanctions by foreign countries to prevent a hydrocarbon society from exporting oil – as happened with Iraq before, during and after the 1991 Gulf War – can reduce a state to chaos and destitution; but presumably similar sanctions against any export-dependent state, whatever the nature of the exports, could be relied upon to produce similar levels of penury. If the West in its wisdom – with or without the rubber stamp of the UN Security Council – ever decides to impose a total oil blockade on Libya such a move would clearly have a catastrophic effect on the national economy, and so on the lives of the Libyan people.

In the pre-coup years that followed independence there was first a low level of economic activity in Libya, which gradually increased through the 1960s as the oil resource came on line. Until the 1960s there was massive dependence on the Western powers for training, weaponry and direct financial aid. Libya's first petroleum law, enacted in the mid-1950s, gave a hint of the independent line that was already significant under Idris and which Gaddafi was to develop, with global consequences, in the post-coup years. The 1950s legislation enabled Libya to largely escape the dominance of the oil companies that they had managed to impose over other oil producers: by contrast, Libya was charting a route for the effective manipulation of many of the major and independent oil companies.

Throughout the 1960s Libya's dependence on foreign aid diminished as its oil revenues increased. Rents were still paid for the US base at Wheelus Field and for the British base at El Adem, but such foreign payments were increasingly unimportant to a state rapidly developing as a hydrocarbon society. The annual increase in oil revenues was dramatic, with the 1969 income from oil twenty times that of 1962 (see Figure 5.1). During this period oil consumers could purchase petroleum products in circumstances of oversupply where the oil companies operating in Libya saw it as profitable to sell crude oil at less than the official posted price. The Libyan government distributed funds to aid development in various areas of the social and commercial infrastructure, with emphasis given to private enterprise; but strains developed in the regulation of both public and private activity, and the government was unable to achieve balanced growth in important commercial sectors. Agriculture, as always, faced a host of intractable problems, whether the enterprises were state-run and state-funded or privately owned and enjoying massive state subsidies: it was not always

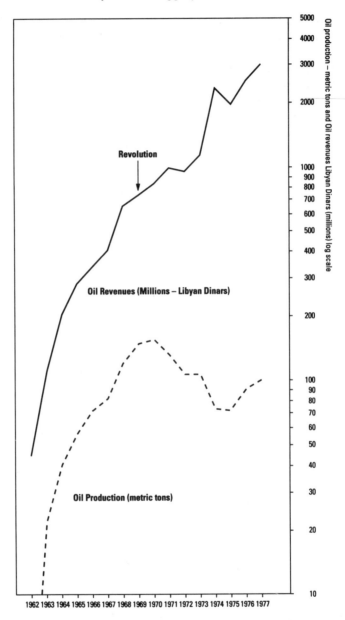

Figure 5.1   Libyan Oil Production and Oil Revenue, 1962–78

Source: J. A. Allan, *Libya: The Experience of Oil* (London: Croom Helm, 1981) p. 69.

obvious how oil money could be used to overcome the perennial Libyan problems associated with insufficient fertile land and limited water resources.

It has been suggested that Libya's painful resource-management lessons through the 1960s were largely ignored by the post-coup administrators.[6] At the same time Gaddafi managed – in part by building on a pre-coup oil policy – to secure a range of oil price increases both for Libya and for other suppliers; and Saudi Arabia also pushed for oil price rises in 1973 and 1974 in the uncertain circumstances of the October War and the changed commercial and political relationships that followed. In the 1970s, because of price rises, oil revenues continued to grow as fast as they did in the 1960s, despite the cuts in production in 1970. It was now evident that Libya was applying a sensible policy of oil conservation but an 'equivalent wisdom' was not to be found in the equally important management of water and land for agriculture, nor in the efforts to link labour and capital to aid industrial development.[7] However, by the end of the 1970s Colonel Gaddafi and Major Jalloud were urging the prudent and thorough research of development schemes before they were implemented, with implementation then to occur with the singular constraints of an Islamic socialism. In the immediate post-coup years the problematic impact of vast oil revenues on a country with a poor resource base soon became apparent.

The development of oil in Libya was helped by its geographical position: Libya is nearer to the key European and North American markets than are some of the most important oil producers, notably those of the Middle East. Thus Libya found itself on the 'market side' of a Suez Canal closed by the Middle East war of June 1967. The oil companies then worked to expand their Libyan activities rather than simply relying on the earlier policy of consolidation. It was cheaper by far to ship oil from the Mediterranean to Europe and North America than to travel from the Persian Gulf round the Cape of Good Hope. In these circumstance there was a rush to obtain Libyan oil: the companies invested in the handling facilities to make increased exports possible, resulting in a fifty per cent increase in oil production between 1967 and 1968, and a similar increase over the following year. Thus in the two years before the 1969 coup Libyan oil production had doubled. If the Suez Canal had stayed closed Libya could have become the world's third largest oil producer, behind only the United States and the Soviet Union.[8] However, it was also the case that Libya had an interest in limiting production, partly for conservation reasons and partly as a mechanism for controlling prices. Libya was already set upon a course of limiting production when it nationalised a range of foreign assets in 1973 and when the same policy was adopted by many of the other Arab oil-exporting nations. Thus in 1974 Libyan oil production was only half that of the peak production year of 1970, and production continued to fall throughout the decade.

Throughout the 1970s it became increasingly clear that oil production and export could be manipulated to serve a variety of commercial and political ends. Libya was one of the key nations in pioneering a new relationship between the oil-producing states and the oil companies (the 'majors' and the 'independents' – see below), a ground-breaking change that was to have global significance for the balance between oil-rich Third World countries and the oil-hungry developed economies of Europe and North America. Throughout the 1980s and 1990s the prodigious oil reserves of the Middle East would continue to have global significance: Libya has one of the twelve mega-fields (those with reserves over 1000 million barrels) in the area (see Table 5.1), and this circumstance will continue to be a central shaping factor in the Libyan economy in the decades ahead.

Libya is only one of the several hydrocarbon societies of the Middle East but its circumstances have given it a unique significance. Its geographical position, its colonial history, its strategic importance, the unique character

Table 5.1   The Twelve Mega-fields of the Middle East

Location	Year of Discovery
Iran	
Agha Jari	1938
Gach Saran	1928
Marun	1964
Bibi Hakimeh	1961
Ahwaz	1958
Iraq	
Kirkuk	1929
Rumeila	1953
Kuwait	
Burgan	1931
Saudi Arabia	
Ghawar	1948
Safaniya	1951
Abqaiq	1940
Libya	
Sarir	1961

of the Gaddafi revolution – all these factors have combined to make Libya a particularly influential state in modern history. It is useful to survey the unique features of Libya's oil experience in more detail.

BEGINNINGS

Oil in any substantial quantities was discovered in the Middle East for the first time at the beginning of the twentieth century, and by the start of the Second World War the region was producing only five per cent of the world's oil; by 1980 this had become forty per cent. One of the first boosts to the young industry came in 1911 when Winston Churchill, then First Lord of the Admiralty decided to change the fuel of the ships of the Royal Navy from coal to oil. From that time until the early 1970s the expanding oil industry was effectively controlled by initially seven, and later eight, major international oil corporations. The original 'seven sisters' were Standard Oil of New Jersey (later Esso/Exxon), Royal Dutch Shell (Shell), British Petroleum (BP), Gulf Oil (Gulf), Texas Oil (Texaco), Standard Oil of California (Socal/Chevron), and Mobil Oil (Mobil). In due course Compagnie Française des Pétroles (CFP) became sufficiently influential to be added to the list of the 'majors'. Until the late 1960s the majors controlled about three-quarters of the world oil industry and more than eighty per cent of oil production in the Middle East. During the 1950s and 1960s the grip of the majors on the global industry loosened slightly with the emergence of the 'independents' (around thirty relatively small companies, some private and some state-owned, able to offer better terms to the producer companies). However, the arrival of the independents scarcely affected what was in essence of global oil imperialism operated by a handful of large corporations backed by their home governments (American, British, Dutch and French). The majors controlled virtually every aspect of oil production, refining and marketing; and moreover often employed highly questionable methods to preserve their lucrative trade. The oil specialist Mana Saeed al-Otaiba gives one example of such practices: 'Iraq, for example, was threatened with dismemberment of the Mosul Province from its territory unless the government agreed to grant a concession to the then Turkish Petroleum Company.'[9] In subsequent years oil interests caused the collapse of the Iranian Mossadeq government in 1953, and the 1991 Gulf War in which a quarter of a million Arabs were killed.

Libya achieved its independence at a time when the corporate grip on the international oil industry seemed assured; but it was Libya, aided by certain other factions in the oil-producing countries, that managed to develop oil policies that shifted the power balance away from the majors and in the direction of the oil-producing (usually Third World) countries. This success, resented by the large oil corporations and their home governments, may yet be the undoing of the Libyan government.

The first hydrocarbon deposits in Libya were found in 1914 when, at a depth of 480 feet during the drilling of a water well at Sidi Mesri, near Tripoli, methane gas was detected. During the 1920s and 1930s the Italians drilled in many locations in their search for underground water supplies; some of these drillings revealed hydrocarbon deposits but they proved of little economic value. A comprehensive geological map of Italian North Africa was made by Professor Ardito Desio who decided in 1935 to watch for signs of oil and gas in the water wells then being drilled. In 1937 he detected both methane and drops of crude oil while supervising the drilling of a well near Tripoli; a year later he had collected enough crude oil to fill a bottle. In 1940, following Desio's recommendations, the Italians moved rigs into the Sirtica to hunt for oil, but the equipment was inadequate in the hostile terrain and the war soon brought to an end the tentative explorations.

After the war, with Italian settlers still in North Africa but with any Italian prospecting initiatives ruled out, two Standard Oil geologists conducted a survey of Libya. The movement towards independence delayed any further foreign prospecting activities, though the oil corporations still had an eye on the region. In 1953 a Minerals Law was enacted which resulted in prospecting permits being given to nine major international companies; teams of geologists were soon active in the desert. Now Italy, which had begun the search for oil in the pre-war years, was out of the picture.

In 1955 oil was struck at Edjeleh in the Algerian Sahara, suggesting for the first time that North Africa might have large oil deposits; and in the same year Libya passed its first Petroleum Law (Royal Decree no. 25). The Libyan legislation proved to be highly significant for the future of the international oil industry. Here, for the first time, an effort was made to prevent any single large cartel gaining a grip over a country's oil resources. The new law suggested that oil production in Libya would be managed very differently to how it was in, for example, Saudi Arabia where the ARAMCO Group had received a concession covering the entire territory. The Libyan law declared that all subsurface mineral resources were the property of the state, and that specific rules would govern the granting of concessions. Concession terms, rents and other conditions were specified; in particular, the government was to receive fifty per cent of the income from company operations after the deduction of operating costs.

At the time the Petroleum Law was passed (18 July 1955) no substantial oil deposits had been found in Libya. There was some evidence that oil would be found, but surface signs were absent: there were no indicative gas fires as in Iran, no sluggish asphalt ponds as in Iraq. When the first concessions were granted in November 1955 the outcome was still uncertain but for geographical and political reasons the possibility of finding oil in Libya was very attractive: the tankers would not have to pass through the Suez Canal, and Britain and the United States still had useful treaty agreements with the Idris government. In the 1950s Libya was the 'big play'.[10] Seismic operations began in 1956, though the first signs were not encouraging. Apart from the difficulties of the harsh desert terrain, a principal problem was the extent of the unexploded mines sown across the territory: an estimated four million mines had been laid by the British, Germans and Italians between El Alamein in Egypt and Mareth in Tunisia, and as late as 1957 it was reckoned that some three million mines remained untouched. Some of the minefields extended for a hundred miles, and clearing parties were necessary to establish 'safe lanes' for the geological teams.[11]

The drafting of the 1955 law had been supervised by Libyan Prime Minister Mustafa ben Halim relying on a team of experts that included N. Pachachi, later the secretary of OPEC (the Organisation of Petroleum Exporting Countries), a Dutch petroleum consultant, oil company representatives, and government officials. It is significant that the 'independent' oil companies had a hand in the drafting of the law: they were keen to penetrate the oil industry and many of their suggestions were congenial to the Libyan government advisors. A limit was put on the number of concessions and the total areas to be granted to any one interest; concessions had to be surrendered if they remained unused after a specified period of time; and the government reserved the right to offer relinquished concessions to fresh bidders (some relinquished areas yielded spectacular oil strikes). Such arrangements meant that there would be a rapid turnover of concessions and that the oil companies would be forced into competitive bidding. Within twelve months after the enactment of the Petroleum Law, fifty-one concessions were granted to seventeen companies. The Libyan oil rush had started.

The map of Libya had been divided into grids with the irregularly shaped concession areas superimposed on them. The majors made it clear that they wanted territory near to the Mediterranean to minimise the length of the pipelines. Ben Halim, himself an engineer and contractor, had anticipated this requirement, so the sizes of the concession plots nearest to the coastal ports were limited to 30,000 square kilometres each. The sites down in the Sahara, far from the coast and so bringing many transportation problems, were much larger. This meant that many oil companies were forced to compete on plots close to the Mediterranean, a circumstance that brought increased revenue to the Libyan government.

The rapid spread of concessions over the next three years resulted in 55 per cent of the land area of Libya being allocated by 1958 to fourteen international oil companies. Oil had already been found in Algeria, so Libyan territory close to the Algerian frontier was seen as an attractive possibility: thus Esso spent a year on geological surveys in Concession One, between the Ubari Sand Sea and the Algerian frontier, and in June 1957 the company decided on the first drillings. A subsequent Esso report spoke of terrain 'rough enough to test even camels', and the need for a 'special truck-trailer, using giant, oversized tires that could maneuver over both sand and hard rock'.[12] Even so, it was necessary to travel 980 miles to reach a well site that was only 480 miles from Tripoli on the map. The first two drillings in Concession One found nothing, but in early 1958 the Atshan Number Two hole began producing oil at the rate of 500 bpd (barrels of oil per day), though the remoteness of the well made it uneconomic. Further drillings in Concession One were unsuccessful.

Esso began drilling in Concession Six, which lay between the Gulf of Sirte and Gebel Zelten, in 1958 though by the end of the year no significant strikes had been made. By 1959 the companies had together spent a total of £42 million, with little to show for this considerable investment: the Atshan strike was far from the coast and the few other oil-producing wells were of little commercial significance. But in 1959 the picture was transformed.

On 18 April a test carried out at an exploration in Esso's Concession Six, near Bir Zelten, gave good results. This C1–6 well, Zelten Number One, was measured on 11 June as producing 17,500 bpd, an output that compared well with the highly productive Kuwaiti and Saudi Arabian oilfields; in August a further major discovery was confirmed with Zelten Number Two tested as producing 15,000 bpd. A rich oil-bearing stratum had been discovered at Zelten less than 6000 feet below the surface, so giving the clearest sign yet of the abundant oil supplies in the Sirtica. In this same *annus mirabilis* there were a number of other highly successful strikes in the region. Drillings by the Oasis Group (the Libyan operator for the consortium of Continental Oil, Amerada, Shell and Marathon), the first producer in Concession 59, soon had oil flowing at 7000 bpd in what was to become known as the Waha Field; and soon after, Oasis drillings in Concession 32 located the Dahra Field. At the same time the Esso Sirte/Libam/Grace group, drilling in Concession 17, found the Mabruk Field; and in September Amoseas (the group working for Texaco Overseas and California Asiatic), operating in Concession 47, achieved the first oil producer in the Beida

Field. On 1 November Mobil-Gelsenberg, a German–American consortium, started producing oil in Concession 12 from the Amal Field.[13] Major Sirtica oilfields had been discovered within a period of months, but in the following year there were few new discoveries. 1960 was a year of consolidation; it was also the year in which OPEC was born.

THE 1960s

In the immediate post-war years Venezuela had pioneered arrangements whereby the oil-producing countries and the international corporations shared the profits from oil: similar agreements were later introduced in the Middle East. Venezuela was also one of the principal instigators of the creation of OPEC (Organisation of Petroleum Exporting Countries) in 1960. One of the main aims of the Organisation was to maintain oil prices despite the growing abundance of resources being discovered and being exploited by the global oil corporations. It also wanted to improve the tax yields levied on the companies by the member states. In OPEC's early days the oil-exporting countries lacked a co-ordinated policy, and the Organisation achieved only limited success. It was at the time of the formation of OPEC that Libyan oil began to flow into the international market.

In 1950 the United States had passed mandatory import quotas to prevent cheap oil from ruining the US market, a move that a former chief economist at the Bureau of Mines reckoned had cost the American taxpayer around $5 billion. The producing countries were now being paid a royalty based on the 'posted price', but in circumstances of oversupply this figure was constantly being undercut: for example, three of the majors cut their prices to retain the Indian market against Russian competition; and in response to the world oil surplus that was starting to emerge around 1960 they cut the posted price in the Middle East by 18 cents a barrel, a decision that cost the oil-producing companies around $132 million. These were the sorts of circumstances that forced the oil producers to create OPEC, what the Venezuelan oil minister dubbed 'a very exclusive club'. The first reaction of the oil companies was to ignore the new Organisation, refusing to trade with 'this so-called OPEC'. The companies still sought to make their deals with the individual governments, at the same time urging President Kennedy to waive the antitrust laws so that OPEC could be fought in the name of 'national security'. The aim was for the global corporations to confront OPEC to safeguard their rich pickings. In fact throughout the 1960s OPEC was largely kept in line, though it was clearly pointing the way to a new framework of relationships between the companies and the oil-exporting states.

In 1961 Abd al-Karim Kassim, having overthrown the Iraqi monarchy in 1958, moved unilaterally to increase his revenues from Iraqi oil. He issued Law 80 designed to expropriate without compensation the whole of the Iraq Petroleum Company concession area apart from the 0.5 per cent of this plot that was already being worked. The company refused to accept the decision of the Iraqi government and in response drastically cut back production, so that for some years Iraq lost its position among the major Middle East producers. The companies had proved, as they had done with Mossadeq in Iran in 1953, that they would not be trifled with. The individual oil-producing states were in no position to act unilaterally to gain control over their own oil resources: OPEC was to show how, by acting in concert, they could achieve results.

In 1963 OPEC moved to propose a new royalty formula that was more favourable to the producing states: the idea was that the royalty received by the governments from the companies should be seen as a cost rather than as part of a tax on profits. The majors were soon working to see how the new formula could be turned to their advantage. Libya had become an OPEC member in 1962, and now the companies put pressure on the Idris government to amend the Petroleum Law so that the independents would have no statutory advantage over the majors; if Libya agreed, the companies would then give consideration to the OPEC formula. The majors couched their offer in such a way that Libya would gain increased revenues but the independents would be hard hit.[14] The independents were horrified to learn that the Idris government was considering adopting the proposals put by the majors.[15] Libya was accused of breaking contracts; of encouraging the companies to undertake exploration and then, when oil strikes were made, to change the concession agreements. The independents also pointed out how they had helped to locate vast oil reserves in Libya and how they had developed European outlets for Libyan oil. The Idris government hesitated and then announced that biddings would soon begin for fresh oil concessions all over the country, including in the highly desirable area of the Sirtica: seventeen items for determining preference were specified. Posted prices would be required as a basis for determining royalties; the government would be able to demand more than fifty per cent of the profits, with other 'benefits' to government to be defined; and the companies would have to indicate their willingness to establish refineries and petrochemical plant in Libya. The scheme aimed to swing the balance of power away from the international companies and towards the oil-producing state: Gaddafi would work to build on this initiative in the post-revolution years. Then the Libyan government agreed to accept the majors' proposal. Now all the companies, including the independents, would be taxed in the same way; the independents protested that they could not afford higher taxes, but the new Petroleum Law was passed in 1965. The next initiative, on behalf of one of the independents would be made by Dr Armand Hammer (see below).

When the new bidding round opened, offers were submitted by several dozen company groups from seven different countries; about a hundred top executives from many different companies attended the formal opening of six crates of bids. There were few contenders for the unpromising areas of Fezzan and Tripolitania, but in the areas where massive oil strikes had been made there were many offers. One of the leading industry journals, *Petroleum Intelligence Weekly*, suggested that likely winners would be European companies that gave the impression of not being 'under the thumb of the international majors'.[16] The new pricing arrangements were included in a Royal Decree that incorporated the OPEC formula, and the government indicated that it intended to impose a quick acceptance of the new terms. The independents resisted for a time but capitulated before the expiry of the deadline: the majors had forced the independents into line.

The new concessions were then announced and the Oil Minister Fuad Kabazi stated that the list showed 'where our interests lie and which way we intend to go'.[17] Awards were won by five West German companies, by Italy's ENI, and by the Spanish/French/American Hispanoil group. There were also fourteen newcomers to Libya, firms with no previous oil experience abroad. The prestigious *Oil and Gas Journal* described some of these organisations – Circle Oil, Lion Petroleum, Libya Texas, Bosco Middle East and others – as 'paper companies'.[18] Such criticisms led three of the members of Libya's Higher Petroleum Council, which had studied the offers, to submit their resignations; and at the same time the King's private secretary issued a statement denying as 'baseless rumours' certain charges that Idris himself had supported bids from two of the companies.

Libya was now a major oil exporting state: Fuad Kabazi had observed how the 'legend' of Libyan oil was set to 'outpace imagination'. Five major oil terminals were opened between October 1961 and early 1968. The new concessions awarded after the passing of the 1965 Petroleum Law required that 25 per cent of the concession holdings be handed back five years after being granted, so giving the government further control over exploration on its own territory. Two important concessions, 102 and 103, announced in February 1966, went to Hammer's Occidental of Libya Inc.; and within fifteen days seismic operations had begun. Within months major strikes were made, and by the end of April 1967 the seven Augila wells were together producing around 61,000 bpd.[19] In May 1967 another successful strike was made in Concession 103, a former Mobil holding. The scale of the new find, augmenting Occidental Augila production, encouraged the company to develop its own transportation system and to build a terminal. The Tripoli *Sunday Ghibli* called the new 'Idris Field' a 'humdinger'. Occidental took less than a year to build a 135-mile, 40-inch pipe (now Libya's biggest) from the Idris Field to Zuetina on the Gulf of Sirte; the new terminal was inaugurated by King Idris in April 1968. Another enormous Occidental well, just south of Idris, required the building of a supplementary spur-line to join the main Zuetina pipe. By contrast, many other companies drilled in Libya for years and found nothing.

The Libyan government was well aware, despite the changes introduced by the 1965 Petroleum Law, that its economy was effectively in the hands of the foreign oil companies. At the same time the companies were increasingly dependent upon the rapidly escalating Libyan output. In April 1968, partly to gain increased independence, the government formed the Libyan General Petroleum Corporation (LIPCO) to allow the government an area for independent initiatives in national oil development. LIPCO was expected to engage 'in all aspects of the oil industry, both within and outside Libya either on its own or in participation with others'. A main interest was in the setting and maintenance of price levels. On 5 April, as soon as the new organisation had been set up, it was announced that LIPCO would work with the French ERAP and SNPA groups on oil exploration and exploitation in Libya. The French were to fund most of the original effort, with the Libyan government satisfied with a 25 per cent share of profits rising later to fifty per cent. Some other foreign companies expressed dismay at what they saw as terms disproportionately favouring the Libyans.

In early 1967 the Libyan government began to take a number of pricing initiatives, which led to a wrangle with various companies (and which had the unusual effect of uniting the majors and the independents). Four companies had unilaterally decided to fix a lower price for Libyan crude oil on the grounds of its higher wax content. The Oil Ministry accused the companies of acting illegally, though at the same time admitting that there were gaps in the law (in particular, in the relevant terms of Regulation 6). The companies were worried that government involvement in price fixing would lead 'to complete control before long'.[20] There were fundamental issues at stake.

The June War of 1967, and the subsequent closing of the Suez Canal, exposed the vulnerability of the Libyan economy to external events. Libya, on the 'right side' of the Canal, may have been expected to benefit from the hostilities; but the two-month selective embargo on exports showed how vulnerable Libya was to political pressures. The Libyans, in concert with other Arab states, blocked shipments to the West as a sign of political solidarity with the Arabs: the Libyan economy was almost brought to a halt. The Libyans had no alternative marketing outlets, but the deprived western countries were able to turn to Venezuela, Iran and the United States to make up the oil shortfall. With the prudent ending of the embargo, Libya was able to benefit from the closing of the Suez Canal, but not before some salutary political truths had been learned.[21] The post-war situation had some lasting benefits for Libya: new trade patterns were consolidated to link western oil consumers with well situated oil producers. Nigeria and Libya were perceived as being closer than the Middle East suppliers to the European states, and when the Nigerian civil war disrupted oil production Libya was left in a favourable position.

By mid 1968 Libyan oil output amounted to about 85 million barrels a month; in July Libya overtook Kuwait which that month had produced 80 million barrels. By 1969 Libya was supplying a quarter of all European needs. Now Libya was the world's sixth oil producer and the fourth oil exporter; the expansion in the Libyan oil industry was such that Libya was expected to be the third producer by 1970. West Germany was the biggest buyer, with Britain, France and Italy also important customers. From being one of the poorest countries in the world in 1960, Libya had moved in less than a decade to being one of the economically most important.[22]

REVOLUTION AND AFTERMATH

The revolution in September 1969 did nothing to interrupt the supply of oil down the pipelines. The new regime went to great pains to notify the governments of Britain, France and the United States that all existing agreements would be honoured, a prudent move if the new government were to be secure in its early days. The oil companies made a few public protests at the overthrow of the congenial Idris monarchy, but company executives had little doubt that 'the normal processes leading to national-isation of the oil industry in Libya have been accelerated by the September Revolution'.[23] Such sentiments, expressed in an internal memorandum of the Oasis Group, were shared by many external observers: even under Idris, a broadly pliant collaborator with the companies, there had been developing trends for greater Libyan independence; few observers doubted that a Gaddafi government would put greater pressure behind such movements. It was recognised that the government organisation (LIPCO) could be used as a 'tool to exercise greater influence on actual operations'; and that 'Once the regime is stable it will launch a frontal attack on the oil industry. Driven by missionary zeal of secure absolute economic sovereignty, the regime will use every possible means of "persuasion" but it is unlikely that it will resort to outright expropriation.'[24] Doubtless, it was hoped, Gaddafi would be deterred from any 'extreme' measures by the fate of Mossadeq in Iran where oil production was interrupted for more than three years after the 1951 nationalisation. However, Gaddafi was in no doubt that Libya had been exploited by the companies during the 1960s, with Idris more interested in preserving accord than in gaining control over Libyan resources. The situation would have to change.

Gaddafi moved quickly to regain what he saw as national assets given away to foreigners. He began negotiations with the Soviet Union to sell Libyan oil in the East and, with the help of Prime Minister Dr Suleiman Maghrabi, who had once worked as an Esso lawyer, started to play the independents off against the majors. He told Hammer to cut Occidental ('Oxy') production from 680,000 to 500,000 barrels a day, so signalling that he intended to use control over production as a means of maintaining prices. Hammer tried to enlist Esso's support against Gaddafi but the contempt of the major for the Oxy independent was greater than Esso's desire to begin building a common front against the new Libyan government. Hammer had no choice but to agree the new Libyan terms, and the old company-run price structure was breached for ever. OPEC was given a shot in the arm and the oil companies were forced to agonise over their trading policies. It did not help that the large international banks, profiting from the massive investments of 'petrodollars', were content to encourage a soft line towards OPEC. In the period 1967 to mid 1972, before the new relationships had been pioneered by Libya, oil company profits rose a mere nine per cent a year; between the third quarter of 1972 and the second quarter of 1974 they increased about 150 per cent. Even the oil companies began to see that the impact of a reinvigorated OPEC, keen to stabilise prices, even at times of oil glut, had much to commend it.

Within weeks of the new regime being established the government announced that it would press for increased oil prices. A government committee was working out a strategy for confronting the oil companies while they too were considering their position. One option was for the companies to increase their production in their non-Libyan fields so that they would become less dependent on Libyan output; but some companies (particularly Oxy), with the vast bulk of the production focused on Libya, did not have this option. As negotiations began in early 1970 between the companies and the Libyan government, the Libyans announced that they were imposing cutbacks in various fields, an obvious political ploy; and at the same time, in circumstances that remain unclear, a Syrian bulldozer happened to disrupt the Trans-Arabian pipeline (Tapline), so putting further pressure on the companies. These circumstances combined to reduce oil output from Tapline and Libya by about a million barrels a day; and then the Libyan government tackled the companies one at a time. Occidental quickly capitulated, but Shell (with a sixth share in Oasis) refused to agree a settlement, whereupon Libya shut down the Shell terminal. Now there was growing dissent within the industry and confusion in the various national governments. British Petroleum agreed to raise the price of Libyan crude oil but insisted that the company was not influenced by the negotiating events in Tripoli. Other companies were prepared to settle, and the British Foreign Office suggested to Shell and BP that it would be helpful if they changed their position. Soon Libya had achieved a price – $2.53 a barrel – that was the highest outside the US: this, Libya announced, was no more than a rectification of past injustices. There was still scope for further price reforms.

The American companies were by now thoroughly alarmed at developments, and so turned to the legal advisor, John Jay McCloy, who had served them on and off in recent years. McCloy, now in his mid-seventies, had represented all seven of the sisters and also most of the largest independents. Soon after Occidental had reached agreement with the Libyan government, McCloy went with various heads of the oil companies to talk to the State Department in Washington. It was agreed that the situation was serious but no decision was reached. A fortnight later the heads of the British companies BP and Shell (Sir Eric Drake and Sir David Barran, respectively) lunched with the British Foreign Secretary, Sir Alec Douglas-Home, who was attending the United Nations in New York; here the gravity of the crisis was discussed.[25] Again, little came of this meeting: the Europeans were clearly not keen to put at risk their Libyan oil supplies.

The companies, divided on policy, now perceived that the demand for increased oil prices would soon spread beyond Libya. Soon Iraq, Algeria, Kuwait and Iran were all claiming an increased tax rate of fifty-five per cent; on 9 December 1970 OPEC members met in Caracas with fresh optimism but some disquiet. The OPEC official Abdul Amir Kubbah later observed that 'The Libyan success was an embarrassment to other OPEC countries. It rendered further silence almost impossible.'[26] The Caracas meeting noted the 'change of circumstances' in the world market situation, and quickly adopted a range of new proposals: the tax on profits would be at least 55 per cent; there would be higher posted prices; and all discounts for companies would be abolished. And even this was not the end: soon after the Caracas resolution had been agreed, Libya demanded an increase of fifty cents a barrel, with 'retroactive claims' and a further twenty-five cents for the 'reinvestment requirement'.[27] On 11 January 1971 the representatives of twenty-three oil companies met in the New York offices of John McCloy to see what action could be taken to stop the avalanche. One problem was that the companies would soon run up against the anti-trust laws if they tried to collaborate in an anti-OPEC strategy. In an attempt to overcome this difficulty McCloy had also invited Jim Atkins from the State Department and Dudley Chapman from the anti-trust division to visit his offices: he explained that he would inspect any agreement drawn up by the companies and then wait for a clearance from the Justice Department. McCloy clearly perceived the need for the companies to organise a united front against OPEC: 'The idea that you can't confront a highly organised cartel of sovereign states is rather silly.'[28] It soon became apparent that the anti-trust provisions were an inconvenience that could be abandoned in time of crisis.

The companies then organised their own cartel and drafted the secret *Libyan Producers' Agreement* specifying that none of the members would make any agreement with the Libyan government without the agreement of the other members, and that if the Libyans ordered a cutback then all the members would share the cutback in specified proportions. The US government had agreed an effective waiving of the anti-trust laws (at the time the head of the US anti-trust division, Richard McLaren, was waging an anti-trust battle against ITT). McCloy also invited the government to become involved, to suggest to the oil producing states that they should 'moderate their demands'. Jack Irwin subsequently flew to the Middle East bearing a message from President Richard Nixon. The situation quickly escalated, a host of other players were drawn onto the stage, and fresh meetings took place in Iran, Libya and elsewhere.[29] Two key agreements in Teheran and Tripoli, between the oil companies and the producers, were intended to last for five years, until 1976; they survived for two. The Libyans had pressed harder than the Iranians, and so secured better terms; in consequence the Shah was furious and the situation was again unstable.

In June 1973 an OPEC meeting in Geneva insisted in a further oil price rise because of the fresh devaluation of the dollar. The militant states – Algeria, Libya and Iraq – were now urging a unilateral control of price: prices were increased by twelve per cent, and Sheikh Yamani of Saudi Arabia commented that this would be the last time that prices were negotiated with the companies. In September 1973 OPEC, in a strong bargaining position, invited the oil companies to a meeting in Vienna on 8 October to consider 'substantial increases' in the price of oil. And at the same time the Libyans contemplated further militant steps, the expropriation of particular concessions. In June 1973 Gaddafi nationalised the concession granted to Bunker Hunt, declaring that the United States deserved 'a good hard slap on its cool and insolent face'.[30] In September, celebrating the fourth anniversary of the revolution, he declared that he would nationalise 51 per cent of all the oil companies operating in Libya (including the subsidiaries of Esso, Mobil, Texaco, Socal and Shell); two days later the Libyans announced that Libyan oil would now cost $6 a barrel, almost twice the price of oil from the Gulf. Gaddafi also threatened to cut off all exports to the United States unless the US stopped supporting Israel, and the foreign ministers of the Arab oil exporting countries (OAPEC) met to consider using oil as a political weapon against the United States. President Nixon then gave a televised warning to Libya reminding them of Mossadeq's fate twenty years before, but no-one took the threat seriously. Ian Seymour in the New York Times was able to ask: 'could it really be that the President of the US had not yet grasped the predominant fact of life in the energy picture over the coming decade, that the problem is not whether oil will find markets, but whether markets will find oil'.[31]

It now seemed clear that 'OPEC's opportunity was created in Libya'.[32] The West had watched the growing confidence of OPEC with alarm through the 1960s, but the 1969 Libyan revolution massively increased the stakes in ways that were never anticipated. Increasingly the management of prices was taken over by the oil-producing states: the West seemed relatively powerless to act here, as it was similarly unable to resist the Libyan nationalisations of 1973. The oil companies could not 'black' nationalised oil as they had managed to do in Iran two decades earlier; but it would be a mistake to believe that the story is complete. In 1991 and its aftermath Iraq learned the consequences of defying Western oil interests, and there remains a deep resentment in the West about what Libya has done to invigorate OPEC and to press its own interests in the international oil market. It is a central theme of the present book that in a 'new world order' framed by the United States, independently-minded countries such as Libya are far from secure (see Chapters One and Eight).

THE HAMMER IMPACT

A principal impact of Dr Armand Hammer was to help Libyan efforts to erode the powers of the majors to exercise unilateral control over national oil resources. As head of Occidental ('Oxy'), Hammer had a great interest in the success of a leading independent; Oxy had been immensely fortunate in its granted concessions, and Hammer was just the man to turn this to advantage. Hammer has been depicted as, in commercial terms, one of Gaddafi's 'greatest friends' in the United States.[33] However, the aid that Hammer and Oxy gave to the new Libyan regime must be reckoned as incidental to Hammer's commercial ambitions: he was given few favours by a Libya intent on regaining control of its own national resources.

Armand Hammer was born on 21 May 1898 in New York City. His paternal grandfather was a Russian émigré who had gained and then lost a fortune in the Russian shipbuilding industry; his father, a gynaecologist and general practitioner, began a drugstore business in New York. In 1921 Armand graduated in medicine with top honours from Columbia University; perhaps he was the first medical student 'ever to earn a million dollars while still in school'.[34] During the civil war in the Soviet Union, Hammer bought a surplus US Army field hospital and transported it to Moscow. Soon he was offering surplus American wheat in exchange for caviar and furs; he also agreed to build a pencil factory for Lenin, and in the 1920s he was supplying Russian oil to the Germans. Such initiatives were early demonstrations of how he could make imaginative deals across political divides. Lenin welcomed Hammer's capitalist contribution in the Soviet Union's ravaged state: as late as the 1960s Hammer made a grand gesture in the Soviet Union by offering a Goya painting to the Hermitage Museum in Leningrad (now, again, St Petersburg). Lenin offered Hammer the concession of an asbestos mine, and Hammer went on to lubricate many deals between the new Soviet government and such capitalist firms as Ford, US Rubber, Allis-Chalmers and Underwood Typewriter. In 1930 Hammer left his prestigious Brown House in Moscow, taking with him a vast collection of Russian art treasures and Soviet promissory notes that were later honoured in full by the commissars. After investing in whiskey distilling, cattle and broadcasting, he moved to California in 1957 with thoughts of retirement. A friend then suggested that he finance two oil wells being drilled by the Occidental Petroleum Company in Bakersfield, California. He then bought up the stock, financed the drilling, and took a stock option: when two of the wells brought up oil, Hammer became president and chairman of the company. In such a fashion he began the long journey to prodigious oil successes and an impact on the global oil industry that would in time put powerful political weapons in the hands of a revolutionary Arab leader in North Africa.

The impact of Armand Hammer on Libya and the global oil industry began with the Libyan concession awards of 1966, well described by Wilbur Eveland, a former CIA officer and oil-company consultant.[35] Eveland himself won a contract in Libya for the Vinnell Corporation (not an oil company), and he knew well the 'oil company greed, internecine rivalries, subordination of corruption' that obtained in Libya at that time. It is likely that Hammer himself was forced to go through the same corrupt mill in putting forward concession bids that stood any chance of success. We do know that he wrapped his bid in an appeal to Libyan chauvinism – literally: he tied up his bid in red, green and black ribbon, thus flaunting Libya's national colours. In addition he made a number of offers calculated to appeal to the government of the day, including to invest five per cent of profits in a scheme to irrigate the desert around the Kufra oasis, the birthplace of King Idris and at one time a desert stronghold of Omar al-Mukhtar. Hammer also paid close attention to the fourteen preferential factors stipulated by Libya's Petroleum Council for the bidding companies. Oxy was quick to incorporate a number of the crucial factors in the bid: for example, the oil minister would be notified of all contracts worth more than half a million dollars; local funds would be kept in local banks; and Oxy would build refineries, petrochemical plants and other installations in Libya that would help the country escape from the stifling Western controls.[36] And Hammer also promised that if he secured an attractive concession he would try to use Libyan natural gas, being simply burned off by the other oil companies, to provide a fertiliser facility.[37] He also decided to pay the necessary 'commission fees' – to the Libyan Minister of Labour, Taher Ogbi, and to the influential Minister at Court, Omar Shelhi. Both were to receive a royalty of three per cent of the sales price of every barrel of oil that Oxy exported from Libya, with the revenues to be paid to a Swiss bank. A certain Pegulu de Rovin later tried to sue Occidental in a Libyan court, claiming that he was entitled to a fee for introducing Ogbi to Occidental (he admitted already receiving $100,000), but the case was dismissed.[38] When all these factors are considered – chauvinistic ribbons, promises to build copious 'downstream' installations, the eagerness to out-manoeuvre the majors, the copious bribes – it is hardly surprising that Hammer managed to secure his attractive concessions, some on land sacrificed by the majors. What could *not* have been predicted was how successful Oxy would become on the Libyan plots: for a time Occidental was the biggest producer in Libya, a circumstance that was not happily viewed by the majors. Thus the American Ambassador, David Newsome, later remarked: 'I think it is safe to say that the advent of Occidental on the scene was not warmly welcomed by all of the other companies.'[39]

Hammer had carefully put all the pieces in place, cannily appealing to Libyan nationalism and diligently cultivating influential men who surrounded the King. An effort was made to gain the sympathy of the Libyan Oil Minister, Fuad Kabazi, who finished up arguing Oxy's case before the

monarch, at times communicating in secret code with Occidental staff.[40] All
that Hammer needed now was good luck, and this was not long in coming.
One of the Oxy wells on land relinquished by Mobil yielded 70,000 bpd on
test, this strike alone converting Occidental overnight into a major international oil company. By the time of the 1967 war Hammer's small firm of
1957 had expanded to a net worth of $300 million with net earnings of
around $22.7 million. Soon after the 1969 revolution Occidental had sales
of more than $2 billion with earnings estimated at around $175 million.[41]
Hammer soon realised that the successful Libyan strategy could be used
elsewhere: when Peru nationalised Exxon's oil fields, Hammer offered to
run them on a service contract, as the Soviet Union was doing for the
expropriated oil fields in Iraq and elsewhere. Occidental was also successful in finding oil in Nigeria, Venezuela, Ghana and the North Sea, so
reducing the scale of its former dependence on Libyan resources.

It is also significant that Hammer thought it prudent to cultivate the
Americans, who were already deeply resentful of Libya's impact on the
global oil industry. So he made a donation of more than $100,000 to
Nixon's 1972 presidential campaign: Hammer himself handed over $46,000
in cash and fed another $54,000 through the office of the former governor
of Montana, Tim Babcock, then a Washington-based Oxy executive.[42] At
the same time Hammer continued to develop the Libyan business: Exxon
had changed place twice with Oasis as lead exporter of oil from Libya by
1969, and in 1970 Oxy was challenging Exxon for second place, after only
two years of oil production. By means of a complex raft of tactics, Hammer
had carved out a lucrative trade in a Libya run as a traditional monarchy: in
the 1970s he would have to contend with Libyan leaders with a different
approach to politics and world trade.[43] However, the new regime had clearly
benefited from some of the policies pioneered under Idris: 'Libya was
always different, always a special case. Its approach to the development and
production of its oil resources was always revolutionary, even before political revolution overtook the country and threw Colonel Muammar el-Qaddafi
onto the centre of the world stage.'[44]

One of the first consequences of the 1969 revolution was the renaming
of the main Occidental field in Libya: formerly Idris it now became Intisar,
as it remains today. Idris himself had pressed for increased profits for oil
but apart from such haggling he never represented a real threat to the
companies. By contrast, Gaddafi 'was willing to nationalise the oil fields
and boot the companies out of the country. That, you might say, is a
difference of style.'[45] Hammer was well aware than in the early days he was
entirely dependent upon Libyan resources, and so had to accede to Gaddafi's
terms without argument. This in turn weakened the bargaining power of the

other companies, majors and independents alike: Gaddafi was astute enough to recognise Hammer as the Trojan Horse in the camp of the oil companies. Thus when the Libyan government ordered Hammer to reduce oil production as a mechanism for price control there were consequences for the whole of the industry.

Hammer found the Libyans polite but tough negotiators; and sometimes there was a hint of threat. At the start of one testing series of negotiations he admitted to being 'momentarily thrown' by the warmth of his welcome by the Libyans, but the atmosphere changed somewhat when the fiery Prime Minister, Abdel Salem Ahmed Jalloud, purposefully placed a revolver on the table between them (Hammer: 'He smiled. I smiled. Then I tried to compose myself. I had conducted business negotiations in some strange circumstances before, but never over the dully gleaming barrel of a .45!'). The upshot was a compromise price increase of thirty cents per barrel. The other companies were outraged, a Shell man reported as declaring, 'From that point on, it was either a retreat or a rout.' The companies were soon forced to follow Oxy's lead, despite the hasty meetings in New York and elsewhere and despite the nominal backing the companies obtained from their respective governments. The oil producing countries, bolstered by the Libyan success, quickly followed suit – to the predictable horror of the oil corporations: Iran, Iraq, Algeria and Kuwait all demanded a 55 per cent increase in their tax rates, and got it. The subsequent talks between the company heads, organised by John McCloy in New York, came to nothing. The Libyans refused to negotiate with the companies *en bloc* and, unexpectedly, the more moderate Iranians adopted the same position. The companies had again been out-manoeuvred: the collective strategy was abandoned, despite the willingness of the US government to waive the anti-trust laws, and the producer countries were again able to negotiate with the companies on an individual basis. The patterns and compromises agreed by Occidental in Libya were now helping to shape the global industry.

The possibility that Gaddafi would move to nationalise company operations in Libya further concentrated corporate minds. Hammer himself announced his intention to reduce Oxy's Libyan operation considerably, and he even contemplated taking the Libyan government to international arbitration in Paris to recover expropriated assets. Hammer then decided to hold monies nominally due to Libya, as a means of putting pressure on Gaddafi; Hammer was advised to wear a bulletproof vest, 'and our security people got a price for an armor-plated car for me'.[46] In due course a deal was done that satisfied both sides. Then followed the 1973 expropriations. Hammer considered himself lucky to be offered $136 million in cash for fifty-one per cent of his Libyan operations; other companies were paid with their 'own' oil, and some were nationalised with no element of compensation at all. The companies pressed ahead with plans to become totally independent of Libya, a plan that eventually led to a reduction in OPEC's share of the world oil business.

Hammer himself perceived that it was 'just too dangerous for the corporation's health that more than 90 per cent of our oil should come from a country which was so constantly at odds with the rest of the world, *especially America*' (my italics). Massive investment was put into exploration around the world, and there were many successes. By the time that President Reagan broke off diplomatic relations with Libya in 1981, Occidental had considerably reduced its dependence on Libyan oil; and when, under Reagan's instruction, American nationals were withdrawn from Libya Oxy's operations there were run by employees from other countries, mainly Britain. In June 1985 the Austrian state oil company, OMV AG, bought twenty-five per cent of Occidental's remaining interests in Libya. When Reagan ordered a ban on all US trade with Libya in January 1986 Oxy's Libyan operations represented less than one per cent of the company's worldwide trade. The explorations elsewhere in the world had come up trumps, one in particular being both timely and immensely lucrative: in January 1973, in the year of the Libyan nationalisations, the *Ocean Victory* rig penetrated the Piper Field, one of the biggest strikes in the North Sea. Even if Gaddafi were to close Occidental down completely, the company could still continue to supply customers (Hammer: 'Piper made Occidental safe from Qaddafi'). By January 1987 Hammer was engaged in further operations that the Libyans can scarcely have welcomed: he had begun drilling for oil in Israel ('we have nearly half the State of Israel under license'). The game had changed since the heady Libyan days of the early 1970s.

By 1985 OPEC's share in the global oil trade had fallen by more than sixty per cent. The companies, having learned the lessons, had invested massively in the worldwide hunt for oil. In 1973 the Yom Kippur war was accompanied by a devastating oil embargo by seven oil-exporting countries against the United States, Japan and a number of European states. The developed oil-consuming nations would not be put at such a disadvantage again. The corollary, for our purposes, was that the strength of Libya's bargaining position was progressively diminished throughout the 1980s. Today Libya – though continuing, sanctions apart, to rely on oil resources – is relatively weaker at the negotiating table; and so more cautious and more vulnerable.

POLITICAL WEAPON

The scale of the international oil industry is unique and unrivalled: no one can doubt that oil is vitally important to every country of the world, a circumstance that puts immense potential power in the hands of the oil-producing countries. But the 'hydrocarbon societies' are as dependent on the smooth operation of the international oil trade as are the oil-consuming nations. If a country relies upon the sale of its oil resources then, if sales are blocked, the country is thrown into chaos and destitution – as Iraq has discovered to its bitter cost in 1991/92. Oil can be used as a potent political weapon, but not always in ways that necessarily benefit the owners of oil reserves.

On 14 November 1974 Henry Kissinger chose to identify oil as 'the world's most strategic commodity'.[47] Deprive a country of oil and it can no longer function in the modern world. America in particular, with its prodigious and disproportionate energy consumption, relies upon oil to sustain its standard of living, its military posture, and its self-appointed global role as the world's sole superpower. If any country, for whatever reason, threatens an international framework that guarantees US access to oil then it had better look to its own security. The bitter US hostility to Libya over the years has nothing to do with terrorism (the US has always supported its own approved terrorists); the hostility stems from the simple fact that Libya was able to rock the international oil industry and, in so doing, embarrass and inconvenience the global corporations.

Libya has long known that oil can be used as a political weapon. Gaddafi himself has used his control over Libyan oil production to support the advancement of Third World countries on the global scene, to develop his own military posture by buying weapons, by funding research into the atomic bomb, and by supporting selected causes in Africa and elsewhere (see Chapter Seven). In the 1970s Libya's role as a militant focus for OPEC members began to decline. By the mid-1970s the high price of oil had temporarily diminished demand, massive tankers rendered Libya's geographical position less important, and there was the growing promise of oil strikes in parts of the world that were more sympathetic to the companies. The Libyans talked of what the 'real' price of their oil should be but in fact were less ambitious in their practical decisions.[48] Gaddafi was forced in 1975 to lift the embargo on oil sales to the United States and to the Caribbean refineries that served the US; at that time Libya was experiencing its first significant financial crisis since the revolution. This led to a political crisis and one of the key members of the Libyan government, Omar al-Meheshi, attempted a coup against Gaddafi.

The Libyans, surprisingly allied to the Shah of Iran, continued to represent the militant OPEC wing, though with diminishing success as new sources of oil were found in Nigeria, the North Sea and elsewhere. Through the 1980s Libya continued to benefit from its oil resources, though the causes that Libya continued to fund caused it be branded – following a range of US initiatives – a 'pariah' nation. Nor did the collapse of the Warsaw Pact and the Soviet Union help the strategic security of Libya. In the late 1980s and 1990s the United States, able to cajole a supine UN Security Council, was able for the first time to make political calculations about Libya without having to consider the possible responses of a potentially hostile Soviet Union. The revolutionary regime in Libya was more insecure than it had ever been, and there were few ways that oil could be used as a political weapon in the changed circumstances.

The United States, its whole *modus operandi* based on oil, never doubted the importance of oil in the global scheme of things. Thus it was no doubt welcome to George Bush to learn that Saudi Arabia's monarchy was happy to manipulate oil production and pricing to support the efforts of a Republican administration in the 1992 elections.[49] Bush was privately assured that the Saudis would pump whatever extra oil was necessary to keep prices down during the critical election year, and there was even an expressed willingness (according to White House sources) to make up the anticipated shortfall in ex-Soviet oil exports. One suggestion is that the 1991 Gulf War, following a rapid rise in oil prices in August and September 1990, helped tip the United States into recession. The Saudi decision to increase pumping may be seen as a prudent effort to help the US through its current economic difficulties. It may also be seen as a reward for a president who manipulated the United Nations and sent 600,000 troops to defeat the (real or imagined) threat from Iraq. In any event the political importance of oil management, whatever the political goal, is not in doubt.

6 Libyan Revolution

Muammar al-Gaddafi has always distinguished between a revolution and a *coup d'état*: the distinction is unremarkable but worth noting. A *coup* is usually nothing more than a transfer of power from one dictatorial group to another, though in some cases this may be accompanied by a change of regime that has wider implications. A revolution, by contrast, involves not only a transfer of power but also a total reshaping of society according to a new philosophy. In this view a revolution represents the end of one system of values and assumptions, a fresh beginning in the history of a nation.[1] There can be no doubt that in this sense Gaddafi made a revolution.

The Libyan revolution was named '*Al-fatih*', a Koranic term which literally means 'opener' or 'conqueror' and which carries also layers of meaning relating to military, social and spiritual achievement. To Gaddafi and his fellow officers this symbolised the conquering of backwardness, ignorance, poverty and national impotence: a rebirth, a new dawn of a day that would never end, encapsulated in the potent slogan, '*al-fatih abadan*' (*al-fatih* for ever). The Libyan revolution was no mere taking of power by ambitious soldiers: it was at once a decisive act that encapsulated a practical and spiritual vision. All the successes, mistakes and failures of the Gaddafi regime should be considered in the context of this original faith.

FRAMEWORK

The Libyan revolution has involved a continuous period of change lasting more than two decades. In a political course that is unique for the region the Libyan leadership has sought to dissolve all pre-existing forms of political and administrative activity, and to replace them with organisations conforming to a fresh approach. This transformation has involved the development of attitudes to Islam, political participation and cultural values: these attitudes have in turn yielded consequences for such social elements as political decision-making, religious observance, the treatment of women, and the conduct of practical economics. The Gaddafi assumption of power was to represent a cultural revolution.

The first phase of the Libyan revolution (a phase dubbed 'Nasserist'[2]) involved the transformation of the country from a pre-capitalist (feudal)

191

society to a state-controlled system involving a predominant capitalist component. The second stage was the period of the socialist *jamahiriya* or 'Era of the Masses' in which the revolution sought to enshrine the concept of a collective political and economic system. The revolutionary leadership, particularly Gaddafi, originally believed that the overthrow of the monarchy would be quickly followed by the effective merging of Libya and Egypt. To this end a Revolutionary Command Council (RCC), derived from the Central Committee of the Free Officer movement, was created as a provisional authority that would last until the unification of the two states had been achieved. It is interesting to reflect that an important theme in the early revolutionary philosophy was not the idea of an independent Libya but of the merging of two nations in the interest of a broad pan-Arabism. Thus in December 1969 the officers issued 'The Provisional Constitutional Proclamation', defining a range of temporary powers that would be exercised during the period of transition. The Egyptian revolution served as a model of social and political change for the new Libya: the RCC introduced a range of measures that were intended to aid the transition to a larger Arab state that would be shaped essentially by the Egyptian revolutionary experience, and when the union failed to materialise the measures stayed in place.

The RCC rapidly introduced a number of radical changes that were to transform the character of Libyan society. The treaties guaranteeing the security of British and American military facilities were annulled, the inalienable rights of the Italian settlers to hold property were removed, and many of the institutions of traditional Libyan society were abolished. The monarchy was destroyed and with it the multifaceted power structure that had depended upon birth and royal assent: by 1971 the new regime had eradicated the power of the pre-capitalist institutions. Even the power and influence of the Sanussi Order was massively curtailed: the *zawiyas* were closed down and the Sanussi leadership, no longer in a congenial symbiosis with the traditional monarchy, was effectively emasculated. A programme of agrarian reform was introduced to abolish the power of the tribal sheikhs and landowners. Behind all these changes lay a dramatic expansion of state control.

The new regime also moved quickly to abolish political parties, trade unions and professional groups and associations (such as the lawyers' union). Within months of the overthrow of the monarchy the press was heavily censored and citizens of the new state were advised not to express public views hostile to the military leadership. When, in December 1969, a planned coup was uncovered the government issued the 'Decision on the Protection of the Revolution', making it a criminal offence to proselytise

against the state, to arouse 'class hatred', to spread falsehoods, or to participate in strikes and demonstrations.[3] The RCC began a series of seminars to
spread its philosophy, and on 11 June 1971 inaugurated the Libyan Arab
Socialist Union (ASU), the organ of 'the working forces of the revolution'
(defined as peasants, labourers, soldiers, intellectuals and national capitalists). The ASU has served as an important focus for national unity.

Within the ASU the RCC served as the supreme authority, responsible
for all policy and for the supervision of the lower levels of the hierarchy. A
biennial General Conference was stipulated but, having no legislative functions, it was confined to the ratification of RCC decisions. At the local level
the *muhafadha*, able to elect the majority of conference delegates, supervised the activities of the ASU sub-district units (the workplace-based
mahalat and the geographically organised *mudiriya*). The RCC initially
found it prudent to enlist the support of local leaders with established
followings, though such leaders too were generally prepared to make pragmatic adjustments to the new Libyan leadership.

Economic policy encouraged collaboration between the state and the
established private sector, though within the framework of a redefined
balance of power. The interests of the state were no longer synonymous
with the interests of the foreign companies and the landowning class. In the
early years of the revolution the RCC opted for state intervention as the
obvious means of securing a transition from the old patterns of colonial (or
neo-colonial) exploitation to a system of state capitalism operated in what
the RCC perceived to be the interests of the country. Again this process was
based on the Egyptian model; however, the next phase of the Libyan
revolution was to represent a significant departure from anything that Nasser
had attempted.

The need for a new social and political direction was signalled by
increasing discontent with how the local administrations were working.
Gaddafi perceived that the revolution was failing because 'pecuniary lust is
rooted in the hearts of officials':[4] a new way had to be found. Gaddafi
decided to initiate what was in effect a cultural revolution, inaugurated on
15 April 1973. His supporters began the task of reshaping the framework of
district and municipal administration. Peoples' committees, now being ac-
countable through elections, were established to take over the district and
municipal services. A wider section of the population was able to participate in political activity but this in turn led to tensions between the influential commercial sector and factions that were ready to applaud the change
of direction. This produced further state intervention and, in consequence,
a serious outflow of funds from the economy; and at the same time state
interference in university elections led in January 1976 to clashes on the

campus of Benghazi University. In April 1976 the Libyan army was involved in fighting in Guarian, Misrata and Yefren.[5] A power struggle within the RCC led to the collapse of a faction opposed to Gaddafi: he emerged with firm control of the RCC and the security services, now able to pursue the new course with little opposition.

The new sociopolitical model was outlined in 1973 at a symposium in Paris, and further developed in the three published instalments of the Green Book. The new conception of social organisation, designated the 'Third Universal Theory' – in contrast to the earlier bureaucratic and élitist route – emphasised the importance of the masses in decision-making and administration. This mode resembled the *umma* social philosophy urged by the Prophet Mohammed in the seventh century, but it remained to be seen whether a Libyan *umma* (community of the faithful) could serve as a realistic model in the modern world. Gaddafi himself saw the *umma* as 'natural socialism' based on God-given natural laws but corrupted in the modern world by the emergence of class society. In Part 1 of the Green Book Gaddafi states:

> Natural law has led to natural socialism based on the equality of the economic factors of production, and has almost brought about among individuals consumption equal to nature's production. But the exploitation of man by man and the possession by some individuals of more of the general wealth than they need is a manifest departure from natural law and the beginning of distortion and corruption in the life of the human community. It is the beginning of the emergence of the society of exploitation.[6]

The similarity in this to Marxist orthodoxy is obvious, despite such clear differences as the supposed divine source of the moral law and the contribution to be made by the early Koranic writings. To Gaddafi, socialism is concerned with the 'happiness of man, which can only be realised through material and spiritual freedom', which can only be achieved if your needs are 'neither owned by somebody else, nor subject to plunder by any part of society'.[7] Gaddafi has drawn on his Bedouin roots to derive a version of socialism that is relevant to the requirements of a modern Arab state. Thus in interview he has stated how Bedouin society led him to discover natural laws and natural relationships, 'to discover the truths that I have presented in the Green Book'.[8]

The Third Universal Theory was intended to convey a version of politics and government distinct from (and above) capitalist democracy and bureaucratic state control (this may be seen as nicely meshing with what some

Western social democrats have dubbed 'democratic socialism'). The theory involves the provision of institutions of collective democracy which together enshrine the 'authority of the people'. There is no longer a requirement for a militant revolutionary vanguard, as was embodied in the RCC, but instead people's congresses will work to establish a majority position. The basic people's congresses (BPCs) are intended to send member secretariats to form the General People's Congress which serves not as a legislature but as a national assembly; the Congress also includes the executive committees of the local people's committees, and the secretariats of the various occupational and professional organisations. The system was comprehensively structured to ensure that 'no section of population was disenfranchised'.[9]

The move to the new political system began with Gaddafi's anniversary speech in September 1975. His followers began to replace the basic units of the ASU with the basic people's congresses; and in January 1976 Gaddafi and Jalloud moved to reconstitute the General Conference of the ASU. The transition to the new system culminated on 2 March 1977 with Gaddafi's announcement, before a 970-member meeting of the General People's Congress in Sebba, of the 'Declaration on the Authority of the People': at this time the Libyan Arab Republic became the *Socialist People's Libyan Arab Jamahiriya*. Changes to the economic structure of the country began a year later. The General People's Congress voted for the replacement of private ownership by 'producer partnerships', a type of workplace cooperative. On 1 May 1978 Gaddafi declared that 'the revolution should be carried on and your march should continue until the workers take over the management completely in all institutions in which they work'.[10] By 1979 the ownership and control of the industrial base had been transformed; and in the early 1980s domestic private trade was phased out, to be replaced by people's distributive committees supplied by the state General Marketing Company. The local agricultural market, the last remaining area of private exchange, was taken over early in 1987.

Opposition to the changes was encountered at every stage. The well-placed merchant class resented the new egalitarianism; and the clerical establishment including the Sunni *ulama*, protested at the theological implications of Part 2 of the Green Book. The clerics saw no basis in the Koran for many of Gaddafi's political and economic changes, and he was accused of being a communist. Gaddafi responded to the developing opposition by creating the 'revolutionary committee' movement, comprising ideologically committed activists keen to serve as cadres of the revolution. This group began with agitation and educational activities but came to acquire coercive and security responsibilities: the 1979 General People's Congress granted the revolutionary committees a range of powers to supervise the elections in the basic people's congresses, to nominate and veto candidates for office in the people's committees, and to dispense 'revolutionary justice'. The revolutionary committees came to serve as one of the main bulwarks for the security of the Gaddafi regime.

It had taken Gaddafi little more than a decade to transform the social, political and economic framework of a traditional Arab society that had been enmeshed in old tribal practices for centuries. The new patterns and practices, not least because of the foreign policy decisions that they inspired, have attracted wide-ranging criticism and hostility, often from self-interested sources; but even many of the regime's critics have found the Libyan revolution 'interesting'.[11] It is useful to look at some of the social and political transformations in more detail.

POLITICS

In his explanation of the character of revolution Gaddafi has declined to talk about specific beginnings. Revolutions, paradoxically, evolve through time; whereas a coup (*inqilab*) is 'a casual event occurring at the pleasure of senior officers'.[12] A revolution may resemble a military coup but it has a different character, growing 'naturally in the consciousness of the society as a whole'; and the very social circumstances produce 'a man of revolution, a man of comprehensive and complete change, a man who is as if born again in a new age'. The revolution, like a coup, may or may not be secure. It may only partially take over the reins of power, encouraging factions sympathetic to the old order to take steps to restore the old regime; so any steps to restore the *status quo ante* must be prevented by speedy and resolute action. In fact on 1 September 1969 Gaddafi quickly arrested officers above the rank of major and pensioned them off or posted them abroad. He also incorporated the purged security forces into the army, which was still further expanded by a systematic recruitment programme. It was vital to secure at the start the basis of security whereby effective transformations in society could be begun. When it was clear that the monarchy had been overthrown and that the new regime was in total control of the country, the new government was soon recognised by the foreign powers. After a few days recognition was offered by Britain, France, the United States and the Soviet Union (the regime had been instantly recognised by Iraq, Syria, Egypt and the Sudan); other countries quickly followed the lead of the major powers.

The first communiqué of the Revolutionary Command Council defined the objectives of the new regime:

1 All legislative councils of the old regime are abolished. They are deprived of all power as from 1 September 1969. All attempts by the old leaders against the revolution will be vigorously suppressed.

2 The Council of the Revolution is the only body entitled to administer the affairs of the Libyan Arab Republic. This being so, all government departments, officials, and armed forces of law are henceforth at the disposal of the Council of the Revolution. Any contravention will come before the courts.

3 The Council of the Revolution wishes to express to the people its will and its determination to build a revolutionary Libya, a socialist Libya, rooted in its own characteristics and rejecting all doctrine, confident in the reality of historical progress which will turn Libya, now underdeveloped and badly governed, into a progressive country which will fight against colonialism and racism and will help colonised countries.

4 The Council of the Revolution attaches great importance to the unity of the countries of the Third World and to all efforts directed towards the overcoming of social and economic under-development.

5 It believes profoundly in the freedom of religion, and in the moral values contained in the Koran, and it promises to defend these and to uphold them.

Gaddafi himself went to some lengths to explain the three concepts – liberty, socialism and unity – on which the revolution had been based (this must be set against the circumstance that no effort was made to develop a thorough-going socialist politics and economics until several years into the revolution). *Liberty* meant that Libya would be free of poverty, colonialism and the presence of foreign military forces; *unity* was effective pan-Arabism, the 'unity of all the Arab peoples', in a form that would depend upon circumstances; and *socialism* meant Arab socialism, Islamic socialism ('We are a Muslim nation. We shall therefore respect, as bidden in the Koran, the principle of private property. But the nation's capital will be encouraged, in order to help the country's development' – in these early days Gaddafi had no stomach to move against traditional private property). On 14 October

1969, in an interview on Egyptian television, Gaddafi identified the under-development of the Arab world as the 'essential dynamic' of the revolution; he also pointed to the corrupt cliques of the old regime, and how foreign power had ascendancy over every Libyan citizen: 'Libyan society . . . was in the cruel grip of an intellectual and cultural imperialism which crushed our minds and dominated everything including even our way of writing; one could not even have a visiting-card printed unless it was done in bilingual form: Arabic and some foreign language. There is no need to underline the humiliation of all this, and its damage to our pride . . . the Libyan citizen did not even receive the minimum living wage necessary to any human being.' In Tripoli, on 16 October, Gaddafi appealed for freedom for all Arab peoples; and on 6 November he was urging the liberation of Palestine.

It was inevitable that much of the early optimism that surrounded the overthrow of the monarchy would be frustrated, but even a year into the revolution Gaddafi was able to list a number of positive achievements:

The doubling of the minimum salary.
The start of numerous industrial and agricultural projects.
The re-organisation of the country's administration.
Economic and social legislation to ensure a better distribution of wealth.
The distribution of land title deeds as part of land reform.
The evacuation of foreign bases.
The nationalisation of banks and some oil-linked companies.
The departure of the Italian colony.
The raising of oil prices.[13]

A few months later, on 11 June 1971, the RCC inaugurated the Arab Socialist Union, the 'popular political organisation in the Libyan Arab Republic'; eight principles were adumbrated to define its role:

1 To stimulate every potentiality for creation and production.
2 To indicate and eliminate the undesirable legacy of the past.
3 To respect the ethics and the essence of Islam and the integrity of the Arab character.
4 To fight against all attempts at foreign or reactionary infiltration.
5 To eschew both the conservative right and the parasitical left, since both are of their nature reactionary; to encourage reflection, in the light of a true knowledge of life and of the Universe as revealed in the divine message and by the lives and actions of the Prophets, for therein alone can truth be found.

6 To fight against negativism, opportunism, deviation and improvisation.

7 To propagate the necessity of recognising and accepting Arab unity.

8 To work for the recognition and acceptance of socialism.[14]

However, despite all the enunciations, despite all the declarations of principle, it soon became apparent that a nation's people did not necessarily share the revolutionary zeal of the leadership. On 7 October 1971 Gaddafi gave a speech in Sabrata in which he castigated the Libyan people for their apathy. It was not, he declared, a matter of only a few individuals (a few 'could be dismissed or sent into retirement') but 'the mentality of hundreds, even of thousands of people, which is at issue . . .'. Gaddafi had encountered the plight of every revolutionary: how to infuse the masses with the necessary political commitment, the selfless zeal without which the revolution would falter and collapse. Nobody, he perceived, was doing anything 'except for the sake of remuneration . . . save in exchange for some reward'; in consequence, all production had edged towards bureaucracy, and this in turn was making 'inroads into hearts and minds'. He realised he could not liberate the mentality of people 'with a stroke of a pen . . . But there will have to be a real change of heart among Libyans: the revolution of 1 September was only a beginning'. Gaddafi returned to the same theme on 19 December, in an address given at the Tripoli Mosque. Here he spoke for the first time of the need for a cultural revolution, a notion which he did not take from China ('It has been foreshadowed in Islam for centuries').

On 23 July 1972, in a speech to students at a camp in Masrata, Gaddafi announced a plan for union between Libya and Egypt. A short time later, on 29 August, a common statement was made by the two countries on how the proposed union was to be brought about; early in the evening Radio Cairo broadcast a long declaration of the unified Egypto-Libyan political Command's thirteen resolutions for the establishment of a unified Arab state that was to be created on 1 September 1973. The Egyptian President Sadat had accepted the principle of total amalgamation of the two countries, as shown by the solemn agreement undertaken at Benghazi on 2 August 1972, but during the course of the preparatory year the Egyptians often expressed doubts about the plan (a detailed chronology of the discussions and unexpected events of this period is given by Bianco, *op. cit.*). At one stage Gaddafi even announced that he was resigning; the RCC refused to accept his resignation and threatened to resign en bloc if he did not withdraw it. Gaddafi reluctantly withdrew his resignation and returned to the Egyptian question: 'amalgamation with Egypt is inevitable, even if it means civil war . . . corruption, favouritism, censorship and bureaucracy still have power today in Egypt . . . All these must go, and the means to this end must be the people's revolution. This alone reflects the people's will . . . Nasser himself was convinced of its necessity.' A fortnight later a high-level delegation led by the Egyptian Deputy Prime Minister, Abdel Qader Hatem, travelled to Tripoli for prolonged discussions; soon after, Gaddafi arrived in Cairo for four-hour *tête-à-tête* talks with Sadat. The upshot was that Cairo withdrew from the agreement, for reasons that have never clearly emerged. Sadat may have been alarmed by Gaddafi's radical political programme, in particular the dramatic implications of the Third Universal Theory, a doctrine that was alien to Egyptian experience; he may also have been alarmed that Libyan radicalism might have been imported into Egypt, an alarming possibility for an Egyptian leader who lacked Nasser's revolutionary vision. It has also been suggested that Egyptian public opinion was concerned that the progress made by women would be set back under the philosophy espoused by Gaddafi (see below). In any event it was now obvious to Gaddafi that the seductive vision of pan-Arabism would have to be approached by another route. The immediate task was for Gaddafi to consolidate the Libyan revolution.

In a new five-point scheme, issued in April 1973, Gaddafi demanded:

the suspension of existing laws: in future all civil and criminal cases would be judged on their merits, according to the precepts of *sharia*;

the elimination of 'political illnesses' in the country, particularly Communism, the Muslim Brotherhood and Ba'athism;

the arming of the population to secure 'the defence of the revolution';

an 'administrative revolution' to bring the bureaucracy back to the people;

a cultural revolution to purge universities of 'the demagogic spirit and foreign cultural influences'.

He identified particular groups – the legal profession, political groups, the army, the bureaucracy and the intelligensia – as needing attention; and he urged 'every village, town, college, factory and school' to form 'popular committees under the control of the masses to fulfil the five points'. Soon after this declaration he was urging students at Benghazi University to 'trample under your feet' any bureaucrat who restricted access to government offices; and to destroy any imported books that did not express Arabism, Islam, socialism and progress.

In May elections were held to establish the people's committees that would thenceforth run government departments, schools, universities, factories, businesses and public services. The aim was to create several thousand committees, each comprising between sixteen and twenty members, throughout the country. Reuter reported on 7 May that the elections were supervised by 'neutral groups whose members have no right to stand for election themselves. After the elections the Revolutionary Command Council . . . sends a delegation to make sure the elections were freely held.'[15] A few days later, at a youth gathering on 14 May, Gaddafi described the features of the Third Universal Theory that underlay the five principles announced in the Zwara Declaration. The Theory ('or ideology') was conceived as a political doctrine but also as a religious exhortation: it was essential that people be called to return to the 'Kingdom of God', to be rearmed with faith to confront the evils of the world. Gaddafi took pains to emphasise the humanitarian aspects of the ideology, its interest in combating the racial theories that were 'designed to bring destruction to the world'. The Third Universal Theory was not a philosophy invented by man but truth, 'firm and unchangeable'.

The political essence of the Theory demanded socialism, as an Islamic rather than a Marxist doctrine ('For Islam and socialism are indivisible'). Private ownership would be allowed to continue when it was judged to be harmless, but there was no place for wealth and poverty co-existing in the same society: Islam, on the side of the working classes, has always set its face against poverty. Godless governments, whether capitalist or communist, were to be opposed equally: Islam would underwrite the brotherhood of man without which men and states would be 'no better than the wild beasts of the forests'.

The character of the Libyan revolution was further revealed by Gaddafi's remarks at the founding conference of the Arab Socialist Union (ASU) in April 1972. Here he suggested that trade unions have nothing to do with politics, and that it was no business of the revolution to set about building a conventional democracy. If, Gaddafi argued, workers were consulted as part of the decision-making process in a democracy then it was inevitable that policies would be formulated in the interests only of working people, and this would be unfair for other sections of the society. Moreover, 'The larger the number of people consulted, the more it is done at the expense of revolutionary transformation.' The Prophet Mohammed had been prepared to consult the people but, more importantly, he relied on guidance from God.

Gaddafi was keen to encourage debate as a mechanism for refining the ideology to which he was already committed. To this end he organised the various sessions of the Libyan Intellectual Seminar, held in Tripoli in 1970; and he encouraged respected intellectuals and clerics to visit him for talks. Some observers have remarked on Gaddafi's intellectual limitations and the narrowness of his reading, less than remarkable in a man born to an illiterate family in a poverty-stricken Bedouin tribe. Thus Mansur Kikhia, Gaddafi's Foreign Minister in 1972/3, observed that Gaddafi had read only two or three books but that he knew all Nasser's speeches by heart. Others have maintained that Gaddafi read widely: an Italian journalist noticed an under-lined passage in Gaddafi's copy of a book by the German writer Heinrich Kleist: 'A free man, capable of reflection, does not stay where chance happens to put him. He senses that he can raise himself above his destiny, that he can control his fate.'[16] Teach-ins were organised to aid the develop-ment of his political philosophy, to consolidate his power, and to extend his influence; but Gaddafi did not always convince the clerics, philosophers and politicians that he invited to Tripoli for discussions, again hardly surprising bearing in mind that Gaddafi himself had followed a tempestuous political course outside the practical experience of many of the visiting thinkers and politicians. In November 1973 he visited Paris to discuss political ideas with French academics and politicians in a *colloque* organ-ised by *Le Monde* (in collaboration with *Die Weit, La Stampa* and *The Times*). One speaker likened Gaddafi's commitment to resisting super-power hegemony to the political posture of the then President De Gaulle; when another contributor suggested that the Third Universal Theory resem-bled Marxism, Gaddafi retorted that in that case Marx must have been influenced by Islamic philosophers.

Against such events the practical business of running the Libyan state had to be continued; what was increasingly clear was that the revolution, despite the creation of the people's committees, could only be secured through authoritarian control. Immediately after the 1969 revolution the RCC had felt compelled to decree a law ('Decision on the Protection of the Revolution') making it a criminal offence to agitate against the new regime; the new law warned that 'Anyone who takes up arms against the republican regime of the Revolution of 1st September, or takes part in armed bands for this purpose, shall be sentenced to death.'[17] It is also clear that from its early days the revolutionary Libyan regime was under threat (see Chapter Eight). In May 1970 the discovery of an arms cache in Sebba provided evidence of a monarchist plot centred on Fezzan. This was the so-called 'Black Prince' conspiracy (on account of the dark features of Abdullah al-Sanussi) in which former Sanussi officers were to invade Libya from Chad with an army of two hundred brotherhood members with the intention of seizing Sebba as a prelude to the reconquest of Tripoli and Benghazi. One suggestion was that the Israelis had supported the conspiracy by providing arms.[18] Gaddafi himself saw the plotters as 'reactionary retired police officers and contractors who had profited from the defunct regime'.[19] About twenty individuals were arrested and sentenced to various terms of imprisonment.

However, this conspiracy and other discernable threats to the new regime did little to erode the confidence of the revolutionary leadership. The government moved quickly to consolidate power, to remove all residual signs of colonialism, to begin a social transformation, to expel the foreign bases, to evict the settler Italians, and to confront the oil companies. It is remarkable, bearing in mind the radical nature of this programme, that there was not more internal opposition or concerted moves by foreign governments to depose Gaddafi and instal a more congenial government (such efforts have of course been common throughout the world and perhaps Libya's time will come).

Among the first revolutionary measures was the complete dissolution of monarchical power. At the same time attention was given to such matters as language and religion. For a start the precedence of the Arabic alphabet was reinstated over the Latin: the Italians had named streets and districts, and now all these were changed to Arabic. Many of the Christian churches established during the Italian occupation were closed and the Roman Catholic cathedral that had been consecrated in 1928, during the Italian 'reconquest' of Libya, was converted into a mosque. The sale of alcohol was prohibited (Gaddafi was later to enrage President Sadat by saying in Cairo: 'How do you permit all these bars and night-clubs and liquor and gambling? . . . How can a drunk make progress in his country? How can a drunk battle in Sinai against the enemy?'). The government also moved against foreign firms, imposing a range of restrictions and allowing foreign residents to transfer only sixty per cent of their income; and steps were taken against the Italian settler community.

The new regime refused to accept the legality of Italian-owned property in Libya or the legitimacy of the 1956 Italo-Libyan Treaty designed to guarantee Italian property rights in the country. The expropriation of Italian property began at the end of 1970 and was planned to be complete by the first anniversary of 'Operation Jerusalem', the overthrow of the old regime. The property of Jews (referred to in official statements as 'Israelis'), along with that of the Italians, was also taken over by the state. Italian commercial property – shops, factories, restaurants and night-clubs – was occupied and then closed in the first stage of the process; then the Banco di Roma and the Banco di Napoli were nationalised; and finally the private residences and landholdings of the Italians were nationalised. Within three months of Gaddafi's declaration of intent on 21 July 1970 ('Vengeance Day') more than 12,000 Italian settlers had left Libya, forced to relinquish some 21,000 hectares of farming land, 687 apartments, 467 villas and 548 other dwellings, 1207 vehicles and about LD9 million in frozen capital deposits.[20] On 17 October 1970 Gaddafi announced 'the end of the hated fascist colonisation'.The comprehensive nationalisation of Italian, Jewish and other assets were referred to as 'restoration', the legitimate return to the Libyan people of their national wealth.

Gaddafi was also aware of the desperate need for a programme of social construction in such areas as housing, health and education. According to the Libyan Ministry of Information there were in 1970 about 300,000 shanty dwellings, 'most of which were about to fall down or in urgent need of rehabilitation'. The 1972–5 Three-Year Intermediary Plan, treating housing construction as a major priority, aimed to give every family a housing unit by 1982, a task which involved a six-fold increase in the housing budget between 1970 and 1978. The Libyan authorities claimed that by 1974 more houses were built per thousand population than were being built by Western governments. One independent expert observed that only Sweden and Denmark 'had higher rates above the 13 housing units per thousand in Libya in 1974'.[21] As a symbolic gesture Gaddafi himself bulldozed the last shanty dwelling in 1976; in less than a decade nearly 150,000 housing units had been completed, increasing by fifty per cent the total housing stock in the country. While this investment was in progress the government doubled the minimum wage, introduced statutory price controls, and reduced rents by 30 to 40 per cent.

Health too saw massive injections of investment capital. In 1968 Libya had a total of forty-one hospitals; within a decade the number has risen by fifty per cent, with an increase in the number of beds from 5646 to 13,347 (3.1 beds per thousand population in 1968 had increased to 5.0 beds per thousand in 1978). Over the same period the number of doctors in Libya had increased from 700 to 3000; and within five years of the overthrow of the monarchy, the ratio of nurses to population had been reduced from 1 to 2040 patients to 1 to 240.[22] Malaria was effectively wiped out and there was a massive decline in the incidence of such diseases as trachoma and tuberculosis. A flying doctor service was established so that people living in remote desert regions could receive medical attention. Life expectancy increased: from 45 in 1960 to 53 in 1974.

Education, the third social priority area, also experienced considerable expansion, a principal aim being to transform the monarchical system, designed for the privileged merchant class, into a system designed for universal education. The levels of literacy had been improving under the monarchy but 'most evidence indicates the attainment of higher levels following the overthrow of the monarchy'.[23] Student places at Tripoli University were 1374 in 1969/70, and 5702 ten years later; at Gar Younis in Benghazi there was an increase from 3360 (+ 303 non-Libyans) in 1969/70 to 7481 (+ 1274 non-Libyans) in 1976.[24] The revolutionary committees kept a close watch at all times on university activities and, in one view,[25] the expansion of the university population 'was too rapid for balanced development of teaching and research'. Moreover, there were immense problems, with the limited staff numbers, in developing a university culture that was well suited to Libya's particular socioeconomic needs. Gaddafi himself was keen to declare that education was 'a natural right for every human being' and no one had the right 'to deprive him of this right'.[26]

The investment made by the revolutionary government has been cynically portrayed by Gaddafi's detractors as a means of buying popular support, as if there is a singular virtue in carrying out *un*popular measures. In fact Gaddafi's social investment strategy is hard to fault, though it is always possible to criticise specific policies at any time. Much, but not all, of the criticism of Gaddafi has derived from factions and governments that lost out following the 1969 revolution. Not the least of these were the powers that had formerly enjoyed a colonial or neocolonial control over Libya's assets. It is useful to remember that, for example, it was widely assumed that Britain had a contingency plan for invading Libya in just such circumstances as Gaddafi had created. A secret protocol was attached to the 1953 Anglo-Libya treaty allowing for the invasion of Libya in case of an emergency. Details of this provision, code-named 'Operation Radford', were supplied in 1965 by an archivist at the British Ministry of Defence to the Egyptians, and the plan was subsequently published in full in *al-Ahram*.[27] The Radford plan specified the movement of British troops from Germany, Malta and Cyprus in order to protect the King and restore the monarchy. But Gaddafi had moved too quickly and he had been too successful: the rapid seizure of the reins of power and the secure maintenance of order gave the British (and doubtless also the Americans) no pretext for intervention. The danger of a fresh invasion by colonial powers was averted and, suitably encouraged, Gaddafi moved speedily to expel the British and American forces that were still on Libyan soil. The El Adem airbase was renamed the Gamal Abdul Nasser Airbase, and Wheelus Field was renamed the Okba bin Nafi Airbase, after one of Libya's ancient Arab heroes.

Throughout the period of social reconstruction and the expulsion of foreign forces, the Libyan government embarked upon a course of increasing confrontation with the international oil companies. On 7 December

1971 the government announced the unilateral nationalisation of BP assets in Libya, a prelude to the raft of expropriations that were to come in later years. The British government refused to recognise the nationalisation and asked other OECD countries to boycott oil from the former BP sites; and BP itself began judicial actions to prevent the movement of oil from the Sarir field previously run jointly with Bunker Hunt. In January 1972 BP took action in an attempt to stop crude oil from being shipped to Sincat in Syracuse for processing.[28] All BP's efforts 'failed miserably'.[29] Similarly, the British decision on 14 December to expel Libya from the Sterling Area achieved nothing more than encouraging Staff Major Jalloud to visit Moscow to discuss possible collaborations in trade and other areas. In a treaty signed on 4 March the Soviet Union agreed to help Libya with the development of its oil industry, and crude oil from Libya's ex-BP fields started moving to various East European countries.

Without Libya's increased revenue from oil the ambitious programme of social investment would have been impossible. It was Libya's radical and successful approach to the handling of its most vital resource that laid the basis for the on-going revolution in the turbulent years that lay ahead. Of Libya's handling of the oil question the independent analyst J. A. Allan observes: 'none could argue that the priority was pursued other than energetically and wisely'.[30] This success in turn led to the impressive social projects in construction, education and health: 'By any standards the achievements in the provision of houses, schools, health facilities and communications were dramatic during the 1970s.'[31] However, it was also clear that other important investment areas needed special attention. Oil would not last for ever – some estimates suggested that the Libyan reserves would only last until around 2010 – so it was essential to reduce the importance of the oil industry in the national economy. Attention was given therefore to such matters as the development of agriculture in a water-thirsty land, the possibility of employing more people in industry, and the need to develop a balanced economy that was, as far as possible, self-sufficient. In 1977 the Libyan government began formulating an economic development plan for the period 1980 to 2000.

The Libyan government, despite the revolutionary successes of the 1970s, was far from complacent. It had always been known that Libya would have to survive in a hostile political climate, that the country's revolutionary development was viewed with bitter resentment by various powerful foreign governments. In such circumstances there was a premium on self-sufficiency: it would be highly irresponsible to continue to export oil in return for food, if an oil blockade by the foreign powers could be used to starve the nation. If any lesson were needed, the experience of Iraq in 1991/

92 carried a grim message. Here a formerly rich hydrocarbon society, dependent upon exporting oil for food and high-technology equipment, was being progressively starved by comprehensive sanctions. The revolutionary Libyan government had always been aware of such possibilities, though to take steps to hedge against them was a difficult matter. The key requirement of a developing agricultural sector had been tackled with mixed success.

GREEN REVOLUTION

Agriculture has been an important sector of the Libyan economy from the earliest times, and there is debate about the population it has supported over the centuries; the extent of Libyan dependence on imports, and the changing patterns of development under various foreign influences. It is thought that the Libyan population may have approached one million during the second and third centuries AD, aided by such circumstances as the Severus patronage, derived from Roman power, that channelled craftsmen and resources to Tripolitania.[32] It was not until the twentieth century that the early Libyan population, sustained by a healthy agriculture, was surpassed.

The Italian occupation of Libya that began in 1911 (see Chapter Three) had a drastic effect on traditional agricultural patterns.[33] Many Libyans were killed in battle or relocated to concentration camps. Agricultural land was devastated, the tended oases became neglected and the livestock on which the Arabs depended was systematically slaughtered as a matter of deliberate policy. The Italians made settlements on land that, while not regularly farmed, was essential to local farming practices. When the Italians finally left the country, following their comprehensive defeats in the Second World War, there remained a massively dislocated economy with a mutilated landscape, a ravaged and demoralised people, and a massive confusion with regard to land titles and related matters. This was the chaos that confronted an independent Libya in 1951 and which was not resolutely and comprehensively addressed until after the 1969 revolution.

The Italian exodus began with the granting of Libyan independence. Many of the large farms were sold to wealthy Libyan purchasers, with some of the extensive tracts then subdivided into units that were still substantial; some of the deals were made by wealthy Palestinian immigrants who then invested in citrus planting and ambitious irrigation schemes. This began the growing exploitation of the water resource that could not be sustained by the coastal aquifers. Efforts were made to expand agriculture in the immediate post-Independence years, but before the oil revenues began to come on stream little was accomplished; and it was not until the mid 1960s that the pace and shape of agricultural development saw significant changes. At first the oil revenues were relatively small and in any case still subject to the policy decisions of the oil companies: much of the early oil revenue was focused on further oil exploration, with some diverted to irrigation schemes and the raising of such crops as citrus, melons and tomatoes. But even the relatively small agricultural initiatives led to problems of water shortage, and soon after the revolution the government was forced to cut back on some areas of agricultural development in order to conserve water resources. Many studies, from the Italian period onwards, had demonstrated the vulnerability of the groundwater reservoir to over-exploitation,[34] and this was one of the most difficult problems that the Gaddafi regime was forced to address.

The question of agricultural reform was one of the first topics that Gaddafi confronted after the overthrow of the monarchy. On 22 September 1969, three weeks after taking power, Gaddafi declared in a speech at Sebba: 'the Jefara Plain, the great Jebel al-Akhdar . . . the Fezzan valleys are witnessing the great agricultural revolution that will enable the Libyan people to earn their living, to eat freely . . . the food that was normally imported from overseas . . . this is freedom, this is independence and this is revolution.'[35] The state quickly took over unused land as a prelude to redistribution and measures were introduced to prevent the local sheikhs from acquiring more land: the tribal leaders were prevented from taking over small landholdings and so encouraging the migration of dispossessed farmers to the urban centres. This was seen as an essential first step to inducing the traditional cultivators and herders to stay on the land and remain involved in agricultural production.

The land held by the residual Italian settlers was then confiscated under the decree of 21 July 1970 and placed under the authority of the new Department of Land Reclamation and Agrarian Reform. This land was then reorganised into model farms to be run by fresh graduates from the Libyan College of Agriculture; once the farms had become viable as functional units they were reallocated to smallholders who would be allowed to purchase the land after a production period of fifteen years. In 1973 further measures were introduced that represented a further break with traditional practices.

The revolutionary government had initially preserved a number of the agricultural policies introduced by the monarchy; for example, the RCC had continued to make available interest-free credit and other subsidies to assist capitalist production in agriculture (in 1972 the new Agricultural Bank was offering high levels of interest-free credit to landowners). The traditional policies had increased crop outputs in some sectors but there had been no incentive to expand the area under cultivation. Now, through the mechanism of the 1973–83 Ten-Year Intermediate Agricultural Development Plan, the revolutionary government intended to use effective state capitalism to expand agricultural production. The Plan (involving twenty-seven agrarian projects and working in conjunction with a Three-Year Intermediate Development Plan and a Five-Year Transformation Plan) stimulated the direct development and organisation of agricultural production, encouraging at the same time the establishment of farming settlements.

Areas devastated by the Second World War were quickly brought back into useful production, particularly where adequate annual rainfall could be guaranteed; the scale of damage in the Gebel al-Akhdar, an area of good rainfall, necessitated major redevelopment, with production in dry inland areas still constrained by the shortage of water. Underground water sources in such areas as Kufra and Sarir in the Khalij area of Cyrenaica and in the Maknoussa region of Fezzan were used for extensive irrigation, and studies showed that aquifers in these parts were capable of sustaining wheat and cereal production. (Interestingly enough, the control parameters of the Maknoussa scheme – water distribution, chemical inputs – were initially regulated by a computer sited in the United States.[36])

The ambitious schemes had mixed successes. Some achieved the intended levels of production whereas others fell far short of expectation. Allan comments that the agricultural experiments in south-east Libya were 'expensive failures according to any economic measures'.[37] Important experience was gained by Libyan graduates in agriculture and engineering but there was a serious shortage of development staff at many of the designated sites and lack of management experience served to compound the problems. Foreigners had been encouraged to help with the work, a ploy that often proved counter-productive: communication problems, cultural incompatibilities and the rapid turnaround of staff 'made quite impossible the task of leading and managing the projects effectively'.[38]

The Kufrah scheme was one of the most prestigious, serving as a model for anticipated developments elsewhere in the country. Armand Hammer had originally funded agricultural development in the Kufrah region, its water resources first revealed oil exploration in the 1950s and 1960s. In 1967 the Occidental Company found artesian water near Tazerbu in the Kufrah basin and plans – of the sort pioneered in Arizona and California – were formulated to reclaim land from the desert. An experimental farm was established, to be taken over by the revolutionary government in 1969. The Libyan Ministry of Petroleum was assigned the scheme and discussions began about how to manage the water in the area. (Investigations by

American geologists had suggested that there was enough underground water to develop 50,000 acres of arable land.)

The various development schemes involved building windbreaks, dams, pumping stations and water reservoirs; trees were planted on land close to crop areas as a protection against wind damage. Thus at Wadi Ramil in Jefara windbreaks were built to help the restoration of 57,600 hectares of land; at Wadi Athel and Wadi Mait, dams were built as part of a project to irrigate a total area of more than 80,000 acres; and on the slopes of the Jebel Nafusah terraces were built in a project designed to reclaim 48,000 acres. Various piping schemes, as in the region of Bir Tarfas, were developed to retrieve deep water.[39] Many such projects were linked to the establishment of farming communities: the first began at Kufrah in 1969, and 380 other farms that were started in 1971 were distributed on 25 October 1974 to farmer-proprietors in Sirtica. A week later Gaddafi himself handed over a further 500 farming developments on the Gebel al-Akhdar. At the same time many of the developments failed to attract the necessary labour: there was still a significant migratory flow to the towns. Moreover, schemes designed to make Libya increasingly independent developed a requirement for foreign produce. By the mid 1970s Libya was forced to import half its sheep feed, most of its cattle feed, and all of its poultry feed; and Libya also remained unhappily dependent on supplies of agricultural equipment from the United States. And, paradoxically in post-colonial Libya, there was an increased dependence on foreign technicians and skilled labour (80 per cent of the labour at Kufrah was non-Libyan). Alarmingly enough, output in various agricultural sectors began to fall, partly as a result of the misuse of scarce water resources. In 1976 the government was forced to restrict the production of crops involving a high water consumption, such as citrus and tomatoes, and in some areas there was a subsequent fall in the amount of land under cultivation. It seemed increasingly unlikely in this context that Libya would be able to establish the required levels of food self-sufficiency. New initiatives were needed, particularly in the area of water management: one of the most ambitious of these was the 'Great Man-made River' project, which at an estimated $9 billion investment far outstrips all other schemes.

The Great Man-made River Project, of which Muammar al-Gaddafi is the official 'Architect', is planned to convey many millions of cubic metres of water a year via multiple pipelines from ancient artesian wells in the southern desert, the site of a vast water stratum, to the coastal areas dedicated to agricultural production. The system is intended to feed irrigation facilities covering a third of a million hectares and allow the replenishment of groundwater resources in the Gebel Akhdar and Jefara Plain.[40] The first stage of the project, completed on 31 August 1984, includes a 400 km pipeline conveying water from Tazerbu and Sarir to the coastal region of Ajdabiya on the coast. Later stages are designed to transport water from Fezzan to Tripoli, from Ajdabiya to Sirte, from Ajdabiya to Tobruk, and from Tripoli to Sirte. The whole scheme is financed out of taxation on consumer goods – including cigarettes, oil and oil products – and has largely escaped the firm financial control on investment. Much of the work has been carried out by the Dong Ah construction company of South Korea.

Studies revealed a huge reservoir of fresh water in the 20,000-year-old desert wells of the southern regions, findings that encouraged the allocation of massive amounts of investment capital to the project. To supervise the scheme a public authority, the Great Man-made River Authority, was established on 6 October 1983; and this was followed immediately by the inauguration of the first phase of the project. According to an official Libyan publication, this 'great and important project has called for the largest concentration of construction equipment and machinery ever assembled'.[41]

Four major underground reservoirs have been located in Libya during exploratory drilling for oil. In the south-east the Kufrah basin has an estimated groundwater storage capacity of 20,000 cubic kilometres; this connects with the Sirte basin where the fresh-water aquifer is reckoned to hold some 10,000 cubic kilometres of water; and south of Gebel Fezzan the Murzuk basin has an estimated water capacity of 4,800 cubic kilometres. A massive Palaeozoic aquifer underlies the Hamadah and Jufrah basins that extend from the Qargaf Arch and Jabal Sawda to the coast. Intermittent rain provides some recharge for the reservoirs but calculations suggest that the Great Man-made River Project, even if successful, may run out of water in about fifty years.[42] According to the official publication, the project was designed to initially extract two million cubic metres a day from the eastern wells and one million cubic metres a day from the western wells; and it is claimed that at this rate there will be 'several hundred years of potential production'.[43] At the same time it is acknowledged that only a small amount of recharge will occur 'from the heavy but intermittent rains' in the southern uplands.

Libya also claims that the first steps towards the Great Man-made River Project were taken as early as 1974 when studies revealed how the underground reservoirs might be exploited. The first phase was designed to transport two million cubic metres of water daily to the coastal region where most of the Libyan population lives; in this phase more than a hundred production wells were connected to collector pipelines with valves, limit switches, high-pressure transmitters, flow meters and various safety devices. A steel header tank at Tazerbo has a water capacity of 170,000 cubic metres. Some idea of the scale of the First Phase construction is given by the broad list of the specified materials (including, for example, 250,000 pipe sections) and by details of the 'largest concentration of handling and earth-moving equipment in the history of civil engineering'.[44]

The figures supplied in official publications from Tripoli only provide a partial picture of what is involved in a gargantuan project of this type. A permanent computer and control system (PCCS) is in place and computer facilities are also used to provide calculations on water-flow parameters and on information associated with water use; to monitor water levels and water flow; and to monitor control equipment, maintenance procedures, spare parts, inventory and other ancillary activities. Phase One of the project required about 65 megawatts of electrical power, supplied mainly from a plant built for the task at Sarir. The requirements of the later phases in the project have demanded considerable expansion of the Phase One provision.

The Great Man-made River Project was conceived partly to bring much needed irrigation to many areas; it was also intended to counter the gradual deterioration of many of the traditional water resources at risk through intensive use (one problem is saline intrusion into the waters of the coastal aquifers). In addition, the water from the new project would also allow supplies to be made available for a wide range of industrial uses, and for domestic use in the towns. Again, a key purpose is to lead Libya to genuine independence, particularly through self-sufficiency in food: 'It is planned to utilise more than 86% of the water output for agricultural development, so that the country will become self-sufficient in agricultural products and achieve economic independence.'[45] Strategic crops (wheat, barley, sorghum, sheep fodder) would be given priority, so that the national production of these crops, of beef and mutton, and of milk and dairy products could be expanded while expensive imports were reduced. Food independence may be judged a prudent aim in an uncertain world in which comprehensive economic sanctions could never be ruled out.

In the official text the Project brings a number of clear benefits: agriculture will no longer be at risk from deteriorating coastal aquifers; fresh land will be taken under cultivation; existing cultivated land will be rejuvenated; there will be increased self-sufficiency in food; light industry in rural areas will be encouraged; existing industries will be boosted; both urban and rural services will improve; rural improvements will encourage people to stay on the land; and new fields of employment will develop. It is not difficult to see why the Great Man-made River Project is viewed by many Libyans as 'a dream long cherished by writers and scientists, a dream of an abundance of water'.[46] The Project is already showing many benefits but it will be years before its full significance can be accurately estimated.

ECONOMY

Economic reform was at the heart of the Libyan revolution, though economic *philosophy* has changed from one phase of development to another. The 'Green Revolution', investment in the industrial infrastructure, a radical shift in the management of oil resources – all signalled a departure from pre-revolutionary patterns. The revolutionary leadership took over a nation with only a small industrial base. An early industrial survey, carried out in conjunction with the Egyptian Organisation for Industrialisation, gave details of visits to some 13,310 'industrial plants' in 1971/72; these were however rudimentary enterprises, each only employing a few workers. Under the monarchy little attempt had been made to use oil revenues to expand the industrial base; in the mid 1950s almost ninety per cent of industrial plants employed fewer than ten workers.[47] Most of the industrial plants had been established by the Italian settlers and were based in the main urban centres; one of the largest plants had been built by Anglo-American Tobacco.[48] In this context industry aimed to produce goods mainly for the domestic market, and foreign exchange earnings were extremely low. A private housing boom, focused on a small proportion of the population and linked to the oil industry, stimulated construction in some areas; in 1969, just prior to the coup, two cement factories were completed in al-Khums and Benghazi but these were only expected to supply ten per cent of contractors' needs, the rest being made up by imports.

The monarchy had displayed no enthusiasm for intervention in industrial activity. The Real Estate Industrial Bank, formed in 1965, offered loans but the state did not become involved in the task of capital formation; the commercial bourgeoisie, interested largely in oil, had no anxieties about state interference. Industrial development was sluggish and focused many on enterprises requiring little capital investment; there was still much reliance of traditional craft methods for producing textiles and other domestic goods. At first the revolutionary leadership did not move to overturn many of the familiar industrial and trading practices: there was still an interest in capitalist development but now the state was intervening to encourage industrial expansion. There was no insistence that the private sector be abolished or even curtailed. In 1973 an official publication, issued by the

General Administration for Information, commented that the new policy 'may be summed up as a clear and frank definition of the role of each of the private and public sectors in the execution of projects and helping the former to overcome the difficulties, by providing financial and technical encouragement'.[49]

Two new state institutions were created to support capitalist development: the Industrial Research Centre, established on 1 November 1970 to provide technical and financial services to both sectors, and to undertake industrial and geological research; and the General National Organisation for Industrialisation, founded on 3 August 1970 to supervise state investment and to control industrial projects commissioned from foreign companies. The Organisation contracted thirty-two initial schemes between 1971 and 1973, including a glass factory in Aziziya with Société Mécanique Frères of France, an electrical cable plant in Benghazi with the West German firm Franzkershweild, four pipe producing factories involving other German companies, and three textile mills at Marj, Derna and Janzour. The government moved also to expand the role of the Real Estate Industrial Bank, specifically to encourage Libyan entrepreneurs. An impulse behind such developments was the assumption that oil resources would only last until around 2020, at which time Libya would be forced to rely on other types of industrial activity. Under the monarchy the government had been content to channel vast funds into the pockets of the ruling families and to tolerate a minimal level of industrial development: by contrast, the revolutionary government saw the need to effect a rapid transition from merchant capitalism to productive capitalism, a prerequisite for a wider industrial base.

The Libyan government was now acting as a state capitalist, just as other states – Turkey, Iran, Egypt and Algeria – had moved to support and expand industrial capitalism; neighbouring Algeria, as a hydrocarbon society, provided a useful model for the new revolutionary leadership in Libya. It was soon found that the available supply of labour was inadequate for the required levels of industrial expansion (in 1980 Libya still had a population of under three million), and so foreign manpower was imported at an ever increasing rate. Between 1970 and 1975 Libya's migrant workforce grew from 50,000 to 323,000.[50] By the mid 1970s more than fifteen per cent of the workforce in most economic sectors was made up by foreign labour, with foreigners constituting 58 per cent of Libya's professional and managerial manpower and 77.3 of unskilled labour in the construction industry. This meant that there was a substantial outflow of foreign exchange, which in fact Libya was always able to meet; more important was the demoralising effect on indigenous peoples of the continuing high levels of foreign manpower.

The first measures introduced by the revolutionary government were aimed at the development of a rudimentary capitalist sector that was already in place: there was little talk at this time of the sort of 'socialist transformation' of society that would have appealed to revolutionaries elsewhere in the world. However, the Libyan revolution was still finding itself: there had been no pre-existing blueprint, no received text. In 1977 Muammar al-Gaddafi issued the second volume of his Green Book, this volume (of only around 4000 words) dealing with 'The Solution of the Economic Problem'. Here it is suggested that the goal of society should be 'natural socialism' which was known in an earlier idealised time during which human beings conducted their affairs according to 'natural principles' abandoned in the dissolute modern age.

Gaddafi briefly reviews the condition of workers since the Industrial Revolution; he concludes that there has been little change in the relationship between workers and employers. Workers are still exploited as economic slaves, and to alter this it is necessary for workers to become partners in the production process (hence the slogans that festooned Libya in the late-1970s: 'Partners, not wage earners'). Gaddafi emphasises 'need' as a key consideration: 'Man's freedom is lacking if somebody else controls what he needs'; satisfying such needs, not profit through exploitation, should be 'the legitimate purpose of the individual's economic activity'. Once the basic needs are met there is no requirement for profit or even for money. Gaddafi's 'natural socialism' is set against atheistic Marxism but there are many Marxists who would be happy with talk of how 'the transformation of the contemporary societies from societies of wage labourers to societies of partners is an inevitable and dialectical outcome of the contradicting economic theses prevailing in the world today'.

Gaddafi argues that the world may from time to time change one economic system or ideology for another, but that such processes do not represent real change. The capitalist and Marxist systems may appear different but in fact they are 'the two faces of one coin'. Both systems exploit the workers: in capitalism there are many independent employers whereas in Marxism there is only one (state) employer but the result is always the same. Whatever the nature of the prevailing system the workers are paid specific wages for their labour. In both systems the people toil without being able to manage their own affairs. Moreover the Marxist state was established through violence, and the people would be driven to revolt against such a system.

Economic and social reforms, Gaddafi concedes, may improve a system but the basic problem always remains: that of true human freedom. The reforms, akin to mere charities, do not properly address the real rights of workers. The only solution is for the producers themselves to be the consumers of their products, and this can only be accomplished when ownership is in the hands of all the people, managed by their congresses and committees; and then will the workers become 'partners and not wage earners'. The final solution, concludes Gaddafi, 'is the elimination of wage earning, and hence the liberation of mankind from its enslavement. It is the return to the natural principles which governed human relations before the rise of social classes, forms of government and their imposed legislation . . . Only natural principles can be taken as the criteria, and the sole source and reference of human relations.'

Since 'in need freedom resides', it is inevitable that social struggle will arise 'when one group in society gains control over the needs of others'. One of the principal needs is the home, and a man cannot be free as long as he lives in the house of another, whether he pays rent or not. There are no circumstances in which a man should pay rent (to a private landlord, a real estate firm, or the state): 'No one has the right, therefore, to build any house beyond his need. This is because that house would then embody the need of another person. Building it with the intention of renting it out is the beginning of the process of controlling another person's need.'

Another crucial need, according to the Green Book, is a person's 'livelihood'. A man dependent upon wages or charity is not free. Instead it should be recognised that a man's livelihood is his own private property, 'which you yourself must manage within the bound of satisfying your personal needs – or it must be your share of a product, in the production of which you were an essential participant – and not a wage for a labour rendered to anyone'. Another need is transport: in the true socialist society no individual or company can be allowed to control the transport of others. And similarly with the land: it should belong to no-one in particular but every individual has the right to use it to fulfil personal needs. A person's heirs do not inherit the ownership of land but simply, along with other people, the right to use it. Against the Marxist slogan 'from each according to his ability, to each according to his need', Gaddafi prefers 'from each according to his ability, to each according to his effort': a worker can set aside a portion of what he earns to meet his own personal needs but to hoard wealth is, according to Gaddafi, to hoard 'the need of another person of the wealth of society'.

This is not a thorough-going doctrine of egalitarianism: it is assumed that there will be varying levels of affluence in society. Thus Gaddafi proclaims: 'The share of every individual in the public wealth of society varies only in accordance with the kind of public service he performs, or the excellence of the work he does.' It is recognised that a person's needs varies according to his education and environment, so it is difficult in the final analysis to establish a real standard to determine how wealth should be distributed to people in society. It is hoped that this difficulty will be overcome by each individual controlling the means to satisfy his own needs. Gaddafi calls this control or even ownership 'a sacred right'. He makes an effort to confront some of the difficulties in the theory but it is hard to doubt the impracticalities of many of its aspects.

It is easy to see the influence of traditional Islamic teaching on Gaddafi's economic vision. The Koran prohibits usury (as did mediaeval Christianity), it insists on obligatory welfare alms (*zakat*), and it demands that people 'spend of their wealth in the way of God'. At the same time Gaddafi is influenced by Marx, though he may chose to trace his influence back to earlier Islamic teachers; and many Moslem clerics have been opposed to Gaddafi's views on orthodox Islam (see below). There is debate about the extent to which the ideas in the second volume of the Green Book came to influence the course of the Libyan revolution in the second half of the 1970s and after. There is at least no doubt that Libya's economic philosophy saw a significant shift from the early capitalist developments of the immediate post-coup years. The extent to which this change yielded greater economic success can be considered.

On 1 September 1985, in his Revolution Day speech, Gaddafi called on the Libyan people to be willing to suffer in support of the revolution, a tacit admission of the country's growing economic difficulties. By the end of 1985 Libyan imports had been cut to $7 billion (from $16 billion in 1980) and exports to $10 billion (from $22 billion); and total GDP had fallen to $25 billion. In the 1985 budget the General People's Congress reduced administrative spending by 19 per cent to $5.7 billion.[51] All the signs suggested a pressing need for economies in state expenditures. None-the-less, about $2 billion was spent on arms purchases in 1985, mainly from the Soviet Union.

In the mid 1970s the United States first began economic sanctions against Libya, with many categories of US equipment denied to Gaddafi. A 1982 embargo on imports of crude oil from Libya cut the country's exports of petroleum products to the US by almost a half; but despite the sanctions the US Department of Commerce reported increased US sales to Libya in 1985, mainly in machinery and agricultural products. In November 1985 the US imposed a ban on refined Libyan petroleum products, just as Libya's Ras Lanouf refinery was coming into operation. Again, despite the restrictions, four major US petroleum companies continued to trade with Libya. The Reagan administration legislated in January 1986 under the terms of the International Economic Powers Act for an almost total embargo on trade with Libya; this involved freezing some $200 million of Libyan assets in the United States. Despite the Reagan legislation, as many as 1000 American citizens continued to live and work in Libya and were treated by Gaddafi in 'exemplary' fashion – 'an apparent effort to put the lie to US warnings that American citizens in Libya are potential hostages to Qadhafi's policies'.[52] In 1986, in addition to the various external political difficulties, the Libyan oil industry faced a number of problems: maintenance difficulties began to emerge; safety standards were found to be inadequate; and there remained the pressing problem of a serious shortage of skilled personnel. Petroleum output was lost through mismanagement, and there were various costly disputes between the Libyan National Oil Corporation and foreign producers.

There were also signs that the economic difficulties caused by economic sanctions and other circumstances were resulting in an increase in graft and corruption, the sort of erosion of public and private integrity that had bedevilled the Idris years. Government proclamations and exhortations reflected the growing concern over such phenomena as nepotism, patronage, black marketeering, and the falsification of production statistics to create the impression that output targets were being met. The black market often trafficked in US dollars and by 1986 many items were not available for Libyan dinars. The government responded by purging government to combat corruption, by frequent public exhortations, and by giving particular projects preferential funding. The economic difficulties were by now affecting arms purchases, an area of expenditure close to Gaddafi's heart (see below): a dispute with Moscow had developed over the apparent nonpayment of $7 billion for arms, and Gaddafi was urging that petroleum could be used increasingly to pay for the import of goods and services. Funds continued to flow into the Great Man-made River Project, a pet scheme of Gaddafi's, with some estimates suggesting that it would cost $25 billion, far beyond the officially quoted figure of around $9 billion. It was inevitable that such massive expenditure would have a serious effect on Libyan finances at such a difficult time.

An expansion of private enterprise in Libya in the late-1980s seemingly took the Gaddafi regime by surprise.[53] It seemed clear that a newly emerging business class was operating in ways that had little connection with the political tenets of the Green Book (Volume 2). Gaddafi, in line with traditional religious thinking, had agitated against profit, interest and many of the other characteristic features of the typical cash economy. Worker partnership and barter of goods had been enthusiastically proclaimed as important elements of the Third Universal Theory, but such notions failed to impress the growing commercial factions in Libyan society. On 17 March 1990 a 'revolutionary programme' was adopted at an extraordinary session of the General People's Congress to wrest back political control over the economy. The adopted resolution declares 'the necessity to transform society into one of production by destroying the consumer society and building a *jamahiri* production society'. In a speech to the Congress on 27 March Gaddafi depicted demands for a market economy as a 'colonial programme' which, he declared, was bound to collapse. He noted:

> Whoever wants prices to go up, salaries to go up, inflation to rise, borrowing from the IMF to start, begging from foreign countries to start, exploitation to begin, and dignity and freedom to be humiliated, wants colonialism to return, takes us away from production and directs us towards consumption.

At the same session the Congress also demanded a halt to the 'haemorrhage of foreign currency' and the introduction of progressive taxation. Such proposals run counter to a number of liberalisation policies introduced by Gaddafi in March 1988 and which now will be difficult to swing into reverse.

At the beginning of April 1990 there was a sudden and unexpected collapse in oil prices, a development that was to continue for several months caused largely by OPEC overproduction when average output exceeded 23 million bd (compared with the agreed ceiling of 22.1 million bd) for the first half of the year.* One effect was a plunge in the price of Libyan crude oil from an average of $21/barrel to less than $16/barrel in early June (compared to an OPEC reference price of $18/barrel). This has serious consequences for Libya's earnings from oil exports. In fact Libya had kept reasonably close to its allocation quota of 1.23 million bd for the first half of 1990, producing (according to the Nicosia-based *Middle East Economic Survey*) an average 1.33 million bd, 7.5 per cent above the OPEC quota. The main OPEC overproducers were, significantly enough, Kuwait, Saudi Arabia, and the United Arab Emirates (UAE). On 2–3 May, at the OPEC meeting in Geneva, Libya argued for a reduction in oil output for the May–July period and agreed to cut its own production to the quota

---

*This may be reckoned one of the principal causes of Iraq's invasion of Kuwait and the subsequent 1991 Gulf War (see Chapter 1).

allocation; but throughout May oil prices remained relatively low as the leading OPEC producers failed to abide by the newly-agreed production ceiling: some OPEC members then faced difficulties, and tensions began to grow in the Middle East.

In an interview on 14 May the Libyan Oil Minister, Fawzi Shakshuki, indicated the country's increased production capacity, declaring that the production at the Sarir field in the south east, operated by the state-owned Arabian Gulf Oil Company, was set to more than double its output (from 230,000 bd to 600,000 bd) following a water injection programme.[54] Major new oil discoveries were made in 1990 at the Bu Attifel field, operated by Agip of Italy. Such finds are important and may be expected to enhance the security of Libya's oil-based revenues. However, US sanctions in the 1990s continue to hamper Libya's development efforts in various areas: it is impossible for Libya to resume normal operations with five American companies – Marathon, Conoco, Ameralda-Mess, Occidental and W. R. Grace – and much-needed US technology and spare parts are blocked. Libya wants the United States to co-operate in joint ventures and to train Libyan oil personnel, activities that are prevented by existing sanctions.

On 28 August 1991, three days before the twenty-second anniversary of the Libyan revolution, the first phase of the Great Man-made River Project was completed at Suluq, near Benghazi. About 14,000 people watched the first flow of water running into a massive four-million-litre reservoir, conveyed via a 430-kilometre-long pipeline from 100 underground wells at Tazerno and 125 at Sarir. Gaddafi gave an inauguration speech in which he depicted the Project as the eighth wonder of the world; he also highlighted the fact that other oil-rich Arab states had declined his suggestion that they make a financial contribution to the scheme. Again, the total cost of the scheme is estimated at more than $25 billion, almost three times initial Libyan estimates, and equivalent to around four years' oil export earnings at current production rates and prices.[55]

There is still much debate about the viability of the Project and whether it will have adverse ecological consequences. David Williams, general manager of the London office of Brown & Root, serving as consultants to the scheme, has been quoted as saying that with a flow rate of about two million cubic metres per day the water should last for four hundred years.[56] However, Brian Smith, a British hydrology expert, has commented that the scheme represents 'a one-off use of the resource, and only a short-term solution to the problem'.[57]

In June 1991 the General People's Congress adopted a resolution to create a new committee to review the position of foreign companies working in Libya. A primary concern is that a number of companies have been given money but have failed to fulfil their contracts with local municipal authorities. It was suggested that all money be returned and contracts be terminated. The work of the new committee has not yet been made public, but it serves to highlight the general problem that Libya experiences with foreign companies. There is often an expressed reluctance to become involved in the Libyan economy. US sanctions have deprived Libya of US equipment and technical expertise, and large West European companies (such as BP or Total) have been unwilling to fill the American gap. Some companies find the current exploration and production agreements unacceptable: for example, there is a clause giving Libya's National Oil Corporation (NOC) the right to cancel a firm's operations at any time, even if the company has observed all its contractual obligations. And there is also the prevailing image of Libya, an adequate deterrent to many companies: an oil executive has been quoted as saying that 'as soon as the word Libya is mentioned, thoughts turn to Lockerbie, the IRA, the Rabta scandal – and that's it'.[58]

Libya will continue to rely on its oil resources, despite all attempts at industrial diversification; and here there are mixed expectations. There is no sign of a lifting of American sanctions. Quite the reverse: when Gaddafi inaugurated the Great Man-made River Project (Phase 1 completion) on 28 August he also warned of the possibility of further US bombing raids (see Chapter One). In such circumstances economic development is subject to many constraints: Western experts 'are pessimistic about Libyan oil exports . . . They estimate that Libyan oil production may be halved by the end of the decade as depletion of current fields will outpace the number of new wells coming on stream.'[59] On 1 August the US Treasury Department announced that it was expanding its blacklist of companies owned by, or in some way associated with, Libya: eight companies and twenty-one individuals were added to a list of firms and people banned from dealing with US citizens and companies. The expanded blacklist now includes the Libyan investment company Oilinvest, the Holborn oil refinery, six companies in Malta, and most of Libya's top oil officials. Richard Newcomb, director of the Treasury Office of Foreign Assets Control has commented that 'the recent Libyan economic expansion into Western Europe increases Muammar Gaddafi's ability to promote and finance terrorist activity. The US attitude cannot be business as usual.'[60]

DEMOCRACY

Gaddafi moved to a view of democracy, as he moved to other ideas, through his experience of the revolution. In the popular view Libya is a highly autocratic state, far removed from the parliamentary democracies of the West. One expert commentator urges us not to doubt 'for a moment that Libya has a military dictatorship'; but elsewhere in the same volume conveys well Gaddafi's view of what he would consider to be *genuine* democracy.[61]

In the first place Gaddafi is opposed to both the state and to representative democracy because they necessarily involve a surrender of individual sovereignty. In Volume 1 (sometimes designated Chapter 1) of the Green Book, Gaddafi argues that if you allow someone else to represent your interests you necessarily sacrifice part of your individual sovereignty. This is a matter of great relevance to real democracy (Volume 1 of the Green Book is entitled: *'Solving the Problem of Democracy'*), for how can it ever be just to allow someone else to act as your political proxy? Representation thus can only lead to domination by one individual or group over other people. It is for this reason that political parties are banned in Libya: they are seen as competing for power so that party members and party supporters can gain dominance over people who are not members or supporters. In the same way the dictatorship of the proletariat is no more than the domination of much of society by one part of it. How can this be just? Or democratic? In short, 'representation is fraud!'

Gaddafi claims to have derived his concept of democracy from a single verse of the Koran: 'and their affairs are decided through consultation (*shura*) among themselves'.[62] The concept of *shura* has been crucial in every political system or ideology that claims to be based on Islam: 'It is put forward by every Islamic regime as the basis of its legitimacy. It is presented as the answer to Western democracy.'[63] Sometimes the notion of the *shura* signals a consultative assembly that serves to advise a despotic ruler; or it may denote an assembly of jurists ruling over a traditional Islamic society subject to the holy law. It is obvious that such interpretations of *shura* are hardly consistent with the notion of political power residing in every citizen. It is a mark of Gaddafi's originality that he has taken a traditional Islamic concept and extended it in an unprecedented fashion to every member of society. This is a highly democratic interpretation of the consultative idea that has informed Islamic polity from the earliest times: whether or not it is a practical approach to politics in the modern state is another matter.

To Gaddafi the central problem is how individual sovereignty can be maintained in modern society, 'rather than – as a Western democrat might phrase it – how to ensure that the state does not abuse those fractions of sovereignty each citizen has to give up, except in the general interest'.[64] What Gaddafi describes in Volume 1 of the Green Book, and what to a degree he managed to implement, is a political system with autonomous local districts, a central government with diminished powers, and ministries that are little more than functional secretariats (see Figure 6.1). The aim has been to sustain the sovereignty of individual Libyan citizens through the creation of popular assemblies (*mutamarat*) and committees (*lijan*); in such a system that the committee is pervasive at every political level and in every social sector. Every resident belongs to a sovereign *popular assembly* at the district level; members meet for an annual week of evening sessions to receive reports on local matters and to agree an agenda of important issues (such issues can range widely: from the relation between law and Islam to foreign aid, from policies on expatriates to economic development). The chairman and other mandated delegates carry the findings and conclusions of the meetings to the annual National Assembly which in turn takes its majority decisions to the secretariats.

Every three years each of the *popular assemblies* elects people to serve on fifteen popular committees with responsibility for local services (in such areas as education, health, justice, youth affairs, water, transport and telecommunications): technically responsible to the districts, the committees liaise closely with the secretariats. The *popular assemblies* elect their own executive committees responsible for the day-to-day use of local sovereignty; and the members are in charge of the elections. They supervise the annual assembly meetings, and serve as an effective court of appeal against local administrators. Libya has around four dozen districts and some 170 sub-districts.[65] The idea is that individual sovereignty can be preserved in such a structure. Here the committees and the congresses '*are* "the solution to the problem of democracy"'.[66] At least this is what the official Libyan claim would be: in fact, since chairmen have executive power and come from one of the sub-districts, people from other component sub-districts are in effect represented by men they have not chosen. The dreaded *representation* has not been avoided, even in the Libyan system. Moreover, the secretariats have wide powers of interpretation which necessarily influence the scope of their decision making.

It is easy to point to the shortfall between the Green Book declarations on the principles of individual sovereignty and what has actually been achieved in Libyan society, but it should also be remembered that few other countries would happily face a comparison of idealistic theory and day-to-

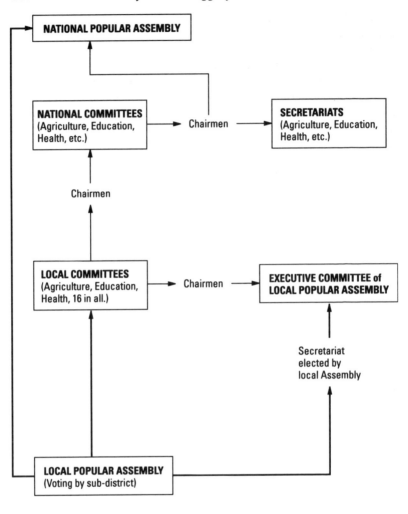

Figure 6.1   The Structure of Committees

Source: John Davis, *Libyan Politics, Tribe and Revolution* (London: I. B. Tauris, 1987) p. 21.

day practice. In some cases the Libyan authorities tried to introduce democratic practices into sectors of the economy which were in the event blocked by expatriate labour. Thus in the oil industry foreign personnel were unwilling to carry our decisions democratically reached by revolutionary workers,[67] and the partial democratisation of the armed forces had to be tackled by the creation of a people's militia rather than through any extension of the committee principle. (Davis has remarked that Gaddafi's reforms in the armed forces 'amounted to universal arming of the population',[68] which itself suggests how secure Gaddafi felt among his own people.)

Gaddafi is opposed to a number of political devices that seem broadly congenial to Western democrats. For example, he is opposed to the plebiscite, seen as yet another form of deception. Anyone asked simply to say 'yes' or 'no', without being allowed to give the reasons for the decision, is being subjected to 'the most cruel and most extreme form of repressive dictatorship': there is an illusion of democracy but no substance. The important task, as set forth in the Green Book, is to point 'the right way for human society to arrive at the society of direct democracy based on the authority of the people'; and to this end, 'People's congresses are the only means of achieving popular democracy. All forms of government in force in the world today are non-democratic until and unless they are guided to this system. People's congresses are the end of a long journey of the masses towards democracy.' Gaddafi's aim is that *every member of society, male and female'* will be able to participate in a direct form of democracy. In contrast to western forms of democracy where it is claimed that the people are able to supervise the government, Gaddafi prefers the concept of a democracy that enshrines 'the supervision of the people of themselves'.

The first volume of the Green Book ends with a warning of what will happen if true liberty for the masses is not achieved:

> Finally the era of the masses is advancing hastily upon us, after the era of republics. It sets feelings ablaze, and dazzles sights! Yet at the same time that it announces the coming of true liberty for the masses, and the happy deliverance from the shackles of old forms of governments, it also warns of an era of social chaos and disintegration if the new democracy, which is the authority of the people is defeated and followed by the rule of any particular individual, class, tribe, confessional group, or political party.

To show that he is aware of empty utopian dreams he concludes by observing that: 'In reality, those who are strong always rule.' In the same spirit, and more recently (at the General People's Congress session held on

17 March 1990), Gaddafi is reported as saying: 'Democracy is good but it needs perseverance.'[69] It is unreasonable in this context to cite the gap between theory and practice to deny that Muammar al-Gaddafi has democratic aspirations.

RELIGION

Gaddafi's writings (brief as they are), his speeches and his interviews suggest that religion is important to him. The Third Universal Theory is rooted in a theistic view of the world, and he is always ready to cite Islamic tradition as justification for his moral and political philosophy. However, he has frequently quarrelled with orthodox Muslim factions in Libya and with strict Muslim groups in other countries; many of the underground Islamic movements will have nothing to do with Gaddafi, believing him to be a false interpreter of the teaching of the Prophet. Gaddafi is apt to cite Islam as a basis for all Libyan actions but most other Islamic governments remain unconvinced. He characteristically ignores caveats from other religious leaders and proclaims that Libya is central to the worldwide resurgence of Islam. His proclamation of the Libyan Republic on 1 September 1969 (see Appendix 8) begins with the words: 'In the Name of God, the Compassionate, the Merciful . . .'. And he is unambiguous about what he perceives as the religious significance of Libya's 'unique example':

> Libya is the unique example of a comprehensive revolution offered to all mankind for the purpose of liberating the human being, whom the Koran calls God's deputy on earth, from all material and spiritual obstacles involving his will. Islam is nothing other than the humanistic revolution: absolute belief in people's innate good powers and capabilities, which enable them to overcome the effects of injustice and aggression that have held them back and which enable them to take the path of progress. Consequently the revolution of the people in the Libyan Jamahiriya is part of the worldwide Islamic movement which, following bleak centuries, is fighting for its fitting place in the world of today.[70]

In subsequent speeches and addresses Gaddafi's religious commitment has been clearly expressed. Thus during a press conference at RCC headquarters in Tripoli in April 1972 he was asked: 'You are a true Moslem, Mr President. What is the role played by religion in your private life? What is the relation between your religious consciousness and the political decisions you have made?' Gaddafi replied that there is 'no contradiction between religious consciousness and political decisions'.[71] A consequence of this view – of the assumed identity of religion and politics – is that political failures can be attributed to human corruptibility, to a sinful departure from the teachings of the Prophet. Gaddafi advised the *Le Monde* correspondent on 8 June 1970 to 'read the Koran or reread it'; here would be found 'the answers to all your questions. Arab unity, socialism, inheritance rights, the place of women in society, the inevitable fall of the Roman empire, the destruction of our planet following the intervention of the atom bomb. It's all there for anyone willing to read it.'

Gaddafi's approach to religious debate was institutionalised on the Supreme Council for National Guidance where mufti from all over the Arab world joined with Libyans to delineate a philosophy of the revolution. *Sharia* law, its relation to the Koran and its application in the modern world were debated, after which the RCC drew up a system of laws supposedly based on the correct interpretation of Islamic doctrine. One of the laws – RCC Decree of 11 October 1972 – stipulated that thieves and armed robbers should be punished by the amputation of hand and foot, though this law was not enacted without much debate. Judges, mufti, journalists and linguistic experts discussed the issue on television and elsewhere. Perhaps a metaphorical interpretation could be agreed: did severing the hand of a thief mean no more than 'interrupting' the hand by removing temptation and social pressure, and by securing a religious conversion? Or was literal amputation the correct Islamic view? The literal interpretation prevailed: amputation would mean amputation, but Article 21 specified amputation by medical methods including anaesthetics, and the many qualifying clauses made the frequent use of the punishment unlikely. In any event this law and the accompanying enactments in the corpus were claimed to be true to correct Islamic doctrine.

Gaddafi himself has been known to interrupt meetings with heads of state so that he could pray at the proper time. He has presented Soviet and other communist leaders, supposed atheists, with copies of the Koran, so adopting the role of an Islamic preacher in high places. One of the earliest decisions of the RCC, under Gaddafi's control, was to create the Islamic Call Society, today an active society for the propagation of Islam in many educational and humanitarian programmes in countries throughout the world. Gaddafi reckons that any materialist civilisation without religious faith is akin to Ad and Thamud in the Koran, which God destroyed because of their corruption.[72] Only Islam, according to Gaddafi, can bring human beings back to the state of society that God willed for the world; only Islam can provide the correct basis for morals and politics in the modern world.

At the first conference of the Islamic Call Society, held in Tripoli in December 1970, Gaddafi asserted that Islam is the last divine address to humanity, with Muhammad the seal of God's messengers to mankind; every Muslim has an obligation to spread this universal faith to ensure that the 'word of God remains uppermost'[73] until the time of the Resurrection. In this view all moral principles and all human knowledge – even that relating to such topics as mathematics and astronomy[74] – have their basis in the Koran. The central question for Gaddafi has always been how the traditional teaching could be made relevant to the conditions of the modern age: 'What is needed is positive change, or progress. By change, however, is not meant altering the basic principles, or essence of the faith or *sharia*, but change in the ways in which they can be applied to today's conditions and problems.' Here Islam is depicted as a universal system capable of answering all human questions and solving all human problems.

There is still scope for interpretation and for adding to the sacred corpus of laws and received doctrine. Thus in an interview with *Qarinah*, a journal published by the Faculty of Literature at the University of Gar Yunis, Benghazi, Gaddafi conceded that other laws could be devised to complement the *sharia*, with the important proviso that human rights and dignity must be safeguarded; some Islamic thinkers have called this open-ended approach to the *sharia* an instance of 'reprehensible innovation'. This highlights the perennial problems that surround the interpretation of any sacred canon: in one context doctrinal departures and expansions can serve a creative purpose in a changing world, but in another context dissensions and schisms may be the only outcome. Gaddafi's Third Universal Theory was prefigured in many of his earlier utterances, not least in those depicting Islam as the divine message of truth. The Theory is not intended as a new message, 'because there is no new message after the message of the apostle Mohammad', but it is necessary to clarify Libyan identity and the path to be followed: 'For any man who follows a way other than the truth will not reach his goal, but will surely go astray.'

Another problem is how religions can be allowed to co-exist in the same community and in the same world: Islam is, after all, a proselytising faith. In Sri Lanka in August 1976 Gaddafi exhorted the Muslims in that pluralistic country to live peacefully with people of other religions ('Since the motto of Muslims is peace, then they must be missionaries of peace everywhere'). At the same time there is a constant *jihad*, though Islam should be spread by persuasion rather than by force. All other religions are incapable of solving human problems; only Islam, with its rich cultural diversity, is suited to all the human societies throughout the world: 'all the religions which came before it were local dispensations. They were concluded with

Islam which is addressed to all humanity.' It is also suggested that despite the spiritual primacy of Islam good can be found in other religions. Gaddafi has praised the Red Cross as well as the Red Crescent, hoping that they will be able to work side by side in the world. Even Christian missionary groups working to spread Christianity are applauded because at least they are preaching religion. Gaddafi insists that he does not wish to turn Christians into Muslims. The central task is to bring religion, of whatever sort, to all the millions of people in the world who have no faith. 'We should seek first to turn these millions of people to religion; then all will be easy.'[75] The ultimate aim is for a 'universal religion' that will come to be recognised by all people.

A Libyan-sponsored Muslim/Christian discussion was held in Tripoli in February 1976; here Gaddafi called for greater understanding between the various followers of divine scripture: Jews, Christians and Muslims. He suggested that the various conflicts between the different religious traditions had only occurred because the various devotees had not been true to their respective sacred texts. Muslims had not followed the Koran as they should, just as Jews had neglected the Torah, and Christians the Gospel; but in the end the Jews and Christians can only recover their faith by turning to the Koran. Until that happens, Gaddafi is keen to promote religious harmony since the main battle is against the unbeliever: 'We must overcome our problems in order that we do not promote atheism among our people and prevent them from abandoning faith altogether.'[76] When Roger Garaudy, the French Marxist who later converted to Islam, visited Gaddafi in May 1978 there was talk of the possibility of *jihad* against the state of Israel. While declaring that such a conflict was necessary, Gaddafi also said that it was impossible to have a war between Muslims and Christians, or between Muslims or Jews, 'because we are all the children of Abraham, our forefather'. In struggling against idolatry in all its forms, 'we are all people of the Book'.[77] However, the Koran also counsels Muslims 'not to take the Jews and Christians as allies, for they are allies of one another. Whoever of you befriends them, shall be one of them'.[78] If Gaddafi wants a reason for preserving his antagonism for Israel and the United States he can find it easily enough in Koranic texts.

On 15–18 March 1982 the 'first intellectual gathering' of Arab students studying in Libya was held in Tripoli. At this meeting Gaddafi declared that the just society safeguards individual rights without violating the rights of God; the primary source of the law of society is the Koran, with the *sunnah* (the example of Mohammad's life) the second source, the *qiyas* (analogical reasoning, for addressing questions about which the Koran and the sunnah are silent) the third, and the *ijtihad* (individual reasoning and scientific knowledge) the fourth. Gaddafi gave as an example of his own *ijtihad* the first part of the Green Book dealing with the law of society: problems were tackled by adapting Islamic philosophy to social circumstances rather than by unthinkingly relying on this or that Koranic text.

The Jamahiriya (or 'popular republic') was created on 2 March 1977, on the Prophet's birthday, and at the same time it was declared that the Koran was the official law (*sharia*) of Libya. This development was consistent with Gaddafi's earlier pronouncements. Thus at a political symposium on 26 October 1972 in Tripoli he had spoken of the 'perfection' of the Koran, how it served as a 'guiding light', able to solve personal problems and to offer answers to international questions. Muslims were exhorted to reject books and political theories that were influenced by the social decadence that characterised the machine age, and to return to the original source of their spiritual strength: 'We are a nation with a special mission, possessing a Book which was sent down from heaven, a Book in which we all believe.' And again there is the insistence that all questions can be resolved by a diligent study of the Koran: 'Anyone who does not know true economics – let him look in the Koran where he will find true socialism. Anyone who wishes to study astronomy should know that its basic principles are to be found in the Koran. Anyone who seeks the laws that govern human societies in times of war and peace, and which govern international relations – let him look in the Koran, for they are there.'[79]

On 3 July 1978 Gaddafi debated Islamic doctrine with a group of Muslim religious scholars (*ulama*) in Tripoli. Much of the talk focused on the extent to which the *hadith* (reports from the Prophet) should complement the Koran as a source of spiritual and social guidance, a central problem being how to know which of the various *hadith* traditions associated with Mohammad to accept. Gaddafi argued that many of the sacred books had been subject to interpolations and alterations, and so could not be trusted in their entirety ('Where is that which the Messenger actually uttered, and where is that which he did not utter?'). This is the familiar problem of theological exegesis: human beings must stand above the texts if they wish to evaluate them; in which case there is the paradox that the text, once evaluated, cannot serve as a *primary* ground for truth. There are many different *hadith* texts: 'If we were now to study the corpus of *hadith* literature, we would find sixty kinds of *hadith*.' Gaddafi was even able to cite seemingly contradictory *hadith* to prove his point: how could it ever be known which, if any, corresponded to the truth? He concludes that for these reasons the *hadith* cannot serve as a basis for determining the law of society. The Koran, by contrast, is the eternal word of God.

The Koran offers precepts and laws that are intended to govern both life on earth and the life to come. It offers practical guidance in such areas as marriage and divorce, alimony and inheritance, theft and adultery. The precepts give guidance on how to build a just and virtuous society, and general principles are available to illuminate such questions as morality, social harmony and goodness. People are exhorted not to transgress against others in this life, to show consideration and to behave without malice. In one section the Koran says: 'O you who have faith, let not any people mock other people, for perhaps they may be better than them. Nor let any woman mock other women, for perhaps they may be better than them. Do not slander one another, nor should you despise one another through name-calling.'[80] Gaddafi interprets this text to mean that no social class should enslave another, and he concludes that in consequence the Koran permits revolution against slavery.

He also cites the Koranic admonition: 'Those who hoard gold and silver, and do not spend it for the cause of God – announce to them a painful torment.'[81] This is taken as support for the socialist ideal, with 'gold and silver' interpreted as including today's hard currencies that are smuggled out of Libya in dollars and deposited in foreign banks. Gaddafi concludes that people should work and eat, work and consume: 'Then anything you have beyond your immediate needs does not belong to you.' Of the Koran's recognition of the differences in society between the rich and the poor, and how this has sometimes been used by Muslims to justify the exploitation of the downtrodden, Gaddafi retorts: 'Is religion then slaves and servants, maidservants and numerous wives? Is it big palaces and tall buildings? Is it spending the fast of Ramadan in Germany and making the *hajj* pilgrimage by way of Rome? Is it big bellies and bulging pockets? Is this religion? No, I seek refuge in God! If this is what religion is, I will abandon it before morning. On the contrary, I am sure that the exact opposite is true! Religion came to abolish all such rotten things.'[82]

In August 1982 Gaddafi discussed the Green Book at the second conference of the Islamic Call Society, exploring the relation of the new text to the Koran and the *hadith* tradition. In fact the *ulama* were angered by the second part of the Green Book which urged the abolition of wages and private property. There had been no precedent in Islam for such measures, and it was at this stage that the *ulama* broke with the regime. Clerics argued also that there was nothing in the *sunnah* to justify the Green Book recommendations on private property. Gaddafi was accused by members of the *ulama* of being a Marxist and of holding heretical views that contradicted the *hadith*. The *ulama* had a practical as well as a theological reason for declaring that the Green Book was contrary to Islam: the clerics had strong links with the commercial sector, many of them related to merchant families and bound to merchant capitalism by complex economic relationships. A prime source of clerical income was the *waqf*, the religious endowment offered by trading families; and the social standing of individual clerics was signalled by the level of endowment made to their mosques by wealthy traders.

Gaddafi responded to the clerical opposition by warning the *ulama*, in a speech at a Tripoli mosque in February 1978, not to form a political alliance with the merchant classes to oppose his policies. He argued that the Green Book was compatible with Islam, and then in May denounced the *ulama* for 'propagating heretical stories elaborated over the course of centuries of decadence'.[83] On 21 May Gaddafi announced an 'Islamic Revolution' and urged the masses to occupy the mosques: they had to be seized from the *ulama* who had introduced 'foreign and non-Islamic ideas'. In July he again engaged in theological debate to uphold the principles of the Green Book, and while acknowledging the primacy of the Koran he cited *ijtihad* in justification for the Third Universal Theory. Gaddafi argued also that every individual had a right to *ijtihad*, the right to think for himself on religious and political questions. He has cited *ijtihad* to alter the calendar so that it began from Mohammad's death in 632 AD instead of the flight to Medina (*hijra*); to deny that the *hajj* (pilgrimage) is an essential element in Islam; and to make changes in the *zakat* (charitable tax). Gaddafi also moved to establish the metaphorical rather than the literal interpretation of the law stipulating the amputation of the hands and feets of thieves. Gaddafi has been depicted as an Islamic modernist rather than a fundamentalist. He is not 'another Mahdi al-Sanussi, rising out of the Libyan desert to create a theocratic empire'.[84]

We can see that Gaddafi is a 'flexible reinterpreter'.[85] interested more in the needs of a modern state than in the demands of orthodoxy. In this he has found himself at odds with fervent Muslims in Libya and in other Arab states. Gaddafi has always been a committed upholder of Islam, but has also tried to reach for a broader religious vision (see Appendix 9) in which other faiths are tolerated; this has not endeared Muammar al-Gaddafi to the assorted fundamentalists that still argue for various versions of orthodoxy throughout the Islamic world.

WOMEN

The third volume (or chapter) of the Green Book is concerned with 'solving the problem of society': social commentary is followed by a discussion of particular social questions, one of which is the position of women. Gaddafi claims, in considering the character and rights of women, to be basing his views on both the Islamic tradition and the specific needs of his own society.

He begins with the useful observation that 'woman and man are both human, without any doubt or disagreement'; it follows that 'women and men are equal in their humanity, and any distinction between them on the human plane is an act of naked and unjustifiable oppression'. However, this suggestion fails to conduct Gaddafi to a position that would satisfy main-stream feminism. Men and women, he argues, have distinct physical differences that dictate different roles in society. At times a woman's biological functions – menstruation, pregnancy and suckling – make her unfit to be a fully active member of society. (In 1973 Gaddafi enraged feminists in Cairo when he suggested that because of certain 'biological defects' women could not hope to succeed in all tasks traditionally performed by men. When challenged that a woman could do any job, Gaddafi retorted: 'In that case you won't complain if we ask women in our army to parachute when they are pregnant.') It is important, according to Gaddafi, that the natural bio-logical functions are respected and allowed to function as God intended; for this reason Gaddafi is hostile to birth control and bottle-feeding. He is also opposed to nurseries as involving coercion and oppression of the child and denying women their human dignity and natural medium of expression. Pregnancy, it is argued, prevents women from undertaking tasks that in-volve great physical exertion, which means that they are unsuited to mining, much factory work and the like. Gaddafi objects in particular to the phrase 'There is no difference between man and woman in anything': the 'in anything' is 'the great deceiver of the woman'. There is no difference between men and women in their common humanity, their rights and freedom; but a woman is only truly free when she is not forced through economic necessity to do unsuitable male jobs; a woman is only truly free when she is allowed to be a female.

Gaddafi emphasises that all societies regard women as commodities: the East sees her as merchandise, and the West looks at her 'not as a female'. By nature, women are intended to bear children and to look after them in the home; women are not precluded from work, providing it is suited to their abilities and to their physical characteristics. Women are limited by their biologies, handicapped by pregnancy and further tied by their need to breastfeed their babies 'for about two years'. Women have as much right as men to fulfilment but this cannot be achieved through violating their god-given natures: 'driving women to do men's work is unjust aggression . . . A woman has full rights to live without being forced to change into a man and to give up her femininity. A woman is tender. A woman is pretty. A woman weeps easily. A woman is easily frightened. In general, woman is gentle and man is tough by virtue of their inbred nature.' It need hardly be remarked that these views are traditional in the Arab world, though departures from orthodoxy should also be noted. Polygamy is banned in Libya, against Islamic tradition; and women are active in the political committees and in such unlikely arenas as the armed forces. The Women's Military Academy was founded in 1978, and in his speeches at the first graduation in 1981 Gaddafi declared that the officers produced by the Academy would have duties spanning the full range of military activities: the women would not merely serve as a corps of auxiliaries as, according to Gaddafi, they do in the American armed forces.

The graduation ceremony was attended by the armed forces commander Brigadier General Abu Bakr Yunis Jaber, the commandment of the Academy, and other armed forces officers. Gaddafi declared that Libya's gradual 'mobilisation' had begun shortly after the air battle with US planes over the Gulf of Sirte on 19 August 1981, as a first step in the 'patriotic mobilisation of all the Arab nations' combat forces'. In broadcasts on Tripoli Radio on 17 and 18 April 1981 Gaddafi expounded on the role of Libyan women in the armed forces.[86] He pointed out that detractors had said it was impossible for women to come forward to join a military academy, but this had been proved wrong: 'Revolutionary transformations have surpassed such mentalities and created a new individual.' It was a source of particular pride that 'the first military academy for girls in the world is today graduating officers in the Jamahariya . . . We in the Jamahariya and the great revolution affirm respect for women and are raising their flag. We have resolved to totally liberate women in Libya, thus . . . removing them from the world of oppression and subjugation, so that they may be masters of their own fate in a democratic milieu where they have equal opportunities with all other members of society.' In this context the Women's Military Academy would serve as a 'cornerstone' for the liberation of women in Libya, the rest of the Arab world, and beyond. A central task would be to liberate the 'oppressed and paralysed' female half of the Arab nations.

It seems clear that Gaddafi, contrary to the facile tenets of the Green Book, had long toyed with a degree of female emancipation that would have been totally at odds with the traditional Islamic practices of pre-revolutionary Libya and the modern societies of Kuwait, the UAE and Saudi Arabia. In 1978 Gaddafi was encouraging the emancipation of the one section of society that was 'not yet free': he declared that 'women are still enslaved and tied by serious social chains, and still suffer injustice because, unfortunately, until now there was no revolutionary tool capable of mobilising women for the revolution of their liberation'.[87] Women cadres were picked to form the basis of a revolutionary caucus, and the Revolutionary Women's Formation was created to advance the cause of Libyan women. This was an immense task in a traditional Islamic culture where women were draped head to foot in public and encouraged not to leave the house (men even shopped so that their wives and daughters could remain incarcerated at home); women were sold by their fathers to the highest bidder and executed for adultery. This was the social context in which Gaddafi moved to his vision of female emancipation.

In 1975 he had created the Libyan General Women's Federation to remove the worst features of social oppression, and by 1979 there were some twenty local branches. The Federation offered support in traditional female areas – helping with hygiene and baby care, running nurseries and kindergartens (against the edicts of the Green Book) – but also expanding female horizons by combating illiteracy, and by helping girls to enter school and university. Health centres had been established to improve the welfare of women and their children: family planning facilities were offered (again contrary to the Green Book), as was medical support for pregnancy, birth and lactation. These centres worked in conjunction with the Social Care and Enlightenment Centres specialising in social work and community health, institutions that were unheard of in pre-revolutionary Libya. In addition, a Centre for the Protection of Women was created in Tripoli to help with the rehabilitation of women such as divorcees, prostitutes, and others abandoned by their families. Under Gaddafi women witnessed for the first time 'a proliferation of educational opportunities'.[88] The People's Committee for Education and the Ministry of Education are prohibited from discriminating on grounds of sex when granting stipends to students. Since the fall of the monarchy the number of females in the educational system has risen at all levels.

In 1970, immediately after the seizure of power, there was legislation (Law no. 58) to affirm the equal status of men and women, and to establish wage parity for male and female workers in the same occupation. In 1972 the passing of Law no. 172 established new rights for women in the areas of marriage and divorce: brides would have to be at least sixteen years old and consenting; brides were allowed for the first time to enter into marriages against their guardians wishes; and the guardians could be similarly overruled by the courts on matters of divorce. Other laws in 1973 gave social security protection to widows, female divorcees over forty, and unmarried mothers. Women who had worked for at least six months became entitled to fifty days' maternity leave, various cash benefits, and an extension of thirty days if there were medical complications during the delivery.

Many unprecedented measures were put in place during the 1970s but they still had to contend with age-old Islamic attitudes. And the inevitable tensions between tradition and emancipation can easily be detected in Gaddafi himself: on the one hand he applauds the familiar domestic role for women but on the other he urges a revolutionary liberation of women throughout the Arab world and beyond. Whatever the theoretical disputation, there can be no doubt that the position of Libyan women has massively improved since the overthrow of the monarchy.

ARMAMENTS

One of the early priorities of the revolutionary Libyan government was to build up a comprehensive arms capability: this began with such items as jet aircraft and armoured vehicles, and continues today – according to some observers – with the stockpiling of chemical weapons, a biological weapons research programme, and ongoing efforts to achieve a nuclear-weapons capability. As soon as Gaddafi seized power the old British arms agreements were renounced and the new regime looked to France to provide military hardware. Mirage aircraft were an attractive option: the Israelis had demonstrated their effectiveness by sweeping across the Nile Valley on 5 June 1967 to bomb the Egyptian MiGs before they had chance to leave their airfields; by the end of the day the Israeli aircraft had destroyed three hundred Egyptian planes and nineteen airbases, and the Israelis were then securely placed to occupy the Sinai desert, the West Bank and the Golan Heights. The technical competence of the Mirages had impressed the world.

President Pompidou found the possibility of supplying Mirages to Libya irresistible: he would at once find a solution to France's pressing oil problems and move into a strategic area where the British and the Americans had become unwelcome. The French decision was resented by the other major powers but French diplomats explained that the Libyans only wanted the sophisticated aircraft as expensive toys, as status symbols for the new regime; in due course the Libyans lent some of their Mirages to Egypt. When Pompidou was criticised during his visit to the United States in February 1970 he attempted to justify the sales of Mirage jets to Libya with the familiar argument of all arms traders: 'There was a vacuum to fill and we thought it was in our interests and – I add – the interests of others to fill it.'[89] The new Libyan regime had managed to acquire modern aircraft but after Gaddafi sent the Mirages to Egypt during the 1973 Arab/Israeli war the West was reluctant to allow any further arms deals with the Libyan government. In consequence Gaddafi looked to the East.,

In 1975 a huge deal was struck with the Soviet Union, said to be worth more than $500 million: this included 2000 tanks and two squadrons of MiG-23 jet aircraft. It was obvious that Libya could not use this quantity of armament and again there was the danger that military equipment would be shipped to other countries.[90] Gaddafi still worked hard to secure what arms he could from Western sources, and some deals were made that were of doubtful value. Once the Israelis had demonstrated the Star-Tron night-seeing device during the 1973 war the Libyans ordered 3000 Star-Trons from a Paris company that had obtained the sales licence. However, the French government prohibited the export and so the company faked the Star-Trons and fed them through the Atlantico arms-dealing company in Madrid. The deal was authorised by a Libyan inspector who promptly disappeared after the money had been paid over.[91] Libya had invested heavily in useless equipment.

Throughout the 1970s, according to the US Arms Control and Disarmanent Agency, worldwide arms exports grew 60 per cent, with thirty-nine per cent of the total coming from the United States and twenty-eight per cent from the Soviet Union. With 'arms' taken to include all support services and construction, the main arms importer was Iran, followed by Israel, Iraq, Libya and West Germany. In all such cases there was always the possibility that purchased hardware might finish up where the original suppliers may not have wished. In fact Libya replaced the eleven MiG-21 jets lost by Uganda in the 1976 Israeli raid on Entebbe. It is known that France, Britain and other suppliers impose few end-use conditions, and we may speculate that military equipment supplied to one country may be intentionally destined for another location. Even if the hardware stays in the purchaser country it may come to be used in ways that the supplier country disapproves, as was demonstrated in the use of Arab squadrons in the 1973 war and by Iraq's use of Western technology in the 1991 Gulf war. France had imposed a few end-use restrictions on the Libyan MiGs but merely complained ineffectually when these were ignored.

US sanctions have been used to block various Libyan efforts to acquire military equipment. In March 1979 the American firm Smith and Wesson were ordered to pay a civil penalty of $120,000 for the unauthorised sale of 283 rifle night-sights to Libya. An order in 1978 for eight C-130 aircraft that Libya had already paid for was blocked by Washington, along with an order for spare parts for aircraft that Libya had already acquired. Gaddafi was however permitted to buy four hundred army-type trucks and he had already obtained Boeing-Vertol Chinook helicopters through Italy.[92] The US aerospace consultant George C. Pritt was quoted at that time in *Aviation Week* as opposing the bans on sales to Libya. He argued that paying Libya $4 billion a year for oil, revenue which could be used to buy aircraft in Europe, was no different in end result from a direct barter of US planes for Libyan oil. However, the bans remained in place and have been intensified in recent years; immediately after the 1969 revolution Libya was not even allowed to purchase US maps and navigation charts.

The Libyan acquisition of 110 Mirages in 1970 had affected the balance of power in the area, and there were further shifts in power and influence to come. Libya had loaned Egypt Mirages during the 1973 war (to be flown by Egyptians as Libya had only twenty-five trained pilots for the aircraft), but when Sadat signalled his willingness to negotiate with Israel he lost Libyan support. Some Egyptian technical staff were expelled from Libya and Egypt itself withdrew others, including the much-needed pilot instructors. Cairo also withdrew two ships and dismantled the surface-to-air missile (SAM) sites that it had placed on Libyan territory; and Egyptian work on the air-defence system around Tripoli, Benghazi and Tobruk was brought to an end. Gaddafi managed to import pilot instructors and technicians from Pakistan, France, Italy and Yugoslavia to fill the gap. He tried to obtain military equipment from the West but was again forced to look to Moscow. A deal was signed in Moscow for the barter of Libyan oil for Soviet SAM batteries. In December 1974 Moscow agreed to supply Libya with Tu-22 supersonic bombers, MiG-23s, the massive MI-8 troopcarrier helicopters, SA-3 and SA-6 batteries, T-62 tanks and antitank missiles. In addition, five hundred Soviet advisors were brought in to train Libyan personnel.

In April 1975 Britain blocked a projected deal for six submarines and thirty-eight Jaguar aircraft, an intended order of around $1.4 billion for British manufacturers, but London remained keen to authorise the sale of other equipment deemed less destabilising: transport aircraft, frigates, tank transports, ammunition and support equipment. However, Gaddafi wanted the full deal and so turned again to the Soviet Union. In May Kosygin arrived in Tripoli and a deal, said by the Cairo newspaper *Al Ahram* to be worth $4 billion, was agreed.[93] Four hundred more T-62s were promised, which would bring the Libyan total up to around one thousand; and submarines, with support facilities at Tobruk and Benghazi, were also included. By 1977 there were 800 Soviet advisors in Libya and 1100 Libyan trainees in the Soviet union. Training remained a problem, as it does today: Sadat, commenting on the rapid build-up of military power in Libya, suggested – drawing on his experience of the Egyptian armed forces – that it would take the Libyans 'twenty to fifty years' to learn to operate their new equipment.

In any event the deal was useful to Moscow: the Soviet Union continued in the 1980s offering 'arms for oil' to Libya (and to Iraq, Algeria and Syria).

In recent years there has been growing concern about the likelihood of nuclear proliferation, an anxiety hightened by such circumstances as the growing Israeli stockpile of nuclear weapons,[94] nuclear research in various Third World countries, and Iraqi efforts to built a nuclear device. Gaddafi himself remarked in 1976 that 'atomic weapons will be like traditional ones, possessed by every state according to its potential. We will have our share of this new weapon.'[95] In 1975 Russia had agreed to build a small nuclear reactor for Libya, with the West taking heart at the belief that a small ten-megawatt facility could never be used to generate enough plutonium for an atomic bomb. It has been said that Libya tried to buy a nuclear bomb from China in 1970 and that since that time he has made many other efforts with the same goal in mind. The Pakistani nuclear-weapons research programme has been partly funded by Libya, with the possibility that Pakistan will one day give Gaddafi a nuclear weapon or the necessary expertise for him to develop his own nuclear research. In March 1986 President Zia ul-Haq made no secret of his view that a Pakistani bomb would belong to 'the entire Islamic world': 'if the Islamic world possessed this technology, it means that 900 million Muslims possess advanced technology. Here comes the aggressive campaign against Pakistan and the aggressive talk about the Pakistani nuclear bomb. It is our right to obtain the technology. And when we acquire the technology, the entire Islamic world will possess it with us.'[96] Libya helped, on at least one occasion, by obtaining 100 tons of yellowcake (uranium) from Niger and then conveying it on to Pakistan.[97] On 22 June 1987 Reuters reported Gaddafi as saying: 'The Arabs must possess the atom bomb to defend themselves, until their numbers reach one thousand million and until they learn to desalinate water and until they liberate Palestine.'[98]

In June 1981 Gaddafi had declared that the production of nuclear weapons must be regarded as a *terrorist* priority: 'As long as the big powers continue to manufacture atomic weapons, it means that they are continuing to terrorise the world . . . I have nothing but scorn for the notion of an Islamic bomb. There is no such thing as an Islamic bomb or a Christian bomb. Any such weapon is a means of terrorising humanity, and we are against the manufacture and acquisition of nuclear weapons. This is in line with our definition of – and opposition to – terrorism . . . this does not mean that we will spare any effort to use atomic energy for peaceful purposes.'[99] This denial of Libya's intention to develop nuclear weapons has been reiterated many times, though his parallel condemnation of terrorism is rightly viewed with scepticism (see Chapter Seven). In the early 1980s it was reported that a West German firm, Kraftwerkunion AG (KWU) was cooperating with Libya in the building of a nuclear reactor facility, one big enough – unlike the Soviet-supplied reactor outside Tripoli – to generate weapons-grade enriched uranium. However, no evidence emerged through the 1980s that the KWU site, at Sebba in Fezzan, was in fact part of a nuclear-weapons research programme.

In the 1970s Gaddafi had even tried to obtain a complete reactor from American suppliers. Executives at Gulf and General Atomics Corporation of Los Angeles had indicated that they were prepared to agree a deal and contracts were drawn up; but when Washington heard about the deal there were speedy moves, apparently involving Henry Kissinger, to block it. Gaddafi then turned to Adera Incorporated, a firm of American consultants, and talks took place in New York, Tripoli and elsewhere. It soon emerged that the Libyans were interested in more than an innocent nuclear-powered generator and Adera too broke off the talks. By the late 1970s Libyan efforts to gain information from the Pakistani nuclear research programme, following generous Libyan financial support, appeared to have ended, partly because of Gaddafi's unwelcome political demands on General Zia. Nor did Libyan approaches to India bear fruit. Prime Minister Indira Gandhi and later Prime Minister Morarji Desai were willing to offer low-grade nuclear-research information to Third World states as part of India's 'atoms for peace' policy, and to allow the state Bharat Heavy Electric Company to build conventional diesel electric-generating stations in Benghazi and Tripoli. At the same time a Soviet-supplied research reactor was being installed at Tajjura near to the Okba bin Nafi Air Base (formerly Wheelus Field). A nuclear engineering facility was established at the al-Fatah University in Tripoli, helped by two leading Libyan scientists Dr Fathi Nooh, educated at the University of California in Berkeley, and Dr Fathi Skinji, trained in India and the United Kingdom; and by at least one American consultant on loan to Libya from a major US university.[100]

There have been many allegations that Libya is attempting to develop nuclear weapons, though such charges generally derive from hostile sources. In February 1992 Hans Blix, the director of the International Atomic Energy Agency, visited Libya to discuss the country's nuclear activities and intentions. At that time the Libyan Foreign Minister, Ibrahim Muhammed Beshari declared that Libya was committed to the peaceful uses of atomic energy, and that no efforts were being made to recruit nuclear experts from the former Soviet Union. It seems unlikely that Libya possesses even a rudimentary nuclear weapon or is investing in nuclear research intended to produce such a weapons capability. Anxieties in the US and elsewhere that the West German company Orbital Transport und Rakenten-

Aktiengesellschaft (OTRAG), which for a while operated a research site in Fezzan, would supply Libya with ballistic missiles capable of carrying nuclear warheads proved to be groundless. An international outcry induced OTRAG to cease its Libyan operations in 1982. The Swedish government agreed in the late 1970s to train Libyans in guided-missile technology but criticism of the scheme led to its cancellation in January 1982: the Libyan students were sent home and the Swedish government made it clear that there would be no further such courses.[101]

Attempts in the 1990s to demonstrate that Libya was developing nuclear weapons appeared to be nothing more than a political ploy of hostile states, but is there evidence that Libya has chemical weapons? In the late 1980s the US was claiming that Libya had acquired chemical weapons, and press reports attributed to British intelligence sources stated that the Soviet Union had supplied Libya with warheads containing nerve gas for its SCUD-B surface-to-surface missiles.[102] In January 1992 the journalist Andrew Stephen, reporting from Washington, declared that US intelligence analysts are convinced that Libya has stockpiled up to 100 tons of chemical weapons, 'a much bigger arsenal than previously believed'.[103] Robert Gates, the new director of the CIA is reported as saying that 'the Libyans have no intention of giving up CW production' and that they are currently building a second plant – 'one they hope will escape international attention'. It is suggested that satellite surveillance and information from CIA sources in Libya has provided evidence that Gaddafi, fearing another air strike, is dispersing his chemical weapons around the country instead of concentrating them in what the US claims is the main production plant in Rabta, forty miles south-west of Tripoli. In early 1992 these American claims had a very familiar ring.

The Libyan revolution has been massively influential, profoundly affecting the culture and history of the nation and dramatically impacting on the lives of its citizens. There remain many imbalances and paradoxes in Libya's ongoing development, mirrored in the confusions and ambiguities of Gaddafi himself: it is an easy matter to note contradictions in Gaddafi's theoretical statements and between aspects of his theory and the practical plans he espouses. In most of his writing and public speeches he is a dedicated socialist but eager in the real world to make pragmatic accommodations with all manner of capitalist organisations; he urges the importance of 'personal sovereignty' but runs a highly authoritarian state; he has a long-standing commitment to pan-Arabism (in 1992 Libya and Egypt are again growing close) but has often offended other Arab leaders; women, he asserts, are gentle and easily frightened but female soldiers form part of his personal bodyguard when he travels abroad; he urges the primacy of the socialist Jamahariya (people's state) but in the 1990s astounded his fellow revolutionaries by proposing the privatisation of schools and the health service; he has always applauded human dignity and human rights but Amnesty International continues to report hundreds of political prisoners held without trial.

In practical matters Gaddafi's huge investment in the welfare of the Libyan people has made him a popular leader. It is generally conceded, albeit reluctantly in the West, that Gaddafi is unlikely to face hostile public demonstrations or to be toppled by a military coup. However, there have been coup attempts and Libya, like any Third World country, remains vulnerable to attack by the developed nations. Gaddafi's domestic policies – in the early days impacting directly on foreign assets – have been enough to make him viewed as a hate figure in the West. But it is his foreign adventures that have made it easy for Western countries – in particular, the United States – to brand Libya a 'pariah nation'. This has proved a useful arrangement in an American culture that has always thrived on the existence of an external enemy. US policy on Libya was also a consideration in efforts to boost George Bush's popularity in the run-up to the 1992 presidential election. It is useful in this context to consider Libya's foreign activities in recent years.

Part III

Terrorism and the US Response

7 International Ambitions

> *By the passage of time, everyone changes, through experience. In the 1970s we supported liberal movements without knowing which were terrorists and which were not. In the 1980s we began to differentiate between terrorists and those with legitimate political aspirations.*
>
> Muammar al-Gaddafi, 1992

FOREIGN POLICY

Libya's foreign policy derives from the views and philosophy of one man. There are various state organisations through which international policy matters are conducted but the ultimate decision-making is Gaddafi's alone. A change in outlook and emphasis over the years can be detected but Libya's international posture continues to derive from an ideology that has been articulated many times. It has been necessary for Gaddafi to make pragmatic and prudent accommodations with many groups, companies and nations that, in the next breath, he may violently condemn. At one time or another he has antagonised African states, most of the Arab world, and the whole of the West. However, this undoubted circumstance needs to be examined with care. Libya's relative isolation in the modern world can be attributed in part to the mercurial and radical temper of its leader, a man prepared to use violence to achieve his goals; but Libya's status as a pariah nation derives equally from the resentment among powerful states that any small country should dare to challenge an international order that upholds the exploitation of the weak by the strong, and that tolerates levels of violence – sometimes reaching genocidal proportions – in defence of that order.

Gaddafi's political philosophy is rooted in an awareness of Libya's colonial past and in the impact of world events in the 1950s and 1960s. He remains acutely conscious of the devastation brought to the region by the French and Italian colonial powers, and became deeply sensitised to the character of international power politics by the struggle of Nasser's Egypt against Israel, France and the United Kingdom. At the heart of Gaddafi's outlook is the belief that the Third World is victimised by powerful nations, often exploiting racial differences to maintain their global hegemony, and that the United States is a principal villain in this corrupt scheme. With such an outlook Gaddafi has been easily depicted as both a local trouble-maker and a threat to world peace, roles that he seems less keen to assume in the post-Cold-War world. Today the military ascendancy of the United States, as sole superpower, gives Gaddafi pause for thought. He is no doubt equally conscious that Libya has not managed to achieve the desired levels of self-sufficiency, that the nation remains painfully dependent upon foreign workers, foreign technical expertise and foreign markets. Libya remains an immensely vulnerable country, a vast area with a sparse population amounting to less than five million people. This too is likely to generate attitudes that the more secure nations, with their long histories of independence, consider to be impolite. Libya's foreign policies and international posture should be considered in the light of the region's history and in acknowledgement of the fact that not all the political structures in the world are just and morally defensible.

Gaddafi's foreign policies derive from an ideology that is frequently rehearsed in interviews and speeches. His aim is to encourage, by any expedient means, all national and international movements fighting what he perceives to be imperialism, the exploitation of peoples by powerful countries. An initial goal is stimulated by pan-Arabist sentiment, the desire to create a unified Arab nation that will then come to influence the shape of global politics. There is no doubt that Gaddafi believes in the universal relevance of his ethical views and his political commitment: the Third Universal Theory is intended to bear on all mankind, the only route to human emancipation and national pride. He is willing, as circumstances demand, to offer diplomatic relations, foreign aid and even the political merging of states – so far unrealised – if such initiatives will further his aims. In much of this, Gaddafi is no different to many other world leaders, but he is unusual in functioning as the sole reference for his country's foreign policies and in the audacity which he has shown in putting them into effect: there have not been many Third World leaders with small populations that have sought to have a global influence. It would be a mistake to believe that Gaddafi's desire to see a universal ethic and a universal polity derive from mere self-aggrandisement. There is obviously a psychological dynamic – as there is with any charismatic and successful leader – but Gaddafi's ideological and spiritual motivation cannot be gainsaid. It is also true that his assumption of a divine mission has alienated many states in Africa and the Arab world that would otherwise have been sympathetic to his message. Gaddafi's flamboyance and rhetoric have likewise not served him well in public relations: too often his promiscuous indignation and poor judgement – witness his support for the Yanayev coup in the Soviet Union ('a brave historical action') – have set back just causes that would have been better served by a more astute political mind.

In summary, Gaddafi has chosen a wide range of policy tools to influence political events outside Libya: he has trained foreign dissidents and insurgents; provided sanctuary for individuals that other states have dubbed 'terrorists'; supplied weapons to subversive factions in many parts of the world; used all manner of front organisations (commercial, educational, journalistic, cultural); organised assassinations in foreign countries; and launched military invasions (for example, in Uganda in 1979 and in Chad at various times – see below). In all such ventures the orthodox diplomatic facilities in Libya and elsewhere have often been exploited with scant regard to international norms of convention and propriety: what Gaddafi would see as justified revolutionary change can only be furthered by the effective exploitation of any means to hand. The imperialists, he would argue, created the diplomatic protocols and the political structures to sustain their rapacious hegemony: this has nothing to do with justice and humanity.

A number of formal bodies are nominally responsible for the implementation of Libyan foreign policy, though they are often peremptorily instructed by Gaddafi or members of his inner circle. The Libyan Foreign Liaison Secretariat is in ostensible control of policy implementation but may be overruled by other bodies in the bureaucracy; policy tasks are carried out also by the Secretariat for External Security, the Secretariat of Justice, the divisions of General Intelligence and Military Intelligence, and the Libyan Special Security Forces. The Revolutionary Committees, virtually a law unto themselves, have their own bureau, a free-ranging body that may seek to undercut the activities of the more orthodox parts of the functioning bureaucracy. The Islamic Call Society can also impact on other state organisations and influence the shape of foreign policy in many aspects of its implementation. Professional Libyan diplomats sometimes face difficulties in foreign countries because they are unaware of subversive initiatives being undertaken by state bodies outside the diplomatic service. Thus diplomats serving at a particular Libyan People's Bureau may be forced to defend the consequences of actions of which they were unaware and about which they may be unsympathetic. Such confusions doubtless serve the revolutionary Libyan government: there can be genuine Libyan protestations of innocence in foreign capitals while the real business of subversion is conducted. (Other states, it is worth noting, often behave in a similar fashion.)

The Secretariat for External Security, created in February 1984 following a directive of the General People's Congress, is responsible for security and intelligence gathering. One of its main tasks is to coordinate other security and intelligence bodies; in consequence, this secretariat is highly influential in the foreign policy establishment. Gaddafi maintains responsibility for its staffing and for how it interacts with other important groups, such as the revolutionary committees.

The revolutionary committees and the people's bureaus have often been involved in subversive activities as part of their foreign policy strategy: in 1985, for example fresh attempts were made to extend Libyan influence into Latin America, partly to attack US interests and partly to increase the Libyan presence in the Third World. Again the 'up-front' diplomacy is one thing, subversive endeavour quite another. Historically, Gaddafi has shown little discrimination in selecting clandestine subversive groups for support: he has been prepared to support equally separatist organisations, mercenary terrorist groups, and national liberation movements. It seems that little effort has been made to assess the viability of any particular group, its revolutionary credentials, or indeed whether it is in accord with Gaddafi's proclaimed ideology. He is particularly interested in the unity and development of the Arab world but keen at the same time to demonstrate that he can support liberation movements across the religious divide (hence his erstwhile support for the IRA – see below). The 'Universal Theory' is held to apply to all groups and movements seeking to free themselves and their people from oppression and exploitation, even if such factions are temporarily unaware of the compelling validity of the 'one true religion'. In this sense Gaddafi is proud of his cosmopolitan support for liberation movements throughout the world, irrespective of race, creed or ideology.

Gaddafi's support for subversion has achieved, even in his terms, mixed success. In some instances he has alienated revolutionary groups by demanding too much in return (intelligence, political commitment, an acceptance of Libyan directives); in other cases he has backed groups that had no chance of success, and so dissipated both resources and credibility. There are signs that Gaddafi has learned from earlier mistakes (or perhaps he has simply grown weary and anxious). It is useful to look at some of the policy-decision areas in more detail but first the question of Arab unity, a principal motivation for the 1969 revolution, should be considered.

ARAB UNITY

The dream of pan-Arabism, the gradual coalescing of the states of the Arab nation, has long motivated aspects of foreign policy in the region. Nasser had hoped that the Arabs would unite around the Palestinian question but their failure in this arena did no more than signal Arab disunity. And if Nasser's pan-Arabism had achieved nothing how could Gaddafi do better? An original impulse behind the 1969 revolution was that Libya and Egypt should merge as a prelude to a greater Arab unity but, as we have seen, the Egyptians drew back for reasons that can be only surmised; perhaps they feared an influx of Libyan radicalism into Egypt, and perhaps they feared a close association with a new Arab leader who, on the international stage, was still an unknown quantity. Gaddafi visited Cairo on 22 September 1970 for what was to be above all a symbolic meeting for Arab unity. However, this historic conference achieved little.

The Nile Hilton Hotel was cordoned off by armed guards, and at least three of the guests – Yasser Arafat, PLO chairman, King Hussein of Jordan and Colonel Gaddafi – wore revolvers in their belts. A principal reason for the meeting was to end the conflict between units of the Jordanian army and PLO guerrillas in Amman, Jordan. Gaddafi seized the opportunity to proselytise on the subject of Arab unity. He declared that Palestine could only be restored by 'the march of the Arab masses, free of fetters, restrictions and narrow regionalism. We will arrive at Palestine, brothers, when we have pulled down the walls which impede the fusion of the Arab people in the battle. We will reach the holy lands only when we have removed our borders and partitions. We shall liberate Palestine when the Arab world has become one solid front.'[1] Arafat responded by dubbing Gaddafi the 'knight of revolutionary phrases'; the leader of the PLO is said by his biographer, Alan Hart, to enjoy telling jokes about Gaddafi. Nasser's aide, Gahazzen Bashir, having found Gaddafi 'dynamic in an irritating way, like a little boy, very erratic', was told by a senior Russian diplomat that Gaddafi 'is crazy'.[2] Gaddafi was at least naive in thinking that Arab unity could be forged with little more than revolutionary slogans and a meeting between a few Arab leaders. He was well aware of the factional disputes between Arab groups and Arab states but at times seemed to believe that rhetorical exortation alone would sweep away all the differences. An early partial success was the Tripoli Pact, signed in December 1969 by Nasser, Gaddafi and President Jaafar Numeiri of Sudan, but this agreement fell far short of the total unity that Gaddafi had always envisaged as a step towards the ultimate creation of one Arab state.

Gaddafi was also disconcerted to perceive signs of political compromise on the part of Nasser, more experienced in statecraft than the heady young revolutionary from across the border. Where Nasser, according to Gaddafi, should have been mobilising to remove the stain of defeat in war he seemed prepared to accept a US peace plan aimed at ending the hostilities between

Egypt and Israel along the Suez canal. UN Resolution 242, seen by Gaddafi as a sell-out but supported by Nasser and King Hussein, declared that territory cannot be acquired by force and demanded that Israel evacuate the Sinai and withdraw to its own permanent and secure borders; there was also reference to a 'just settlement' for the Palestinian refugees and for the ending of the state of belligerency between the Arabs and the Israelis. We can hardly fault Gaddafi's perception that Resolution 242, framed about fifteen years ago, would not bring justice to the Palestinian people; to Gaddafi the only solution to the Arab/Israeli problem was war. Anyone who stood against such a policy was a traitor to the Arab cause and to be condemned. When King Hussein launched a Bedouin army against the Palestinian guerrillas Gaddafi declared that Hussein should be hanged ('I will go on Egyptian television and announce myself that Hussein should be hanged and that the Egyptian government didn't have the courage to do it'). Gahazzen Bashir later observed that he thought then that 'we were dealing with a dangerous young man'.

Soon after Nasser's death on 29 September 1970, from a massive heart attack, the federation between Libya, Egypt and Sudan – 'to hasten and develop integration and cooperation' – was announced. The prospect was a greatly enlarged Arab country with a large population (mostly Egyptian) and vast financial resources (mostly Libyan). Egypt also had considerable military power and technical expertise; it was hoped that the new union would attract other Arab states towards the final realisation of the unity dream. In fact Syria joined the new federation in April 1971 and plans for further integration were drawn up: it was suggested that the four armies could be put under joint control and that a single president would preside over a sixty-member federal assembly. On 1 September 1971, the second anniversary of the Libyan revolution, the peoples of Egypt, Syria and Libya voted 98.3 per cent in favour of the merging of their countries. Work continued on drafting a constitution for the new Federation of Arab Republics, with Syria succeeding in defeating Libyan and Egyptian demands that Islam be made the state religion of the new organisation. Instead the constitution was similar to earlier Syrian constitutions in making Islamic law 'the source' of legislation, with Syria agreeing at the same time that an educational policy would be adopted to create 'a believing generation'.[3] (Syria's decision to join the new federation caused an immediate crisis in the government. Dr Atasi resigned as premier and head of state on 18 October, and General Assad moved quickly – in what has been called his 'second coup' – to arrest army officers and to jail top political leaders. This was, he later commented, not a *coup d'état* but 'a normal development in our party.'[4] On the morrow of the coup Gaddafi arrived in Damascus to support Syria's membership of the Tripoli Federation, and this intervention helped Assad to consolidate his position).

However, despite the popular support and the nominal agreement of the Arab leaders, the Federation of Arab Republics never got off the ground. There were various crippling points of disagreement and contending ambitions. One disabling problem was how communists were to be viewed in the new organisation: Egypt, Sudan and Libya ban the Communist Party but Syria was reluctant to legislate a similar provision. In July 1971 Egypt and Libya invaded the Sudan to crush a pro-communist coup, whereupon General Numeiri executed many communists and fellow travellers. Gaddafi demanded that Assad oust all Communist Party members from the Syrian Progressive Front and from the government. Assad rejected this demand but the Regional Command, at the Ba'ath Party eleventh National Congress (August 1971), presented a draft resolution terming the executed Sudanese communists and pro-communists 'Qasimites, regionalists and false progressives': the Congress then overwhelmingly rejected this resolution. Another resolution upheld the Progressive Front as the only correct model for all Arab countries. Thus Syria was directly challenging the political posture of Egypt and Libya.

Other problems arose out of the different ambitions of the member states. It soon emerged that Sadat was more interested in cooperation than in integration, and that he was more concerned to get his hands on Libyan money than he was with any romantic dreams about pan-Arabism (this was one reason why the West found the pragmatic Sadat a more congenial Arab leader than it did the visionary Nasser). The Syrians, quick to stake their own claim to political independence within the new federation, were worried that the organisation would be dominated by the Egyptians. Gaddafi, as always, preached in a way that irritated his nominal partners, exacerbating rather than closing rifts within the new organisation. When he visited Cairo in 1973 he lectured the Egyptians with seeming indifference to their own views; Egyptian politicians were antagonised and Egyptian feminists were appalled (he instructed the relatively liberated Egyptian women to get back in the home where the Koran told them they belonged). Gaddafi rationalised his failure by denouncing what he saw as the decadent bourgeoisie of Egypt, a corrupt stratum of society far removed from the toiling masses in the villages and urban slums. In September 1973 he tried to march 20,000 Libyans 1500 miles to Cairo, assuming that thousands of Egyptians would then rise up to demand unity; the Egyptians stopped the march at the border and a small group was allowed through to hand in an ineffectual petition.

On 22 December 1972 Gaddafi had spoken at a rally in Tunis to demand union with Libya. President Bourguiba of Tunisia had not been forewarned of this initiative and was shocked when he heard Gaddafi's words on the radio. He rushed to the rally, insisted on taking the microphone, and launched a criticism of the whole unity idea. He commented that the Arabs had never been unified and that he did not welcome a lecture on the subject by the leader of a backward nation. It seemed that wherever Gaddafi turned he could find no Arab leaders to share his pan-Arabist vision. His first disappointment had come with the collapse of the United Arab Republic; separate appeals to individual states had come to nothing; and finally the new Federation, ambitious in concept, had not proved able to surmount political differences and petty rivalries.

President Sadat had been prepared to support union with Libya provided it could be turned to Egypt's advantage, but various difficulties combined to frustrate even cynical calculations of expediency. It was not long before the United States became involved: the Secretary of State, William Rogers, began conciliatory talks with Sadat which quickly aroused suspicions in other Egyptian power centres. The Egyptian Armed Forces Commander in Chief General Mohammed Fawzi informed Sadat that the army was unhappy at the talks with the Americans.[5] The situation deteriorated further whereupon Sadat sacked the Interior Minister Sharamy Gomaa on the ground that his phone was tapped. Senior government officials then resigned and Fawzi, fearing a sell-out to the Americans, urged senior officers to stage a coup; but enough officers remained loyal to Sadat to keep him in power.

This power struggle was concluded on 15 May 1971 with the arrest of the main conspirators against Sadat. This 'Corrective Revolution' had strengthened Sadat's position: with added powers he felt able to act according to his own instincts rather than being pressured by Egyptian factions clamouring for Arab unity. The changed circumstances had consequences for Egypt's relations with Libya. In the summer of 1971 Sadat began secret talks with Saudi Arabia and set up a hotline link between his own house in Giza and the Cairo residence of Kamel Adhem, the director of the Saudi intelligence service (trained by the CIA). Sadat was already establishing links with organisations hostile to the Gaddafi-sponsored unification plans while at the same time he saw advantages in going along with the unity talks. This was a time when, 'Whatever Sadat's real thoughts and intentions may have been . . . he managed to conceal them from more or less everyone.'[6]

When Sadat stopped the 20,000-strong Libyan march on Cairo he sent Hafez Ghanem, Secretary of the Egyptian ASU, to confront Gaddafi but when Ghanem arrived in Tripoli he was told that Gaddafi had resigned and that Sadat was the effective ruler of the two countries. We can surmise that this statement was not taken seriously by the Egyptians. The marchers then began a popular demonstration in support of Gaddafi, and a short time later he withdrew his 'resignation' and declared that he would make fresh efforts to secure union with Egypt ('even if it means civil war'). When Gaddafi and Jalloud flew to Cairo to discuss union they were told that Sadat had departed for talks in Saudi Arabia. When, a week later, they did meet Sadat informed the Libyans that Egypt was not yet ready for 'total union': a planned referendum, to be held on Libya's Revolution Day, was postponed and no new date was set. Sadat was preoccupied with his plans for war with Israel, about which Gaddafi knew nothing: Sadat had his own scheme for Arab unity and, at least in the short term, it left Libya out of the picture, When the war began, there was a further widening in the gulf between the Egyptians and the Libyans. The Libyans were generous in supplying two Mirage squadrons but when their officials visited Cairo they were not given the same preferential treatment as the Saudis. And when Sadat accepted a ceasefire on 25 October Gaddafi remonstrated with him by telephone – and later during a personal visit – to push on into Sinai. Sadat was soon involved in disengagement talks whereupon Gaddafi boycotted the Arab League and withdrew the Libyan diplomatic mission from Cairo. Sadat responded in kind and the proposed union between Egypt and Libya had never looked farther away.

Gaddafi then focused his attention on Tunisia, not for the first time. On 11 January 1974, President Bourguiba, now able to ignore Gaddafi's Tunis speech in December 1972, signed an agreement committing their countries to the formation of a single unified state, the Arab Islamic Republic. This Jerba Declaration, named after the Mediterranean island where the talks were held, represented a dramatic change of mind by the Tunisian president; now Bourguiba seemed to be committed to an arrangement that would give both countries a single constitution, a single army, and a single president. Bourguiba's *volte-face* was not unrelated to the fact that 30,000 Tunisian workers in Libya were making a useful contribution to the Tunisian economy. Moreover, some members of the Tunisian government – notably, the Foreign Minister, Mohammed Masmoudi – were convinced that closer ties with Libya would bring further economic benefits. In 1973 a series of agreements were concluded on trade, customs duties, investment, regulations for migrant workers, social security, and the creation of a joint shipping company. On 1 September 1973 Tunisia was the only country in the Arab world to celebrate the Gaddafi revolution; elsewhere in North Africa and the Middle East the anniversary went unsung. The Tunisian government was not, however, prepared to surrender control of the state:

economic benefit was one thing, a surrender of Tunisian sovereignty quite another.

This meant that Bourguiba had miscalculated: in pledging unity with Libya he had gone beyond what he could deliver. The Socialist Destour Party in Tunisia rebelled against what they saw as 'blank cheque' agreements with Libya, ill-defined arrangements that made no mention of the sorts of political institutions that would develop in the new union. Bourguiba was forced to have crisis talks with other members of the government and with Hedi Noura, a one-time governor of the Central Bank, after which Bourguiba was compelled to abandon the Jerba Agreement. On 12 January 1974 it was announced that the planned referendum would be postponed and any agreement with Libya would only be introduced gradually. The next day Masmoudi, the main pro-union advocate, was sacked; Hedi Noura staged an internal coup; and Bourguiba flew to Switzerland for a rest. Libya's pan-Arabist ambitions were thwarted yet again.

Efforts to cajole Algeria into union were similarly unsuccessful. President Houari Boumedienne, under pressure from Gaddafi, was prepared to declare union as an ultimate aim but at the same time was keen to preserve the Algerian independence won at such great cost in blood by the FLN. Boumedienne had been anxious about the Jerba Declaration, concerned that it would create a powerful state on Algeria's eastern border. To have joined such a union, had it succeeded, would have necessarily compromised the freedom of the FLN in Algeria. Gaddafi remained concerned at the failure to develop ties between Egypt and Libya, and it was obvious to him that his further efforts to develop a union in the area were fruitless. He again travelled to Cairo in a vain effort to pacify Sadat but it was too late: Sadat was now keen to develop relations with Israel and the United States, even to the point that he accused Gaddafi of exerting economic blackmail so that Egypt could attract more US aid. Egyptian civil servants were prohibited from travelling to Libya and Gaddafi responded by banning all Egyptian propaganda about the 1973 war and by closing the Egyptian cultural centre in Benghazi.[7]

Libya was blamed when a Muslim group launched an attack on the Cairo military academy on 18 April 1974 and when, on 26 July, an Alexandria nightclub was blown up. Libya countered by suggesting that Egypt was stirring up trouble among the border tribes, with Cairo alleging that Gaddafi had laid plans for the assassination of the entire Egyptian leadership. Sadat leaked the fact that Libya's French Mirages had been used in the 1973 war, so exposing Gaddafi willingness to ignore purchase conditions. The Egypto-Libyan 'Cold War' was significantly moderated after mediation by Sheikh Zayed, the Federal President of the UAR. Sadat and Gaddafi met briefly in

Alexandria and agreed to behave themselves; a joint committee was established to study the dispute between the two countries and to make recommendations. However, a few months later Sadat commented (in an interview published in the Kuwait newspaper, *al-Siyasah*) that the Libyan leader was 'one-hundred per cent mad' and that he was trying to divide Egypt from other countries. Then Sadat claimed that Libya was trying to annex Egyptian territory, a charge that resulted in Gaddafi expelling 265 Egyptian workers from Libya, which in turn induced the Sadat-controlled Egyptian parliament to demand the withdrawal of the entire Egyptian workforce in Libya. On 10 May 1975 the premises of the Libyan diplomatic mission in Cairo were invaded by a mob. As Sadat prepared for the signing of the second Sinai disengagement agreement the Libyan authorities organised demonstrations against 'the capitulationist Egyptian regime'.[8]

Sadat moved further to the right by deregulating the Egyptian economy in an attempt to attract foreign capital. Laws were introduced in 1974 and 1975 to exempt foreign investment from taxation for a period of five years; foreign merchant banks were offered attractive currency exchange facilities; the Suez canal area was converted into a Free Trade Zone; and steps were taken to dismantle the public sector while encouraging free enterprise. With this *infittah* ('opening up') policy an economic atmosphere was created that soon generated a class of capitalists and entrepreneurs, what came to be known as the 'Sadat class'. There was nothing in this of pan-Arabism or even of Egyptian nationalism: the new entrepreneurs were only interested in profits, their sole allegiance being directed at international capitalism. The possibility of a restoration of Nasserist policies became increasingly remote and the gulf widened between Egypt and Libya. Sadat had progressively eroded Nasser's political achievements, intent above all to make accommodations with the postwar Israelis and the United States. At the same time Sadat developed his relations with the pro-Western regime in Saudi Arabia. The Arab world, far from moving gradually to a pan-Arabist unified nation, was becoming consolidated in a static regionalism, key Arab leaders being content to form alliances with opponents of Arab nationalism. Gaddafi had been sidelined, his fervent rhetoric and unification ambitions ignored in a region increasingly concerned with factional self-interest; Libya was too weak to make a difference.

The relations between Gaddafi and Sadat had deteriorated beyond the possibility of recovery; frequent incidents confirmed that there was no way of reconciling the competing philosophies. On 21 February 1973 a Libyan Airlines plane lost its bearings *en route* for Cairo and began heading over Sinai. The Israelis detected the aircraft on radar and sent up jet fighters to shoot it down: all the passengers and the French crew, a total of one hundred and eight people, were killed. When Gaddafi urged retaliation, Sadat discouraged him, saying that they should conserve their forces for the coming war against Israel. Asked why Egyptian aircraft had not flown to the aid of the Libyan plane, Sadat commented that the weather was bad. Gaddafi retorted by phone that the weather had not stopped the Israeli aircraft from flying, but he decided to take Sadat's advice and take no action. In Libya there were anti-Egyptian protests and the son of Salah Buassir, the former Libyan Foreign Minister and one of the victims, printed leaflets accusing the Egyptians of treacherous cowardice.

Another incident, potentially equally dramatic, caused Egypto-Libyan relations to worsen still further. A group of wealthy Jews and other supporters of Israel had chartered the *Queen Elizabeth II* for a special voyage to celebrate the anniversary of Israel's independence. Gaddafi summoned the commander of a Soviet-supplied submarine, part of an Egyptian naval unit still based in Libya under defence agreements that Gaddafi had negotiated with Nasser. Gaddafi then ordered the young commander to sink the ship on its way to the Israeli port of Ashpod. However, once at sea the commander radioed a report to Alexandria whereupon Sadat was quickly informed of Gaddafi's instructions. Sadat cancelled the plan, waited until the *Queen* reached Ashpod, and then notified Gaddafi that the submarine had been unable to locate the liner. This event served as further confirmation, if any were needed, that Sadat was more interested in maintaining good relations with the Israelis and the Americans than in combatting the traditional enemies of the Arab nation. In one quoted comment from a Libyan émigré the impact of this incident on Gaddafi is made clear: 'Gaddafi at this point became like a different person. He withdrew into the desert, raging at anyone who tried to speak to him. If ever he showed signs of being a manic depressive, it was after the submarine incident.'[9] Gaddafi later flew to Cairo in an attempt to patch up matters, but the time for compromise was gone. The situation would only be resolved, to Gaddafi's satisfaction, with the assassination of Sadat in Cairo on 6 October 1981. There is no evidence that Gaddafi was implicated in the murder of Sadat but no doubt he was pleased with what the assassins had accomplished.

Gaddafi had also struggled to breathe life into the discredited Jerba Declaration, originally intended to consolidate the union of Tunisia and Libya; now the Destour socialists in Tunisia were saying that the document should be seen 'as a political declaration, not as a treaty'.[10] It seemed likely that Algeria's President Boumedienne had discouraged the proposed union, perceiving that an enlarged state on his eastern border might pose a threat; Gaddafi was soon talking of Maghreb leaders 'who stand in the way of inevitable unity', but he was no nearer to achieving such unity with Tunisia or any other country. By March 1976 he had lost patience: 6837 Tunisian workers, said by Tripoli to lack the proper work and residence permits, were expelled; and evidence soon emerged that Gaddafi was beginning a policy of subversion. On 21 March 1976 three members of the Libyan *mukhabarat* (intelligence service) were arrested in Tunis, with Bourguiba announcing that they had come to murder him and his prime minister. Tripoli indignantly denied the charge and expelled eight Tunisian diplomats; more expulsions followed on both sides, though diplomatic relations were preserved.

A fresh problem arose, following an important oil strike, when Tunisia and Libya began a dispute over the offshore median line. The two countries agreed to take their argument to the International Court of Justice at The Hague, but in February 1977 Tunisia sent the *Bourguiba* frigate to stop Libyan drilling in the area. Warning shots were fired to signal Tunisian intent, and the Libyans sent a gunboat. The offshore rig at the centre of this confrontation was the *Scarab Four* being used in a joint venture between the Italian oil company ENI and the Libyan National Oil Company. When the Italians could not get the necessary security guarantees for the seventy-man crew they towed the rig away. The dispute dragged on for several years and, signalling the state of relations between the two countries, a Libya-supported guerrilla attack was launched on Gafsa, a Tunisian phosphate mine, on 26 January 1980. Gaddafi had demonstrated, in familiar fashion, what he thought of the small pro-Western country situated on Libya's shoulder.[11] Gaddafi had failed to cement a union between Tunisia and Libya, as he had failed elsewhere. In the early 1980s he turned his attention to Morocco.

The 1984 Oujda Treaty pledged Morocco and Libya to eventual unity though no plan for implementation was agreed and the treaty was seen as a declaration of intent rather than a firm bond between the two nations. Efforts to build links with other countries in the area had achieved nothing; instead invective was traded as part of the *status quo*. On more than one occasion Gaddafi has warned President Hosni Mubarak of Egypt that he will 'meet Sadat's fate'; and in November 1984 an Egyptian 'sting' operation tricked Gaddafi into thinking that he had successfully brought off a plan to assassinate a former Libyan prime minister in Cairo. There is evidence that Gaddafi retaliated by mining the Red Sea and the Gulf of Suez. Through the 1980s he seemed no nearer to advancing his dream of pan-Arabism: he had managed to sustain a level of friendship with Morocco, Syria, Iran and South Yemen as fellow Islamic states, but even with these sympathetic countries various serious differences emerged from time to time. Gaddafi supported Iran in its war with Iraq, not least because he rightly detected US support for Iraq in its desire to contain Islamic fundamentalism; and most other Arab states condemned Libya on this. Similarly, they are suspicious of Gaddafi's hostility to Yasser Arafat and his (Gaddafi's) support for the more extreme Palestinian factions. Several hundred Libyan troops were stationed in Lebanon in the late 1970s and early 1980s, which led to fresh tensions with Syria but failed to win Libya kudos as one of the committed 'front-line states' against Israel. In fact Libya has at times broken ties, for one reason or another, with Egypt, Tunisia, Morocco, Iraq, Jordan and Saudi Arabia. Gaddafi on one occasion tried to disrupt the Muslim *hajj* (pilgrimage) to Mecca in Saudi Arabia, and he has frequently tried to appeal to the Arab peoples over the heads of their rulers, as he did in April 1985, to 'rise and destroy the submissive traitors who have betrayed our nation'.[12]

On his southern border Gaddafi has attempted to create a bloc of Libyan-dominated pan-Islamic countries in the Sahel region of West Africa. He has claimed territory in a number of states but has only been strong enough to invade and occupy a part of Chad (see below), though he has often threatened Niger and Tunisia. Libyan-trained Sudanese revolutionary committee members were positioned in Sudan in the mid-eighties and Gaddafi's declarations of support for the Sudanese regime were viewed with some suspicion. In August 1981 a tripartite alliance between Libya, Ethiopia and the People's Democratic Republic of Yemen was formed but represented no more than a paper agreement: there was no realistic attempt at a political merging of the states or at the creation of a unified military command (Libya's efforts to improve relations with Somalia resulted in a deterioration in the scope of the Ethiopian connection).

Gaddafi's 'carrot and stick' approach (oil and finance on the one hand, threats and subversion on the other) has influenced a number of states in their attitude to Libya. It has been prudent to remain in a condition of reasonable accord but Gaddafi's rhetoric and unreasonable demands have often led to rifts. It is difficult to fault his Islamic commitment or his fervent wish for the unification of the entire Arab nation: had he moved more diplomatically, and with greater regard for the international protocols he so obviously despises, he might have accomplished more through the troubled 1970s and 1980s. In the 1990s there are signs that, through experience or weariness, he is acting with more circumspection. This is too late to retrieve his reputation in the eyes of the West and many Arab states: Gaddafi remains a force to be considered on the global stage but he has few firm friends.

An extraordinary Arab Summit was held in Baghdad on 28–30 May 1990, intended to discuss the Palestinian *intifada*, the problems of Soviet Jewish emigration to Israel, and items such as 'threats against Iraq and Libya, possible aggression against Jordan, and the assessment of the Arab position *vis-à-vis* recent world developments, in particular in Eastern Europe'. The summit was addressed by Yasser Arafat, PLO chairman who considered the likely escalation of the Arab–Israeli conflict. Syria did not attend the meeting, despite mediation by Gaddafi (and by Egypt, Jordan and Saudi Arabia), and this may be seen as a further set-back for Gaddafi's dream of Arab unity. However, an event earlier in the year seemed, from Libya's point of view, more promising.

On 6 March Gaddafi and Omar Hassan al-Bashir, the military ruler of Sudan, signed an agreement specifying a complete merger of the two countries within four years: this would represent a total integration of their political, economic, social, defence and foreign policies. The declared intention was to create a supreme authority vested in the two heads of state, a general secretariat and a ministerial body; at the same time common authorities would be created for finance, labour, energy, mining and foreign affairs, and a Joint High Command of the armed forces would be created. An earlier union between Libya and Sudan (then under prime minister Sadiq al-Mahdi) had been planned for September 1989, but this was cancelled when General Bashir took over on 30 June 1989, following a military coup.

The unity plans seemed still to be on course when, on 19 June 1991, the first meeting took place to agree the steps towards union. At this meeting of the Arab Integration Ministerial Committee, held at Sirte, an agreement for freedom of movement, residence, work and ownership was signed by the deputy prime minister of Sudan, Zoubeir Mohammed Saleh, and the foreign minister of Libya, Ibrahim al-Beshari. Moves were set in train for the provision of new identity cards, showing dual Libyan/Sudanese citizenship. On 1 July Gaddafi visited Sudan and gave speeches – one to celebrate the second anniversary of General Bashir's National Salvation Revolution – in which he focused on the questions of integration and unity. However, from the outset there were difficulties: the two countries have very different political systems and in 1990 Gaddafi made it clear that he expected Sudan to move towards the *Jamahariya* style of government. By 1992 he was beginning to doubt the sincerity of the Sudanese leadership in this respect, having already observed on 17 July 1991 at the General People's Congress at Sirte that the Sudanese authorities were preparing to hold council and government elections, activities that were incompatible with the *jamahiri* system.

On 8 August a unity document for the Sirte municipality and the Sudanese province of Dafur was signed and Abdel-Rahim Hamdi, the Sudanese Minister of Finance and Planning, declared that Libya and Sudan had agreed that all local goods traded between the two countries should carry no customs and excise duties. A joint protocol was signed for the establishment of the Nile International Bank; and on 23 August an agreement was concluded on Libya's investment of $45 million in the Sudanese/Libyan Holding Company intended to finance the manufacture of plastics and agricultural production. In 1992 it seemed that the Libya/Sudan unity plans were making progress but there were still many problems to overcome, not least the regional influence of Egypt. The Egyptians have been unenthusiastic about developing their own relations with Sudan, and it has been suggested that 'Libya will not jeopardise its friendship with Egypt by fraternising with the Khartoum regime.'[13]

Gaddafi had increasingly looked to post-Sadat Egypt for support, even though he has frequently criticised President Mubarak for his lack of interest in practical steps towards Arab unity. One calculation is that Egypt is well placed to help Libya gain international respectability. Mubarak was a plaint supporter of the Gulf War coalition, induced to conform when the United States cancelled his substantial dollar debt, and so the Egyptian leader is perceived as a useful conduit to Washington and the conservative Arab states. Gaddafi also calculated that Mubarak might be able to provide Libya with a degree of protection against a further US military strike in the context of the Lockerbie issue (see Chapter One). Again the familiar Libyan tactics are fully displayed though, with a new prudence, Gaddafi seems to be relying more on 'carrot' than on 'stick'. Libya is being generous in financing joint ventures and in the terms of other agreements on economic cooperation; it is also significant that Gaddafi has offered to help Egypt's overpopulation problem by funding the resettlement of one million Egyptian farmers in areas of Libya that will be irrigated by the Great Man-made River Project. Egypt also has an interest in curbing Islamic fundamentalism which might come to the fore if Gaddafi were to collapse. In May 1989 a reconciliation took place between Mubarak and Gaddafi in Casablanca and they have met on many occasions since that time: Gaddafi was quick to visit Mubarak for talks when the possibility again loomed, in late 1991, that the United States would launch fresh bombing raids on Libya within a matter of months.

On 4 July 1991 Gaddafi visited Egypt to reach an immediate agreement on the payment of arrears to Egyptian teachers and doctors working in Libya; and after a Mubarak visit to Tripoli in August Cairo ordered the dismantling of all the border customs and immigration posts with Libya. An Egypto-Libyan meeting in Benghazi yielded a number of economic agreements, and Gaddafi expressed his much-rehearsed hope that a union between Egypt and Libya would be the first step towards a wider Arab unity. He again called for a union between Libya, Egypt and Sudan but there is no reason to think that Egypt shares these unity enthusiasms. In an interview on 23 August with the Egyptian journal *Al-Musawwar* President Mubarak commented on his excellent understanding with Gaddafi who had 'kept his word and promises', but he also suggested that true unity between nations could only come when there was a genuine convergence of interests, that this would generate a stronger unity than one imposed by the will of political leaders. He commented that the current Sudanese regime gave cause for concern, so dashing Gaddafi's perennial hope of a tripartite union.

Almost as soon as Egypt abolished the controls on the Libyan border in August 1991 the human traffic escalated to around 10,000 a day. Egyptian consumer goods began to flood into Libya's shops while Libyans surged across the border for goods and entertainment not available under the puritanical Libyan regime. The volume of traffic alarmed both governments and within a week the Egyptian security police established a border post to check the names of all travellers to Libya, while at the same time the Libyan police manned a checkpoint between Tobruk and Mosaid. Furthermore, both Libya and Egypt introduced an 'insurance' charge on each car crossing the border; and on 18 August Mohammed Abdel Halim Moussa, the Egyptian Interior Minister, visited Libya to discuss further controls on the flow of traffic. An agreement, not made public, was signed on 23 August: there has been official comment on the need to stop drug smuggling and to apprehend criminals, but a principal reason is the desire to monitor the movement of political opponents.

Gaddafi has struggled for more than two decades to build Arab unity. Hampered in part by his own mercurial temperament but more by the factional disputes and competing interests in the region, he has made little progress. Islam itself, like any world faith or ideology, is a multi-faceted and evolving system; it lacks the monolithic dynamic that may be used to unite first the Arab and then the entire Islamic world. In one view, all Gaddafi's ambitions derive from his desire for a unified Moslem world that will then seduce by its example the rest of the human race. However, it is an easy matter to point to the perfidies committed in the name of Islam (and in the name of any other missionary faith). It is possible to defend some of the national liberation groups that Gaddafi has supported, but for much of the period of the Libyan revolution Gaddafi sought to intervene, with a promiscuous lack of discrimination, in other countries.

EXPORTING REVOLUTION

The Gaddafi revolution was never an insular affair: to the alarm and resentment of his neighbours and the West every effort was made to spread the message of Islam and the Jamahariya as widely as possible. Here was a model, not just for the Arab world but for the entire Moslem community and ultimately all mankind. It is easy to conclude that such an unconstrained ambition signals no more than megalomania, the rantings of a demagogue; but where is the committed political leader who would not like to see his/her views prevail throughout the world? With the revenue and clout based on oil, Gaddafi set about exporting a revolution that at least had succeeded in transforming independent Libya.

The Arab Liaison Bureau, sited in what was a favourite building of King Idris and is now the People's Palace, functions today as an effective foreign ministry, set up to supervise the foreign bureaus that were designed to replace the old Libyan embassies. In non-Arab countries, such as Britain and the United States, the bureaus are called *People's Bureau*, in Arab countries *Brotherhood Bureaus*; in all cases they have a range of responsibilities, from looking after diplomatic relations to collecting intelligence information. Some observers, able to cite evidence, suggest that the bureaus also have an interest in subversion and sabotage, in agitation and political assassination. It is said that arms and sabotage devices are frequently smuggled in diplomatic pouches to foreign countries. Such activities clearly violate diplomatic protocols but it should never be thought that Libya has a monopoly of such behaviour. The Foreign Liaison Bureau is also concerned with foreign visitors, with the supervision of emissaries sent abroad, and with the recruitment of foreign agents.

The Arab and Foreign Liaison Bureaus work with the Libyan intelligence and security services and operate under the auspices of the *Maktub Tasdir al-Thawra* (literally the 'Bureau for the Export of the Revolution'): for much of the period of the Libyan revolution the desire to spread the revolutionary message was an up-front matter, though the range of practical tactics were necessarily clandestine. Gaddafi intended to export the revolution and there were government departments set up for the task.

SUPPORTING TERRORISM*

There can be no doubt, despite Gaddafi's protestations, that he has supported a wide range of terrorist organisations throughout the world. The
past is unambiguous on this matter though today the position is unclear: in
a 1992 interview with *The Observer* editor, Donald Trelford, Gaddafi
declared that there were times in the 1970s 'when we might have behaved
in a way that was not in accordance with international law, but not now'.[14]
In the same interview Gaddafi claimed to have changed 'through experience . . . In the 1980s we began to differentiate between terrorists and those
with legitimate political aspirations.' We need hardly remark that this is a
highly contentious claim: few people would argue that a genuinely oppressed nation would not be justified in using force – 'terrorism' – to
achieve liberation, and so the distinction between terrorists and 'legitimate'
political activists is hard to sustain. However, whatever Gaddafi's current
position his earlier support for terrorism throughout the world is well
established.

Gaddafi has given both funds and rhetorical support to Sinn Fein and the
Irish Republican Army in Northern Ireland, to the Armenian Secret Army,
to the Basque Separatist Movement, to the Red Army Faction in West
Germany, and to the Popular Forces of April 25 in Portugal. Such international terrorists as Carlos Ilyich Ramirez and Abu Nidal have received
financial support from Gaddafi and been offered sanctuary in Libya: in
1987 Abu Nidal opened a huge terrorist training camp in the Libyan desert,
100 miles south of Tripoli, but today Gaddafi claims that he has renounced
international terrorism and that the camp is no longer in his country.[15]
Similarly, the German Bader-Meinhof gang has at times received support
from Gaddafi and been offered asylum in Libya. The Palestinian Black
September and Abu Musa factions, the Japanese Red Army, the Philippine
Moro National Liberation Front, and various black groups in the United
States have also received rhetorical and financial support.

According to a detailed Israeli intelligence report,[16] Gaddafi was supporting in 1986 some 'fifty terror organisations and subversion groups, in
addition to more than forty radical governments in Africa, Asia, Europe and
America'. Help is given to almost all the terrorist groups of the Middle East,
such as George Habash's PFLP, Ahmed Jibril's PFLP–GC, Naif Hawatmeh's
Democratic Front, the Saiqa, the Popular Struggle Front, and the Abu Nidal

---

*I use the word *terrorism* for the sake of convenience and no moral connotation should be
assumed. The platitude 'one man's terrorist is another man's freedom fighter' suggests that
violent political acts have to be considered on their individual merits.

organisation.[17] Gaddafi has also funded terrorist groups working against what he takes to be the reactionary regimes of the Arab world; so while he has tried at one level to build unity between Libya and such states as Tunisia, Sudan and Egypt he has been prepared at another level to organise acts of subversion in those countries. He has maintained close and sympathetic links with such groups as ETA in Spain, Action Directe In France, and the SIM group in Sardinia. Name almost any terrorist or revolutionary group and you will find Gaddafi's fingers in the pie. He has supported the Tupamaros in Uruguay, the revolutionary groups (principally the FSLN) in El Salvador (where an end to the war was agreed early in 1992), and the one-time Sandinista government in Nicaragua. In such countries as Chad, Senegal, Zaire and Tunisia, help has been offered by Gaddafi to groups trying to destabilise pro-Western or reactionary governments. The Israeli report claimed that in 1986 some 7000 terrorists were being trained – by Syrians, Cubans, Russians and East Germans – in camps across Libya: for example, the Al Hilal camp west of Tobruk; the Al Jadayim camp west of Tripoli; the Al Jaghbub camp west of the Egyptian border; the Ghadames camp; the Beda camp south of Sirte; and camps at Kufrah, Misrata, Sidi Bilal, Sebba, Sabratha and Benghazi.

It should be emphasised that the various Israeli intelligence organisations have different opinions and make different factual claims about the Libyán funding of world terrorism. In the 1980s Israeli intelligence analysts consistently down-played the risk posed by Libya, saying that if there was 'a mastermind behind international terror, it is President Assad of Syria'.[19] This is an important consideration in view of current Western claims that Libya has *sole* responsibility for the Lockerbie outrage (see Chapter One). Nevertheless, there is no doubt that Gaddafi's revolutionary ambitions have had effects, albeit usually minimal, in dozens of countries throughout the world.

Many countries – among them Egypt, Sudan, Tunisia, Algeria, Senegal, Nigeria, Lebanon, Gambia, Mauritania, Mali, Malaysia, Indonesia, Thailand and the Philippines – have at one time or another accused Gaddafi of supporting dissident or subversive groups in their countries. In the early 1970s Gaddafi supported the Eritrean rebels against the reactionary Ethiopian government of Haile Selassie, but changed sides in 1974 when President Mengistu took power in a military coup. Gaddafi also supported Idi Amin through the 1970s because he was a Muslim who had expelled the Israeli advisors from Uganda. In an interview with Oriana Fallaci, an Italian journalist, Gaddafi declared in 1979: 'Amin's internal policies do not interest me; what I am interested in is Amin's position in the field of international relations.' He admitted that Amin's 'private personality . . .

might not be to my liking' and that he might disagree with particular policies, but he disliked even more: 'the interference of France and Tanzania and worst of all I dislike the support provided by the Westerners to Israel'. When in 1978 Tanzania, with the support of Ugandan exiles, invaded Uganda, Gaddafi provided 2500 troops, tanks and other vehicles in support of Amin. The invading force was defeated and the Libyans were expelled, having lost more than four hundred dead.

Connections have been established between various subversive groups acting in Europe, the Middle East and elsewhere. Thus evidence emerged in the 1970s of links between the Italian Red Brigades and the Revolutionary Cells Movement in West Germany; in Athens the CIA station claimed to have discovered similar connections between France's Action Directe and the Greek Revolutionary Group for International Solidarity. All such groups have used explosives provided by Libya; and in many cases the groups have benefited from training provided in the Libyan camps set up for that purpose. A key task was to train terrorists who could then journey to foreign countries to kill political activists opposed to the Libyan regime. In 1980 Gaddafi threatened his own opposition abroad that they 'would be liquidated wherever they were'.[20]

On 11 April 1980 the journalist Mohammed Mustafa Ramadan was shot dead outside a London mosque, and a fortnight later the lawyer Mahmud Nafa was killed outside his house. The businessman Mohammed Salem Rtemi was shot by Libyans in Rome, his body found in the trunk of his car a month later. On 19 April 1980 three Libyans shot and killed a textile wholesaler, Abdul Jilal Aref in the Café de Paris on the Via Veneto, just as the Libyan Aballah Mohammed el-Kasmi was shot twice in the head by a Libyan in the Hotel Torino in Rome and the former Libyan diplomat Omran Mehdawi was shot and killed in Bonn. Such murders serve to highlight the character of Libyan terrorist methods but they also illustrate that Gaddafi has had as much interest in attacking Arabs as he has had in subverting Western or Israeli institutions or individuals. An American report, published in 1986, suggests that Gaddafi has not been particularly active in attacking Israel or the United States.[21] Instead he has focused on dissident citizens of his own country, on moderate Palestinians, and on Arab and African countries with which he has political disagreements. A chronology of Libyan support for specific terrorist acts in the period 1980 to 1985 shows, according to the US report, that Gaddafi carried out five anti-West terrorist acts and forty-six against Arab and African targets. The attempt to assassinate Ambassador Eilts in Cairo has been interpreted as more an attack on Sadat and US/Egyptian relations than as an attack on the United States (Eilts himself has remarked that 'It was nothing personal . . .').

A report from Tel Aviv University similarly suggests that Libya's support for international terrorism in the 1980s was less than often supposed.[22] Out of a total of more than four hundred terrorist incidents in 1985 Libyan hit teams were responsible for only eleven, and these involved eight *Libyan* victims; by contrast, the Shiite Islamic Jihad were responsible for thirty-five hits, and Abu Nidal twenty-four. Dennis Pluchinsky, an expert in the Threat Analysis Division of the Bureau of Diplomatic Security in the US State Department, recorded about seventy-five terrorist attacks that produced sixty-five deaths and more than 500 injuries: most of the attacks were against Arab or Palestinian targets and, interestingly enough, there were six attacks against Libyan targets and only five against American. There is in fact a terrorist campaign against Gaddafi and the Libyan regime.[23]

The statistics should be interpreted with care. It may well be true that Libyan hit squads have themselves only attempted a relatively small number of terrorist acts; it remains the case that Libya has funded, and supported in many other ways, the terrorist activities of many other groups, some of which in their terms have been successful (Patrick Seale gives details in his book *Abu Nidal, A Gun for Hire*, 1992, of the extent of Gaddafi's support for one of the world's most notorious terrorists.). A mere listing of Gaddafi's foreign interventions is also likely to be misleading. His is essentially a scattergun approach: his financial and manpower resources, although clearly significant, have been spread thinly in the international arena of subversion. He may have accomplished more if he had adopted a focused attack in particular areas, in perhaps Africa or the Middle East. His efforts to recruit, train and shelter terrorists had some success but it is difficult to point to changes of regime or alterations in a country's political direction that such recruitments achieved.

It has been claimed that Gaddafi at one time or another set in train plans for the assassination of particular world leaders: for example, Sadat of Egypt, King Hussein of Jordan, and Ronald Reagan of the United States. At one time the CIA station chief in Rome, Duane R. Clarrige, received what he believed to be reliable reports that Gaddafi was planning to kill President Sadat. The source was a Clarrige contact in DIGOS, the Italian anti-terrorist squad that had maintained strong contacts in Libya. Aziz Shenib, in 1982 the Secretary of the Libyan People's Bureau in Jordan, has related how he was asked to recruit 'fanatics' from the Palestinian refugee camps, to assassinate King Hussein, and to obtain a rocket for firing at the Israeli nuclear reactor at Demona in the Negev desert.[24] According to Shenib, Gaddafi had wanted to get rid of Hussein since 1970, holding him responsible for the loss of the West Bank to the Israelis in 1967. Gaddafi proposed that Hussein's private jet could be shot down one weekend by a ground-to-air missile that could be obtained from the Syrians. Shenib ('I have a lot of respect for Hussein') decided to defect and inform the King of the plan; he then visited Khaddam in Damascus to see if the Syrians would take the bait. Assad reckoned the scheme 'ridiculous and childish' and the plot was cancelled, but Hussein remained high on Gaddafi's hit list. The plot against Reagan, if there ever was one, was also abandoned (see Chapter Eight).

If Gaddafi had little success in eliminating foreign leaders he had more in controlling domestic dissidents (it has to be said that because of Gaddafi's personal standing in Libya the dissident problem is less significant than in regimes with less popular leaders). Throughout the period of the Libyan revolution there have been violations of human rights, as there have been elsewhere in the Arab world without the compensation of massive social investment. Libyan dissidents have been arrested, imprisoned without trial, and then 'disappeared' without official explanation. In the United States Admiral Bobby Ray Inman, an intelligence expert, provided William Casey, CIA Director, with information about torture in Libya. Inman, head of the NSA, had pinpointed in 1981 the old Ministry of Planning buildings in Tripoli as the country's main torture-centre. Here, Inman claimed, victims suffered electric shocks, hooding, mock executions and other inhuman treatment. Through the 1980s the situation improved: 400 political prisoners were freed in 1988 and legal reforms were promised to safeguard human rights. However, on 26 June 1991 Amnesty International noted a deterioration in the human-rights situation, claiming that 'hundreds of political prisoners have been jailed in the past two years, including prisoners of conscience, and that arbitrary arrests and secret incommunicado detention are continuing'. The whereabouts of several hundred political prisoners arrested in 1989 and 1990 were not known to their families, and in some circumstances prisoners remain 'extremely vulnerable to torture and ill-treatment'. Perhaps the most celebrated disappearance in Libya was that of Iman Moussa Sadr, founder of the Amal Militia, who went missing in Tripoli in 1978 and who was never seen or heard of again.[25]

While Gaddafi's hold on power in Libya seems secure most of his foreign ambitions have been thwarted. In many cases initially promising links with other countries have been torn asunder by Gaddafi's caprice or by incompatible ideologies and contending political objectives. Dom Mintoff of Malta, no lover of Western imperialism, had a long honeymoon with Gaddafi but relations collapsed when, in June 1980, Gaddafi cut off the preferentially-priced oil shipments to Malta. The situation was exacerbated by a dispute about jurisdiction over the waters between Malta and Libya in connection with drilling rights. The Libyans were expelled from Malta, and when Maltese neutrality gained international recognition they were effectively prohibited from returning. Again a promising connection between Libya and another state had crumbled.

Most of Gaddafi's foreign policy initiatives have come to nothing. Some have had mixed success. Perhaps only one has been generally viewed as – from Gaddafi's point of view – successful. Chad is a special case, However, here too there are ambiguities and uncertainties.

CHAD

Libya has long had an interest in Chad, the poverty-stricken desert country to the south of Fezzan. For centuries the two countries traded and the Sanussi Order established military, religious and commercial centres in northern and central Chad in the nineteenth century. Nomads travelled between the two countries with scant regard for lines drawn on a map. The Sanussi and their Muslim friends had vigorously resisted French expansion in the area, and Chad was one of the first African countries to win its independence.

The many ethnic and regional factions in Chad have always tended to weaken the country's central authority, a circumstance which has made it relatively easy for Libya to press its own interests in the area. One key concern has been control of the Aouzou Strip, a 40,000 square-mile border zone. The Strip was effectively given to Libya under the terms of the unratified 1935 Franco-Italian Treaty, but after the Second World War the French colonial government tried to integrate the zone within Chad. When the French were forced to withdraw from Fezzan in 1954, King Idris tacitly accepted the annexation by agreeing the 1955 Franco-Italian Treaty; but after the fall of the monarchy Gaddafi moved quickly to restore Libyan sovereignty in the region.

The border originally drawn by the French had no ethnic or religious significance: there were strong kinship and commercial links between the inhabitants of southern Libya and northern Chad. The largest ethnic group in the region were the Tebu, occupying the land from Kufrah in the north to the shores of Lake Chad in the south. The 70,000 Tebu were largely nomadic, moving freely over a vast area but mostly concentrating in the Aouzou Strip. The Tebu tribe, converted to Islam by Ould Suleyman Sanussi in the late nineteenth century, was not of Arab origin but black Caucasians intent on retaining part of their animist heritage and characteristic tribal structures. They were divided primarily between the northern Tedas and the southern Dazas, keen to recognise the overall authority of the *Derde* (judge) chosen from leaders of the Tomagra clan. The French tried to restrain the wandering Tebu in defined areas, to give credibility to the colonial territorial claims but such efforts were unavailing: the Tebu continued to migrate, as they had always done, between Chad and Libya. At the same time there were Arab migrations to the south: Arab settlements and sultanates were established in Chad and when independence was achieved in 1960 the ethnic Arab population was estimated at around 40,000.[26] While the vast majority of the Arabs were locally born, they continued to owe political and religious allegiance to their ancestral lands of Libya and Sudan. The Sanussi tried to exploit these commitments when in 1972 they made Chad their base for the planned royalist overthrow of Gaddafi.[27]

The French had not succeeded after eight decades of colonial occupation – up to Independence Day in 1960 – in constraining the wandering tribes within the arbitrarily defined Chadian borders. The occupying authorities, in familiar colonial mode, ruled the territory piecemeal by inviting the collaboration of local tribal leaders. The country remained divided between nearly two hundred tribes with no clear sense of national unity. A rudimentary infrastructure was established by means of a network of military garrisons which have evolved into the principal Chadian towns of today. Efforts were made to adjust the borders to give Chad some sort of territorial integrity – for example, the French tried to annex the Tebesti mountains to the Chadian area – but the tribes, particularly the Tebu, remained recalcitrant and uncooperative.

The colonial authorities were interested mostly in developing the land to defray the costs of the colonial administration. Crops were introduced into fertile areas to provide an export potential: the *cordes des chefs* plantations were worked by farmers of the Sara people, the most populous minority in Chad. The French hostility to the slave trade in the area derived mainly from the need to keep the plantations supplied with labour. The crops, particularly cotton, came to have real economic significance for the region, and after the Second World War the metropolitan government continued the process of development through irrigation, locust control, and increased mechanisation on the land. One consequence was that the Sara people began to achieve political ascendancy within the colonial structure. However, when the local chiefs inadvisedly appropriated an excess of the produce rebellions broke out and the French were forced to abandon the *cordes des chefs* programme.

The local farmers and traders then founded the Parti Progressiste Tchadien (PPT), similar to the Parti Démocratique de la Côte d'Ivoire (PDCI) of Felix Houphouet-Boigny: the party wanted to achieve political independence but was still prepared to collaborate with the French authorities. The PPT leader, Gabriel Lisette, led his party to victory in the 1957 elections and, as the new Chadian Prime Minister, looked set to lead the country to independence. However, in 1959 Lisette was ousted by the Sara trader, François Tombalbaye, who was soon endorsed by the Sara-dominated national assembly. Tombalbaye was accepted by the French and became first head of the government and then head of state. When independence was granted in 1960, he set about creating a Chadian nation based on the southern Saras, a shortsighted policy that quickly led to the disaffection of the Arabs and the Tebus in the north, whereupon the Arab sultans and tribal leaders created the Parti National Africain (PNA) to rival the Sara PPT.

There followed a period of unrest throughout the country. The French-backed Tombalbaye had imposed a virtual military regime on the south to replace the departing French colonial forces. This led to areas of popular unrest in what should have been a secure PPT power base. Various groups were now organising to oppose the Sara-imposed regime that by now was enjoying little popular support throughout the land. Thus the Union Nationale Tchadienne (UNT), led by Arab and Muslim intellectuals, began preparations for an uprising in central and northern Chad, following Tombalbaye's suppression of political opponents in 1962/3. New tensions developed between Tombalbaye and the Tebu *Derde* when the government refused to appoint the son of the *Derde*, Goukouni Ouaddai, to a government post. Then the *Derde*, with a thousand tribesmen, sought refuge in Libya as the guest of King Idris while the Chadian rebellion grew across the border.

In 1966 a Chad exile, Ibrahim Abatcha, founded the Front de Liberation Nationale du Tchad ('Frolinat') in Khartoum. This brought together various groups and parties (the UNT, the FLT, other northern oppositionists, etc.) in a common organisation dedicated to what was increasingly perceived as a Chadian dictatorship, one moreover backed by the previous colonial power. A principal aim of Frolinat was to organise the Tebu tribes of the north to liberate the ancestral homeland of the south. Abatcha – with his lieutenants Djabalo Othman and Mohammed Ali Taher – travelled the world in search of recruits and support for the liberation war. He managed to recruit students in Cairo, some of whom went with him to North Korea for training in guerrilla warfare. On returning to Chad, Abatcha founded the First Liberation Army which set about inaugurating popular councils comprising military commanders and political organisers, and launching raids into southern Chad, burning cotton plantations and sabotaging communications. In 1968 the government army of Felix Malloum, Chad's French-educated president, killed Abatcha in battle and paraded his head through the northern villages on the point of a spear.

This was a set-back for the liberation forces but the armed struggle continued, led by the surviving lieutenants of the First Liberation Army. Taher launched Frolinat operations in the Tebu areas, and in March 1968 the Tebu Noman Guard in Aouzou mutinied in sympathy and killed their southern officers. Tombalbaye, seeing that the situation was rapidly deteriorating, invoked the 1960 mutual defence treaty with France. The French invaded the northern territories and quickly restored the situation and in August forced the Tebu Nomad Guard to surrender, but as soon as the French had withdrawn in November the Tebu rose again and quickly gained control of much of the north. This time the French decided to focus their attention on the strategically more important area of central Chad. By the time the Idris monarchy collapsed most of the Aouzou Strip had been liberated from Chadian government control. There had as yet been no Libyan invasion of Chad but the Libyans had already become involved in the war of liberation.

In 1966 Frolinat had established a presence in Sebba and begun a recruiting drive among Chadian students at the Islamic University at al-Beida; Idris, reluctant to become involved, was nonetheless forced to show some sympathy with his co-religionists among the Tebu and Arabs south of Fezzan. He stopped short of providing weapons or open support for the rebels but they derived some material support from the Libyan monarchy. At the same time, to the anger of Frolinat, Idris signed a number of agreements – on communications, the support of Islamic institutions in Chad, and the position of Chadian workers in Libya – with the Tombalbaye regime.[28] The border issue was not discussed.

Once the Idris monarchy had been overthrown Gaddafi addressed himself to the Chadian question. At first he was circumspect, offering arms and funds to Frolinat but unwilling to become involved in direct confrontation with the Tombalbaye government. Frolinat's new chief, the successor to Abatcha, was Dr Abba Seddik who had both a European and a traditional Muslim education and who was bitterly hostile to the non-Muslim neocolonial black power in the south of Chad. Some observers saw Seddik as a more conservative figure than Abatcha: he had been friendly with Idris and seemed to favour a campaign of national liberation rather than a bloody war of liberation. This seemed to suit Gaddafi who initially had no interest in being drawn into a war beyond his borders, nor in seeing the establishment of a robust Tebu force in the Aouzou Strip that would be sure to oppose Libyan claims on the area.

When divisions emerged in the liberation organisation Gaddafi backed Seddik. A Second Liberation Army (the Forces des Armées du Nord, FAN) had been formed by the *Derde*'s son, Goukouni Ouaddai, and this now challenged Siddik's leadership of the Frolinat movement. Gaddafi responded by clapping Ouddai in jail but this only made matters worse. When Ouddai was eventually released in October 1972, a reorganised FAN (now the Conseil de Commandant des Forces des Armées du Nord, CCFAN) came under the sway of Hissène Habré who was to emerge as an implacable enemy of Gaddafi. As relations between Gaddafi and Tombalbaye deteriorated further, Tripoli moved to offer Frolinat enhanced facilities: Siddik himself was provided with an office and communication facilities, and Frolinat was offered official recognition. Tombalbaye responded immediately by declaring that he would give similar facilities to the forces planning the overthrow of Gaddafi (the 1972 Sanussi plot to overthrow the Libyan government showed that the threat was not empty). However, the President of Nigeria, Hamami Diori, then came to serve as an intermediary between the two countries: negotiations took place and the threat of war was averted. In fact at that time Libya and Chad achieved an unexpected accommodation. On 12 April 1972 it was declared that both countries were resuming diplomatic relations; the Frolinat leadership was expelled from Tripoli, and Chad broke all its links with Israel, including the presence in its territory of Israeli military advisors. The principle of a Chadian/Libyan 'zone of solidarity' was incorporated in a formal treaty signed on 23 December 1972 in Tripoli. In 1973, under cover of the treaty, Libyan troops moved into the Aouzou Strip and they have been there ever since. To sweeten what may have seemed a bitter pill to Tombalbaye, Libya announced in March 1974 the creation of a joint bank to provide the Chadian regime with investment funds. However, it has been suggested that the promised funds never materialised and Gaddafi's support for Frolinat continued.[29]

The Libyan/Chad accommodations, whatever their character, became seriously threatened with the fall of Tombalbaye on 13 April 1975. He was deposed by a military group, led by General Felix Malloum, that called itself the Conseil Supérieur Militaire: the new junta, with French backing, had no interest in agreeing Gaddafi's claim to the Aouzou Strip. The Libyan Foreign Secretary, Dr Ali Treiki, visited Ndjamena for discussions with Malloum who preferred to seek a negotiated settlement with all the interested parties (Siddik and Habré included) rather than simply agreeing to Tripoli's demands. A confrontation between a Habré force and Libyan troops in northern Chad in June 1976 indicated the shape of things to come. In the same year a Libyan-backed coup attempt failed to topple General Malloum.

There now developed a nationwide civil war between the Malloum regime established in the south and the Frolinat forces, backed by Libya, in the north. By 1978 it was clear that the superior Libyan-supplied fire-power was having its effect: Faya Largeau, the largest town in northern Chad, was liberated by Frolinat, and by that time almost half the Chadian army had been lost in the fighting. But not all the Frolinat factions were enthusiastic about the growing Libyan influence in Chad: for instance, Goukouni Ouaddai, now head of FAN, even proposed to Malloum 'a national truce to confront the Libyan occupation'.[30] Such an arrangement never transpired and Gaddafi was content to assume the role of peacemaker between the contending factions.

In March 1978 he persuaded Frolinat and the Malloum government to sign an armistice that entitled Frolinat troops to travel through Chad to 'check on the presence of foreign troops', allowing the liberation forces to ascertain any residual colonial presence.[31] Malloum was forced to agree a range of concessions that effectively institutionalised Libyan intervention in Chad. Thus Gaddafi was able in July 1978 to divide Chad across the 14th Parallel into Libyan and French zones of influence. Gaddafi commented to the French: 'If you give me the Muslims in the north, I will give you the blacks in the south.'[32] Habré remained unhappy about the deal and broke away from Frolinat to develop his own faction, which led before long to a coalition between Malloum and Habré's FAN. This union, which Gaddafi called 'colonial and Fascist', did not last long.

Malloum, contrary to the negotiated agreement, had not renounced all his military ties with France and this gave Ouaddai the excuse to launch a further onslaught on the south. A further Libyan-sponsored peace conference never took place, and Gaddafi was soon forced to give fresh support to the Frolinat faction. Malloum again invoked the defence agreement with France and the French seized the chance to intervene yet again in the Chadian conflict. French airforce Jaguar bombers attacked Frolinat forces advancing towards the Chadian capital and the offensive was stopped. Goukouni Ouaddai split from the commander of the main Frolinat army, Ahmed Acyl, and a new power struggle developed in the movement. A Third Liberation Army, this time backed by Nigeria, entered upon the scene under the leadership of Abu Bakr Abdul Rahman; and at the same time there were splits in the Sara factions in the south, hampering Malloum's capacity to exploit the growing divisions within Frolinat.

In March 1979 Frolinat forces marched south and managed to take Ndjamena. Ouaddai became provisional President of Chad and tried initially to rule in conjunction with Habré but this alliance crumbled and yet another civil war began. With Ouaddai's position becoming increasingly insecure he desperately requested Libyan assistance, the sort of invitation that Gaddafi had been waiting for. Seven thousand Libyan troops attacked

Habré in the south and Gaddafi's Russian tanks travelled across 700 miles of desert to crush pockets of resistance in Ndjamena. Gaddafi had won his first significant military victory. Habré fled to Cameroon and the French, who had always assumed their right to a continuing influence in Chad, were humiliated. Moreover, Gaddafi could always claim that he had been invited into Chad by the provisional president.

In addition to the 7000 regular Libyan troops a further 7000 members of the Islamic Legion took part in the fighting. There were some serious Libyan losses but the remnants of Habré's 4000-man army were forced to flee to Sudan. The Islamic Legion continued to attack the fleeing forces in Sudan until President Sadat threatened that 'if one Libyan soldier enters Sudan, Egypt will act with its own forces'. In March 1981 Gaddafi commented from Tripoli: 'We have no wish to send our troops beyond Chad. We are bringing all confrontations to an end, including the one with Sadat's army.'[33] For the first time Gaddafi appeared to have tightened his grip on the whole of Chad; his victory would prove to be short-lived.

In 1981 Gaddafi was again looking to the possibility of merging two independent nations, with strong hints that Ouaddai would be executed if he refused to comply. The possibility of merger aroused horror in Chad, and Habré redoubled his efforts to organise a military force strong enough to expel the Libyans. Gaddafi again attracted international criticism and abuse, Libyan officials were expelled from many African countries, and the Organisation of African Unity (OAU) – seeing the Libyan plans as an unwelcome Arab penetration of the continent – condemned the proposed merger. Ouaddai declared from Paris that Libya and Chad would remain two separate countries and then, having asked the Libyans to enter his country, asked them to leave. Gaddafi, now being criticised by the OAU for imperialism and perceiving that Ouaddai was gaining considerable international support, abruptly pulled out of Chad in October 1981. An African peace-keeping force moved in but soon the country was again involved in civil war. This time Habré was backed by France and the United States: he moved back into Chad from Sudan, drove Ouaddai out of Ndjamena, and became president. Ouaddai was forced to flee to Cameroon, and Chad settled down to a brief period of peace. Then Ouaddai managed to raise support among the northern tribes and what has been called the 'Third Civil War' began.

This time the United States decided to become involved, sending two AWAC planes and eight F-15s to monitor and control Libyan air activities, and supplying also $10 million in other types of military aid. France, for the third time, sent troops and aircraft to Ndjamena. Habré was rescued and flown out on a Red Cross plane, just before Ouaddai and the Libyans captured the area on 11 August 1983. The French troops drew their own 'Red Line' across Chad, effectively dividing the country: Habré controlled all the territory to the south, under French and US protection; and Ouaddai controlled everything to the north, helped by the Libyans. Gaddafi consistently denied that his forces were in Chad, despite photographic and eyewitness evidence that they were. The US aircraft carrier *Coral Sea* had been despatched to join the *Eisenhower* off the Libyan coast; despite the French involvement in the conflict they were still able to suggest that Reagan was 'obsessed' by Gaddafi.

The stalemate lasted for a year. There were three thousand French troops and a full squadron of Jaguar aircraft at Ndjamena while Libyan troops were established at Faya Largeau. The OAU tried to mediate in Addis Adaba in January 1984 but the attempt collapsed when both sides insisted on their right to fly the Chadian flag. Meanwhile secret talks were being conducted between the Libyan and the French, leading to an agreement in September 1984 (to many Chadians, the 'great betrayal') that both sides would withdraw their troops. Against the wishes of Habré the French withdrew their troops from the south but Gaddafi's 'non-existent' army stayed entrenched in north (the US State Department claimed that there were still 5500 Libyan troops in Chad). Faya Largeau continued to fly the Libya flag and was recognised in the mid-1980s as a part of greater Libya. On 16 November President Mitterrand met Gaddafi in Crete, with the Green prime minister Papandreou serving as a mediator. Here Gaddafi repeatedly declared that all Libyan troops had been withdrawn; the next day Mitterrand admitted in Paris that Gaddafi had lied to him but declined to order French troops back to Chad. The country then enjoyed two years of peace, during which time the French and the US were building up Habré's forces and the Libyans were constructing roads and airbases in southern Libya and northern Chad. It did not take long to prepare the ground for the 'Fourth Civil War'.

It began, according to western commentators, with an attack in February 1986 by Ouaddai and his Libyan allies across the 'Red Line'. French aircraft were soon in action and the attack was beaten back. A further stalemate was established until Ouaddai took the unexpected initiative of proposing a peace with Habré. Ouaddai, apparently seen by the Libyans as betraying their cause, shot and wounded him in Tripoli on 30 October while he was 'resisting arrest'. This led to the Tebu changing sides and invited Habré to come to their rescue: he began mobilising his forces and moving north. On 11 December Libyan jets flew south to attack Ndjamena and a month later French aircraft struck at a Libyan airbase in Northern Chad. On 2 January Habré launched a ground attack, using four-wheel-drive trucks mounted with heavy machine-guns or anti-tank guns. They were supported by troops loyal to Ouaddai using Libyan weapons that they had brought with them when they changed sides. Habré succeeded in capturing six Italian anti-aircraft guns and dozens of Soviet T-55 tanks from the Libyans; armoured Libyan columns were ambushed and Habré claimed to have killed 800 Libyans in two major encounters. Libyan enclaves were successfully attacked and captured. The French and the Americans provided massive quantities of arms for the offensive, and the French provided also logistical support, transporting weapons and munitions up to the northern front.

As many as 1200 Libyans were killed at Faya, the Chadians taking them completely by surprise, and an immense quantity of booty was captured, including scores of Tupolev fighter-bombers, MiG-21s, helicopters, three Soviet SAM 13 batteries, Soviet Radar, and more than one hundred tanks. One estimate was that this booty was worth between $500 million and $1 billion. By the end of March it was claimed that 3603 Libyans had been killed and 1165 wounded, with losses of thirty-five Chadians. It was found that many of the dead and captured 'Libyans' were in fact mercenaries: Sudanese, and 1700 Druse militiamen from Lebanon, hired out by Walid Jumblatt at a monthly rate of $500 to $2300, their families assured of $50,000 if they were killed.[34] Habré then proceeded to expel the Libyans from the rest of the country. In June 1987 he visited President Reagan in Washington and was promised $32 million in aid, including Stinger anti-aircraft missiles in exchange for a selection of the captured Soviet military equipment, of much interest to US specialists.

In August, Habré succeeded in driving the Libyans out of the Aouzou Strip but the Chadian occupation of this area could not be sustained. The French had refused to provide air cover and the fresh confrontation was too far from Habré's own bases. The Libyans retook the Strip and flew foreign journalists to the region to demonstrate their success. But this again was swiftly countered when Habré sent a column more than sixty miles into Libyan territory to destroy the major Libyan airbase at Matan as-Sarra. The Chadians claimed a further 1700 Libyan fatalities and 312 prisoners while losing sixty-five of their own men. The OAU managed to organise a ceasefire for 11 September 1987 but not before Gaddafi had lost, according to US estimates, one-tenth of his army, 7500 men killed, and around $1.5 billion in equipment destroyed or captured.[35]

This was not the end of the matter. Both sides again began preparations for war, with the Libyans building fresh airbases and military installations in the Strip and Habré taking delivery of his US-supplied Stinger missiles and continuing to benefit from annual French aid amounting to around $70 million. The French, despite some earlier assurances continue to maintain troops in Chad and a squadron of Jaguars in maintained at Ndjamena. At a

OAU conference in May 1988 Gaddafi announced that he would recognise Habré as the legitimate president of Chad, 'as a gift to Africa', but said nothing about evacuating the Aouzou Strip. Habré, for his part, declared that he would not return an estimated 2000 Libyan prisoners-of-war, or send the French forces home, until Gaddafi had vacated the Strip. In August 1989 Libya and Chad signed a peace agreement and a number of meetings of the Libya/Chad Commission were subsequently convened to discuss the Strip and the question of Libyan prisoners-of-war, though deadlock has always resulted. The meetings were also overshadowed by periodic outbreaks of violence between government forces and pro-Gaddafi rebels entrenched in Sudan's Durfar Province. On 27 March 1990 Chad's foreign minister Sheikh Ibn Oumar declared to the BBC correspondent Brice Ndoumba that Libya was using the rebels to destabilise his country. Fresh incidents involved military clashes and the stopping of ten Libyan lorries travelling between Libya and Sudan. In May Libya called on the UN Security Council to intervene to settle the dispute.

At the beginning of 1991 President Habré was deposed by the Libyan-backed Idris Déby, according to one journalist, 'a leader satisfactory to all'.[36] Déby, a French-trained officer, was quick to pledge friendship to both Libya and France, and to announce democratic reforms. However, Habré had managed to escape into Niger with 3000 to 4000 of his troops intact, and in early January 1992 he returned to the country in force and captured two towns on Lake Chad. Now, it seems, the French are protecting Chad against Habré: the 1400 French troops in the country have been supplemented in early 1992 by 450 more sent from France and bases elsewhere in Africa. The French foreign ministry declared that the troops were there to protect the 3000 French nationals in the country, but soldiers have still been deployed to key installations. France has also expressed support for Deby's democratic reform programme and is seemingly not keen to see a Habré return. In late 1991 there was a further coup attempt against Déby, so perhaps he too will be submerged by the quagmire of Chadian politics. In 1992 the French continue to support the Déby administration, with French officers assigned to help the Chadian armed forces. Colonel Gaddafi, across the border, is keeping a low profile.

SUDAN

Sudan is of current interest because it remains the target of Gaddafi's unification plans and because it has been alarmed at Libyan incursions into Chad. The Sudan's western regions of northern and southern Darfur, bordering Libya and Chad, were included within the territory of Sudan according to a 1919 agreement. Darfur is a poverty-stricken area remote from Khartoum; social deprivation often led to protest which had to be suppressed by government forces. A revolt in January 1981 was not originally blamed on Gaddafi, though the area, the least developed region of Sudan's Muslim north, seemed to invite the attention of the Bureau for the Export of the Revolution. Throughout 1981 President Numeiri and Gaddafi traded insults, each saying that the other deserved to be put to death by his own people; and the Sudan was one of the African countries working hardest to get Libyan forces out of Chad. On one occasion Gaddafi sent a plane to bomb Khartoum, never forgetting that Darfur would serve as an excellent springboard for operations against Chad.[37]

In 1975 Libya hired mercenaries to attempt a coup in Sudan; the attempt was brutally crushed, with almost one hundred people summarily executed. Numeiri became increasingly autocratic, imposing the *sharia* with great severity and growing increasingly unwilling to compromise on what he took to be Islamic principle: adulterers were stoned to death, thieves had hands and feet amputated, and all alcohol (even that intended for medical uses in hospitals) was banned. Tensions in the country began a civil war in 1983, fomented in part by the Sudan People's Liberation Army led by Colonel John Garang, a US-educated Christian Dinka. At the same time the United States poured in aid ($77.4 million in 1989 and much more in military assistance) to ensure the loyalty of the country. Earlier, in 1985, the US, Britain, West Germany and Saudi Arabia had all suspended aid because of the drastic need for reforms in the country; and when President Reagan resumed aid, no reforms having been put in place, in 1985 it was too late. There were riots, mass demonstrations and a general strike: the army staged a coup on 6 April, whereupon the new government quickly resumed diplomatic relations with Libya. Today Sudan accepts large-scale aid from Libya, though this is not always welcome: the suspicion prevails that Gaddafi wants to annex Sudan and even a small incident – such as a confrontation between Libyan and Sudanese troops on the border – can spark riots against the Libyans. After the 1985 coup the army staged elections in April 1986 and power was won by the Umma Party under Saddiq el-Mahdi, the great-grandson of the Mahdi.

Conflict has continued between the new government and Garang's SPLA. In December 1987 the government forces claimed to have killed more than 3000 rebels, but Garang's army has been estimated as having up to 30,000 men and he has greatly extended his power base beyond the Dinka tribe. The Sudanese army ventures out of secure garrisons to attack the SPLA and in such unsettled circumstances the Sudan exists in a state of chaos (in 1988 more than three million people were dying of starvation). The government had little regard for human rights and it has been charged with deliberately starving whole sections of the rural population. The United States ever mindful of the needs of *realpolitik*, has refrained from criticising the abuses emanating from Khartoum for fear of pushing Mahdi into the arms of Gaddafi; but the Washington ploy has failed in its purpose. In recent years the Sudanese government has been happy to grow closer to Libya. In 1988 Mahdi visited Libya and signed an agreement for the merging of the two countries: again it seemed that Gaddafi's perennial dream for an enlargement of the country, with a view to the ultimate unification of the Arab world, was at last being realised.

However, the Sudanese army could not tolerate a union with Libya. The economy continued to worsen, the war dragged on, the famine in the south persisted, and on 30 June 1988 the army again took power. The coup was overtly welcomed by Egypt and covertly by Britain and the United States, none of which wanted to see an enlarged Libya. In February 1989 the US State Department commented that between 100,000 and 250,000 people had starved to death in southern Sudan, 'after elements of the armed forces on each side interfered or failed to cooperate with efforts to deliver food supplies to regions controlled by the other side'.[38] However, none of this was enough to totally disrupt Gaddafi's plans for a merger between the two countries. The unification steps taken by Mahdi were not wholly repugnant to Sudan's new military ruler, Omar Hassan al-Bashir, despite the earlier position of the army.

On 6 March 1990 Bashir and Gaddafi signed an agreement for a complete merger of the two countries within four years; the plan provided for a complete integration of their political, economic, social, defence and foreign policies, with a supreme authority vested in the two heads of state, a general secretariat and a ministerial body. Joint authorities would be created in such areas as foreign affairs, finance, labour, energy and mining; and the armed forces would have a joint High Command. By 1992 the scheme had developed further and the intention of full integration of the two countries was still on the agenda.

WESTERN SAHARA

One effect of the Second World War was to destabilise all the colonial territories of North Africa. The Algerian National Liberation Front (FLN) began its war against the French occupation in November 1954, and in

Morocco an Army of Liberation started operations to achieve an independent republican state. The French removed the sultan of Morocco, Mohammed V, in August 1953 and installed a new compliant monarch. However, following the country's rapid descent into chaos the French, wanting to concentrate on Algeria, gave Morocco and Tunisia their independence. Spain too was forced to abandon its territory in Morocco, leaving the north immediately and agreeing to vacate the south as soon as an independent Morocco could take over. Under attack by the Army of Liberation the Spanish were then pushed out of Ifni, Spanish Sahara and Spanish South Morocco (though the Spanish army later returned to a small strip around the village of Sidi Ifni).

The Army of Liberation was perceived as a threat to the Moroccan monarchy, as it was to the local interests of Spain and France. After an Army attack on French positions in Algeria and Mauritania, France launched Operation Hurricane to crush bases of the Army of Liberation in Mauritania and the Spanish Sahara. Spain, with this military support from France, found that it could retain part of Spanish Sahara, though when Mauritania gained its independence in 1960 both Mauritania and Morocco lay claim to the Spanish Sahara. Morocco's claim to this region was first declared in 1974, by which time an anti-colonial movement had been created by student Saharawis influenced by the radical Arabs. These students from Moroccan schools and universities founded the Polisario Front in 1972 (the *Frente Popular para la Liberation de Saguia el-Hamra y Rio de Oro*, the Saguia el-Hamra a river in the north of Spanish Sahara, Rio de Oro the southern area). Polisario began its guerrilla war in 1973, supplied with arms by Gaddafi.

The Americans and the French opposed Polisario on principle because of its leftist leanings but the Spanish, still under Franco, decided that it could work with the Polisario Front. The United Nations sent representatives to Spanish Sahara and were everywhere greeted with demonstrations in support of Polisario. On 15 October 1975 the UN mission declared that most of the people of Spanish Sahara were in favour of independence; it was clear also that Polisario would be the people's choice for the new administration. On 16 October the International Court of Justice ruled that no 'tie of territorial sovereignty' existed between the territory of Western Sahara 'and the Kingdom of Morocco or the Mauritanian entity'. King Hassan of Morocco decided to ignore the judicial ruling and was supported in this by France and the United States. Spain severed all links with Polisario, began talks with Hassan on 21 October, and a week later began leaving the territory (even to the point of removing a thousand bodies from the Spanish cemetery at Villa Cisneros): soon the Moroccan army and

Polisario units were fighting each other for control of the region. Some 40,000 Saharawis fled their homes while Morocco and Mauritania divided up the territory between them.

The military wing of Polisario (the Saharawi People's Liberation Army, SPLA) continued to fight against what it saw as an illicit occupation of its land, and it now enjoyed the support of Algeria and Libya. El-Ouali Mustapha Sayed, the founder and secretary-general of Polisario, was killed in a raid on the Mauritanian capital in June 1976. He was succeeded by Mohammed Abdel Aziz who, in the early 1990s, was still Polisario's secretary-general. Through the 1980s the SPLA won a number of important victories against Morocco but was unable to erode Morocco's position in the OAU or the United Nations because of the position of the Western powers. Most of the Arab states, out of a sense of ethnic solidarity, also supported Morocco. Gaddafi vacillated: having opposed Morocco, he then swung round and signed a unification treaty with Hassan, only to swing the other way two years later.

In August 1988 UN Secretary-General Perez de Cuellar proposed a truce between the SPLA and Morocco, to be followed by a plebiscite in the Western Sahara; and on 27 December Hassan, reversing his 13-year-long policy, declared his willingness to talk to the Polisario Front. In 1992 the United Nations is still trying to establish the terms of the proposed referendum. The Polisario Front has accused the Moroccans of trying to gerrymander the result by artificially inflating the pro-Moroccan vote. Today the problem still sits on the desk of UN Secretary-General Boutros Ghali. Gaddafi, having dumped Polisario in 1984 and then taken up the cause again in 1986, is saying little.

PHILIPPINES

The Muslims in the Philippines, though racially indistinguishable from the Filipino Christians, are known as the Moros (from 'Moors'). They live mainly in the southern islands, Mindanao and the Sulu archipelago. They never accepted the rule of the colonial Spanish but during the American period Mindanao and Sulu were brought firmly under Manila's control. The authorities, with American support, have encouraged landless peasants from Luzon to settle in the southern islands, with the result that there are now fewer Muslims than Christians in Mindanao. The principal Moro grievance is that they fear being submerged by the Christian influx, their land taken and their rights ignored. In 1968 a group of Moros, inspired by

Muslim nationalism in Indonesia and Malaysia, founded the Moro National Liberation Front (MNLF). In the early 1970s they began looking to Arab states – including Libya – for moral and practical support. The MNLF has launched terrorist attacks and on occasions full-scale military operations in an attempt to secure the independence of the Muslim provinces. The Moros have claimed that ten per cent of the Filipino population of 50 million is Muslim (President Marcos used to declare that the Muslim proportion was much less). The Islamic Conference has shown interest in the rights of the Moros, though it seems that Gaddafi has been the main supplier of arms and funds. By 1974 the MNLF was able to put between 50,000 and 60,000 guerrillas into the field, with arms from Libya pouring in via Malaysia. An embargo on Arab oil was also threatened.

By 1977 the guerrilla war was occupying two-thirds of the army's combat units, and no end seemed in sight. Marcos decided to sign the 'Tripoli Agreement', granting the Moros a measure of independence. This satisfied much of the MNLF leadership but a hardline faction, led by Nur Misauri, continued to demand complete autonomy for Mindanao, Sulu, Basilan and Palawan, as much as a third of the national territory of the Philippines (Misauri has claimed that throughout the 1980s some 100,000 Moros were killed). In 1976 President Marcos, believing that Gaddafi was the main supporter of the MNLF, decided to send his wife Imelda to Libya 'to charm' Gaddafi into helping to find a solution to the Moro problem.[39] Talks were launched between Philippine government representatives, Nur Misauri, and envoys from the Islamic Conference, leading to the signing of a 'preliminary' accord on 30 December 1976.

The Moros were nominally given their own institutions, including a representative assembly and Muslim courts, but these would remain under the control of Manila. It was declared that the various parties to the agreement would return to Libya to sign a final document in early 1977 while a commission – comprising MNLF and Philippine representatives and a four-man committee from Libya, Somalia, Senegal and Saudi Arabia – was delegated to control the cease-fire. However, on 4 January the Philippine government announced that a referendum would be held in the southern provinces to ascertain which wanted to be autonomous; other areas could have their own referenda, so diluting the Muslim character of the south. Gaddafi did not like the sound of this, and the MNLF flatly rejected the idea of a referendum. To sweeten the pill Marcos promised a conditional amnesty for Muslim rebels in the south and then promulgated new laws for a Muslim court system. The fresh talks in Tripoli collapsed, the Marcos envoy returned to Manila, and the MNLF threatened to resume hostilities; by now the Moros were demanding their own flag, their own army, and the incorporation of three Christian provinces (offering offshore oil and good farmland) into the Muslim area. On 7 March 1977 fighting resumed between the MNLF and government forces whereupon Imelda Marcos was sent back to Tripoli. In one account the chemistry between Imelda and Gaddafi 'evidently worked, because Gaddafi stopped funding the Moros after Imelda's second visit'.[40] The head of the CIA, William Casey, visited Imelda Marcos to debrief her.

Gaddafi then offered a fresh peace plan involving the granting of a new autonomous area and a provisional administration to monitor the referendum (still rejected by the MNLF). He suggested to President Marcos that such an agreement would 'open a new page in the relations between the Philippines and the Islamic States'; and in a marathon television and phone-in broadcast on 29 March Marcos declared that Christians would predominate in the provisional administration, that it would be subordinate to the martial-law regime, and that Gaddafi would persuade the MNLF to accept the plan. In fact Misauri, in exile in Tripoli, stated that he disapproved of the entire scheme. When the referendum was held it was claimed that 97.93 per cent of votes were *against* autonomy under MNLF rule, though perhaps such a figure should be viewed with some circumspection. Subsequent talks in Manila broke down, the Islamic Conference condemned the role that Marcos had played, and Misauri declared that now the MNLF would battle for complete independence.

However, the MNLF then split into two (and later three) factions. Misauri, still with Libyan support, stayed in Tripoli; his aide, Hashim Salamat, began separate MNLF activities in Cairo; and later a third group of Moro exiles enjoyed congenial asylum in Saudi Arabia. King Hassan of Morocco then stepped in to say that he would help in any way he could, while Gaddafi, perceiving that the whole situation was becoming unmanageable, decided to opt out. He was further discouraged by reports that the Moros had become associated in the early 1980s with the Maoist New People's Army, a branch of the banned Philippines Communist Party (PKP). Gaddafi has never welcomed the contamination of Muslim movement by atheistic communism.

When President Aquino took power in 1986 she quickly arranged a truce with the MNLF and persuaded Nur Misauri to return to the Philippines. A new constitution was drawn up in 1987 to offer a degree of autonomy for the Moros in Mindanao, but the new scheme was never implemented. Manila has exploited divisions in the MNLF, offering political posts and other jobs to Moro leaders and so exacerbating splits in the movement. The Libyan-backed dream of an independent unified Muslim state in the southern provinces of the Philippines is dead.

IRISH REPUBLICAN ARMY (IRA)

Gaddafi's support for the IRA began more than two decades ago. In 1970, at a meeting with Nasser and Mohammed Heikal, Gaddafi declared that he had decided to help the IRA in order to fight British colonialism. At that time Heikal protested that the IRA was not a genuine liberation movement, but Gaddafi was not convinced.[41] In June 1972 he gave a speech declaring his support for the 'revolutionaries of Ireland who oppose Britain and are motivated by nationalism and religion'. Here Gaddafi was keen to advertise his 'pan-religious' philosophy, proud of his capacity to support committed theists even though they were not Moslems: any religion, in this view, is better than none at all. In August, two members of the Provisional IRA flew to Warsaw to meet a representative of Libya's Foreign Ministry, and Ed Moloney of the *Irish Times* later described the 'quite extraordinary' deal that was agreed. The Libyans suggested that the IRA representatives be established on a permanent basis in Tripoli with semi-diplomatic status; and at the same time substantial economic aid was promised. In due course three IRA people went to Tripoli in the guise of English teachers.[42] In January 1973 the new 'diplomats' began the negotiations that were to yield the *Claudia* gun-running fiasco.

In March 1973 the Irish navy halted a fishing vessel, the *SS Claudia*, off the south-east coast of Ireland. When the ship was searched the authorities found rifles, other small arms, and anti-tank weapons, along with Joe Cahill, a leading IRA figure later sentenced to three years' penal servitude but released because of ill health. According to a German businessman, the middle man in the deal, three IRA men in Tripoli had made the necessary arrangements but the deal had not worked out: 95 tons of arms out of the planned 100 tons had gone missing. Also, as the *Claudia* approached Ireland, Gaddafi invited the IRA men in Tripoli to broadcast their revolutionary message on the radio, an act of bravado that probably alerted the British and Irish authorities.

On an earlier occasion a freelance arms dealer flew a batch of arms from Libya to Ireland. He landed his plane on a small remote airfield where the guns were unloaded. Then, against the advice of his colleagues, he took off with the intention of flying to the United States. His plane disappeared over the Atlantic and it is assumed that he ran out of fuel and crashed.[43] In 1986 a large cache of Libyan arms was found in the Republic of Ireland; and in 1988 the French navy intercepted a Panamanian ship, the *Eksund*, carrying a cargo of 150 tons of Libyan arms for the IRA; this cargo included surface-to-air missiles, Kalashnikov rifles, and large quantities of explosives. However, despite such evidence it has been suggested that Libyan aid for the IRA had been relatively small in scale.

After the *Claudia* episode Gaddafi seems to have halted the bulk of his attempted arms shipments to Ireland and to have confined himself to his much-declared 'moral and political' support for the IRA. A senior officer in Scotland Yard's anti-terrorist squad had commented that Libyan support for the IRA has been 'very minor indeed. It can be counted in the thousands of pounds, but certainly not in hundreds of thousands and any talk of millions of dollars is ludicrous.'[44] Noraid, the US group supporting the IRA, has contributed very much more than Libya over the years.

Members of the Ulster Defence Association (UDA) also visited Libya in an effort to gain support of one kind or another. They achieved little but claim to have opened the Libyans' eyes as to the real nature of the IRA ('We told them . . . that the Provos weren't just shooting military targets, but ordinary Protestant people as well').[45] The IRA itself sent some young recruits to Libyan training camps but was uneasy about links with what was seen as a fundamentalist Moslem country that was at the time building up its Moscow connection. It appears that the Libyan supply of arms dried up, and even when equipment arrived there were often problems: one batch of Libyan rocket launchers arrived with detailed instructions printed in Arabic. There was also the matter of interpreting arms finds accurately: Libyan arms found in Eire or Northern Ireland may not have been sent by the Libyans but may have come from the illegal gun markets of the world. However, there can be no doubt that Prime Minister Margaret Thatcher was ready to support Ronald Reagan's bombing of Libya in 1986 because of Gaddafi's oft-stated support for the IRA.

There are many signs that Gaddafi has moderated his attitudes in recent years. When Donald Trelford, editor of *The Observer*, visited Gaddafi in 1987, soon after the American air strikes, Gaddafi declared that he had increased aid to the IRA as a means of retaliating against Britain. But in 1992 the tone was completely different: 'The IRA commit acts that we consider to be terrorist and we do not approve of them. We give political support to Sinn Fein, but nothing to the IRA.'[46] Some observers may see this as a specious distinction but there are other signs that Gaddafi has changed his views (see below).

LIBYA TODAY

The most important features of modern Libya are oil and Gaddafi. In an oil-hungry world it is impossible to relegate Libya, with its prodigious oil resources, to the margins of the world economy. For almost two decades the United States has maintained a tight economic squeeze on Libya but has not been able to prevent other Western states from purchasing Libyan oil. Libya's economic survival is as much guaranteed by the perceived self-interest of certain developed countries as by any policies that may be adopted by its revolutionary leadership. Oil has enabled Libya to fund social reconstruction, to buy weapons on a massive scale, and to finance terrorists and revolutionary groups throughout the world. Libya remains dependent on foreign companies and foreign labour (5500 specialists from Britain alone) and there is no sign that it will achieve the desired levels of self-sufficiency in the short or medium term.

The development of the Libyan economy, dependent to a large extent on foreign goodwill, necessarily impacts on Libyan foreign policy. Relations are cultivated – as far as international political pressures will allow – with states deemed important to Libyan investment and growth. Hundreds of Western firms have contracts for projects in Libya, from irrigation schemes to construction, from oil-product development to the building of communication networks. Thus in 1991 the Swedish company Ericsson agreed terms for building a 30,000-line communication network for the Murzuk region. The Libyan market, as a well-situated hydrocarbon society, is an attractive prospect for foreign contractors, though it appears that payments for work are sometimes delayed when disputes arise. An outstanding claim for payment by the Turkish Libas company which carried out $700 million of construction work in Libya has recently been settled and outstanding payments will be made; but in late 1991 the Yugoslav companies Hidrgardnja and Unioninvest were still waiting for advance payments, due within one month of signature, on contracts signed in 1990 for irrigation work. The Spanish firms Watt, Ferrovial, Cisa and Agroman completed their work in 1986, and expect to receive outstanding payments in 1992. The settlement follows the decision of the Spanish government to allow the Libyan subsidiary, Oilinvest Espana, to invest $10 million in building a network of petrol and service stations in Spain.[47]

Libya remains massively dependent on foreign contractors, foreign technicians and foreign labour for all large-scale development in the country. Dozens of firms are involved in the Great Man-made River Project (GMR) and the complexity of this vast scheme means that there are frequent difficulties and delays to be overcome. Thus in 1992 a dispute between the

GMR authority and the Brazilian firm Braspetro was referred to the Paris-based International Chamber of Commerce (ICC) for arbitration. In this case filters supplied by the Brazilian company broke down, allowing contamination of the water: so far it has been found that seventy-six wells, out of 126 drilled in the Safir area, will have to be repaired or rebuilt.

However, occasional delays in payment and other contractual disputes appear not to discourage foreign contractors seeking work in Libya. For example, contractors are currently discussing irrigation and farm complexes to be built in the Sirte and Benghazi areas; and many international companies expect automatic renewal of contracts upon termination. Such economic deals must be considered a vital part of Libya's foreign-policy posture in the international trading community. In recent years a number of European countries (Italy, Germany, France, Britain and Yugoslavia) have been happy to increase their volume of imports (mainly oil) from Libya, and others (Netherlands, Spain, Greece, Belgium, Austria and Switzerland) have continued to take Libyan exports in substantial volumes. Libya itself takes substantial imports from such countries as Italy, Germany, Britain, France and Japan (Italy remains its principal trading partner, perhaps because of the indelible historical links between the two countries but mainly because of their geographical proximity).

Libya's economic links with Europe (Table 7.1) may be seen as providing a basis for Gaddafi's evident attempts to improve his image in the international community. Over the last two years he has entertained a range of European dignitaries, considerably moderated his revolutionary rhetoric,

Table 7.1   Libya: Main Trading Partners, 1989–90 ($ million)

	Exports		Imports	
	1990	1989	1990	1989
Italy	4716	3072	1083	1150
Germany	2186	1622	748	679
Spain	1163	776	66	82
France	762	466	378	355
Turkey*	487	286	221	227
UK	281	186	437	392
Belgium/Lux.*	269	190	148	92
Austria*	262	152	76	60

*OECD figures.

Source: Middle East Economic Digest, 28 June 1991

and largely observed the protocols of international law, whatever the British and the Americans may see (see Chapter One). In April 1991 Gaddafi helds talks in Tripoli with the French Foreign Minister Roland Dumas; and in June with the Italian Prime Minister Giulio Andreotti. A foreign oil executive has been quoted as saying: 'It may not have the best press in the world, but at the moment Libya is looking a more appealing business proposition than Algeria.'[48] On the occasion of the 1988 anniversary of the revolution Gaddafi stated his own version of the economic liberalisation that was sweeping the world. The impulse to nationalise all trade had disappeared: local merchants would be allowed to import and export without restraint, and the state's control over small-scale industrial enterprises would be reduced. All this tokens a pragmatic accommodation to the prevailing climate of world opinion.

A growing range of 'decadent' goods – French perfumes, Swiss watches and Japanese electronic goods – are appearing in Libyan shops. Employee partnerships are being formed for the first time in small commercial ventures. In April 1988 the Executive Authority for Partnerships and Small Industries was established to oversee the transfer of control of small state enterprises to employees; today employees can buy shares in a company or can obtain partnership loans. In theory it is now possible for mixed-sector ventures to be created in all commercial areas, with the exception of the oil and steel industries. One published source suggested that 292 small and medium-size industrial ventures with total assets of $62 million had passed into employee hands by 1991 in the Tripoli municipality alone.[49] The state continues to control the vast bulk of the economy, and members of the revolutionary committees have protested at the modest economic reforms. A recent article in the Libyan press, condemning consumerism and personal wealth, was headed: 'Fancy villas with satellite dishes: time for the bulldozer.' The economic changes have however signalled Gaddafi's cautious response to world changes that appear to have discredited massive state involvement in national economies.

Gaddafi is also working to improve his relations with the rest of the Arab world. In the past he has condemned President Mubarak as a Western stooge, with Cairo an 'occupied capital' because of the presence of an Israeli embassy. Today Gaddafi and Mubarak meet regularly with Gaddafi seeking Egyptian protection from the extremes of US policy. Mubarak has recently supported Gaddafi in the Libyan claims that the Rabta plant is a pharmaceutical and not a chemical-weapons factory, and in Gaddafi's insistence that Abu Nidal has never been in Libya. During the 1991 Gulf War, in circumstances where Gaddafi might have been expected to adopt a radical posture, it was significant that he chose to exert a moderating influence: 'Unfortunately, by entering Kuwait, Iraq presented the region on a plate to American imperialism.' A number of international observers have been keen to emphasise what they see as an important shift of emphasis in Gaddafi's attitudes to foreign relations. Such disparate Westminster MPs as Tam Dalyell, Bernie Grant and Teddy Taylor have been impatient with a British government determined to ignore the changes. And the French Foreign Minister Roland Dumas has commented: 'Our position towards Libya should be more positive'; and an Andreotti aide, commenting on the June 1991 discussions, remarked that the talks 'are a turning point, which should allow the start of correct relations with not only us but the whole of Europe'.

Gaddafi has also made a number of conciliatory gestures to Britain and the United States: all such approaches have been spurned. In May 1991 the Libyan Foreign Minister Abrahim Mohammed Beshari declared (of Britain and the US): 'They have their position, we have ours, but that should not prevent the establishment of normal relations . . . in the framework of mutual respect and non-interference in internal affairs.' In response a UK Foreign and Commonwealth Office statement read: 'There cannot be any improvement until there is convincing evidence that Libya has renounced international terrorism, including support for the Irish Republican Army'; and the US State Department commented in June 1991 that 'We have not seen any particular change. Libya is still supporting terrorism, destabilising regimes and pursuing development of dangerous weapons systems. We will need very strong signals before a review of relations can take place.'[50]

In mid 1991 Gaddafi also made apologies and conciliatory gestures for the shooting of Woman Police Constable Yvonne Fletcher, after serious demonstrations in London, from a window of Libya's embassy in 1984.[51] A number of concessions were made by the Libyans, including a cheque for £250,000 sent to a police charity. Sir Teddy Taylor, who helped to secure the Libyan concessions, remains convinced that news of the cheque was 'selectively leaked' in Britain to produce a negative response.[52] The phrase 'Blood money' was used in many British newspapers, even though it was Taylor and not Gaddafi who had suggested the possibility of a payment in recompense. The upshot was that the Libyans were treated with 'discourtesy and contempt' and Gaddafi understandably declared that Britain and the United States could 'go to hell'. Taylor subsequently released a copy of the Libyan note, signed by Gaddafi that he had received:

> With regard to relations with the IRA, and similar organisations, Libya has frequently declared, and I herewith confirm, its condemnation of terrorist activities whose victims are innocent people, and on this basis

Libya believes the so-called IRA is not worth (*sic*) for us to have any contacts with, or to give it any support or backing. And that applies to any organisation that uses terrorism as a means to further its aims.

The British government confirmed that there would be 'no response' to the Libyan leader.[53]

After a visit of the British M.P. Bernie Grant to Libya in August 1991, he and Sir Teddy Taylor issue a joint statement. It included the words:

Sir Teddy and I have both now visited Libya and had serious discussions with senior figures in that country. I believe that they are serious in having changed their position on a number of key issues, especially on the matter of their past support for certain groups, and that progress should now be made towards the restoration of diplomatic relations with Libya. I note also that they have already shown a willingness to pay compensation in relation to the death of WPC Fletcher.

Britain now appears to stand alone in Europe in its unwillingness to work for change in its relationship with Libya. Numerous senior European politicians have now visited Libya and are in the process of taking steps to bring Libya back into the community of nations. They recognise that the situation in North Africa is of great importance for the future of Europe, and in particular the question of immigration from the Magreb countries has to be addressed. It is my view that Britain should not isolate itself from Europe on this issue.

There can be little doubt that the Libyan position has changed in many areas, though debate is still possible about the extent of the transformation. Economic policy has discernibly shifted in the direction of liberalisation, there is an evident move away from moral and practical help for dissident groups throughout the world, and constructive steps have been through discussion and real initiatives to improve relations with other countries.

It is equally clear that many countries have shown a willingness to respond to the changed posture adopted by Colonel Gaddafi. There has been an evident improvement in Libyan relations with a number of European countries – notably, Italy and France (though the disputed bombing of the UTA DC-10 over the Ténéré desert has had, and continues to have, an adverse impact); and it is obvious that relations with various Arab countries have improved. There is still talk of a merger with Sudan, and Egypt is emerging as a principal friend of Libya, though it is unlikely that Mubarak would support Libya over the United States. Such developments suggest that there is great scope for constructive dialogue with Gaddafi and the rest of the Libyan leadership. Where this fails to take place it is clear that certain nations are following their own hidden agenda, a set of priorities that are never publicly expressed but which none-the-less come to shape the character of political events. We can learn something of such covert political pressures by considering the troubled history of relations between Libya and the United States.

8 United States versus Gaddafi

Why don't we give him AIDS.

George Shultz, US Secretary of State, 1986

THE US AND THE THIRD WORLD

The United States has long been accustomed to intervening in the Third World for strategic or economic reasons. The celebrated Monroe Doctrine was one of the clearest signs that the US considered itself entitled in the nineteenth century to intervene in the world wherever its emerging hegemony would allow. The Monroe Doctrine was not the first overt expression of this presumed right, nor was it the last; but it signalled a resolution that weaker nations ignored at their peril. On 2 December 1823 President James Monroe declared to the US Congress that the United States was to run the western hemisphere, that interlopers from Europe had no right to 'extend their system' to the New World. From the 1850s onward it was assumed that the Monroe Doctrine entitled the United States to invade any country of Latin America whenever it wished and for whatever reason. This principle had a convenient simplicity and focus: it was to be refined and enlarged for application many times in the nineteenth and twentieth centuries.

In 1962 Secretary of State Dean Rusk presented a State Department list, 'Instance of the Use of United States Armed Forces Abroad, 1798–1945', in order to cite precedents for the use of military action against Cuba. The following examples appear in the list:

1852–3   Argentina: marines landed and occupied parts of Buenos Aires.
1853   Nicaragua: invasion to 'protect American lives and interests'.
1853–54   Japan: warships used to compel the opening of ports to the US.
1853–54   Ryukyu and Bonin Islands: invasion to secure a coaling concession.

1854	Nicaragua: destruction of San Juan del Norte to avenge an insult to the American Minister to Nicaragua.
1855	Uraguay: invasion to 'protect American interests'.
1859	China: invasion 'for the protection of American interests in Shanghai'.
1860	Angola: invasion to 'protect American lives and property'.
1893	Hawaii: invasion to 'protect American lives and property'.
1894	Nicaragua: invasion to 'protect American interests'.

Thus by the time of the twentieth century the United States was a fully fledged imperialist power, keen to use military forces to acquire or protect overseas properties. Its presumed right to act in such a fashion was reiterated many times, most famously by President Theodore Roosevelt in 1901: 'Speak softly and carry a big stick; you will go far.' In the nineteenth century people throughout the world felt the weight of the American 'big stick'; countless more were destined to do so in the twentieth.* The culture had been well prepared, America's industrial magnates and military leaders eager to support a policy of economic and territorial expansion. Captain A. T. Mahan, a popular US Navy propagandist, spoke for many when he observed that the countries with the biggest navies would inherit the earth ('Americans must now begin to look outward'). The then Senator Henry Cabot Lodge of Massachusetts commented that 'for the sake of our commercial supremacy in the Pacific we should control the Hawaiian Islands and maintain our influence in Samoa'; furthermore, 'the island of Cuba . . . will become a necessity'. He declared that the great nations were absorbing 'all the waste places of the earth', and that the United States should not be left behind: 'It is a movement that makes for civilisation and the advancement of the race.'[1] On the eve of the Spanish–American war the *Washington Post* celebrated the mood of the people: 'The taste of Empire is in the mouth of the people even as the taste of blood in the jungle.'[2] The historian J. A. Hobson, in a classic text,[3] noted the capitalist need for imperial expansion: 'It was Messrs Rockefeller, Pierpont Morgan, and their associates who needed Imperialism and who fastened it upon the shoulders of the great Republic of the West. They needed Imperialism because they desired to use the public resources of their country to find profitable employment for their capital.' And he added, with uncommon prescience, that

---

*The United States, not uniquely perfidious, has simply exploited the *de facto* privileges that are characteristic of all hegemonic powers.

'Cuba, the Philippines, and Hawaii were but the *hors d'oeuvre* to whet an appetite for an ampler banquet.' Hobson, writing in 1902, was already charting the course of the decades to come.

At the end of the nineteenth century the US Navy Department observed that the possibility of war in Cuba was encouraged 'by the contractors for projectiles, ordnance, ammunition and other supplies, who have thronged the department'. The banker Russell Sage, in comfort and security, declared that if war came there would be no question 'where the rich men stand'; it was reported that Astor, Rockefeller and Ryan were 'feeling militant', and that Morgan reckoned that further talk with Spain would be pointless. In March 1898 an advisor to President McKinley declared that all the big corporations would welcome war.[4] Soon afterwards the US invaded Cuba; the Spanish forces collapsed within three months, after what John Hay, the US Secretary of State, had dubbed 'a splendid little war'. American business moved quickly to take over Cuban assets, and the war also had other consequences. The United States took Puerto Rico by military conquest and in July 1898 annexed the Hawaiian Islands. Wake Island, on the route to Japan, was occupied; as was the Spanish possession of Guam, near to the Philippines. By 1899 the United States had forced Spain to hand over Guam, Puerto Rico and the Philippines. On the acquisition of the Philippines President McKinley remarked that 'there was nothing left for us to do but to take them all and to educate the Filipinos, and uplift and civilise and Christianise them . . .' The upshot was a bloody war of conquest fought by the superior US forces against ill-equipped guerrilla bands. General Arthur MacArthur admitted that the guerrilla tactics of the peasant Filipinos 'depended upon almost complete unity of action of the entire native population'. It was a pattern that American commanders would learn to recognise throughout the world.

It is obvious that US imperialism was well entrenched before the start of the twentieth century. In addition to the interventions cited by Dean Rusk, and the major nineteenth-century invasions of Cuba and the Philippines, we can also mention without comment the military incursions into Korea (in 1871, 1888 and 1894–6), into Panama (1865 and 1886), into Columbia (1868, 1873 and 1895), into Brazil (1894), and into Egypt (1882). The US development of an imperialist culture is often acknowledged by American observers. Thus J. William Fulbright, one of the most distinguished and influential senators, wrote of the 'arrogance of power'[5] and the 'price of empire';[6] and the celebrated American writer Steele Commager observed that it was the West, not Communist countries, 'that invented imperialism and colonialism . . . We should remember that in the eyes of the 19th century world it was the United States that was pre-eminently an expansionist and aggressive nation . . . in half a century we trebled our territory at the expense of France, Spain, Mexico and Britain.'[7]

The American experience of imperialist expansion in the nineteenth century came to have increasing relevance in the twentieth. The way had been prepared, the slogans conjured, the military technologies massively improved. A procession of US governments rejoiced in their Manifest Destiny, assumed the burdens that Fate had put on the shoulders of God's Own Country, and resolved – 'whatever the price' – to uphold freedom and democracy throughout the world. Sometimes the words slipped into absurdity – as with 'intervening to preserve independence' or justifying (as did Francis P. Matthews, the Secretary of the US Navy, on 25 January 1950) the US role as 'aggressors for peace'. However, the slogans were less important than the practical actions in the world. Here we cannot profile the many US interventions throughout the twentieth century but it is worth recalling such events as the intervention in Guatemala in 1954 to overthrow the democratically elected Jacobo Arbenz government, the use of the CIA to overthrow the Iranian Prime Minister Mossadeq in 1951, the imposing of the military dictator George Papadopoulos in Greece in 1967, the invasion of Lebanon in 1958, support for the anti-Sukarno coup in Indonesia in 1958, the provision of arms between 1975 and the 1990s for the Indonesian occupation and suppression of East Timor, support for the 1961 invasion of Cuba, support for the overthrow of Patrice Lumumba in the Congo in 1960, CIA involvement in the sacking of the Labour premier Gough Whitlam in Australia in 1975, support for the military coup against President Joao Goulart of Brazil in 1964 and the democratic Chilean leader Dr Salvador Allende in 1973, the invasion of the Dominican Republic in 1965, and efforts to destabilise the elected government of Michael Manley in Jamaica through the 1980s.[8] It is clear that US intervention can take many forms, involving diplomatic pressure on governments, the manipulation of international bodies, economic sanctions and blockade, the arming and supply of military proxies ('freedom fighters'), and the use of American covert or overt forces. The United States, like other nations, relies upon comprehensive intelligence services and is willing, like other nations, to spread lies via pliant or manipulated media in the furtherance of its objectives.

The US strategy against Colonel Muammar al-Gaddafi of Libya has so far involved the spreading of disinformation (lies), economic sanctions, and the bombing in 1986 of major cities. It is important, in considering the ongoing US intervention in Libyan affairs, to remember the context of American involvement throughout the world in recent decades. The Libyan question is not an isolated event, but part of a broader picture in which a powerful hegemonic state adumbrates to itself the right to define moral right and international law in its own perceived interests. This is the context in which US policy on Libya will unfold, in circumstances in which the constraints on the freedom of action of the world's one superpower – following the collapse of the Soviet Union – have been massively reduced. The consequences of the US-defined New World Order (see Chapter One) will be increasingly felt across the globe, but most of all in the Third World.

FIRST LIBYAN/US CONFLICT

The first confrontation between Libya and the United States (1801–5) resulted from the US refusal to increase payments of tribute to the pasha of Tripoli for the protection he offered against pirate raids. At that time the trade between Europe and North Africa (the Barbary states) was flourishing: stones were obtained from Leptis Magna for the building of Versailles and St Germain des Prés.[9] The Barbary states derived a substantial income from their pirate ships as well as from the wide-ranging commerce that served as an extension of Turkish naval strategy in the region.[10] The activities of the pirates were supported by local rulers, such as Yusuf Karamanli of Tripoli, who provided political support and an effective market for the pirate loot. The rulers in turn benefited from the acts of piracy, acquiring treasure and produce from the seized European and American ships, and obtaining slaves and hostages for their own purposes: erstwhile crews could be forced into labour or sold as hostages. It was difficult to defeat the pirates in naval confrontation since they were relatively close to their own bases and in any case enjoyed the support of the local tribal leaders. The other option was for traders (or their governments) to pay protection money: in 1799 the administration of President John Adams began the practice of paying annual tribute to the local rulers in North Africa to guarantee immunity for US merchant ships. At that time Yusuf Karamanli was receiving $18,000 a year for that purpose.

In September 1800 the frigate *George Washington* was sent by Adams to Algiers with tribute for the dey, the Ottoman sultan's representative. Captain William Bainbridge was then ordered by the dey of Algiers to carry an ambassador and tribute to the sultan in Constantinople. Bainbridge refused, whereupon the dey declared: 'You pay me tribute, by which you become my slaves. I have a right to order you as I may think proper.'[11] Bainbridge, under threat of death, was forced to accept the mission, a prelude to further demands that would be made by the local potentates. Early in 1801 Karamanli increased the annual tribute to $250,000, which, quite apart from representing a considerable burden on the US treasury, began to dent American pride. President Thomas Jefferson objected to having to pay protection money to distant pashas and pirates, and so decided to result to the type of military means that had worked well elsewhere in settling disputes with foreigners.

In 1804 Jefferson sent a fleet of US ships to punish the Barbary pirates and their protectors, but efforts to blockade Tripoli and the rest of the Libyan coast were generally seen as unsuccessful. The US frigate *Philadelphia* was trapped outside Tripoli when the ship hit a shoal whereupon the crew and vessel were captured by the Libyans. In February a commando raid led by Lieutenant Stephen Decatur succeeded in infiltrating the harbour and blowing up the *Philadelphia*, so rendering it unusable by the Libyans as a gunship guarding the harbour. This early raid by the US Marine Corp inspired the words 'from the shores of Tripoli' in their celebrated hymn. The raid, successful in its mission, stimulated resistance by the Libyans and prolonged fighting began. The American ships subjected Tripoli to a massive bombardment with Karamanli, supported by the Ottomans and the Knights of St John, well protected by thick walls. The crew of the *Philadelphia* were set the task of reinforcing the ramparts while the fighting continued.

The US government then sent reinforcements. The former US consul in Tunis, Cyrus Eaton, was asked to carry out a plan for the overthrow of Yusuf Karamanli and to put his older brother Hamed in his place (Hamed was ambitious and prepared to accept help from any quarter). In 1805 Eaton, Hamed and a bunch of mercenaries marched with the US marines from Alexandria westwards across six hundred miles of desert. The US ships continued to bombard the coast, and in due course the mixed military force managed to capture the Cyrenaican port of Derna. Karamanli then perceived the wisdom of negotiations, dropping his demand for regular tribute payments but asking $60,000, half his original demand, for the ransom of the *Philadelphia* crew. The United States, though denied outright victory, decided to accept the deal and brought to an end the American support for Hamed (puppets could always be abandoned with shifts in US policy). A qualified success had been achieved, though the Libyans had managed to secure some further bounty. The pirates continued to operate off the Barbary coast; and US operations against the corsairs were staged until 1815.[12]

For well over a century the United States had little further interest in the area. It was not until the Second World War, when the Allied armies fought against the Axis forces in North Africa, that Americans would again confront Libyans, this time the collaborators with Benito Mussolini. This in turn led to the US acquisition of the Italian airbase that was to be re-named Wheelus Field, a secure site until the collapse of the pro-West Idris monarchy.

GADDAFI AND THE US

When Gaddafi assumed power in Libya in 1969 he moved quickly to attack what he saw as the nation's colonial inheritance. In 1970 the property of Italians and non-resident Jews was appropriated; the Italian Foreign Minis-ter Aldo Moro – later assassinated by the Red Brigades supported, some say, by the Libyans – protested but the expropriations went ahead and much of the 13,000-strong Italian community left the country in the summer of 1970. At the same time Gaddafi was snubbing the West by insisting on an improved price for oil, and urging the colonial powers to vacate their military bases in Libya. In September 1970 Gaddafi broke off diplomatic relations with the pro-West King Hussein of Jordan after Jordanian troops had attacked Palestinian guerrillas in Jordan. By 1971 Gaddafi had nation-alised foreign banks and imposed various regulations on other foreign companies operating within the country. Diplomatic ties with another pro-West government, that of King Hassan in Morocco, were broken off after Gaddafi gave premature support to an anti-monarchy coup attempt. How-ever, the Western policy had not yet settled down into its resolute anti-Gaddafi mode. The United States was prepared to tolerate and even support (see below) the new Libyan regime: Gaddafi was, after all, just the sort of authoritarian anti-communist that Washington tended to welcome on the world stage. For a time Gaddafi enjoyed some US support, being allowed to purchase western weapons and even being warned against coup attempts. The honeymoon did not last long.

Within a short time Gaddafi had demonstrated that he was far from being a pliant puppet of the West, the usual role adopted by anti-communist authoritarian leaders in the Third World. He nationalised the Libyan hold-ings of British Petroleum in December 1971, and followed this with further nationalisations in 1972–3. He further irritated the British by supporting Dom Mintoff in his dispute with Britain over bases in Malta; and by declaring in June 1972 that 'We are making war on Great Britain, and if the Irish revolutionaries want to liberate Ireland we will back them to the hilt.' Gaddafi was rapidly developing as a thorn in the Western flesh, a role that he now finds it hard to live down as a more moderate leader in the 1990s.

The United States had been prepared to offer Gaddafi a measure of protection immediately after the fall of the Idris monarchy, but it seems that Gaddafi paid no attention to this in organising his domestic and foreign plans. In 1977 the Americans learned about a Libyan-supported assassination plot against Herman Frederick Eilts, the US ambassador in Cairo seconded to work with Henry Kissinger on Sadat's ground-breaking shift to collaboration with the United States. Gaddafi was upset at what he saw as a betrayal of the Arab cause. One theory was that a 'mole' in Gaddafi's terrorist organisation had learned of the assassination plans and informed Washington. President Carter thereupon sent a personal letter to Gaddafi, informing him that he knew of the plot and offering details to substantiate the claim. It was hoped that this bare communication would be enough to thwart the scheme. For a time Gaddafi hesitated and then protested that the charge was absurd: there was no such plot, the accused Libyans were innocent, and Gaddafi himself was obviously the victim of disinformation. Whatever the truth, 'Operation Eilts' never got off the ground; but it served in particular to establish the framework within which US/Libyan relations would be conducted in the years ahead. Carter had decided that Gaddafi could not be trusted and no American leader was prepared to dissent from this judgement. In 1980 President Carter wrote: 'There are few governments in the world with which we have more sharp and frequent policy differences than Libya. Libya has steadfastly opposed our efforts to reach and carry out the Camp David Accords between Israel, Egypt and the United States, signed in 1978 and 1979. We have strongly differing attitudes toward the PLO and the support of terrorism.'[13] Carter's personal approach to Gaddafi had in fact impressed him, and in 1977 he had attempt to improve cooperation with the United States, to little avail.

In March 1978 the Libyan Foreign Liaison Bureau had launched a series of 'people-to-people' visits which it was hoped would improve the US/ Libyan diplomatic climate. Gaddafi was particularly keen to secure the granting of US export licences for Boeing 727s which the American administration insisted had military potential. It was these circumstances that led to the *Billy Carter Hearings* and to President Carter's declaration of policy differences with Libya.

The Libyan Bureau decided to contact President Carter's brother, Billy, in the hope that his opinions would carry weight with the US administration. He was eventually contacted via a circuitous route by the former Libyan ambassador to Italy, Jibril Shalouf, who had worked at cultivating Billy's business partners.[14] Billy naively accepted an invitation to Libya, having been told that such a visit would be useful to his own business ventures. In January 1979 he hosted Libyan dancers in Georgia and established the Libyan Arab Friendship Society. At the same time, by seeming chance, the US administration decided to issue export licences for the Boeing 727s. In November the Libyan government attempted to influence the Iranian authorities into releasing the US hostages in Teheran. The attempt failed and relations between Libya and the United States went into a steep decline towards the end of the Carter presidency. One key factor was the burning of the US embassy in Tripoli on 2 December, a reaction to the US decision to freeze Iranian assets.

On 7 May 1980 Washington expelled members of the Libyan People's Bureau on the ground that they had been persecuting dissident students; and in August, Washington announced – as an obviously provocative act – that it intended to hold Sixth Fleet exercises in the Gulf of Sirte which Libya claimed as sovereign waters. When, one month later, the exercises began the fleet was ordered to stay outside the zone claimed by Libya but a US C-135 electronic surveillance plane 'flying at the edge of Libyan airspace' and escorted by an F-14 fighter squadron, was confronted by Libyan jets twice in a week. The aim on that occasion was to send a clear signal to Gaddafi without starting a military conflict.

When in January 1981 Ronald Reagan took over the White House (which may not have happened had Gaddafi been able to secure the release of the US hostages), the relations between Libya and the United States, already on the slide, worsened still more. Washington was already smarting from a number of foreign-policy reverses: the humiliating failure of the helicopter rescue mission, which crashed to abject disaster in the Salt desert; the fall of the Shah of Iran; the collapse of the Somoza dictatorship in Nicaragua; the burning of the US embassy in Pakistan; and a pro-Soviet coup in Afghanistan followed by an invasion by Soviet troops. Ronald Reagan came to the White House in an atmosphere of chauvinism and militancy, determined to ensure that the United States 'walked tall' again. The scene was set for a dramatic reassertion of the global authority of the US, which in practice meant no more than bullying weaker nations into acquiescence when confronted with American demands. A key task, in the 1990s being systematically implemented throughout the world, was to establish American dominance over the developing countries, to demonstrate the unambiguous power of the US over the Third World. At the start of the Reagan presidency in the early 1980s this may have seemed a daunting task: the existence of a still powerful Soviet Union, prepared to fund anti-West subversion, represented an unavoidable brake on Western initiative. One of Reagan's first tasks was to launch a campaign against Soviet-sponsored terrorism, and at the same time Gaddafi came in for special attention.

Libya was dubbed 'a base for Soviet subversion', with Gaddafi himself 'the most dangerous man in the world'.[15] Psychological pressure was put on Gaddafi by spreading rumours about assassination attempts against the Libyan leader, and provocative naval manoeuvres were begun in March 1981 off the coast of Libya. This time the Sixth Fleet moved within the disputed Gulf of Sirte: for a period of four days exercises were conducted by two US aircraft carriers, ten other ships and several squadrons of carrier-borne F-14 aircraft. The Libyans took care to avoid a military confrontation. Next Washington tightened the noose around Libya by promising to fund anti-Gaddafi forces in Africa: on 8 July 1981 Chester Crocker, the Assistant Secretary of State for African Affairs, declared to Congress that the US government would provide arms for African opponents of Libya 'to help those who see the problem as we see it'.[16] The US administration moved to supply arms to factions across Libya's borders that could be relied upon to present a military threat to Gaddafi. Thus Washington announced its willingness to provide Tunisia with fifty-four M-60 tanks; and Frank Carlucci, the Deputy Defence Secretary, visited Algeria to whip up anti-Gaddafi feeling and to offer to supply C-130 transport aircraft for the Algerian air force.[17] American strategists also speculated on how the US might take over the Libyan oilfields, observing that it would be preferable to assume control of Gaddafi's oil resources than to take over the oilfields in the Gulf.[18]

The mounting US hostility to Libya also had a broader purpose. Gaddafi, it was widely assumed, had funded anti-American subversive groups throughout the world, so any destabilisation policy directed at the Libyan government would indirectly help American client states across the globe. In recent years the US administration had already witnessed the fall of Somoza in Nicaragua and the Shah of Iran; to attack Libya would be seen as a worthwhile demonstration of Washington's commitment to surviving US puppets. With a more robust government in Washington it would be harder, so the argument ran, for Gaddafi to encourage the collapse of unpopular pro-US regimes in Central America, Africa, Asia and elsewhere.

The provocative naval exercises off the Libyan coast, thousands of miles from the United States, were deliberately designed to lead to a military confrontation; and in this aim they succeeded. A massive Sixth Fleet battle group, including the nuclear-powered aircraft carrier *Nimitz*, sailed into the Gulf of Sirte. On 19 August two Libyan SU-22 bombers took off to monitor the movements of the US battle formation – and were promptly shot down by *Nimitz*-based fighters. The Pentagon subsequently admitted that it had no evidence that the Libyan pilots had received orders to act in a hostile way, and it has been suggested that the Libyans' MiG or Mirage aircraft would have been better suited than SU-22 bombers for offensive action.[19] It was also significant that the Americans gave various inconsistent accounts about their proximity to the Libyan coast. Having earlier declared that the incident occurred sixty miles out, Rear Admiral James E. Service stated that 'About the closest we came was about 25 miles to their coast.'[20] Few independent observers doubted that the American posture throughout this period was intentionally provocative, designed to give Gaddafi a 'bloody nose'.

There was also evidence that Washington was encouraging a military confrontation between Egypt and Libya. Sadat was said to favour a military incursion into Libya though some of his senior officers opposed the idea; when some of these officers, including the Defence Minister General Ahmed Bedawi, were killed in a mysterious helicopter crash on 2 March 1981 Sadat's position was strengthened.[21] French intelligence sources were quoted in July as stating that an Israeli working group was helping Sadat produce a plan for the invasion of Libya, and it had already been made clear that Sadat could reasonably expect US support in the implementation of such a plan. When Sadat was assassinated in October 1981 the idea of an Egyptian invasion of Libya was dropped: Hosni Mubarak, seen in the 1990s as a friend of Gaddafi, was confronted with a domestic crisis and would have had no stomach for any inherited plan for hazardous foreign adventures.

On 10 March 1982 President Reagan, in a further move to isolate Libya, declared an embargo on the US importation of crude oil from Libya. At the same time he also initiated a ban on the export to Libya of a wide range of technological products, a move designed to weaken not only Libya's military capability but also its capacity for industrial development. It was suggested by Washington that Libyan 'hit squads' were loose in the United States with a mission to assassinate Reagan himself: the FBI later admitted that no signs of such groups had ever been detected. Nonetheless the import embargo and export ban remained in place in the hope that these would seriously impact on the Libyan economy. At the time the United States had been buying about a third of Libya's crude oil and it was assumed that Libya would be drastically affected by the loss of such a significant market. In the event other markets were found and the damaging consequences were contained. US oil companies were encouraged to bring home their personnel working in Libya and in due course the pressure from Washington was strengthened by a presidential edict: 3000 Americans came home though nearly a half of these subsequently returned. It was clear that the American workers and technicians had little sympathy with the pressure from Washington. The companies responded 'reluctantly and under protest',[22] and when one observer visited Tripoli just before Christmas 1981, 'several hundred of the Americans had glumly complied. None said they felt threatened in any way.'[23] The Libyan Oil Ministry was soon recruiting Iranian, Canadian, Arab and European oil technicians to take the place of the departed Americans. Since the economic measures were clearly having little effect the Reagan administration again looked to the possibility of military action.

In February 1983 Reagan responded to President Numeiri's claim to have uncovered a Libyan conspiracy against him by initiating a massive military confrontation with Gaddafi. AWAC surveillance aircraft were immediately despatched to Cairo West airfield for reconnaissance missions over Libya. Then *Nimitz* and its associated battle formation again sailed towards the Gulf of Sirte, encouraging speculation that this time an actual invasion would take place. Suddenly however the US backed off, with rumours of arguments with the Egyptian government. A senior Egyptian official commented: 'We are furious. The Americans are trying to implicate us in things that do not involve us.'[24] In the same spirit the Egyptian Defence Minister, Field Marshal Abdul Halim Abu Ghazala, declared that he could not see any sign of 'Libyan aggression against the Sudan'.[25] The Americans had made little effort to check the veracity of Numeiri's accusations against Libya: it was enough that the Sudanese leader had provided a pretext for a further US confrontation with Gaddafi.

A few months later the Americans were again mobilising against the Libyan regime, this time using the excuse of Gaddafi's involvement in Chad. The USS *Eisenhower* sailed towards the Gulf of Sirte and AWACs were again active; but yet again the Egyptian government could not be relied upon to engage in military action against the Libyans.[26] In March 1984 further Sudanese claims of Libyan hostility stimulated yet more US manoeuvres and on this occasion Egyptian forces were sent to support Numeiri, but Mubarak still made it clear that he wanted to avoid a military confrontation with Gaddafi.[27] There was also evidence that the US was trying to lure Gaddafi into a confrontation with Numeiri so that Washington could righteously respond with a 'justified' attack on Libya, just as Egypt would be compelled to observe the terms of its 1975 defence pact with Sudan. One observer commented that Gaddafi 'prudently ignored the bait offered him'.[28]

By the mid 1980s the Reagan administration had done all it could, short of a US invasion of Libya, to topple Gaddafi. At that time, as doubtless today, there did exist a plan for the US forces with Egyptian support to invade Libya, though the Egyptian government was not prepared to co-operate in such a scheme.[29] There were evident tensions between Egypt and Libya but Washington was never able to exploit these to the point of generating an actual military conflict. That would come – with the 1986 bombing of Benghazi and Tripoli – but before profiling that onslaught on Libya it is useful to record the paradox of US *support* for Gaddafi set against the escalating campaign for the destabilisation of the Libyan regime, a campaign run by the CIA and other institutions at the heart of the American establishment. After the brief honeymoon with Washington, Colonel Gaddafi became increasingly insecure through the 1980s.

US SUPPORT FOR GADDAFI

For a brief period after the fall of the pro-West Idris monarchy there were elements in the US administration prepared to see Gaddafi as a nationalist and anti-communist, and as such a force that could be viewed with sympathy (we have already seen that mainstream opinion in Washington was hostile to the new Libyan leader). It has even been emphasised that the US and Western European intelligence services protected Gaddafi from his enemies, 'and most assuredly helped him to remain in power'.[30] In the early days of the Libyan revolution, some factions in Washington were pleased to note that Gaddafi was taking a number of anti-Soviet and anti-communist actions. He was wont to criticise the Soviet Union, a self-proclaimed atheist society, in his early speeches and in particular he had condemned the involvement of the Soviets in the 1971 Indo-Pakistan war as signalling 'Soviet imperialist designs in the area'. He also criticised the 1972 Soviet/Iraqi treaty, even though Gaddafi himself had signed a trade and technical (though not yet an arms treaty) with the Soviet Union a short time earlier. (It is significant that Gaddafi was to side with Iran in the Iran/Iraq war as a further sign of his resentment of great power influence – this time Washington's – in the region.) The US was pleased to note also that Gaddafi had applauded Sadat's expulsion of Soviet military forces from Egypt in July 1972. There were even signs in these early days of 'CIA protection of Qaddafi's regime and person'.[31]

The evident US protection of Gaddafi was demonstrated when splits began to appear in the Revolutionary Command Council (RCC) soon after the fall of the monarchy. Two Libyan colonels, late appointees to the RCC, were arrested after the US had warned Gaddafi that they were plotting against him: Adam al-Hawaz and Musa Ahmed were seized after the CIA warned the Libyan leader that the two men, pro-Western officers, could not be trusted.[32] At around the same time an Arabic translation of a Soviet book highly critical of Islam began circulating in Tripoli. The Soviets did not deny the book's authenticity but declared that it had only been intended for use in the Soviet Union. Such events combined to create the impression that Gaddafi was prepared to conspire with US schemes in the region. To some limited extent the impression was accurate. Gaddafi had sent aircraft to Pakistan to counter the Soviet support for India in the 1971 war; and he had forced down in Libya a plane carrying communist coup plotters against President Numeiri (they were subsequently hanged in Khartoum). Gaddafi himself, in banning all political parties, had prohibited all political meetings between socialists, communists and other groups hostile to the United States: this all had a pleasant ring to Washington. Perhaps Gaddafi was a bit wild in his support for the Palestinians and terrorists elsewhere but there were influential factions in Washington prepared to see Gaddafi's authoritarian anti-communism as one of the blessings of the area. In such circumstances it was surely worth protecting Gaddafi from attempted coups in his own country.[33]

The Libyan leader was also greatly assisted by erstwhile CIA operatives, a set of free enterprise initiatives that eventually incurred the wrath of Washington. Such events relied upon the relationship between the CIA and the clandestine operations of the Sydney-based Nugan Hand Bank, an employer of retired CIA agents and heavily involved in drugs trafficking.[34] The Bank became involved with a network of former CIA agents run by Edwin Wilson and conveniently situated in Libya. Himself formerly with the CIA, Wilson prospered in the private sector.[35] Between June and September 1976 Ed Wilson was able to supply Libya with thousands of CIA-designed bomb timers and in excess of twenty-one tons of Composition C-4, the 'most powerful non-nuclear explosive in America's arsenal'.[36] Wilson also recruited US Green Berets to train Libyan commandos, and is even said to have arranged assassinations in various countries for Gaddafi.[37] The CIA was informed of Wilson's activities by one of his erstwhile CIA employees, Kevin Mulcahy, but Theodore Shackley, then CIA deputy director of clandestine services and an old friend of Wilson, decided to block any internal investigation. In such a fashion the CIA, against the policy thrusts of other departments of the US administration, protected Gaddafi and sanctioned his acquisition of the accoutrements of modern terrorism.

In April 1977 *The Washington Post* publicised Wilson's activities and commented that he 'may have had contact with one or more current CIA employees'. The article stimulated the new CIA director Admiral Stansfield Turner into launching his own enquiry, which in due course led to the transfer of the high-ranking Thomas Clines and Theodore Shackley to lower-grade jobs. Soon afterwards Clines resigned from the CIA, borrowed $500,000 from Wilson to create his own company, and won a $71 million contract with Egypt for the delivery of arms; Shackley resigned soon after and became a consultant. Wilson himself was eventually convicted of supplying Gaddafi with explosives, timing devices, and military training.[39]

The US support – overt or clandestine – for Colonel Gaddafi must be seen as a brief distraction from the main business. Elements in Washington had flirted with the idea that Gaddafi could be promoted as a useful anti-communist tool, and some small quantities of military hardware were exported from the US to Libya over the years. In 1970 Gaddafi was supplied with eight Lockheed C-130 Hercules aircraft, in 1978 with a Bell-121 helicopter, and in 1981 with two further C-130 Hercules aircraft; but such deliveries were inconsequential departures from the principal policy that has now been sustained for more than two decades. Few in Washington doubted that the only sane policy was to target Gaddafi for destabilisation.

TARGETING GADDAFI

Just five days after the start of the first Reagan administration, on 26 January 1981, CIA chief William Casey visited the White House to give his first full presentation since accepting office. His theme was the world-wide threat of terrorism and how it was being fomented by states like Syria, Iran and Libya. Casey, well aware of what appeared to be a new vigour in the White House, had decided to seize the moment; now, if ever, was the time to reassert American dominance across the world. This was to be the start of the US resurgence, the beginning of new policies that would arrest the drift and disasters that had been all too plain under the previous administration. Casey was to be preoccupied with the 'Libyan question' on many occasions through the 1980s. In 1984 it was alleged that Gaddafi's hand was discernible behind unrest in Egypt, Tunisia and Algeria; and his People's Bureaus were fomenting trouble in capitals across Europe. In the White House a sub-group created by Robert McFarlane, Reagan's new National Security Advisor, was preparing plans for covert action against Gaddafi, or against anyone else who threatened the interests of the United States. One of the most vocal voices in the sub-group was that of Oliver North.

In May 1986 William Casey reiterated the familiar claim that 'Libya, Syria and Iran use terrorism as an instrument of foreign policy.' Such countries 'hire and support established terrorist organisations . . . These countries make their officials, their embassies, their diplomatic pouches, their communications channels and their territory as safe havens for these criminals to plan, direct and execute bombing, assassination, kidnapping and other terrorist operations.'[40] It was by now part of the conventional wisdom that Libya, along with one or two other states, should be viewed as a 'pariah' nation, to be combated in every way possible. The Heritage Foundation, one of the main foreign policy advisory bodies to the Reagan administration, called for the overthrow of nine governments: those of Nicaragua, Angola, Cambodia, Afghanistan, Laos, Vietnam, Ethiopia, Iran and Libya.[41] In fact this demand was simply reiterating established US policy: as early as March 1981 William Casey, talking to a sympathetic administration, had presented detailed plans for covert operations against Nicaragua, Afghanistan, Laos, Cambodia, Grenada, Iran, Cuba, and Libya.[42] In July 1981 a CIA plan had been presented for the specific overthrow of Colonel Gaddafi,[43] though, as we have seen, Egypt refused to go along with plans that involved them. Then psychological warfare was chosen as a major tool for the destabilisation of the Libyan regime. This 'psyops' campaign against Gaddafi finally led to the resignation of Bernard Kalb, State Department spokesman and highly regarded journalist, in protest against the deliberate lies about Libya being disseminated by a compliant US press.

The systematic propaganda campaign against Libya was part of a larger programme of deception aimed at linking Middle East terrorism to Nicaragua, Cuba and the Soviet Union. Thus in 1985 Reagan declared to the American Bar Association: 'Most of the terrorists who are kidnapping and murdering American citizens and attacking American installations are being trained, financed and directly or indirectly controlled by a core group of radical and totalitarian governments, a new international version of Murder, Inc.' The core group of governments were Iran, Libya, Cuba, Nicaragua, and North Korea, an identifiable confederation of outlaw terrorist states engaged in outright war against the United States; Reagan also noted the involvement of the Soviet Union.[44] In 1986 the capital of Nicaragua, Managua, was portrayed by the Reagan administration as a place where Palestinians, Libyans, Cubans and Iranians plotted against innocent US citizens and for the overthrow of the US government.[45] In this way Nicaragua has been characterised as a major base for Libyan operations in the Western hemisphere.

In the early summer of 1986 various US intelligence reports were made available to the British Foreign Office to suggest that Libyan terrorists and the surrogates were planning to hit targets in Europe and US targets in Malta and Crete. British diplomats were given the impression that the US government 'intended to take further military action against Libya'.[46] The Foreign Office was not impressed with the 'evidence', which was moreover accompanied by 'wild assertions'.[47] The bombing of Libya had taken place a few months before (see below) and now, the bombs having failed to kill Gaddafi, the US administration was contemplating further raids. In fact the principal US strategy was to destabilise the Libyan regime by suggesting that Washington and Gaddafi were again on a collision course. The military strike had failed and something had to be done. In August, Admiral John Poindexter, the US National Security Advisor, sent President Reagan a secret memorandum recommending a 'disinformation' programme involving 'a series of closely co-ordinated events involving covert, diplomatic, military and public actions'. This was the latest phase in Washington's strategy for the subversion of the Libyan regime. In fact at the time the Americans were forced to admit that Gaddafi was not active in world terrorism. Poindexter had been forced to admit in his memo to Reagan that Gaddafi was 'temporarily quiescent in his support of terrorism' – but no doubt this evident quiescence could not be relied upon ('he may soon move to a more active role'). So Gaddafi was damned if he supported terrorism and equally damned if he did not.

Some of the National Security Council staff (including Oliver North) hoped that the policy of disinformation would scare Gaddafi and possibly even inspire a coup. However, the Washington press establishment became alarmed when Bob Woodward of the *Washington Post* suggested that the US administration had succeeded in planting this disinformation on the front page of the *Wall Street Journal* (25 August 1986). The planted lie was that the United States and Libya were again on a 'collision course', with the implication that soon Washington would be forced to act. Now however the cynical policy of manipulating the press had been spelt out in a government memorandum that had reached the public domain, and this 'touched off a furor'.[48] Reagan compounded the situation by seeming to endorse the policy of lying to the press: 'Our position has been one which we would just as soon have Mr Qadhafi go to bed every night wondering what we might do.'[49] But he had misjudged the public feeling and soon there was talk of possible House and Senate investigations into the NSC disinformation campaign on Libya.[50] The Woodward revelations were not quite on the Watergate scale but again the complacent assumption of the White House that lies make good policy had been shaken. In fact Bob Woodward has taken pains to chart Washington's confused and mendacious policy on Libya over many years.[51]

As early as 1980 the then Director of the CIA, Admiral Stansfield Turner, had suggested covert operations to topple Colonel Gaddafi. On one occasion, without reference to the White House, he had asked the Deputy Director of Operations what steps would be taken to remove three leaders who threatened US interests: Fidel Castro in Cuba, the Ayatollah Ruhollah Khomeini in Iran, and Muammar al-Gaddafi. At that time the assassination of foreign leaders was banned, following an executive order signed by President Ford and reaffirmed by Carter. What Turner had in mind was the provision of funds or supplies to groups outside the countries in question: if such groups managed to kill the particular leaders then that was another matter, nothing to do with Washington. In the event the DDO decided at that time that there were no groups that could be usefully supported (some money was being passed to anti-Khomeini factions but the overthrow of the Ayatollah was deemed unlikely).[52] However, it was not long before candidates emerged who were seen as suitable recipients for American aid designed to accelerate the fall of Gaddafi. Hissène Habré in Chad (see Chapter Seven) was, amongst others, reckoned a likely candidate.

There were some doubts about Habré. Some congressman pointed out that he had been involved in massacres, others that he had on occasions expressed admiration for Castro, Mao and Ho Chi Minh. He had even demanded 'revolutionary ferment in all of Africa'. In the past he had been supported by Gaddafi and, some argued, it could not be assumed that similar accommodations would not be made in the future. Differences between the House committee members resulted in a letter of protest being sent to President Reagan, and before long reports were appearing about policy disputes concerning an unnamed state in Africa. Clement J. Zablocki, the then Chairman of the House Foreign Affairs Committee and a member of the House Intelligence Committee, leaked to the press a story which *Newsweek* titled 'A Plan to Overthrow Qaddafi'. Here it was claimed that the CIA was soon to launch 'a large scale multiphase and costly scheme to overthrow the Libyan regime . . . To members of the House Intelligence Committee who reviewed the plan, that . . . seemed to imply Qaddafi's assassination.' William Casey, then CIA chief, was incensed at the leak. A detailed plan had been drawn up, with France and Egypt already implicated, so the White House decided to deny the *Newsweek* story. This did not stop massive amounts of military aid going to the anti-Gaddafi forces in Chad. If covert CIA plans were put into effect they did not succeed in toppling the Libyan leader.

The US administration continued to be preoccupied with the 'Libyan question'. The Libyan diplomatic and intelligence codes had been cracked and Gaddafi often spoke on insecure telephone lines: soon the CIA had built a bulging file on Gaddafi. It was known, for example, that the ostensible passenger and cargo air carrier, United African Airlines (UAA), was the air transport facility of the Libyan armed forces and the Libyan Intelligence Services (LIS).[54] CIA reports suggested that Gaddafi was working to acquire a nuclear weapon: the Soviets had delivered enriched uranium to a research centre outside Tripoli and uranium yellowcake was being obtained from Niger (one secret intelligence memo of 5 July 1981 was headed 'Niger: Libya's next target'[55]). There then followed the first of the military confrontations in the Gulf of Sirte (see above).

The US intelligence services were soon claiming to have uncovered a host of anti-American plots concocted by Gaddafi. It was declared that he was sending hit squads to kill Reagan and other leading members of the administration; he was about to launch terrorist attacks against American targets in Europe and elsewhere; there was a Libyan plan to kidnap or murder Maxwell Rabb, the American ambassador to Italy; and Gaddafi was about to launch a suicide mission against the *USS Nimitz*, off the coast of Libya. An 'informant with demonstrated access to senior Libyan intelligence personnel' declared that Libyans had been sent to attack the US embassies in Paris and Rome; six days later the informant added the embassies in Athens, Beirut, Tunis, Madrid and London to the target list.[56] Libyans were reported in Rome, and Rabb was flown back to the United States for his own safety. An informant who said he was from one of Gaddafi's training camps – and who passed a polygraph test – declared that if Reagan proved too difficult a target the Libyans were expected to go after Vice-President Bush, Secretary of State Haig or Defence Secretary Weinberger. Moreover, Gaddafi's support for such radical states as Ethiopia and South Yemen was adding further irritation to a US administration that seemed powerless to control what it saw as the wild posturing of a Third World upstart.

On 4 December 1981 *The New York Times* reported that a five-man Libyan hit squad had entered the United States; within three days reports upped the squad to ten men. The Immigration and Naturalisation Service sent detailed instructions to airport offices and major border-crossing points; and composite sketches of five of the alleged would-be assassins were shown on television. Fresh reports that there were now fourteen Libyan hit men in the United States were leaked by the US administration and anti-sniper patrols were seen crouching on the roof of the White House.[57] Reagan and Bush were protected by such artifices as decoy limousines and phony motor-cycle escort convoys.

The reports of Libyan assassins were never confirmed by any real-world events; no Libyans were ever arrested and no Gaddafi-inspired assassination attempts were ever uncovered in the United States. To many foreign observers the hit-squad claims were little short of ludicrous. However, together with the more likely reports of Libyan terrorist and political moves elsewhere in the world, they served to justify further plans for the overthrow of Gaddafi. Defence Secretary Haig quickly approved an option presented to him by Robert C. 'Bud' McFarlane, a former marine lieutenant colonel who had been given the job of co-ordinating the policy on Libya: 'Work with the Defense Department and CIA to develop responses to Libyan provocations that involve US and Egyptian forces in covert, tactical air and commando operations.'[58] Haig wanted to discourage a 'major ground force operation' but all other options were open.

Surveillance flights over Libya were to be increased and other measures were put in train: Reagan asked for plans to be developed for 'a military response against Libya in the event of a further Libyan attempt to assassinate American officials or attack US facilities'. Haig, Carlucci and Casey drafted a TOP SECRET memorandum on 'counter-terrorist planning toward Libya', intended to cover all relevant aspects: from a plan for handling the media and Congress to economic sanctions against Libya. The President was urged to 'immediately direct the Joint Chiefs of Staff to ready assets to carry out military action against Libya in self-defense, following a further Libyan provocation'. A TOP SECRET chart showed the 'graduated responses': these involved a direct attack on terrorist training sites in Libya; a strike at Libyan airfields; a strike at Gaddafi's naval forces; the destruction of his military-equipment stockpiles; and a Navy Seal attack on Libyan naval vessels in port.[59]

On 6 December 1981 Colonel Gaddafi appeared on the live ABC Television show *This Week with David Brinkley:* from Tripoli, Gaddafi denied all the American charges concerning hit squads and assassination teams, and he challenged the administration to produce the evidence. He called the Americans 'silly people' and Reagan 'a liar', remarks that provoked a response from the Vice-Chairman of the Senate Intelligence Committee, Daniel Patrick Moynihan, that Gaddafi was a liar and a mad dictator. Reagan said publicly that 'I wouldn't believe a word [Gaddafi] says if I were you'; and then sent a TOP SECRET EYES ONLY threat to the Libyan leader: 'I have detailed and verified information about several Libyan-sponsored plans and attempts to assassinate US government officials and attack US facilities both in the US and abroad. Any acts of violence directed by Libya or its agents against officials of the US at home or abroad, will be regarded by the US government as an armed attack upon the US and will be met by every means necessary to defend this nation in accordance with Article 51 of the United Nations Charter.'[60] It seemed that the threat bore fruit: within a week a Libyan envoy had visited the United States to say that Gaddafi was 'desperate' to open a channel to the United States and that there would be no terrorist operations.

Before long the Americans themselves were expressing doubts about the accuracy of the earlier reports on Libyan terrorist activities. The CIA suddenly decided that a former 'excellent source' had a credibility that was 'open to question'; reports of Libyan plans to attack US personnel were 'most later discounted', with the observation that it was likely that 'reporting breeds reporting where the US is perceived to have an interest'. Now it was decided that *'all the hit-squad reports may have been misinformation feeding off itself'* (italics added).[61] In short, a massive deception had been planned to justify the possibility of a military attack on Libya. The US administration was party to a wide-ranging fabrication that was to yield results in the future: a climate had been created in which the American people would be quick to applaud the bombing of Libya in 1986.

The American intelligence community continued to collect information about Libya, much of it of dubious accuracy and dubious value. Some anti-Gaddafi successes were chalked up – for example, seventy tons of weapons and ammunition destined for Nicaragua were intercepted – but the Libyan leader seemed as secure as ever. The possibility of enlarged economic sanctions was contemplated but it was acknowledged that the relatively primitive Libyan economy was hard to hurt. Communication intercepts, satellite information and some human testimony revealed that Gaddafi was intervening in Sudan and had designs on Egypt. He had also signed a naval agreement with Greece, a NATO member, which suggested to the Americans that Gaddafi would soon have access to vital Western secrets. The FBI claimed to have concrete evidence that a Libyan students' committee in a Washington suburb was deeply involved in terrorist activities and intelligence work. Yet another report, 'Countering Libyan Terrorism' – this time initiated by Schultz's deputy, Kenneth W. Dam – was produced by the State Department's intelligence branch. The options ranged from 'do nothing' to such possibilities as 'Mount a programme of covert actions . . .' and 'Seek a regime change'. Soon the CIA, the DIA and the NSA were busy estimating the threat posed by Gaddafi to US interests, identifying his weaknesses, and estimating how US policy might be designed and implemented to have an impact. Attention was given to Gaddafi's own psychology, his life style, his relations with neighbouring countries, and the strength of the anti-Gaddafi factions in exile.

In March 1985 William Casey issued 'Libya's Qaddafi: The Challenge to the United States and Western Interests', a Special National Intelligence Estimate. This again suggested that before long Gaddafi would be stirring up trouble across the globe; already intelligence had revealed that Libya provided 'money, weapons, a base of operations, travel assistance or training to some 30 insurgent, radical or terrorist groups'.[62] On 14 June TWA Flight 847 taking off from Athens was hijacked by two Lebanese men who forced the plane first to land in Beirut and then to fly to Algiers. William Casey was quick to point the finger at Gaddafi though the CIA chief was not yet certain who was behind the hijacking. Here was an event that served nicely to confirm the predictions in the March report: an elaborate fold-out map of the world showed how Gaddafi was infiltrating dozens of countries across the globe. On 30 April President Reagan signed a National Security Decision Directive, 'US Policy Toward North Africa', in which a special group was charged with the task of containing 'Qaddafi's subversion activities'; one key order was that the Department of Defence would review the Stairship Exercise for naval manoeuvres off the coast of Libya. Extensive surveillance revealed Libya's arms build-up and confirmed that Libyan exiles posed little threat to Gaddafi's security: despite this, the CIA 'Tulip' covert operation (under the 'Flower' range of anti-Gaddafi plans and operations) was developed to topple Gaddafi by providing support to anti-Gaddafi exile movements. The Ford ban on the assassination of foreign leaders would be circumvented: 'The President said that they should not worry about the assassination prohibition. He would personally take the heat on that if Qaddafi were killed.'[63] A speech was drafted for Reagan to announce a 'preemptive or retaliatory' attack on Libya.

Two days after Christmas 1985 there were terrorist attacks at the Rome and Vienna airports; nineteen people were killed, including five Americans. It was suspected that Abu Nidal, then in Libya, was responsible. The CIA and the National Security Council were keen to implicate Gaddafi but the only evidence they had was a transfer of $1 million made by Gaddafi agents to an Abu Nidal bank account in Bulgaria some years earlier. The US administration began to lay plans for the bombing of Libya though there was some concern expressed at the presence of 1500 Soviet advisors in the country: what would happen if some of them were killed in a US air strike? The decision to bomb Libya was postponed.

On 14 March 1986 President Reagan ordered three carrier battle groups to assemble off the Libyan coast for Operation Prairie Fire. If Gaddafi were to attack any of the US planes and ships converging on Libya there would be a proportionate response from the American forces. If there was a single US casualty the President would authorise the bombing of military targets; and if Gaddafi were to adopt generally aggressive tactics then US aircraft would bomb a range of Libyan targets inland, hitting oil pumping stations and other economic facilities. There was debate within the US administration as to how hard the American forces should hit the Libyan military: one view was that there should be no unnecessary destruction but others counselled that if the Libyan military were hard hit there may be an armed-forces rebellion against Gaddafi. In the event, gale-force winds in the Gulf of Sirte delayed the start of Operation Prairie Fire to 23 March, when a vast American armada appeared off the coast of Libya: forty-five ships, 200 aircraft, and nuclear-powered submarines. More than one hundred US air-craft   flew overhead to protect the fleet.

The Libyans, facing impossible odds, launched two SA-5 missiles at US reconnaissance planes; these missiles, and subsequent ones, all missed their targets. Then the American forces responded by launching HARM missiles to lock on to Libyan radar and destroy the sites, and by sinking over the next two days at least two Libyan patrol boats. US intelligence reports suggested that seventy-two Libyans had been killed, against no American casualties. On 26 March the Prairie Fire operation was terminated.

The American forces had flexed their muscles, destroying military equip-ment and killing a few dozen Libyans. However, the Libyan regime was intact: there had been no rebellion against Gaddafi and he seemed as secure as ever. A more drastic course of action was needed.

REAGAN, TERRORISM AND NATO

A key element of the Reagan Doctrine was that the United States should be prepared to intervene in the Third World whenever there was a perceived threat to American interests. The American establishment was still smarting under the impact of the 'Vietnam syndrome' (still not exorcised despite the crushing of Iraq) and there were other reverses, not least the bomb blasts in Lebanon in 1983 that killed 236 American servicemen and officials. The Reagan response in these circumstances was not to concede the limits of American power (and certainly not to examine the ethical or legal propriety of US interventions across the globe), but simply to up the ante. The ratchet of the Cold War was turned another notch, the 'evil empire' was pro-claimed, and a virtual Third World War – against Soviet-backed 'terrorism' in the Third World – was declared. The Reagan Doctrine demanded that terrorists ('freedom fighters') be supported wherever they were struggling to overthrow left-leaning governments, and that freedom-fighters ('terror-ists') be crushed wherever they were striving to topple right-leaning re-gimes. Thus the policy involved supporting terror and subversion in such countries as Nicaragua, Angola, Cambodia, Laos and Afghanistan; and working to overthrow regimes such as Colonel Gaddafi's in Libya. The support for various Libyans-in-exile groups and the US military actions against Libya were part of a global pattern, the reassertion of American power by a macho US administration subconsciously troubled about its virility. The US response to the Beirut killings was the invasion of Grenada; the response to terrorists acts in various countries was the flamboyant Prairie Fire operation and the later onslaught on Libya that was dubbed Operation El Dorado Canyon (see below).

The United States was now evolving a mode of military response that would be more politically acceptable than the deployment of large numbers of men and vast quantities of armaments. Large-scale conflict with the Soviet Union was ruled out (there were less costly ways of subverting that regime), and instead there would be 'brush-fire' conflicts, 'low-intensity' actions, 'policing' initiatives and the like. The United States would assess a threat to its interests, decide a course of action, and cite UN resolutions or Charter articles (as appropriate) to sanction this or that military intervention in this or that Third World country. Where Reagan claimed to have evidence of a conspiracy of 'terrorist' states he actively sought a collaboration of 'contra' forces drawn from various areas of conflict. Thus in June 1985 'contras' from Nicaragua, Angola, Laos and Afghanistan met in Angola to form what came to be known as the 'Democratic International': the meeting was organised by multimillionaire Lewis Lehrman, a close friend of Reagan, who later declared 'their goals are our goals'. A principal aim was to develop a capacity for 'low-intensity warfare' so that pro-West terror and subversion could be sustained whenever deemed necessary. This was, according to the US Army, the 'limited use of power for political purposes'.[64]

The American military actions against Libya served various purposes. Macho elements in the administration and the armed forces were temporarily mollified (Reagan himself had been known to pretend to draw imaginary six-guns when given the results of the latest confrontation); military procedures and weaponry were conveniently tested in real-world situations; the American public was shown American 'walking tall' (which gave a pre-election Bush a reason in 1991/92 for further confrontation with both Saddam Hussein and Muammar Gaddafi); and allies and client states of America were forced to concur with US policy, becoming 'locked in' to Washington's Third World policies. This last *desideratum* inevitably meant that NATO, originally set up to contain what was proclaimed to be an expansionist Soviet Union, was to become an accomplice in Washington's Third World War against 'terrorism' in poor countries across the globe. Britain, as a leading NATO member, was thus induced to conspire with the United States in the 1986 bombing of Tripoli and Benghazi (below). Thus the British government agreed to a NATO exercise at US bases in England to mask the preparations for the attack; this involved disguising the work involved in loading the American F-111 aircraft with hundreds of bombs. Independent observers of such events were confirmed in their suspicions that NATO in the 1980s was moving towards a Third World 'policing' role in defence of Western interests. The collapse of the Warsaw Pact and the Soviet Union, and the associated 'democratisation' of Eastern Europe, meant that the easy certainties of the Cold War could no longer be used to justify the existence of a NATO alliance designed primarily to sustain American hegemony. The hapless Third World was selected as the new and improved justification. It was clear in the late 1980s and early 1990s that Britain and the United States were increasingly willing to countenance a NATO 'out-of-area' role. Iraq and Libya were and remain (in 1992) the main beneficiaries of this developing policy.

OPERATION EL DORADO CANYON

Prelude

In the mid 1980s a number of events combined to concentrate the collective mind of the US administration. Gaddafi remained a thorn in the flesh of the world's most powerful nation and the resulting irritation stimulated one reaction after another in the body politic. The naval and air confrontations had done no more than tweak Gaddafi's nose and Washington had much greater ambitions than that. The important task was to find a pretext for a more effective military attack, one in which Gaddafi's 'fortuitous' death would nicely conform with the Ford edict banning the deliberate murder of foreign heads of state. The hijacking of TWA Flight 847 to Beirut by Arab gunmen in June 1985, when twenty-nine Americans were held hostage, had effectively humiliated the Reagan administration. There was a pressing need to find some face-saving course of action; the requirement was for a target that could be attacked with low risk to American personnel, and with good chances of improving the image of the United States in the world. Libya fitted the bill.

Washington had no doubt that Gaddafi had funded terrorism all over the world. It was of little concern that no Libyan link with the TWA hijacking had been discovered; Gaddafi was guilty enough on other counts. The journalists Lou Cannon and Bob Woodward, with access to officials in the administration, drew attention to how the TWA incident brought Libya back into the limelight: 'Sources said it was the TWA hijacking that brought anti-Libyan and anti-terrorist policies together. The secret planning led to a number of military options in which Libya was increasingly singled out as the main target, even though several other nations, notably Syria and Iran, were also considered to be centres of terrorism.'[65] The US right was urging reprisals against the Arabs; it seemed that *any* Arabs would do. George Shultz was one of the influential protagonists who was constantly pressing for military action against Arabs who sought to frustrate US plans in the area.[66] He was supported by Zionists, certain business interests and Republican militarists. In July 1985 Reagan signalled his acceptance of the Shultz position by giving his notorious 'misfits and loony-tunes' speech, in which he denounced the 'terrorist' states of Iran, Cuba, Nicaragua, North Korea and Libya.

It was easy to list the terrorist events but more difficult to demonstrate the guilt of any particular faction or state. The US administration, horrified by particular terrorist actions (such as the TWA hijacking, the take-over of the Italian cruise liner *Achille Lauro* by a PLO faction, the hijacking of an Egyptair flight to Malta, and the Abu Nidal killings at the Rome and Vienna airports), exploited such events to prepare the ground for an attack on Libya. Direct Libyan involvement in most of the terrorist events could not be demonstrated by the US administration, but 'Libya's guilt was largely pre-determined'.[67] In January 1986 Washington published a document headed 'Libya Under Qadhafi: A Pattern of Aggression': here were listed various acts of violence that were attributed to the Gaddafi regime, though only the 1979 sacking of the US embassy in Tripoli was cited as evidence of Libyan violence against Americans. The document claimed that Gaddafi uses terrorism 'as one of the primary instruments of his foreign policy', but no concrete evidence was provided; the story of Libyan hit squads in the US was reiterated with no reference to the many expressed doubts that any such teams ever existed. Libya was again being selected for special attention, not because it had a terrorist record demonstrably worse than that of certain other states but because it was a convenient target. The black propaganda had done its work. Who could complain if a 'loony-tunes' character such as Gaddafi was bombed from the air and perhaps even killed?

After the staged intimidation of Libya by the Prairie Fire armada in the Gulf of Sirte (and the killing of seventy-two Libyans), Washington surmised that Gaddafi might try to retaliate by organising terrorist acts. It was reported that the security service in Tripoli sent coded instructions to a number of its People's Bureaus urging them to make preparations for attacks on US military targets.[68] One of these messages was allegedly sent to the People's Bureau in East Berlin. Soon afterwards, a bomb exploded in La Belle discotheque in West Berlin, a place frequented by American servicemen: this explosion, on 5 April 1986, killed three and injured 230 others. The US administration quickly claimed that interception of coded messages proved Libyan involvement in the atrocity, a claim that has since been questioned by many independent observers (see below). Washington had been desperate to pin some terrorist act on Gaddafi, and now it claimed to have the smoking gun. The pretext for the bombing of Libya had been established.

The Bombing

President Reagan, famously fond of Rambo feature films, had been saying to aides for more than a year that he was looking for 'a clean shot' against terrorism. Now he had his opportunity. On 9 April he attended a press conference and demonstrated his remarkable communication skills by denouncing Gaddafi as 'the Mad Dog of the Middle East'.[69] The countdown was on.

For some time the president's aides and the military planners had been preparing for an attack on Gaddafi, but they wanted to discourage speculation. Oliver North therefore set about creating the correct climate of minimum expectation, telling the NSC aide Johnathan Miller (who enjoyed good press relations) that action against Libya was unlikely: the United States did not want an incident, the right ships were not available, and in any case the French would not approve overflights. Miller then called John McWerthy, the State Department correspondent for ABC News, to offer details of the story. The ABC anchorman then included a report in his show stating that a retaliation against Gaddafi was unlikely. Oliver North remarked to Miller afterwards: 'That was the best disinformation I've ever seen.'[70]

On 15 April 1986, at 2 a.m. Libyan time, aircraft from the US Air force and Navy struck at six main targets in Tripoli and Benghazi. The US officially stated that a total of thirty-six people were killed, but journalists in Tripoli estimated that there were more than 100 dead and twice as many wounded.[71] The casualties included Gaddafi's wife Safia and three of the couple's children, all of whom suffered pressure shock from a 2000lb bomb which hit their accommodation. The injured children were rushed to hospital and some hours later Gaddafi's sixteen-month-old adopted daughter, Hanna, died from severe brain damage. His two sons, Saef al-Islam and Khamees, were kept in intensive care for several days.[72] Gaddafi survived unhurt but was emotionally shaken.

The American bomber force comprised F-111s flying from British bases and A-6s flying from aircraft carriers in the Mediterranean. The targets included the Aziziya Barracks where Gaddafi and his family were sleeping; the Al Jamahiriya Barracks which houses the Muslim League, a paramilitary force of many nationalities; two airfields; and anti-aircraft sites.

France and Spain had refused to allow use of their airspace and so the UK-based F-111 bombers were forced to fly 2800 nautical miles across the Atlantic and through the Gilbralter Straits; thirty KC-135 tankers were used en route for refuelling purposes. Television viewers were shown horrifying pictures of the dead and the wounded and of the damage to property (the TV broadcasts were later condemned by Tory MPs keen to support the American action). Several houses were destroyed and the French, Austrian and Finnish embassies were damaged. Eight or nine F-111s had intended to drop their laser-guided bombs on Gaddafi's compound but the planes had mechanical problems and only two of the bombs were dropped as planned; one F-111 bomber and its two crewmen were lost. The much-lauded 'smart' bombs had succeeded in demolishing ordinary houses, killing innocent civilians, and damaging foreign embassies. Gaddafi was alive but few people doubted that the US raids were an assassination attempt.

President Reagan had claimed that 'we were not out to kill anybody', an assertion that was amply contradicted by his own officials. Sources within the US administration have revealed that the bombing of the Aziziya Barracks, in the first wave of a two-wave attack, was intended to kill Gaddafi.[73] Officials of the National Security Council had drafted a prior statement describing Gaddafi's death as 'fortuitous',[74] and an administration official who had been intimately involved in planning the bombing raids admitted that 'We hoped to get him. But nobody knew his whereabouts.'[75] There was also the hope that, if the raids failed to kill Gaddafi, his reputation would be so weakened that the Libyan army would stage a coup. Secretary of State George Schultz observed that the targets were chosen to leave an 'impression' on the Libyan military and that a coup would be 'all to the good'.[76] Military sites had been attacked to give the Libyan officers their chance: they did not take it. The bombing raid had failed in its primary purpose and the US administration had again misjudged Libyan politics.

The Thatcher Role

At the beginning of 1986 Prime Minister Margaret Thatcher issued a warning against what she regarded as illegal measures that might be used to combat international terrorism. The terrorist attacks at the Rome and Vienna airports had occurred not long before and it was already clear that opinion was being whipped up in the United States for a raid on Libya. Michael Heseltine had resigned the day before Thatcher spoke to American correspondents, and she had her own problems to contend with. Reagan was urging a united NATO stand against Gaddafi but Thatcher, at that time, refused to join the stampede towards hasty action. They declared that sanctions 'don't work' as an instrument of foreign policy and in any case there would be no chance of getting a European consensus. However, she stressed in particular her opposition to a military strike against Libya: 'I do not believe in retaliatory strikes that are against international law.' Such measures might produce 'much greater chaos' than terrorism itself: 'Once you start to go across borders then I do not see an end to it. I uphold international law very firmly.'[77]

In early April President Reagan informed Thatcher, following the Berlin outrage, that he intended to strike against Libya. He declared that the action would proceed, whatever Thatcher's opinion, but that it would be useful to be able to fly the F-111 bombers from their British bases. This would, Reagan claimed, mean fewer casualties in Libya since the F-111s could achieve more accurate results than the carrier-based aircraft in the Mediterranean. It seemed clear that Reagan was asking Thatcher to conspire in actions that she had only recently denounced as violations of international law.

Suddenly Thatcher seemed less concerned about legal obligation, seeing the immediate task as being able to find a way of justifying the proposed American action. The British Attorney-General Michael Havers was asked whether the proposed bombing of Libya might not be accommodated by Article 51* of the UN Charter, which permitted military action for the purpose of self-defence. The advice was seemingly that such action could be justified under the Charter, whereupon Thatcher had no problem agreeing to the proposed bombing raids. However, she did suggest that only 'terrorist' targets should be hit and that civilian casualties should be kept to a minimum, her only concessions to the demands of international law that she had viewed very differently a short time before. Only a small number of British cabinet ministers – Foreign Secretary Howe, Defence Secretary Younger and Lord Whitelaw – were involved in the decision, and they all had reservations. When Geoffrey Howe voiced some Foreign Office doubts about the plan, Thatcher interrupted him, according to one minister, 'shrieking about the need to support the Americans and the need not to be fair-weather friends'.[78] Younger broadcast some of his anxieties on a Scottish

---

*Article 51: 'Nothing in the present Charter shall impair the inherent right of individual or collective self-defence if an armed attack occurs against a Member of the United Nations, until the Security Council has taken measures necessary to maintain international peace and security. Measures taken by Members in the exercise of this right of self-defence shall be immediately reported to the Security Council and shall not in any way affect the authority and responsibility of the Security Council under the present Charter to take at any time such action as it deems necessary in order to maintain or restore international peace and security.'

radio programme, and Whitelaw tried to make a distinction between agreeing a request from an ally and enthusing about every action that an ally might take. When the rest of the cabinet were told about the American request Chancellor Nigel Lawson and party chairman Norman Tebbit expressed reservations, as did a number of other Tory ministers. Soon after this wide range of dissent had been expressed, Thatcher declared that it would have been 'inconceivable' to have turned down the American request.

Debate in the House of Commons showed Thatcher vigorously defending an American policy that she had roundly condemned a few months before. One characteristic exchange was with Leo Abse, MP for Torfaen:

Mr Leo Abse (Torfaen): Is it not clear from all the statements the Prime Minister has made that her passionate political infatuation with Reagan is leading her to the misjudgments of a giddy girl? Why is she feeding the paranoia of Gaddafi? Why is she providing him with corroboration of his crazy conspiratorial theories? Why does she provide him with a theatre in which he can place his self-immolating terrorists and allow them, as they obviously now will, to come into this country? Is it not abundantly clear that the real immediate effect of her collusion is inevitably the importation of greater terrorist violence into Britain?

The Prime Minister: The United States stands by the NATO alliance, this country and Europe in defence of freedom. For that purpose it keeps hundreds of thousands of troops in Europe. In that capacity, American forces have been subject to terrorist attacks: and the complicity of Libya in these attacks is beyond doubt. Yet the Hon. Gentleman is asking me to refuse the United States, in the face of those attacks and planned terrorist attacks, any right of self-defence, to use its own planes and its own pilots to defend its own people. It would be ridiculous to refuse it.[79]

It was clear that Prime Minister Thatcher would hear no criticism of the American decision to bomb Libya, despite her earlier comments on international law: Reagan, at least according to Thatcher's public utterances, could do no wrong. But Thatcher did not escape criticism on this issue: her position on Libya – along with her deceits over the Belgrano and Westland affairs – were most tellingly exposed by the tenacious Labour MP, Tam Dalyell.[80]

Dalyell (MP for Linlithgow) quotes the Thatcher speech justifying the American action and then subjects her remarks to scrutiny.[81] He explores in particular her suggestion that UK-based F-111 bombers had to be used in order to minimise 'collateral' (civilian) damage in Libya: was Thatcher really acting on humanitarian grounds? She was trying to argue that 'containment of killing' was her justification for agreeing the use of British bases sited in the United Kingdom. Dalyell draws attention to American sources to indicate the real reasons for the use of the F-111s, especially the need to provide a proving ground for weapons. An ex-Pentagon analyst is quoted: 'The budget, in short, is the mission. "It all comes back to the budget," says one ex-Pentagon analyst. "For years we've being saying that radar, infra-red, and smart bombs are the way to go. We've spent billions on night-mission avionics, so we had to try to use them, even if a daylight strike would have been better." '[82] In a similar vein, one reputable aviation journal noted that the attack on Libya 'provided a good proving ground for the F-111s to be flown in the Mediterranean, and gave the Air Force a chance to demonstrate its capabilities'.[83] Nor was it true, as Thatcher had implied, that the F-111s were superior to the carrier-borne A6s and A7s: both were equipped with the high-technology TAM system or its equivalent.

There were also other influential considerations that Thatcher failed to cite in her attempted justification. There was, for example, the inter-service rivalry between the US Navy and the US Air Force. Dalyell instances the words of a senior Pentagon official quoted in *Aviation Week:* 'Understandably, after the all-Navy action in Libya last month, the Air Force wanted a piece of the action.' Moreover, a powerful Pentagon lobby was pushing the idea of joint-service operations, particularly the use of land-based aircraft in support of naval operations. And there were other aspects of internal American politics that received no acknowledgement in the Thatcher justification. Again Tam Dalyell highlights the comments of Rear Admiral Eugene Carroll Jr of the Center for Defense Information in Washington. When asked whether it would have been practical *to use the F-111s and ask the British afterwards* the Rear Admiral replied: 'That was the basis on which the plan was prepared.'[84] The implication was that the United States could act in any way it pleased, using the territory of an ally as necessary and without prior consultation, with the assumption that the ally could be bounced into compliance after the event.

Tam Dalyell raised other matters of crucial importance, not least the reason advanced by Washington in justification for their bombing strikes: namely, the supposed Libyan complicity in the outrage at La Belle discotheque in West Berlin. Even if the Libyans were involved there was the matter of proportionality of response but that consideration can be left on one side: if Libyan complicity could not be established then no US action, proportionate or not, could – even in Washington's terms – be justified. Were the Libyans involved in the bombing of La Belle discotheque?

La Belle Justification?

After the naval actions of March 1986 the US searched for signs of Libyan-inspired terrorist activities. We have seen that Washington claimed to have intercepted messages from Tripoli to various People's Bureaus, leading to the suspicion that Libya was working to organise further terrorist outrages. One message in particular was seen as crucially important, a coded instruction allegedly received by the People's Bureau to East Germany in East Berlin. The American claim is that on receiving this instruction the Libyan security personnel at the Bureau felt authorised to proceed with a terrorist operation against US servicemen in West Berlin, and La Belle discotheque was chosen as the target. The day before the incident, the East Berlin bureau had reportedly sent a message to Tripoli informing the security authorities that they would 'be very happy' when they saw tomorrow's headlines.[85] A further message, sent within minutes of the explosion, said – the US alleges – that an operation 'was happening now'.[86] President Reagan claimed that the intercepted and decoded cables were 'irrefutable proof' of Libyan involvement in the terrorist outrage. However, sources within the US administration and what was claimed to be a West German translation of the intercepted cables testified that the Libyan leadership neither authorised the bombing nor specified the target.[87]

The US authorities have been unwilling to clarify the precise nature of the Libyan involvement in the West Berlin outrage, or to release the full text of the decoded and translated cables. Such reticence is conveniently explained by Washington in terms of national security, but there is a widespread suspicion that the US administration has deliberately sought to obscure the wording of the intercepted messages because they cannot be relied upon to support an interpretation that would have gone some way to justifying the bombing of Libya. In one interpretation, 'President Reagan merely inferred the responsibility of the Libyan leadership from evidence his advisors knew to be ambiguous.'[88] Washington tried to secure a trade embargo against Libya, following the discotheque bombing, but could not secure the agreement of its European allies: the Bonn government, for example, expelled two Libyan diplomats but would not agree to a trade embargo. A frustrated White House decided that a military strike – Operation El Dorado Canyon – was the only option: five days later, Tripoli and Benghazi were bombed.

Tam Dalyell has also worked to expose the weakness in La Belle Justi-fication. In particular, he reproduces a timetable prepared by Richard Ware and Christopher Bowlby, impartial scholars in the British House of Commons Library. This important chronology is headed 'Progress of investigations into responsibility for bomb at La Belle discotheque in Berlin on 5 April 1986'; it serves to show the fragility of the US justification for the air strikes on Libya. It is useful to quote some of the elements of this chronology:

5 April 1986:	Bomb at La Belle discotheque in Berlin.
14–15 April 1986:	US raid . . . Reagan asserts 'irrefutable' evidence of Libyan connection with terrorism and refers to intercepted messages . . . 'The evidence is now conclusive that the terrorist bombing of La Belle discotheque was planned and executed under the direct orders of the Libyan regime.'
17 April 1986:	Bomb attack on El Al plane foiled at Heathrow airport.
18 April 1986:	Arrest in London of Nezar Hindawi in connection with El Al attempted bombing; Ahmed Hasi arrested in Berlin on suspicion of involvement in La Belle attack.
21 April 1986	*Der Spiegel* quotes Berlin state security chief Manfred Ganshow's statement to a *Bundestag* home affairs committee that the Libyan connection is still only one important lead among several. Christian Lochte, head of the Hamburg *Verfassungsschutz*, is quoted as saying that there is as yet 'no concrete evidence' of Libyan involvement . . . Local criminal police are investigating 'in all possible directions', including the theory that rival disco-owners or drug dealers might have had a motive for the attack on La Belle.
25 April 1986:	The West Berlin *Morgenpost* reports that the documents found in Hasi's flat 'have turned out to be insufficient grounds for keeping Hasi in jail' . . . unidentified police sources tell Associated Press that there has been 'no progress' on solving La Belle bombing.

27 April 1986:	*The Observer*, drawing on Washington and Bonn sources, reports that the US administration has 'massaged' the intercepts . . . in order to make their relevance more clear-cut.
6 May 1986:	West German police do not now think that (Hasi and his associate Salameh) were involved in La Belle attack.
22–23 May 1986:	. . . *Die Welt* and *Bild* report an alleged connection between the La Belle bombing and a Libyan shot dead in East Berlin . . . According to unidentified Intelligence sources Mohammed Ashour, a former Libyan diplomat, was killed on the orders of Colonel Gaddafi because he had passed information on La Belle bombing to the CIA. US diplomatic sources and the West German government discount the story . . .
17 November 1986:	. . . the *Guardian* correspondent reports that 'the La Belle investigations have reached a dead end'.
18 January 1987:	. . . *Morgenpost* cites anonymous justice department sources as saying that a letter found on . . . Hindawi . . . referred both to the La Belle discotheque and a Syrian intelligence agent . . .

These chronological extracts are quoted, not to demonstrate that a clear solution to the discotheque bombing is at hand but, quite the reverse, to show that it is impossible at this stage to establish that any group of individuals – or any state – is uniquely culpable. It is obvious that Reagan's 'irrefutable' evidence was no such thing. This should be borne in mind in considering the 1991/92 claims of the Bush administration that there was irrefutable evidence of Libya's sole responsibility for the Lockerbie outrage (Chapter One).

The Response

The international response to the bombing of Libya was to a large extent predictable. President Reagan had made clear, in characteristic fashion, what his purposes were: he had bombed Libya as a way of 'contributing to an international environment of peace, freedom and progress within which our democracy – and other free nations – can flourish'.[90] However, the US administration had not been confident enough of the US public's reaction to the bombing to neglect necessary attention to news management. The 1986 air attack on Libya 'was a brilliantly staged media event, the first bombing in history scheduled for prime-time TV, for the precise moment when the networks open their national news programs'.[91] Anchor men were able to switch at once to Tripoli so that the exciting events could be viewed live. Then followed the carefully conceived news conferences and White House statements. It was firmly explained that the bombing of Tripoli and Benghazi was 'self-defense against future attack',[92] a measured reaction to the discotheque outrage in Berlin ten days before. The media knew that the evidence for Libyan complicity in the discotheque bombing was slight but such an inconsequential detail was suppressed in the general applause for Reagan's decisive action.

In fact a report from Berlin, just half an hour before the US attack, had stated that US and West German officials had no evidence, only 'suspicions', of Libyan involvement. This contradicted earlier government claims of certain knowledge, again a minor inconsistency that the White House press corps resolutely ignored. Within a short time leading West German publications, and obscure ones in the United States, carried the information that the German intelligence team investigating the bombing at La Belle discotheque had no knowledge whatever of any Libyan complicity. This information was largely suppressed in the United States. And there was more. The US administration had put out a story that, having intercepted the Libyan messages, efforts were made to warn the US servicemen at the discotheque but that the alert called in West Berlin had failed by fifteen minutes. The West Berlin police informed the BBC that no alert had been called: the American story was pure fabrication. Yet the pliant US media continued to carry the disinformation. Thus the Pentagon correspondent of *Business Week* was able to write that 'by ordering the 1986 bombing of a West Berlin disco in which two American servicemen were killed, Qadaffi provoked a violent response – a massive air raid'.[93]

The systematic campaign of disinformation and news management achieved its purpose. Reagan's popularity in the United States soared as he was engulfed in a wave of adulation. High-technology weapons had been given their first trial by fire and, despite the unimpressive results, arms stock prices shot up immediately after the bombing. Liberal opinion in America might have been shocked by the US onslaught on a sovereign state but the action had supposedly had 'chilling effect on state-sponsored terrorism and had demonstrated the President's resolve to the world'.[94] The response in Britain to the bombing of Libya was mixed, with a substantial number of observers sceptical or disapproving. Even some committed Conservative columnists withheld their support from the Thatcher-approved American action. Thus Ferdinand Mount, who had run Thatcher's policy unit for two years bridging the 1983 election, ridiculed the idea that 'carefully selected targets' designed to minimise civilian casualties, could include a site right in the centre of Tripoli; and he commented that perhaps the event would cost the Tories the next election. A resolution introduced in the US Congress had offered Thatcher the 'highest praise and thanks' for supporting the American action but in the UK the episode made her deeply unpopular. There was concern that Libya would retaliate with terrorist operations: not much happened but pro-Libyan activists killed two British hostages, Leigh Douglas and Philip Padfield, and the American Peter Kilburn in Beirut.[95]

The response in Europe was deeply hostile. A round-the-clock protest was begun outside the US embassy in London; two thousand people held a candlelit vigil outside Downing Street; and there were demonstrations outside government buildings and at the four US bases – Upper Heyford, Lakenheath, Fairford and Mildenhall – from which the F-111 bombers had flown. About 10,000 people demonstrated in West Germany, and in Italy 3000 people attended a Communist Party youth protest. Polls suggested that 65 per cent of people in Britain and 75 per cent in West Germany opposed the bombing; in France 66 per cent were in favour but 63 per cent approved the government's decision not to let the US bombers use French airspace (by the end of April the figure opposing the American attack had risen to 56 per cent with 79 per cent approving the ban on the use of airspace).[96] The day before the US bombing the European Economic Community had underlined 'the need for restraint on all sides', and when the bombing went ahead there was speedy condemnation from many European capitals. Bettino Craxi said that the action ran the risk of 'provoking a further explosion of fanaticism, extremism, criminal and suicide actions', and other leaders joined the Italian Prime Minister in condemning the US attack. Spain, Greece, Austria, Denmark and the Netherlands expressed various degrees of criticism, some 'deplored' the action. The Greek government accused Britain, with its foreknowledge of the attack, of 'violating the moral rules of political co-operation'; and Leo Tindemans, the Belgian Foreign Minister, demanded an explanation from Geoffrey Howe.[97] The official French and West German reactions were more guarded.

There was widespread Arab condemnation of the American attack, perhaps the most predictable foreign reaction of all, but this did nothing to dent the enthusiasm of the American public for President Reagan's 'resolute' stand. The way was open for further anti-Libyan initiatives.

THE CONTINUING CAMPAIGN

Soon the US administration, frustrated at their failure to kill Colonel Gaddafi, were again considering possible options. Such key players as CIA chief William Casey and Secretary of State George Shultz 'were determined to finish what had been started in Libya'.[98] Meetings were held between representatives from the CIA, the State Department, the White House, and the Department of Defence to discuss the possible courses of action. Perhaps the Pentagon could send planes to generate sonic booms just off the Libyan coast to unnerve Gaddafi. Casey volunteered: 'Humiliate him.' How could this be done? How could Gaddafi's perceived paranoia be fed, in the hope that he would fall apart? The State Department acknowledged that the Libyan exile groups were weak and that the US must rely upon its own direct covert action. Further disinformation plans were considered. 'Deception' should be arranged to suggest that US planes were crossing Gaddafi's 'line of death' in the Gulf of Sirte, and there could be foreign media placements. 'Articles should be placed to show the following: Libyan military dissent; the existence of an underground in the Libyan Army; combined operations planned against Libya; Soviets planning a coup; Libyan intelligence should be provided with photography of Libyan dissidents meeting with Soviet officials in Paris, Baghdad, etc.; US coup planned with senior Libyan help.'[99] Use could be made of clandestine radio, and rubber rafts could be dropped on Libyan beaches to make it seem that a coup was underway.

In August 1986 William Casey received a TOP SECRET memorandum from John Poindexter in which further possible actions against Colonel Gaddafi were set down. Internal dissidents could be encouraged to act, there could be fresh covert action, rumours could be spread that the US was about to take further military action, there could be fresh joint military exercises (designed to 'spook' the Libyan defences), and there could be further 'deception operations'. The 'temporarily quiescent' Gaddafi must be stopped before he moved 'to a more active role'. On 14 August President Reagan met with Shultz, Weinberger, Casey, Poindexter and Admiral William Crowe, the Chairman of the Joint Chiefs of Staff, to consider further actions against Gaddafi. Poindexter praised the bombing raids and urged the need for a fresh disinformation campaign. Crowe wondered whether it was sensible to spread rumours about possible American actions and not carry them through. The President was soon offering his own contribution:

'Reagan quipped, "Why not invite Qaddafi to San Francisco, he likes to dress up so much."

Shultz retorted, "Why don't we give him AIDS."

The others laughed . . .'[100]

The meeting considered many different 'harassment' options but did not at that stage consider terrorism or fresh military options. Two days later President Reagan authorised a deception and disinformation program designed to 'dissuade Qaddafi from engaging in terrorism; bring about a change of leadership; minimize the possibility of Soviet gains in Libya'. The classification was TOP SECRET and coded 'VEIL'.[101] Soon afterwards elements of the disinformation plan were put into effect: *The Wall Street Journal* talked of the 'collision course' between Libya and the United States, declaring that Gaddafi was plotting fresh acts of terrorism and that the US was preparing for another air raid. Poindexter publicly endorsed the story and White House spokesman Larry Speakes declared it 'authoritative'.

Such events should be borne in mind when we consider the Western accusations made against Colonel Gaddafi through 1991 and 1992.

It remains to be seen whether the new Clinton presidency will represent a genuine 'new beginning' or whether it will remain true to the broad thrust of US interventionism that has been maintained, virtually without pause, for more than a century. We did not have to wait long to be given a clue as to what to expect. On 4 November 1992 President-elect Clinton declared: 'America has only one president at a time . . . and even as America's administrations change, America's fundamental interests do not.' There would, he said, be 'essential continuity of American foreign policy'.

Appendix 1

Summary of Documents Issued to the United Nations by US, UK and France to Record Charges Against and Demands on Libya

All the documents are cited in UN Security Council Resolution 731 (Appendix 2).

Document S/23306 – issued by France (20 December 1991)

Covering letter plus Annex

The Annex notes the attack on the UTA DC-10 and demands that the Libyan authorities 'cooperate immediately, effectively and by all possible means with French justice in order to help to establish responsibility for this terrorist act'. Libya is called upon

'To produce all the material evidence in its possession and to facilitate access to all documents that might be useful for establishing the truth'.

'To facilitate the necessary contacts and meetings, *inter alia*, for the assembly of witnesses'.

'To authorise the responsible Libyan officials to respond to any request made by the examining magistrate responsible for judicial information'.

Document S/23307 – issued by the United Kingdom (20 December 1991)

Covering letter plus text of the statement made by the Scottish Lord Advocate on 14 November 1991, text of the Foreign Secretary's statement in the Commons on 14 November 1991, and test of a statement issued by the British government on 27 November 1991

The Lord Advocate's statement records the issuing of warrants for the arrest of the two named Libyan nationals, details the charges (including the alleged chronology of events), and declares that this 'does not mark the end of the police investigation . . .'

The Foreign Secretary's statement notes the details of the Lockerbie bombing, notes the issuing of warrants by the Lord Advocate, and comments that 'the investigation has revealed no evidence to support suggestion of involvement by other countries . . .'

The British government statement notes the issuing of warrants and demands that the Libyan government: surrender for trial those charged; accept complete responsibility for the actions of Libyan officials; disclose all it knows of the crime; and pay appropriate compensation. 'We expect Libya to comply promptly and in full.'

Document S/23308 – issued by the United States (20 December 1991)

Covering letter plus statement from US government and joint declaration from government of United States and United Kingdom

The statement notes that the indictments have been conveyed to the Libyan government and introduces the joint declaration. The declaration demands that Libya: surrender for trial those charged; accept responsibility for the actions of Libyan officials; disclose all it knows of the crime; and pay appropriate compensation. 'We expect Libya to comply promptly and in full.'

Document S/23309 – issued by France, the United Kingdom and the United States (20 December 1991)

Letter plus tripartite declaration condemning terrorism and noting the demands on Libya. 'Libya must promptly, by concrete actions, prove its renunciation of terrorism.'

Document S/23317 – issued by the United States (23 December 1991)

Covering letter plus copy of the indictment handed down by the United States District Court for the District of Columbia on 14 November in connection with the bombing of Pan Am flight 103. The indictment lists the alleged chronology of events, gives details of the alleged conspiracy, describes the manner and means used by the alleged conspirators, records specific alleged acts, and names the alleged conspirators. The indictment also lists all the victims of the Lockerbie bombing and lists separately the nationals of the United States who died as a result of the bombing.

Appendix 2

UN Security Council Resolution 731 (1992)

Also before the Council is a draft resolution *(Document S/23422)* sponsored by France, the United Kingdom and the United States, which reads as follows:

'The Security Council,

'Deeply disturbed by the world-wide persistence of acts of international terrorism in all its forms, including those in which States are directly or indirectly involved, which endanger or take innocent lives, have a deleterious effect on international relations and jeopardise the security of States,

'Deeply concerned by all activities directed against international civil aviation and affirming the right of all States, in accordance with the Charter of the United Nations and relevant principles of international law, to protect their nationals from acts of international terrorism that constitute threats to international peace and security,

'Reaffirming its resolution 286 (1970) in which it called on States to take all possible legal steps to prevent any interference with international civil air travel,

'Reaffirming also its resolution 635 (1989) in which it condemned all acts of unlawful interference against the security of civil aviation and called upon all States to cooperate in devising and implementing measures to prevent all acts of terrorism, including those involving explosives,

'Recalling the statement made on 30 December 1988 by the President of the Council on behalf of the members of the Council strongly condemning the destruction of Pan Am flight 103 and calling on all States to assist in the apprehension and prosecution of those responsible for this criminal act,

'Deeply concerned over results of investigations which implicate officials of the Libyan Government and which are contained in Security Council documents that include the requests addressed to the Libyan authorities by France, the United Kingdom of Great Britain and Northern Ireland and the United States of America in connection with the legal procedures related to the attacks carried out against Pan Am flight 103 and UTA flight 772 (S/23306*; S/23307*; S/23308*; S/23309*; S/23317),

'Determined to eliminate international terrorism,

'1. Condemns the destruction of Pan Am flight 103 and UTA flight 772 and the resultant loss of hundreds of lives;

'2. Strongly deplores the fact that the Libyan Government has not yet responded effectively to the above requests to cooperate fully in establishing responsibility for the terrorist acts referred to above against Pan Am flight 103 and UTA flight 772;

'3. Urges the Libyan Government immediately to provide a full and effective response to those requests so as to contribute to the elimination of international terrorism;

'4. Requests the Secretary-General to seek the cooperation of the Libyan Government to provide a full and effective response to those requests;

'5. Urges all States individually and collectively to encourage the Libyan Government to respond fully and effectively to those requests;

'6. Decides to remain seized of the matter.'

Appendix 3

First Report (S/23574) on Libyan Crisis by UN Secretary-General Dr Boutros Boutros Ghali (11 February 1992)

1. This report is being submitted pursuant to paragraph 4 of Security Council resolution 731 (1992), which requested the Secretary-General 'to seek the cooperation of the Libyan Government to provide a full and effective response' to the requests referred to in that resolution.

2. Following consultations with the Libyan authorities, the Secretary-General sent Under-Secretary-General Vasiliy Safronchuk as his Special Envoy to Libya on 25 January 1992. The next day, Mr. Safronchuk called on the Libyan leader, Colonel Qaddafi, and delivered to him a personal message from the Secretary-General together with the text of resolution 731 and the related records of the Security Council. In his message to Colonel Qaddafi, the Secretary-General noted that he was encouraged by the assurances given to him by Minister Jadalla Belgasem El-Talhi that Libya was ready to cooperate with him. Further, while expressing the earnest hope that the matter in question could be resolved quickly so that peace could prevail, the Secretary-General emphasised that he was acting under the terms of paragraph 4 of resolution 731 and not as a mediator between the Security Council and the Libyan authorities.

3. In responding, Colonel Qaddafi asked the Special Envoy to reiterate to the Secretary-General his readiness to cooperate with him. Following receipt of the charges against two Libyan nationals, Colonel Qaddafi stated that the Libyan authorities had immediately started legal proceedings against them and appointed a judge to try them. He added that the two Libyan nationals had hired lawyers to represent them. Colonel Qaddafi said that the Libyan judges would require further information and that this should be provided by the Governments of the United States and the United Kingdom. He further suggested that if those two Governments were dissatisfied with the Libyan judges, then they should send their own judges. With specific reference to the requests contained in resolution 731 (1992), Colonel Qaddafi stated that he could not take any action which would contravene the legal system of Libya. He suggested, however, that the Secretary-General invite to Libya judges from the United States, the United Kingdom and France, as well as representatives of the League of Arab States, the Organisation of African Unity and the Organisation of the Islamic Conference to observe a trial in the event that the Libyan judges decided to try the two Libyan nationals.

4. After careful consideration of this response, the Secretary-General on 30 January 1992 once again received the Permanent Representative of Libya in New York

and informed him that he would now need to report to the Security Council. The Permanent Representative indicated that he would like to have a further discussion with his leadership. He proposed to the Secretary-General to allow him five to six days during which he would fly to Tripoli and consult with his leadership on its final position. Upon returning from Tripoli, the Permanent Representative met the Secretary-General on 11 February and indicated that he was mandated by his leadership to convey the following reply:

(1) Libya had decided to accept 'the French demands since they were in conformity with international law and did not infringe upon the sovereignty of Libya'. Libya requested, therefore, that the Secretary-General inform the French Government of that decision. The Libyan authorities further requested that the Secretary-General either take the initiative of setting up a mechanism for the implementation of this aspect of the resolution or ask France and Libya to negotiate such a mechanism among themselves.

(2) As far as resolution 731 as a whole was concerned, Libya was ready to cooperate fully with the Security Council and with the Secretary-General 'in the light of the statements made in the Security Council and in a way that would not infringe upon State sovereignty nor violate the Charter of the United Nations and principles of international law'. It was thus his country's view that 'a mechanism should be created for the implementation of resolution 731 and, therefore, Libya invited the Secretary-General to create such a mechanism or to call upon the parties concerned to discuss among themselves and eventually agree on the setting up of the mechanism in accordance with the spirit of resolution 731'.

5.   The Secretary-General explained to the Ambassador that his own role under resolution 731 was determined by the provisions of paragraph 4 of that resolution. He added, however, that he would inform the Security Council fully of the position of the Libyan authorities.

Appendix 4

Second Report (S/23672) on Libyan Crisis by UN Secretary-General Dr Boutros Boutros Ghali (3 March 1992)

1.   The present further report is being submitted pursuant to paragraph 4 of Security Council resolution 731 (1992), by which the Council requested the Secretary-General to seek the cooperation of the Libyan Government to provide a full and effective response to the requests referred to in that resolution.

2.   Following the circulation of the Secretary-General's earlier report on this subject, 1/ the Secretary-General met with the Permanent Representatives of France, the United Kingdom of Great Britain and Northern Ireland and the United States of America on 17 February 1992. They requested the Secretary-General to convey to the Libyan leader, Colonel Muammar Qaddafi, Leader of the First of September Revolution, the following points on behalf of their Governments:

(a)   The three Governments consider that the statement by the Libyan Government delivered to the Secretary-General of the United Nations through the Permanent Representative of the Libyan Arab Jamahiriya in New York, in which the Libyan Arab Jamahiriya expresses its readiness to abide by the Security Council resolution and to cooperate fully with their request as referred to in resolution 731 (1992), represents a step forward only if it is supported by action;

(b)   In this connection, the three Governments support the request of the French Government and would like to be informed of the mechanism by which the Libyan authorities will hand over the records and documentation requested, and whatever else may be requested by the French examining magistrate, and of where and when the Libyan authorities intend to do so;

(c)   The Governments of the States in question would further like to know the time, place and modality of the hand-over by the Libyan authorities of the two persons charged and the information and evidence requested and the precise measures that the Libyan Government intends to take in order to end support for terrorism in all its forms;

(d)   The three Governments have no objection to the hand-over of the suspects and the information requested taking place through the Secretary-General of the United Nations in accordance with paragraph 4 of resolution 731 (1992);

(e) The three Governments believe that their requests are clear and precise and that they do not require further clarification;

(f) With regard to the question of compensation, the three States seek to obtain assurances from the Libyan Arab Jamahiriya with regard to its responsibility in this connection.

3. Following consultations with the Libyan authorities, the Secretary-General again sent Under-Secretary-General Vasiliy Safronchuk to Tripoli to convey to Colonel Qaddafi a second message containing the above points and he asked the Libyan Leader to give him a precise and detailed reply.

4. Mr. Safronchuk first met with Colonel Qaddafi on 24 February 1992. He then travelled to Geneva on 25 February in order to report to the Secretary-General Colonel Qaddafi's reaction to his message. He then returned to the Libyan Arab Jamahiriya and met again with Colonel Qaddafi on 27 February. In the course of the two meetings the head of the Libyan State made the following points:

(a) There are constitutional obstructions preventing Colonel Qaddafi or the Libyan administration from handing over Libyan citizens abroad for trial in the absence of an extradition treaty;

(b) He may address an appeal to the Libyan people through the People's Committee, which might result in the removal of these obstructions. He did not indicate how long it would take to overcome the existing constitutional hurdles;

(c) Once the constitutional problems were solved, the Libyan Arab Jamahiriya could be inclined to consider France as the possible venue for a trial of the Libyan citizens; however, France had not requested that any suspects be handed over to it for trial;

(d) Although the Libyan authorities could not forcibly hand over the suspects for trial in a foreign country, the suspects were free to hand themselves over voluntarily and the Government of the Libyan Arab Jamahiriya had no intention of preventing them from doing so;

(e) The possibility of handing over the suspects to the authorities of third countries for trial may be considered. In this context Malta or any Arab country were mentioned by the Libyan Leader;

(f) Improvement of bilateral relations between the Libyan Arab Jamahiriya and the United States would make it possible to hand over the two suspects to the United States authorities;

(g) The Libyan Arab Jamahiriya is prepared to cooperate in every way possible to put an end to terrorist activities and sever its relations with all groups and organisations that target innocent civilians. It will not allow its territory, citizens or organisations to be used in any way for carrying out terrorist acts directly or indirectly. It is prepared to punish most severely anyone proven to be involved in such acts;

(h) It is premature to discuss the question of compensation, which can result only from a civil court decision. However, the Libyan Arab Jamahiriya will guarantee the payment of compensation awarded as a result of responsibility of its suspected citizens if they are unable to pay it themselves;

(i) The Libyan Arab Jamahiriya agrees to the French request. As a means of giving effect to these requests, the Libyan Arab Jamahiriya agrees to act on the French proposal that a judge come to the Libyan Arab Jamahiriya to investigate the case as he may see fit. It agrees to provide the French judge with a copy of the minutes of the investigation carried out by the Libyan judge;

(j) The Secretary of the People's Committee for Foreign Liaison and International Cooperation of the Libyan Arab Jamahiriya, Mr. Ibrahim M. Bishari, on 27 February 1992 addressed a letter to the Secretary-General of the United Nations in which some of these points are reiterated (see annex I). The Secretary-General received a second letter from the Secretary on 2 March 1992 (see annex II, enclosure).

5. On 26 February, while in Geneva the Secretary-General met with a special envoy of Colonel Qaddafi, Mr. Yusef Debri, Head of Libyan Intelligence, with whom the entire situation was reviewed.

6. From the foregoing, it will be seen that while resolution 731 (1992) has not yet been complied with, there has been a certain evolution in the position of the Libyan authorities since the Secretary-General's earlier report of 11 February 1992. 1/ The Security Council may wish to consider this in deciding on its future course of action.

Annex I

Letter dated 27 February 1992 from the Secretary of the People's Committee for Foreign Liaison and International Cooperation of the Libyan Arab Jamahiriya addressed to the Secretary-General

[*Original:* Arabic]

Proceeding from the adherence of the Great Jamahiriya to the rules of international law and to respect for the provisions of the Charter of the United Nations,

In its desire to promote international peace and security, to strengthen friendly relations between States, to ensure stability in international relations, to condemn all modes of the threat or use of force and to condemn international terrorism,

· Seeking to cooperate closely with the United Nations and its Secretary-General, and basing itself on the human rights covenants and laws that regard the right to litigation before a fair and impartial court as an essential guarantee of justice,

Understanding the role entrusted to the Secretary-General of the United Nations, and seeking to demonstrate its sincerity in meeting its international obligations,

The Jamahiriya, despite all the technical, legal and judicial difficulties raised by its national legislation, by international agreements, by the principles of sovereignty and by the Charter of the United Nations, with which we deem Security Council resolution 731 (1992) to be incompatible, nevertheless expresses its full readiness to cooperate with the Secretary-General of the United Nations in facilitating the task entrusted to him under paragraph 4 of Security Council resolution 731 (1992),

To that end, the Jamahiriya proposes the following mechanism:

1. It has no objection in principle to handing over the two suspects to the Office of the United Nations Development Programme in Tripoli for questioning.

2. The Secretary-General of the United Nations should undertake to form a legal committee made up of judges whose probity and impartiality are well attested in order to inquire into the facts, ascertain whether the charges made against the two suspects are well founded and conduct a comprehensive inquiry.

3. Should it become evident to the Secretary-General of the United Nations that the charge is well founded, the Jamahiriya will not oppose the hand-over of the two suspects, under his personal supervision, to a third party, while stressing that they should not again be handed over.

4. The Secretary-General of the United Nations should endeavour to provide all legal and judicial guarantees for the conduct of a just and fair trial based on the International Bill of Human Rights and the principles of international law.

With regard to the French requests

Libya agrees to the French requests. As a means of giving effect to these requests, the Jamahiriya agrees to act on the French proposal that a magistrate should come to Libya to investigate the case in the manner that he deems fit. It agrees to provide the French magistrate with a copy of the minutes of the investigation carried out by the Libyan judge.

With regard to the issue of terrorism

The Jamahiriya affirms its outright condemnation of terrorism in all its forms and whatever its source, and it denies the allegations concerning its involvement in any terrorist acts. Accordingly, it is prepared to undertake the following:

1. The Jamahiriya, denying this allegation, has no objection to the Secretary-General or his representative investigating the facts in the Jamahiriya in order to refute or confirm it. The Jamahiriya undertakes to provide all the facilities and information that the Secretary-General or his representative may deem it necessary to have in order to arrive at the truth. The Jamahiriya is of the view that it is possible to draw up an agreement, or bilateral or multilateral agreements, designating the ways and means necessary for the elimination of international terrorism, and it is prepared to enter into bilateral or multilateral discussions to that end.

2. Libya expresses its readiness to cooperate in any matter that may put an end to terrorist activities and to sever its relations with all groups and organisations which target innocent civilians.

3. Libya shall not, under any circumstances, permit the use of its territory, its nationals or its institutions for the perpetration, directly or indirectly, of any terrorist acts, and it is prepared to impose the severest penalties on those against whom involvement in such acts can be proved.

4. Libya undertakes to respect the national choices of all States and to build its relations on a foundation of mutual respect and non-interference in internal affairs.

The proposals contained in this draft shall be binding on Libya if they are accepted by the other party. The results arrived at, whatever they may be, shall be binding on all, a new chapter shall be opened in relations between the two sides, State terrorism against Libya shall end, there shall be a halt to threats and provocations against it, its territorial integrity, its sovereignty and the integrity of its territorial waters shall be guaranteed, the economic boycott shall be ended, its political choices shall be respected and its name shall finally be removed from the roster of terrorism.

With regard to compensation

Despite the fact that discussion of the question of compensation is premature, since it would only follow from a civil judgement based on a criminal judgement, Libya guarantees the payment of any compensation that might be incurred by the responsibility of the two suspects who are its nationals in the event that they were unable to pay.

The Jamahiriya stresses to the Secretary-General and to the Security Council that all parties must contribute to cooperation and not one party alone. To this day, despite all the cooperation that the Jamahiriya has evinced and has demonstrated in practice, the three States in question have not responded to its legitimate request for them to provide it with the dossiers of the investigation on the basis of which the parties concerned presume to make charges against the two suspects. Saddened as it is at the lack of cooperation on the part of these parties, it requests you and the Council to intercede with them in this matter.

In conclusion, the Jamahiriya appreciates your role and salutes your contribution, and it affirms once more its readiness to cooperate in such a manner as to ensure the success of your endeavours.

> *(Signed)* Ibrahim M. BISHARI
> *Secretary of the People's Committee for*
> *Foreign Liaison and International Cooperation*

Annex II

Letter dated 2 March 1992 from the Permanent Representative of the Libyan Arab Jamahiriya to the United Nations addressed to the Secretary-General

[*Original:* Arabic]

I have the honour to transmit to you herewith the text of a letter addressed to you by Mr. Ibrahim M. Bishari, Secretary of the People's Committee for Foreign Liaison and International Cooperation.

> *(Signed)* Ali Ahmed HOUDEIRI
> Permanent Representative

Enclosure

Letter from the Secretary of the People's Committee for Foreign Liaison and International Cooperation of the Libyan Arab Jamahiriya addressed to the Secretary-General

Since the announcement of the presumed suspicion of two Libyan nationals in the matter of the regrettable incident involving Pan Am flight 103 – in which innocent people were victims and with regard to which, as before, I can only express the grief invoked in me by the incident and by the victims who died in it – the popular authorities in the Jamahiriya have taken the measures required in such cases by the law and by international covenants. The United Kingdom and the United States, however, submitted to the competent Libyan authorities requests for the extradition of the two Libyan nationals for the purpose of bringing them to trial themselves, and they have constantly insisted, despite the proposals made by the competent authorities in the Jamahiriya, on requesting extradition and nothing else, thereby overstepping the limits of our domestic law and international rules and customs.

As you know, the United Kingdom and the United States convened a meeting of the Security Council on the regrettable aircraft incident and succeeded in having the Council adopt a resolution urging the Jamahiriya to respond to their requests with regard to the relevant legal procedures. Following the adoption of the resolution, the Jamahiriya announced that it would respond in a manner in keeping with its sovereignty and the rule of law, and it took practical steps for the implementation of the resolution as it related to legal investigations.

In this connection, I should like to say that the Jamahiriya, a State Member of the United Nations, did not refuse extradition in itself. The domestic institutions of the Jamahiriya, however, whether administrative or judicial, were faced with a legal obstacle, namely that the Libyan law which has been in force for more than 30 years does not permit the extradition of Libyan nationals. This is a law which is fully in keeping with all the world's legal systems. The competent authorities in the Jamahiriya could find nothing that would enable them to respond to the requests made by these States other than by violating the law, and this is something that cannot be done in any civilised State which is a Member of the United Nations. It is this that is the obstacle, and it is, as you can see, a legal obstacle and not by any means a political one. The Libyan authorities cannot bypass this legal obstacle or violate the rights of citizens protected by the law.

You are aware that the United Kingdom and the United States are intimating that they are about to convene another meeting of the Security Council in order to seek the adoption of another resolution on the same matter. It goes without saying that the convening of such a meeting and the adoption of a resolution, whatever its character might be, will change nothing. The legal obstacle indicated above will remain as it is, and it cannot be altered by a decision of the Security Council, whether a recommendation or a binding resolution. It would be pointless to adopt such a resolution because of its futility and the impossibility of its implementation in light of the domestic law in force and of international rules and customs while the competent authorities proclaim that they have no objection to extradition or to trial in any locality.

I have sought to address this letter to you so that we may convey to you a picture of the legal situation as it really is. I should like to advise you, however, that the solution to this matter falls within the purview of the law and not elsewhere and that attempts to bypass the law, even by means of resolutions, binding or non-binding, would seem to be both unhelpful and unwarranted since there is no party that is deliberately raising objections. It is rather the law that has objections, and it is not rational to put pressure on the law by the adoption of resolutions by the Security Council or by any other body.

(Signed) Ibrahim M. BISHARI
Secretary of the People's Committee
for Foreign Liaison and International Cooperation

Appendix 5

Arab League Resolution 5161 (22 March 1992)

Resolution adopted by the Council of the League of Arab States at its Resumed Meeting at the Level of Ministers for Foreign Affairs Convened in Extraordinary Session on 22 March 1992

Threats to the Great Socialist People's Libyan Arab Jamahiriya

The Council of the League of Arab States, meeting in extraordinary session on 22 March 1992,

In conformity with the Pact of the League of Arab States and the covenants and treaties emanating therefrom and supplementary thereto,

Recalling its resolutions 5156, of 5 December 1991, and 5158, of 16 January 1992, affirming support for and solidarity with Libya in the matter of the American, British and French charges made against it,

Having regard for the principles of the United Nations and of the League of Arab States relating to the settlement of international conflicts by peaceful means and in a manner that does not place in jeopardy international peace and security, and particularly for the provisions of article 52 of the Charter of the United Nations,

Welcoming Libya's expression of its readiness to cooperate with the Secretary-General of the United Nations, as regards the legal aspects of Security Council resolution 731 (1992), in an impartial inquiry or an impartial or international tribunal,

Recalling the application submitted by Libya to the International Court of Justice on 3 March 1992,

Having reviewed the most recent developments relating to the incident of the United States Pan American aircraft and that of the French UTA aircraft and the persistence of the United States of America, the United Kingdom and France in escalating their campaign against the Libyan Arab Jamahiriya, decides:

1. To exercise its good offices at all levels for no threats to be directed against Libya and for an attempt to be made to solve the problem by peaceful means;

2.   To affirm its explicit condemnation of terrorism in all its forms, and to welcome the readiness expressed by Libya to cooperate in any international effort to eliminate this phenomenon;

3.   To renew its call to the Security Council to resolve the conflict through negotiations, mediation and a judicial settlement, in accordance with the stipulations of Chapter VI, Article 33, of the Charter of the United Nations;

4.   To urge the Security Council to avoid the adoption of any decision to take economic, military or diplomatic measures that might increase the complications and have an adverse impact on the region, to await a decision by the International Court of Justice on the case submitted to it on 3 March 1992 and to allow an opportunity for the efforts to be made by the committee established by the Council of the League;

5.   To establish a ministerial follow-up committee consisting of Algeria, Egypt, Libya, Mauritania, Morocco, Syria and the Secretary-General of the League to be entrusted with the task of establishing all necessary urgent contacts with the parties concerned, with the President of the Security Council, with the States members of the Council and with the Secretary-General of the United Nations with a view to seeking a solution to the crisis in accordance with the provisions of the Charter and the principles of international law;

6.   To consider the Council as being in continuous session, and to request the Secretary-General to follow up the implementation of this resolution and submit a report to the Council on developments in the situation.

Appendix 6

UN Security Council Resolution 748 (1992)

The Security Council this morning voted to impose aerial, arms and diplomatic sanctions against Libya on 15 April, until that Government complied with requests to cooperate fully in establishing responsibility for terrorist acts against Pan Am flight 103 and UTA flight 772.

Acting under Chapter VII of the Charter, the Council decided that, as of that date, all States must cut air links with Libya, except those based on humanitarian needs; prohibit the supply of parts or servicing to Libyan aircraft; prohibit the provision of arms-related material, advice or assistance to that country; significantly reduce the level of Libyan diplomatic representation in their territory; prevent the operation of all Libyan Arab Airlines offices; and deny entry to or expel Libyan nationals suspected of involvement in terrorist activities.

The Council took that action by adopting resolution 748 (1992), by a vote of 10 in favour to none against, with 5 abstentions (China, Cape Verde, India, Morocco and Zimbabwe).

The Council requested all States to report to the Secretary-General by 15 May on the measures they take in response to the resolution. It established a Committee of the Security Council to examine those reports, decide upon approval of humanitarian flights, consider information concerning violations of the resolution and recommend appropriate responses to such violations. The Council will review, every 120 days, the measures contained in the resolution.

Also by the resolution, the Council said the Libyan Government must commit itself definitively to cease all forms of terrorist action and all assistance to terrorist groups, and that it must promptly, by concrete actions, demonstrate its renunciation of terrorism.

Speaking before the adoption of the resolution, which was co-sponsored by France, the United Kingdom and the United States, Ali Ahmed Elhouderi (Libya) said his country had reaffirmed its readiness to cooperate with the Council in a manner that would not harm its sovereignty or violate international law. The current impasse was due to the refusal of attempts aimed at a neutral and fair investigation. He expressed concern that the rejection of all of Libya's initiatives and the efforts to smear his country's reputation were attempts to lead the way to further action against Libya.

Thomas R. Pickering (United States), one of the resolution's three co-sponsors, said the international community was sending clear signals that it was prepared to take concerted political action against the continuing defiance of international obligations and norms of behaviour represented by Libya's State-supported terrorism.

Sir David Hannay (United Kingdom) said the Council would be ready to respond positively in the event of Libyan compliance, adding that a verbal commitment to renounce terrorism would be inadequate, as such statements had been made in the past, 'yet the Libyan authorities, by their own admission, continued to give direct assistance to terrorists'.

Jean-Bernard Merimee (France) said the measures called for were selective and appropriate and did not target the Libyan people. He hoped the Libyan authorities would make proper use of the time left before the deadline of 15 April.

Also taking part in the Council's discussion were the representatives of Jordan, Mauritania, Iraq and Uganda, and the observer for the Organisation of the Islamic Conference.

The following Council members also explained their positions: Cape Verde, Ecuador, Zimbabwe, India, China, Morocco, Japan, Hungary, Austria, Russian Federation, Belgium and Venezuela.

SECURITY COUNCIL RESOLUTION 748 (1992)

Also before the Council is a draft resolution (document S/23762), sponsored by France, the United Kingdom and the United States, the text of which reads as follows:

'The Security Council,

'Reaffirming its resolution 731 (1992) of 21 January 1992,

'Noting the reports of the Secretary-General (S/23574) and (S/23672),

'Deeply concerned that the Libyan Government has still not provided a full and effective response to the requests in its resolution 731 (1992),

'Convinced that the suppression of acts of international terrorism, including those in which States are directly or indirectly involved, is essential for the maintenance of international peace and security,

'Recalling that in the statement issued on 31 January 1992 on the occasion of the meeting of the Security Council at the levels of Heads of State and Government the members of the Council expressed their deep concern over acts of international terrorism and emphasied the need for the international community to deal effectively with all such acts,

'Reaffirming that, in accordance with the Principle in Article 2, paragraph 4, of the Charter of the United Nations, every State has the duty to refrain from organising, instigating, assisting or participation in terrorist acts in another State of acquiescing in organised activities within its territory directed towards the commission of such acts, when such acts involve a threat or use of force,

'Determining in this contest that the failure by the Libyan Government to demonstrate, by concrete actions, its renunciation of terrorism, and in particular its continued failure to respond fully and effectively to the requests in resolution 731 (1992), constitute a threat to international peace and security,

'Determined to eliminate international terrorism,

'Recalling the right of States, under Article 50 of the Charter of the United Nations, to consult the Security Council where they find themselves confronted with special economic problems arising from the carrying out of preventive or enforcement measures,

'Acting under Chapter VII of the Charter of the United Nations,

'1. Decides that the Libyan Government must now comply without any further delay with paragraph 3 of resolution 731 (1992) of 21 January 1992 regarding the requests contained in documents S/23306, S/23308 and S/23309;

'2. Decides further that the Libyan Government must commit itself definitively to cease all forms of terrorist action and all assistance to terrorist groups, and that it must promptly, by concrete actions, demonstrate its renunciation of terrorism;

'3. Decides that on 15 April 1992 all States shall adopt the measures set out below, which shall apply until the Security Council decides that the Libyan Government has complied with paragraphs 1 and 2 above:

'4. Decides that all States shall:

'(a) Deny permission to any aircraft to take off from, land in or overfly their territory if it is destined to land in or has taken off from the territory of Libya, unless the particular flight has been approved on grounds of significant humanitarian need by the Committee established by paragraph 9 below; and

'(b) Prohibit, by their nationals or from their territory, the supply of any aircraft or aircraft components to Libya, the provision of engineering and maintenance servicing of Libyan aircraft or aircraft components, the certification of air-worthiness for Libyan aircraft, the payment of new claims against existing insurance contracts, and the provision of new direct insurance for Libyan aircraft;

'5. Decides further that all States shall:

'(a) Prohibit any provision to Libya by their nationals or from their territory of arms and related material of all types, including the sale or transfer of weapons and ammunition, military vehicles and equipment, paramilitary police equipment, and spare parts for the aforementioned, as well as the provision of any types of equipment, supplies and grants of licensing arrangements, for the manufacture or maintenance of the aforementioned;

'(b) Prohibit any provision to Libya by their nationals or from their territory of technical advice, assistance or training related to the provision, manufacture, maintenance, or use of the items in (a) above;

'(c) Withdraw any of their officials or agents present in Libya to advise the Libyan authorities on military matters;

'6.   Decides also that all States shall:

'(a) Significantly reduce the number and the level of the staff at Libyan diplomatic missions and consular posts and restrict or control the movement within their territory of all such staff who remain; in the case of Libyan missions to international organisations, the host State may, as it deems necessary, consult the organisation concerned on the measures required to implement this subparagraph;

'(b) Prevent the operation of all Libyan Arab Airlines offices;

'(c) Take all appropriate steps to deny entry to or expel Libyan nationals who have been denied entry to or expelled from other States because of their involvement in terrorist activities;

'7.   Calls upon all States, including States non-Members of the United Nations, and all international organisations to act strictly in accordance with the provisions of the present resolution notwithstanding the existence of any rights or obligations conferred or imposed by any international agreement or any contract entered into or any licence or permit granted before 15 April 1992;

'8.   Requests all States to report to the Secretary-General by 15 May 1992 on the measures they have instituted for meeting the obligations set out in paragraphs 3 to 7 above;

'9.   Decides to establish, in accordance with rule 28 of its provisional rules of procedure, a Committee of the Security Council consisting of all the members of the Council, to undertake the following tasks and to report on its work to the Council with its observations and recommendations:

'(a) To examine the reports submitted pursuant to paragraph 8 above;

'(b) To seek from all States further information regarding the action taken by them concerning the effective implementation of the measures imposed by paragraphs 3 to 7 above;

'(c) To consider any information brought to its attention by States concerning violations of the measures imposed by paragraphs 3 to 7 above, and in that context to make recommendations to the Council on ways to increase their effectiveness;

'(d) To recommend appropriate measures in response to violations of the measures imposed by paragraphs 3 to 7 above and provide information on a regular basis to the Secretary-General for general distribution to Member States;

'(e) To consider and to decide upon expeditiously any application by States for the approval of flights on grounds of significant humanitarian need in accordance with paragraph 4 above;

'(f) To give special attention to any communications in accordance with Article 50 of the Charter of the United Nations from any neighbouring or other States with special economic problems which might arise from the carrying out of the measures imposed by paragraphs 3 to 7 above;

'10. Calls upon all States to cooperate fully with the Committee in the fulfilment of its task, including supplying such information as may be sought by the Committee in pursuance of the present resolution;

'11. Requests the Secretary-General to provide all necessary assistance to the Committee and to make the necessary arrangements in the Secretariat for this purpose;

'12. Invites the Secretary-General to continue his role as set out in paragraph 4 of resolution 731 (1992);

'13. Decides that the Security Council shall every 120 days, or sooner should the situation so require, review the measures imposed by paragraphs 3 to 7 above in the light of the compliance by the Libyan Government with paragraphs 1 and 2 above, taking into account, as appropriate, any reports provided by the Secretary-General on his role as set out in paragraph 4 of resolution 731 (1992);

'14. Decides to remain seized of the matter.'

Appendix 7

UN Resolution on Independence of Libya (21 November 1949)

1   That Libya, comprising Cyrenaica, Tripolitania and the Fezzan, shall be constituted an independent and sovereign state;

2   That this independence shall become effective as soon as possible and in any case not later than January 1, 1952;

3   That a constitution for Libya, including the form of the government, shall be determined by representatives of the inhabitants of Cyrenaica, Tripolitania and Fezzan meeting and consulting together in a National Assembly;

4   That for the purpose of assisting the people of Libya in the formulation of the constitution and the establishment of an independent government, there shall be a United Nations Commissioner in Libya appointed by the General Assembly and a Council to aid and advise him;

5   That the United Nations Commissioner, in consultation with the Council, shall submit to the Secretary-General an annual report and such other special reports as he may consider necessary. To these reports shall be added any memorandum or documents that the United Nations Commissioner or a member of the Council may wish to bring to the attention of the United Nations;

6   That the Council shall consist of ten members, namely (a) One representative nominated by the government of each of the following countries: Egypt, France, Italy, Pakistan, the United Kingdom and the United States; (b) one representative of the people of each of the three regions of Libya and one representative of the minorities in Libya;

7   That the United Nations Commissioner shall appoint the representatives mentioned in paragraph 6(b), after consultation with the administrative powers, the representatives of the governments mentioned in paragraph 6(a), leading personalities and representatives of political parties and organisations in the territories concerned;

8   That, in discharge of his functions, the United Nations Commissioner shall consult and be guided by the advice of the members of his Council; it being understood that he may call upon different members to advise him in respect of different regions or different subjects;

9 . That the United Nations Commissioner may offer suggestions to the General Assembly, to the Economic and Social Council, and to the Secretary-General as to the measures that the United Nations might adopt during the transitional period regarding the economic and social problems of Libya;

10 That the administering powers in co-operation with the United Nations Commissioner: (a) Initiate immediately all necessary steps for the transfer of power to a duly constituted independent government; (b) Administer the territories for the purpose of assisting in the establishment of Libyan unity and independence, co-operate in the formation of governmental institutions and co-ordinate their activities to this end; (c) Make an annual report to the General Assembly on the steps taken to implement these recommendations;

11 That upon its establishment as an independent state, Libya shall be admitted to the United Nations in accordance with Article 4 of the Charter.

Appendix 8

Proclamation of the Libyan Republic on 1 September 1969

In the Name of God, the Compassionate, the Merciful, O great Libyan people: To execute your free will, to realise your precious aspirations, truly to answer your repeated call demanding change and purification, urging work and initiative, and eager for revolution and assault, your armed forces have destroyed the reactionary, backward, and decadent regime whose putrid odour assailed one's nose and the vision of whose attributes made one's eyes tremble. With one blow from your heroic army, the idols collapsed and the graven images shattered. In one terrible moment of fate, the darkness of ages – from the rule of the Turks to the tyranny of the Italians and the era of reaction, bribery and intercession, favouritism, treason and treachery – was dispersed. Thus, from now on Libya is deemed a free, sovereign republic under the name of the Libyan Republic – ascending with God's help to exalted heights, proceeding in the path of freedom, unity and social justice, guaranteeing the right of equality to its citizens, and opening before them the doors of honourable work – with none terrorised, none cheated, none oppressed, no master and no servant, but free brothers in the shadow of a society over which flutters, God willing, the banner of prosperity and equality. Extend your hands, open your hearts, forget your rancours, and stand together against the enemy of the Arab nation, the enemy of Islam, the enemy of humanity, who burned out holy places and shattered our honour. Thus we will build glory, revive our heritage, and revenge an honour wounded and a right usurped. O you who witness the holy war of Omar al-Mukhtar for Libya, Arabism, and Islam, O you who fought the good fight with Almad al-Sharif, O sons of the steppe, O sons of the desert, O sons of the ancient cities, O sons of the upright countryside, O sons of the villages – our beloved and beautiful villages – the hour of work has come. Forward.*

Middle East Journal, vol. 24, no. 2 (Spring 1970), from a set of translations of proclamations, statements, addresses, and interviews.

Appendix 9

Telegram sent by Gaddafi to World Leaders at New Year, 1975

The people of the earth, and even the angels of heaven have despaired of the meaningless exchange over hundreds of years of the greeting, 'Happy New Year!' Every ruler repeats this greeting, and yet goes on striving to make the year one of misfortune, rather than happiness. Can we, therefore, stop for a moment to ponder some verses of the scriptures: The Koran, the Torah, and the Gospels? The Koran says, 'Assist one another in works of righteousness and piety, and assist not one another in works of wrongdoing and transgression.' Let us remember how Christ reproached people because they forgot the Word of God, and instead gave themselves to conceit. He upbraided the priests for their neglect of God's word and for their greed. He reproached the scribes for spreading false teachings, and for abandoning the law of God. All this he declared in his first sermon which he preached in Jerusalem. Now because we are without a Christ to reproach the conceited, the greedy, those who propagate false teachings and those who oppose God's law, we must reproach one another for our sins. We must realise that we are far removed from the teachings of Christ, and are instead close to the teachings of Satan. The superpowers spend large sums on producing nuclear bombs and the development of intercontinental missiles. They are engaged in the conquest of space and the spread of propaganda and psychological warfare, while the rest of the people of the globe suffer the scourges of disease, hunger, and rocketing inflation. In reality, these nations are guided by Satan and his scriptures and by the theories of Marx, and not by any holy scripture. We are in great need of the teachings of Christ which would command us saying, 'Lift your hands from Palestine, the birthplace of Christ, peace be upon him, from Ireland, Southeast Asia and your colonies in Africa!' How greatly in need is the world today of Christ, in order that it may turn away from bars and from vain pleasures on every Christmas and New Year. People should instead turn to houses of worship to offer prayers, seek God's forgiveness and reflect upon His law.

With season's greetings.

Notes

Notes to Chapter 1: Lockerbie, Libya and the West

1. The Pentagon has drawn up a list of wars it may have to fight in the 1990s and beyond. It makes reference to possible Resurgent/Emergent Global Threats (REGTs) that may have to be combated and to possible 'war scenarios' that may have to be faced: see the report in, for example, *The Independent* (London), 18 February 1992. There is also the possibility that nuclear weapons will be targeted on Third World countries: see *The Sunday Times* (London), 9 February 1992.

2. I owe most of these details to David Leppard, *On the Trail of Terror: The Inside Story of the Lockerbie Investigation* (London: Jonathan Cape, 1991) Chapter 2; see also *The Times* (London), 23 December 1988.

3. David Blundy and Andrew Lycett, *Qaddafi and the Libyan Revolution* (London: Weidenfeld and Nicolson, 1987) p. 8.

4. *Ibid.*, p. 10.

5. *Ibid.*, p. 11.

6. Peter Pringle, 'View from Washington', in Kaldor and Anderson (eds), *Mad Dogs: The US Raids on Libya* (London: Pluto Press, 1986) p. 54.

7. Ian Mather and Farzad Bazoft, 'How Could It Happen?', *The Observer* (London), 10 July 1988.

8. *Ibid.*

9. Adrian Hamilton, *The Observer* (London), 10 July 1988.

10. *Ibid.*

11. Patrick Cockburn, 'US Ship Was in Iran Waters', *The Independent* (London), 12 December 1991.

12. *Ibid.*

13. *Private Eye* (London), 22 November 1991, p. 12, suggested that 'President Bush certainly takes the Scottish police, the Lord Advocate, the Foreign Secretary, and, with one or two exceptions, the entire British press for blithering idiots – and that he is absolutely right in that assessment'.

14. *Ibid.*

15. *Hansard*, 21 March 1989.

16. Jack Anderson and Dale Van Atta, *The Washington Post*, 11 January 1990.

17. Alfred W. McCloy, *The Politics of Heroin: CIA Complicity in the Global Drug Trade* (New York: Harper and Row, 1991).

18. *The Sunday Times* (London), 17 November 1991.

19. David Leppard, 'Lockerbie Trail Leads to Sweden', *The Sunday Times* (London), 12 November 1989; David Leppard describes the Lockerbie enquiry, *op. cit.*

20. David Leppard, 'Lockerbie Police Widen Net', *The Sunday Times* (London), 10 December 1989.

21. *Ibid.* The same report notes that relatives of the Lockerbie victims, dissatisfied with the course of the investigation, were considering taking the British

Government to the European Court of Human Rights; and that Cecil Parkinson, the then new transport minister, had turned down requests for a full enquiry.

22. Michael Evans, Thomas Prentice and Michael Binyon, 'Embassy Bulletin Told of Terror Plot', *The Times* (London), 23 December 1988.

23. David Leppard, 'Revealed: The Lockerbie Plot', *The Sunday Times* (London), 5 November 1989, pp. 1–2; Leppard, 'Lockerbie, the Tangled Trail', p. A15.

24. Additional reporting by John Cassidy (Washington), Marie Colvin (Tehran), and James Adams (London).

25. David Leppard and Nick Rufford, 'Police Close in on Lockerbie Killers', *The Sunday Times* (London), 17 December 1989; 'Lockerbie, the Final Reckoning', pp. A14–15.

26. Leppard (1991), *op. cit.*, p. 164.

27. *Ibid.*, p. 210.

28. Quoted by Leppard, *ibid.*, p. 212.

29. *Ibid.*, p. 212.

30. *Ibid.*, p. 213.

31. These five documents are referenced S/23306–9 and S/23317.

32. Dilip Hiro, *The Longest War* (London: Paladin, 1990) p. 73.

33. *Krasnaya Zvezda* (Red Star), 26 October 1980.

34. *The Daily Telegraph* (London), 19 January 1983.

35. Baghdad Radio, 19 January 1981.

36. Tripoli Radio, 9 October 1980.

37. Hiro, *op. cit.*, p. 119.

38. *Newsday*, 22 May 1984; quoted by Hiro, *ibid.*, p. 120.

39. These grievances, here neither endorsed nor disputed, cannot be explored in the present book. Useful accounts are given in Micah L. Sifry and Christopher Cerf (eds), *The Gulf War Reader: History, Documents, Opinions* (New York: Random House, 1991); Pierre Salinger with Eric Laurent, *Secret Dossier: The Hidden Agenda behind the Gulf War* (translation of *Guerre du Golfe: Le Dossier Secret*, Orban) (Harmondsworth: Penguin, 1991); Dilip Hiro, *Desert Shield to Desert Storm* (London: Paladin, 1992).

40. *The Washington Post*, 4 August 1990.

41. *Ibid.*, 18 January 1991.

42. *The Guardian* (London), 18 January 1991.

43. *The Washington Post*, 3 September 1990.

44. Adel Darwish and Gregory Alexander, *Unholy Babylon: The Secret History of Saddam's War* (London: Victor Gollancz, 1991) pp. 287–8.

45. The United States was now depicted as a world 'policeman' (or by some observers, e.g. Noam Chomsky, as a mafia don running a protection racket). Typical headlines: 'Sheriff of the Whole World's Posse' (*The Guardian*, London, 27 August 1991); 'Unrivalled Bush Set to Police the Planet' (*The Observer*, London, 25 August 1991).

46. John Cassidy and Garth Alexander, 'CIA Girds Itself to Repulse the "yellow peril"', *The Sunday Times* (London), 16 June 1991.

47. Andrew Stephen, *The Observer* (London), 9 February 1992.

48. Adrian Hamilton, *The Observer* (London), 3 November 1991.

49. Rupert Cornwell, 'Bush Considers Saudi Plan to Bomb Saddam', *The Independent* (London), 20 January 1992.

50. James Adams reports in *The Sunday Times* (London), 9 February 1992, of how MI6 is joining the CIA 'in secret war to topple Saddam': Bush 'wants Saddam out before the election in November'.

51. Noam Chomsky, *Deterring Democracy* (London: Verso, 1991) p. 3.

52. *American Policy vis-à-vis Vietnam*, Memorandum of Law prepared by Lawyers Committee on American Policy towards Vietnam, New York, inserted into the Congressional Record by Senators Wayne Morse (Oregon) and Ernest Gruening (Alaska) on 23 September 1965 (p. 42).

53. Daniel Patrick Moynihan, *A Dangerous Place* (New York: Little, Brown, 1978).

54. Associated Press, 20 December 1989

55. Leonard Doyle, 'UN Raises Stakes on Arms in Confrontation with Iraq', *The Independent* (London), 20 February 1992, p. 11.

56. Bob Woodward, *The Commanders* (New York: Simon and Schuster, 1991) pp. 333–4.

57. *Ibid.*, p. 334.

58. *The Independent* (London), 12 February 1981, p. 1.

59. Robert Fisk, 'US Withholds Death Toll from Red Cross', *The Independent* (London), 5 August 1991.

60. Victoria Brittain, 'Allies Accused of Violating War Laws', *The Guardian* (London), 18 November 1991.

61. In early 1992 the United States rejected a Syrian request, as a reward for its Middle East peace efforts, to be dropped from the US list of states which sponsor terrorism: see *The Guardian* (London), 17 February 1992.

62. *Le Monde*, 23 September 1991. Earlier claims as to Libya's involvement were published in *L'Express*, 27 June 1991, and in *Le Point*, 6 July 1991.

63. Judge Jean Louis Bruguière had worked on 'Action Direct' from 1981 to 1986, had conducted the investigation into the Eksund trawler arms shipment to the IRA, and had investigated the 1991 murder of the former Iranian premier Bakhtiar.

64. Simon Tisdall, *The Guardian* (London), 14 November 1991.

65. Duncan Campbell, Nikki Knewstub and Martin Walker, 'Libya Told to Give Up "bombers"', *The Guardian* (London), 15 November 1991.

66. Michael Sheridan, Rupert Cornwell, David Black and Annika Savill, 'Libya Blamed for Lockerbie', *The Independent* (London), 15 November 1991, p. 1.

67. *Ibid.*

68. Tim Kelsey, 'Relatives Greet Decision with Mixed Emotions', *The Independent* (London), 15 November 1991, p. 2.

69. *Ibid.*

70. Nicholas Wapshott and Patrick Brogan, 'Allies Prepare Libya Sanctions', *The Observer* (London), 17 November 1991.

71. *Ibid.*

72. James Adams, David Leppard, David Hughes and Nick Rufford, 'Lockerbie Suspects Boasted about Plot', *The Sunday Times* (London), 17 November 1991.

73. Ian Black and Richard Norton-Taylor, *The Guardian* (London), 19 November 1991.

74. Quoted by David Hirst, 'Reprisal Plan for Lockerbie Divides Arabs', *The Guardian* (London), 21 November 1991.

75. *Ibid.*
76. *Ibid.*
77. *Ibid.*
78. Annika Savill, 'The Demands Facing Libya', *The Independent* (London), 27 November 1991.
79. *Ibid.*
80. Carol Berger, 'Gaddafi Attempts to Avert US Action', *The Independent* (London), 29 November 1991.
81. Adrian Porter and Con Coughlin, 'US Planes in Dry Run to Bomb Libya', *The Sunday Telegraph* (London), 1 December 1991.
82. Deborah Pugh, 'Libya Says It Holds Two Over Lockerbie', *The Guardian* (London), 5 December 1991.
83. Sarah Helm and Safa Haeri, 'West and Libya Reaching Stalemate over Lockerbie', *The Independent* (London), 6 December 1991.
84. Pierre Salinger, 'Accused Libyans Deny Any Role in Lockerbie Bombing', *The Guardian* (London), 7 December 1991.
85. 'Dismay over Support for Libya', *The Independent* (London), 7 December 1991.
86. John Mullin, 'American Anger at Visit to Gadafy', *The Guardian* (London), 14 December 1991.
87. Reuter Report, *The Independent* (London), 13 December 1991.
88. David Connett, 'Libya to Seek Out Jet Bomb Evidence', *The Independent* (London), 14 December 1991.
89. Leonard Doyle, 'Britain to Seek International Ban on Flights to Libya', *The Independent* (London), 19 December 1991.
90. David Pallister, 'Gadafy Makes Trial Offer', *The Guardian* (London), 28 December 1991.
91. Douglas Hurd, 'Making the World a Safer Place: Our Five Priorities', *The Daily Telegraph* (London), 1 January 1992.
92. Douglas Hurd, 'Little Peace for the Peacekeeper', *The Guardian* (London), 13 January 1991.
93. *Hansard*, 20 January 1992, pp. 153–62.
94. Ian Williams, *Tribune* (London), 17 January 1992.
95. *Ibid.*
96. *Ibid.*
97. Richard Norton-Taylor, 'Lockerbie Report Implicates Syria', *The Guardian* (London), 21 January 1992.
98. Marc Weller, 'Lockerbie, the Law and Power Politics', *The Independent* (London), 24 January 1992.
99. Leonard Doyle, 'UN to Demand Lockerbie Suspects', *The Independent* (London), 21 January 1992.
100. Weller, *op. cit.*
101. Jane Rosen, 'UN Demands Pan Am Suspects', *The Guardian* (London), 22 January 1992.
102. Donald Trelford, 'Gaddafi Bids to Do a Deal with the West', *The Observer* (London), 26 January 1992.
103. Annika Savill, 'Libya Denies Killing of Lockerbie Suspects', *The Independent* (London), 12 February 1992.
104. *Ibid.*

105. *Ibid.*
106. BBC Radio, 11 February 1992.
107. ITN Television, *News at Ten*, 14 February 1992.
108. *The Independent* (London), 15 February 1992.
109. David Hirst, 'Judge Rules Out Extradition of Libyan Lockerbie Suspects', *The Guardian* (London), 19 February 1992.
110. Patrick Lockburn, 'Extradition Demand "bolstering Gaddafi"', *The Independent* (London), 21 February 1992.
111. *Ibid.*
112. Marie Colvin, 'PLO Links Iran with Lockerbie', *The Sunday Times* (London), 23 February 1992.
113. Wafr Amr, 'PLO Says It Can Prove Libya Not to Blame for Lockerbie Bomb', *The Guardian* (London), 17 February 1992.
114. Marie Colvin, David Leppard and Safa Haeri, 'Hitmen Hunt Lockerbie "supergrass"', *The Sunday Times* (London), 1 March 1992.
115. *Le Figaro* (Paris), 24 February 1992.
116. Deborah Pugh, 'Mubarak Seeks Neutral Venue for Lockerbie Trial', *The Guardian* (London), 25 February 1992.
117. Julian Nundy, 'Mubarak Denies Lockerbie Mediation', *The Independent* (London), 27 February 1992.
118. Marie Colvin, David Leppard and Safa Haeri, 'Hitmen Hunt Lockerbie "supergrass"', *The Sunday Times* (London), 1 March 1992.
119. *Ibid.*
120. Susan Morgan, 'Fundamentalists Wait in the Wings as US Targets Gaddafi', *The Observer* (London), 1 March 1992.
121. Deborah Pugh, 'Libya Offers Deal on Suspects', *The Guardian* (London), 2 March 1992.
122. Saad Muhber, 'Guilty Till Judged Guilty', *The Guardian* (London), 4 March 1992.
123. Patrick Cockburn, 'Libya Wins Friends and Influences People', *The Independent* (London), 5 March 1992.
124. *Ibid.*
125. Leonard Doyle, 'Ghali Finds Merit in Tripoli Shift', *The Independent* (London), 5 March 1992.
126. Tony Walker, Mark Nicholson and Michael Littlejohns, 'Libya Shifts Assets from Europe', *Financial Times* (London), 5 March 1992; see also Tony Walker and Mark Nicholson, 'Much of Libya's Money Has Long Been on the Move', *Financial Times* (London), 6 March 1992.
127. Martin Walker, 'Gulf Alliance Eyeing Iraq's Foreign Assets', *The Guardian* (London), 6 March 1992.
128. Quoted in Patrick Cockburn, 'Nasser's Friend Voices Arab Humiliation', *The Independent* (London), 11 March 1992.
129. Hella Pick, 'Britain Advises Nationals to Quit Libya as UN Acts', *The Guardian* (London), 18 March 1992.
130. Robin Oakley, 'Why I Know We Will Beat Labour', *The Times* (London), 20 March 1992.
131. 'Libya Says Islamic States Weigh Pullout from UN', *International Herald Tribune* (New York), 21–2 March 1992 (*source:* Reuter, AFP).

132. 'Arab League Role Proposed in Handover of Lockerbie Two', *The Guardian* (London), 23 March 1992 (*source:* Reuter).

133. Hella Pick, 'Libya to Hand Lockerbie Suspects to Arab League', *The Guardian* (London), 24 March 1992.

134. *Ibid.*

135. Leonard Doyle and Carol Berger, 'Libya Agrees to Hand Over Accused Men', *The Independent* (London), 24 March 1992.

136. Patrick Cockburn and Leonard Doyle, 'UN Hands Libya an Ultimatum on Suspects', *The Independent* (London), 25 March 1992.

137. Patrick Cockburn, 'Tripoli Hardens Stance on Lockerbie Suspects', *The Independent* (London), 26 March 1992.

138. Sarah Lambert, 'Libya "will not bow to blackmail"', *The Independent* (London), 27 March 1992.

139. Leonard Doyle and Sarah Lambert, 'US Tells China to Back Libya Vote or Pay the Price', *The Independent* (London), 28 March 1992; see also 'China Gets Warning on Libya Sanctions', *The Guardian* (London), 30 March 1992.

140. Leonard Doyle, 'UN Votes to Impose Sanctions on Libya', *The Independent* (London), 1 April 1992.

141. Patrick Cockburn, 'Gaddafi Seems Ready to Turn and Fight Back', *The Independent* (London), 4 April 1992.

142. Michael Simmons, 'Security Council Envoy Will Discuss Embassy Damage', *The Guardian* (London), 4 April 1992.

143. Julie Flint, 'Gadaffi Raises Islamic Banner', *The Observer* (London), 5 April 1992.

144. *Ibid.*

145. Simon Tisdall and Deborah Pugh, 'Arafat Comes Out of Own Desert Storm', *The Guardian* (London), 9 April 1992.

146. Nick Rufford, Tim Raymont, David Leppard and Ian Burreli, 'Gadaffi Builds Huge Poison Gas Arsenal at Rabta Plant', *The Sunday Times* (London), 5 April 1992.

147. R. Barry O'Brien, 'Malta Will Accept Lockerbie Bomb Suspects for Trial', *The Daily Telegraph* (London), 15 April 1992.

148. Tom Walker and Michael Binyon, 'World Court Rules Against Libya', *The Times* (London), 15 April 1992.

149. Carol Berger, 'Egypt Offers a Way Through UN Sanctions', *The Independent* (London), 15 April 1992.

150. Geoffrey Robertson, 'Jury Out on Terror Trials', *The Guardian* (London), 30 March 1992.

151. Marc Weller, 'Double Standards at the UN', *New Law Journal*, 13 March 1992, pp. 360–1.

152. 'Sanctions Send Signals' (editorial), *The Independent* (London), 16 April 1992.

153. Charles Richards, 'Hurd Defends Flight Ban', *The Independent* (London), 20 August 1992.

154. Kathy Evans and Richard Norton-Taylor, 'Spain checks Syrian link to Lockerbie', *The Guardian* (London), 6 June 1992.

155. 'German Doubts Over Lockerbie', *The Independent* (London), 20 June 1992.

156. James Adams and Marie Colvin, 'Libya Blows the Whistle on IRA', *The Sunday Times* (London), 14 June 1992.

157. David Usborne, 'US Judges Uphold Right to Snatch Suspects Abroad', *The Independent* (London), 16 June 1992.
158. An extract from this memorandum is given in *Third World Resurgence*, no. 21, May 1992, p. 28.
159. Marc Weller, 'The Lockerbie Case: A Premature End to the "New World Order"?', *African Journal of International and Comparative Law*, no. 4, 1992, pp 1–15.

Notes to Chapter 2: The Libyan Past

1. Gustave Glotz, *The Aegean Civilisation* (London: Routledge and Kegan Paul) p. 57.
2. John Wright, *Libya* (London: Ernest Benn, 1969) p. 30.
3. *Ibid.*, p. 34.
4. Herodotus, *The Histories*, trans. Aubrey de Selincourt (Penguin Classic edition) first published in 1954. Most of the quotations are from Book IV.
5. Charles Daniels, *The Garamantes of Southern Libya* (Harrow: Cleander Press, 1970) p. 20.
6. Ruth First, *Libya: The Elusive Revolution* (Harmondsworth: Penguin, 1974) p. 33.
7. Daniels, *op. cit.*, p. 23.
8. Wright, *op. cit.*, p. 55.
9. *Ibid.*, p. 70.
10. John K. Cooley, *Baal, Christ and Mohammed: Religion and Revolution in North Africa* (New York: Holt, Rinehart and Winston, 1965) pp. 73–9.
11. John Bagot Glubb, *A Short History of the Arab Peoples* (London: Quartet Books, 1978) p. 135.
12. B. G. Martin, 'Kanem, Bornu and the Fezzan: Notes on the Political History of a Trade Route', *Journal of African History*, vol. X, no. 1 (1969) pp. 15–27.
13. Glubb, *op. cit.*, p. 251.
14. Nicola A. Ziadeh, *Sanusiyah: A Study of a Revivalist Movement in Islam* (Leiden: E. J. Brill, 1958) p. 46.
15. H. A. R. Gibb, *Mohammedanism* (London: Oxford University Press, 1949) p. 13.
16. E. E. Evans-Pritchard, *The Sanusi of Cyrenaica* (Oxford: Oxford University Press, 1949).
17. Public Record Office, WO, 18 January 1903, 'Notes on the History of the Sanusi', note by Colonel Count Gleichan, Dir., Intelligence, Egyptian Army.
18. Gentil Lamotte, *Revue de Cercle Militaire* (1902) p. 12, quoted in Cooley, *op. cit.*, p. 180.
19. Peter Mansfield, *Nasser's Egypt* (Harmondsworth: Penguin, 1965) p. 13.
20. H. J. Rose, *A Handbook of Greek Literature* (London: Methuen, 4th rev. edn, 1964) p. 300.

Notes to Chapter 3: The Fourth Shore

1. John Wright, *Libya* (London: Ernest Benn, 1969) p. 122.

2. Enzo Santarelli, in Enzo Santarelli, Giorgio Rochat, Romain Rainero and Luigi Goglia, *Omar al-Mukhtar: The Italian Reconquest of Libya*, trans. John Gilbert (London: Darf Publishing, 1986) p. 25.
3. Francesco Malgeri, *La Guerra Libica, 1911–1912* (Rome, 1970) p. 95.
4. Giorgio Rochat, *Il Colonialismo Italiano* (Turin, 1973) p. 30.
5. Luigi Ganapini, *Il Nazionalismo Cattolico* (Bari, 1970) chapter IV.
6. Wright, *op. cit.*, p. 122.
7. *Ibid.*, p. 124.
8. Ninetta Jucker, *Italy* (London: Thames and Hudson, 1970) p. 47.
9. Quoted in John K. Cooley, *Libyan Sandstorm* (New York: Holt, Rinehart and Winston, 1982) p. 32.
10. Public Record Office, WO, 106/1532, Intelligence Department, War Office, Cairo, 11 October 1913.
11. Public Record Office, WO, 106/1553.
12. Adrian Pelt, *Libyan Independence and the United Nations: A Case of Planned Decolonisation* (New Haven: Yale University Press, Carnegie Endowment for International Peace, 1970) pp. 3–8.
13. E. E. Evans-Pritchard, *The Sanusi of Cyrenaica* (Oxford: Oxford University Press, 1949) p. 155.
14. Wright, *op. cit.*, p. 140.
15. *Ibid.*, p. 142.
16. Benito Mussolini, 'Il solito ricatto', *Il Popolo d'Italia*, 23 March 1919.
17. Santarelli, in Enzo Santarelli *et al.*, *op. cit.*, p. 16.
18. Vittorio Scialoja, *I Problemi dello Stato Italiano Dopa la Guerra* (Bologna, 1918) pp. 296, 299.
19. Wright, *op. cit.*, p. 149.
20. Giuseppe Volpi, *La Rinascita della Tripolitania* (Milan, 1926).
21. John Wright, 'Libya: Italy's Promised Land', in Joffe and McLachlan (eds), *Social and Economic Development in Libya* (1982), quoted by Jonathan Bearman, *Qadhafi's Libya* (London: Zed Books, 1986) p. 15.
22. *Jamahiriya International Report*, quoted in Countries of Italian Colonisation, vol. 2, no. 14, pp. 6–7, quoted by Bearman, *ibid.*, p. 15.
23. Wright, *op. cit.*, p. 154.
24. *Ibid.*, p. 157.
25. Clemente Menzio, *Dieci Anni di Storia Cirenaica*, a typewritten account for the command of the royal corps of colonial troops in Cyrenaica, 25 December 1931; source used by Evans-Pritchard, *op. cit.*, p. 159, and by Rochat, in Santarelli *et al.*, *op. cit.*, p. 41.
26. *Ibid.*
27. Evans-Pritchard, *op. cit.*, pp. 159–60.
28. Menzio, *op. cit.*
29. Quoted by Rochat, in Santarelli *et al.*, *op. cit.*, p. 43.
30. *Ibid.*, p. 45.
31. Menzio, *op. cit.*
32. Santarelli *et al.*, *op. cit.*, p. 48.
33. *Notiziario*, 3 March 1928.
34. *Notiziario*, 7 April 1928.
35. *Notiziario*, 30 June 1928.
36. Quoted by Wright, *op. cit.*, p. 160.

37. Quoted by Rochat, in Santarelli *et al.*, *op. cit.*, p. 69.
38. This phase is well described in Evans-Pritchard, *op. cit.*, pp. 159–73; and in Wright, *op. cit.*, pp. 164–8.
39. Wright, *ibid.*, p. 165.
40. Knud Holmboe, *Desert Encounter: An Adventurous Journey through Italian Africa* (London: Harrap, 1936).
41. *Ibid.*, p. 203.
42. Quoted by Rochat, in Santarelli *et al.*, *op. cit.*, p. 73.
43. Pietro Badoglio, quoted by Rochat, in Santarelli *et al.*, *op. cit.*, p. 76.
44. Rodolfo Graziani, quoted by Rochat, *ibid.*, p. 78.
45. Quoted by Wright, *op. cit.*, p. 166.
46. Badoglio, quoted by Rochat, in Santarelli *et al.*, *op. cit.*, p. 92.
47. Emilio De Bono, quoted by Rochat, *ibid.*, p. 92.
48. Romain Rainero, in Santarelli *et al.*, *ibid.*, p. 145.
49. Giuseppe Bendendo, *Le Gesta e la Politica del Generale Graziani* (Rome, 1936).
50. Rainero, in Santarelli *et al.*, *op. cit.*, p. 146.
51. Rainero includes in Santarelli *et al.*, *ibid.*, as appendices the secret proceedings in the trial at Benghazi, 15 September 1931 (comprising the interrogation of Mukhtar, the typewritten account of the hearing against him, the record of the hearing, and the list of charges); and the clandestine manifesto of the Cyrenaican resistance celebrating the first anniversary of Mukhtar's execution.
52 Quoted by Wright, *op. cit.*, p. 167.
53. Emilio De Bono, quoted by Rainero, in Santarelli *et. al.*, *op. cit.*, p. 150.
54. Chekib Arslan, 'Omar al-Mukhtar', in *el Djihad*, 10 October 1931.
55. Martin Moore, *Fourth Shore: Italy's Mass Colonisation of Libya* (London: Routledge, 1940) p. 132.
56. *Ibid.*, pp. 216–17, 221.
57. G. L. Fowler, 'The Role of Private Estates and Development Companies in the Italian Agricultural Colonisation of Libya', in Joffe and McLachlan (eds), *Social and Economic Development in Libya* (1982).
58. Adrian Pelt, *The United Kingdom of Libya from Colony to Independent State*, UN Bulletin, 15 February 1952.
59. Quoted by Wright, *op. cit.*, p.180.
60. Christopher Hibbert, *Benito Mussolini* (London, 1962) p. 95.
61. See also Richard Griffiths, *Fellow Travellers of the Right* (Oxford University Press, 1983) for details of British support for Mussolini and Hitler.
62. William L. Shirer, *Berlin Diary* (London, 1941).
63. Quoted in Adrian Pelt, *op. cit.*, (1970) p. 41.
64. The ensuing events are well described by Roger Parkinson, *The Desert War* (London: Hart-Davis, MacGibbon, 1976).
65. Alan Moorehead, *African Trilogy (Mediterranean Front – A Year of Battle – The End in Africa)* (London: Hamish Hamilton, 1944).
66. J. F. C. Fuller, *The Second World War* (London, 1948).
67. Denti di Pirajno, *A Cure for Serpents (A Doctor in Africa)* (London: André Deutsch, 1955) p. 250, quoted by Wright, *op. cit.*, p.187.
68. Lillian Haig Harris, *Libya, Qadhafi's Revolution and the Modern State* (London: Croom Helm, 1986).

69. Paper presented by the Institute of Diplomatic Studies to a Geneva-based seminar on 'War Remnants in Libya', May 1981.

Notes to Chapter 4: From Idris to Gaddafi

1. Majid Khadduri, *Modern Libya: A Study in Political Development* (Baltimore, Md: John Hopkins, Press, 1963) p. 33.
2. *Ibid.*, p. 61.
3. John Wright, *Libya* (London: Ernest Benn, 1969) p. 191.
4. Henry Serrano Villard, *Libya: The New Arab Kingdom of North Africa* (New York: Cornell University Press, 1956) p. 24.
5. *Ibid.*, p. 24.
6. Ruth First, *Libya: The Elusive Revolution* (New York: Africa Publishing Co. 1975) p. 62.
7. C. Grove Haines, 'The Problem of the Italian Colonies', *Middle East Journal* vol. 1, no. 4 (October 1947) pp. 417–31.
8. Villard, *op. cit.*, p. 24.
9. John Lindberg, *General Economic Appraisal of Libya* (New York: United Nations, 1952) p. 32.
10. Quoted by Wright, *op. cit.*, p. 204.
11. Official Records, General Assembly, Fourth Session, First Committee, 278th Meeting, 30 September 1949, p. 20.
12. First, *op. cit.*, p. 69.
13. Adrian Pelt, *Libyan Independence and the United Nations: A Case of Planned Decolonisation* (New Haven: Yale University Press, Carnegie Endowment for International Peace, 1970) p. 128.
14. *Ibid.*, p. 168.
15. Adrian Pelt, in Official Records of the UN General Assembly, Fifth Session, 1950, vol. 1, pp. 411–12.
16. First, *op. cit.*, p. 73.
17. Wright, *op. cit.*, p. 212.
18. Quoted by Wright, *ibid.*, p. 226.
19. Quoted by Wright, *ibid.*, p. 227.
20. First, *op. cit.*, p. 74.
21. *Ibid.*, p. 76.
22. Villard, *op. cit.*, p. 44.
23. Robert C. Doty, *New York Times*, 13 February 1954.
24. John Gunther, *Inside Africa* (London: Hamish Hamilton, 1955) p. 167.
25. Khadduri, *op. cit.*, pp. 240–3.
26. This episode is well described in Wright, *op cit.*, pp. 230–1.
27. Richard Carrington, *East from Tunis: A Record of Travels on the Northern Coast of Africa* (London: Chatto and Windus, 1957).
28. Gunther, *op. cit.*, p. 169.
29. 'Dangers of Tribal Unrest in Libya', *The Times* (London), 21 October 1954.
30. Gunther, *op. cit.*, p. 171.
31. Wright, *op. cit.*, p. 231.
32. First, *op. cit.*, p. 81.
33. *Hansard*, 2 August 1956.

34. Egypt Committee, Cabinet Minute, *Action against Egypt*, 7 August 1956, HMA.
35. Wright, *op. cit.*, p. 239.
36. Quoted by Jonathan Bearman, *Qadhafi's Libya* (London: Zed Books, 1986) p. 26.
37. Bearman, *ibid.*, p. 26.
38. Wright, *op. cit.*, pp. 239–40.
39. First, *op. cit.*, pp. 84–5.
40. R. F. Harrison, 'Migrants in the City of Tripoli, Libya', *Geographical Review*, vol. LVII (1967).
41. Hadi M. Bulugna, *Benghazi through the Ages* (London, 1972).
42. Recommendations quoted in J. A. Allan, K. McLachlan and E. Penrose (eds), *Libya: Agriculture and Economic Development* (London: Frank Cass, 1973).
43. Quoted by Bearman, *op. cit.*, p. 48.
44. Ronald Segal, *African Profiles* (Harmondsworth: Penguin, 1962) p. 383.
45. Stephen E. Ambrose, *Rise to Globalism: American Foreign Policy since 1938*, 5th rev. edn (Harmondsworth: Penguin, 1988) pp. 126–7.
46. Quoted by Kwame Nkrumah, *Neo-Colonialism: The Last Stage of Imperialism* (London: Nelson, 1965).
47. Denis Healey, *The Time of My Life* (London: Michael Joseph, 1989) p. 322.
48. David Blundy and Andrew Lycett, *Qaddafi and the Libyan Revolution* (London: Weidenfeld and Nicolson, 1987) p. 57.
49. This section is largely based on Blundy and Lycett, *ibid.*, pp. 33–56.
50. *Ibid.*, p. 42.
51. *Ibid.*, p. 44.
52. *Ibid.*, p. 45.
53. *Ibid.*, p. 48.
54. Quoted by John K. Cooley, *Libyan Sandstorm* (New York: Holt, Rinehart and Winston, 1982) pp. 15–16.
55. Frederick Muscat, *My President, My Son* (Malta: Adam Publishers, 1974) p. 99.
56. The text of Communiqué One is included in Mirella Bianco, *Gadhafi: Voice from the Desert* (London: Longman, 1975) pp. 67–8.
57. Quoted by Blundy and Lycett, *op. cit.*, p. 60.
58. *Ibid.*, p. 61.

Notes to Chapter 5: The Oil Factor

1. John Gunther, *Inside Africa* (London: Hamish Hamilton, 1955) p. 179.
2. Ruth First, *Libya: The Elusive Revolution* (New York: Africa Publishing Co., 1975) p. 141.
3. John Wright, *Libya* (London: Ernest Benn, 1969) p. 268.
4. *Ibid.*, p. 269.
5. John Davis, *Libyan Politics, Tribe and Revolution* (London: I. B. Tauris, 1987) pp. 15–19, and Appendix 1, 'On Hydrocarbon Society', pp. 261–3.
6. J. A. Allan, *Libya: The Experience of Oil* (London: Croom Helm, 1981) p. 24.
7. *Ibid.*, p. 24.

8. Peter R. Odell, *Oil and World Power: Background to the Oil Crisis* (Harmondsworth: Penguin, England, 1970) p. 92.

9. Mana Saeed al-Otaiba, *OPEC and the Petroleum Industry* (New York: John Wiley, 1975) p. 25.

10. Wright, *op. cit.*, p. 246.

11. *Ibid.*, p. 246.

12. *Esso in Libya* (Tripoli: Esso Standard Libya Inc., 1965).

13. Wright, *op. cit.*, p. 248.

14. First, *op. cit.*, pp. 190–1.

15. Wanda M. Jaclobski, 'Libya's Oil Pricing and Tax Dilemma', *Petroleum Intelligence Weekly*, 19 April 1965, pp. 6–9.

16. *Petroleum Intelligence Weekly*, 13 September 1965.

17. *Ibid.*, 28 February 1966.

18. *Oil and Gas Journal*, 5 December 1966.

19. Wright, *op. cit.*, p. 252.

20. *Petroleum Intelligence Weekly*, 9 January 1967.

21. Nasser reached a bargain with the Arab oil states – Kuwait, Saudi Arabia and Libya – whereby all pressure on them to continue their boycott of Britain and the US would be lifted if suitable payments (Kuwait £55 million, Saudi Arabia £50 million, and Libya £30 million) were made to Egypt and Jordan (who would receive respectively £95 million and £40 million) to remove 'the traces of aggression' (i.e. to compensate for lost Suez Canal revenues): see Peter Mansfield, *Nasser's Egypt* (Harmondsworth: Penguin, rev. edn, 1969) p. 85.

22. A detailed analysis of the impact of oil revenues on the Libyan economy is given in Allan, *op. cit.*, esp. Chapters 4, 5 and 8.

23. First, *op. cit.*, p. 199.

24. Oasis internal memorandum, September/October 1969.

25. Anthony Sampson, *The Seven Sisters* (London: Hodder and Stoughton, 1975) p. 214.

26. Abdul Amir Kubbah, *OPEC Past and Present* (Vienna), September 1974, p. 54.

27. Sampson, *op. cit.*, p. 216.

28. *Ibid.*, p. 217.

29. Described in detail in Sampson, *ibid.*, Chapters 10 and 11.

30. *Ibid.*, p. 248.

31. Ian Seymour, *New York Times*, 7 October 1973, quoted by Sampson, *ibid.*, p. 248.

32. Richard J. Barnet, *The Lean Years: Politics in the Age of Scarcity* (London: Abacus, 1981) p. 43.

33. John K. Cooley, *Libyan Sandstorm* (New York: Holt, Rinehart and Winston, 1982) p. 53.

34. *Ibid.*, p. 53.

35. Wilbur Eveland, *Ropes of Sand: America's Failure in the Middle East* (New York: Norton, 1980).

36. Christopher Rand, *Making Democracy Safe for Oil: Oilmen and the Islamic East* (Boston, Mass.: Atlantic–Little, Brown, 1975) p. 251.

37. A subsequent Hammer plan for a fertiliser plant was agreed with the Soviet

Union, but this scheme was interrupted when President Carter blocked agricultural exports to the Soviet Union in retaliation for the Soviet invasion of Afghanistan. Libya never got its promised Hammer fertiliser plant.

38. Rand, *op. cit.*, p. 254.
39. David Newsome, *Multinational Report* (1975) p. 99; quoted by Sampson, *op. cit.*, p. 211.
40. Stanley Penn, *Wall Street Journal*, 8 February 1972, p. 1.
41. Cooley, *op. cit.*, pp. 55–6.
42. *New York Times*, 11 December 1974.
43. Hammer describes his Libyan experiences (and many others) in Armand Hammer with Neil Lyndon, *Hammer: Witness to History* (New York: Simon and Schuster, 1987).
44. *Ibid.*, p. 449.
45. *Ibid.*, p. 465.
46. *Ibid.*, p. 475.
47. Quoted in Ewan W. Anderson and Khalil H. Rashidian, *Iraq and the Continuous Middle East Crisis* (London: Pinter, 1991) p. 55.
48. *Petroleum Economist* (Beirut), vol. 42, no. 8 (August 1975).
49. Martin Walker, *The Guardian* (London), 4 January 1992.

Notes to Chapter 6: Libyan Revolution

1. *al-Sijill al-Qawmi* (writings, speeches and pronouncements of Muammar al-Gaddafi, appearing in yearly volumes under various auspices), vol. 8 (1976–7) p. 89.
2. Jonathan Bearman, 'The Formation and Character of the Contemporary Libyan State', paper presented at the BRISMES Annual Conference, 12–15 July 1987, p. 1.
3. Meredith O. Ansell and Ibrahim Assoud al-Arif, *The Libyan Revolution: A Sourcebook of Legal and Historical Documents*, vol. 1 (September 1969/ August 1970) (London: Oleander Press, 1972).
4. Ruth First, *Libya: The Elusive Revolution* (New York: African Publishing Co., 1975) p. 132.
5. R. F. Nyrop, *Libya: A Country Profile – An Area Handbook for Libya* (Washington: The American University, 1979) p. 199.
6. Muammar al-Gaddafi, *The Green Book*, English edition (Ministry of Information, Tripoli, Libya, 1979) p. 47.
7. *Ibid.*, p. 65.
8. P. Enahoro, 'Heart to Heart with Qadhafi', *New African*, February 1983, pp. 37–46.
9. Bearman, *op cit.*, p. 8.
10. Muammar al-Gaddafi, 'Democracy in Industry', address delivered to a rally on International Workers' Day, 1 May 1978, Arab Dawn Essays, *Arab Dawn* (London, 1978).
11. John Davis, *Libyan Politics, Tribe and Revolution* (London: I. B. Tauris, 1987) p. 258.
12. An 'official history' of the background, planning and execution of the Libyan revolution appeared in Libyan newspapers in serialised instalments in Sep-

tember 1969 and over the next two years; also articles in Tripoli's *al-Yawm*, 5 September 1969; Gadaffi's interview with Egyptian television reported in Libyan newspapers of 15 October 1969; and his interview with the Sudanese *al-Ayyam* reported in Tripoli's *al-Ra'id*, 26 September 1969 and 6 December 1969.

13. Mirella Bianco, *Gadafi: Voice from the Desert*, trans. Margaret Lyle (London: Longman, published in arrangement with Éditions Stock, Paris, 1975) pp. 90–1.
14. *Ibid.*, p. 92.
15. David Blundy and Andrew Lycett, *Qaddafi and the Libyan Revolution* (London: Weidenfeld and Nicolson, 1987) p. 86.
16. *Ibid.*, p. 92.
17. Ansell and al-Arif, *op. cit.*, pp. 113–14.
18. John K. Cooley, *Libyan Sandstorm* (New York: Holt, Rinehart and Winston, 1982) p. 99.
19. Jonathan Bearman, *Qadhafi's Libya* (London: Zed Books, 1986) p. 71.
20. *Ibid.*, p. 72.
21. J. A. Allan, *Libya: the Experience of Oil* (London: Croom Helm, 1981) p. 223.
22. *JIR*, vol. 1, no. 9 (3 September 1982); see also *The Al-Fateh Revolution: Ten Years On* (Tripoli: Secretariat of Information, 1979); and *Facts and Figures* (Tripoli: Secretariat of Information, 1979).
23. Bearman (1986), *op. cit.*, p. 75.
24. Allan, *op. cit.*, p. 229.
25. *Ibid.*, p. 229.
26. *Muammar al-Gaddafi* (Tripoli: Secretariat of Information, 1979) p. 45.
27. *Arab Report and Record*, no. 17 (1–15 September 1969) p. 364.
28. Frank Waddams, *The Libyan Oil Industry* (London, 1980) p. 251.
29. Bearman (1986), *op. cit.*, p. 90.
30. Allan, *op. cit.*, p. 179.
31. *Ibid.*, p. 191.
32. I. M. Barton, 'The Effects of Imperial Favour: Septimus Severus and Lepcis Magna', paper delivered at the Classical Conference, University of London (1978).
33. K. Holmboe, *Desert Encounter* (London: Harrap, 1936).
34. R. W. Hill, 'Underground Water Resources of the Jafara Plain', in S. G. Willimott and J. I. Clarke (eds), *Field Studies in Libya* (University of Durham, 1960) pp. 20–3; C. J. Cederstrom and M. Bertaiola, *Groundwater Resources of the Tripoli Area, Libya* (Tripoli, Libya: USOM Report, 1960).
35. Quoted in Ansell and al-Arif, *op. cit.*, p. 75.
36. S. Birks and C. Sinclair, 'Libya: Problems of a *Rentier* State', in R. Lawless and A. Findlay (eds), *North Africa: Contemporary Politics and Economic Development* (London: Croom Helm, 1984) p. 262.
37. Allan, *op. cit.*, p. 204.
38. *Ibid.*, p. 204.
39. 'LAR's Four Major Agricultural Projects', *Arab Dawn*, December 1974.
40. Adotey Bing, 'Harnessing Desert Waters', *Africa*, June 1985; see also *The Great Man-Made River Project*, Socialist People's Libyan Arab Jamahiriya, the Management and Implementation Authority of the Great Man-made River Project, Tripoli, Libya, 1989.

41. *Ibid.*, p. vi.
42. Bearman (1986), *op. cit.*, p. 274.
43. *The Great Man-Made River Project, op. cit.*, p. 10.
44. *Ibid.*, pp. 14–15.
45. *Ibid.*, p. 19.
46. *Ibid.*, p. 22.
47. M. El Mehdawi, 'The Industrialisation of Libya', in *Change and Development in the Middle East* (London: Methuen, 1981); also quoted in P. Barker, 'The Development of Libyan Industry', in J. A. Allan (ed), *Libya since Independence* (London: Croom Helm, 1982).
48. Pandeli Glavanis, 'State and Labour in Libya', in Lawless and Findlay (eds), *op. cit.*, (1928).
49. *The Revolution of 1st September: The Fourth Anniversary* (Benghazi: General Administration for Information, Annual Yearbook, 1973) p. 52.
50. Birks and Sinclair, *op. cit.*, p. 262.
51. *Africa Confidential* (London), 13 March 1985, pp. 3, 4; reprinted in *Joint Publications Research Service – Near East*, 15 April 1985.
52. Lillian Craig Harris, *Libya: Qadhafi's Revolution and the Modern State* (London: Croom Helm, 1986) p. 117.
53. *Libya*, Country Report, no. 3 (1990), The Economist Intelligence Unit, London.
54. *Petroleum Intelligence Weekly*, 14 May 1990.
55. *Libya*, Country Report, no. 4 (1991), The Economist Intelligence Unit, London, p. 7.
56. *Middle East Economic Survey*, 6 September 1991.
57. *Newsreport*, May/June 1991, published by the Libyan opposition in exile.
58. *Middle East Economic Survey*, 30 August 1991.
59. Libya, Country Report (1991), *op. cit.*, p. 14.
60. *Middle East Economic Survey*, 5 August 1991.
61. Davis, *op. cit.*
62. *Koran* 42:38.
63. Mahmoud Ayoub, *Islam and the Third Universal Theory* (London: Kegan Paul International, 1987) p. 35.
64. Davis, *op. cit.*, p. 20.
65. This information is largely based on Davis, *ibid.*, pp. 19–24.
66. *Ibid.*, pp. 19–24.
67. G Lenczowski, 'Popular Revolution in Libya', *Current History*, vol. 66, no. 390 (1974) pp. 57–61.
68. Davis, *op. cit.*, p. 24.
69. *Libya*, Country Report (1990), *op. cit.*, p. 11.
70. Quoted by Wilhelm Dietl, *Holy War*, trans. Martha Humphreys (New York: Macmillan, 1984).
71. Quoted by First, *op. cit.*, p. 135.
72. *Koran* 7:65ff and 41:13ff.
73. *Koran* 9:40.
74. *Koran* 10:5, 17:12 and 36:40.
75. Quoted by Ayoub, *op. cit.*, p. 68.
76. *Ibid.*, p. 71.
77. *Ibid.*, p. 72.

78. *Koran* 5:53.
79. Quoted by Ayoub, *op. cit.*, p. 77.
80. *Koran* 49:11.
81. *Koran* 9:34.
82. Quoted by Ayoub, *op. cit.*, p. 86.
83. Edward Mortimer, *Faith and Power: The Politics of Islam* (London: Faber and Faber, 1982) p. 281.
84. Bearman (1986), *op. cit.*, p. 164.
85. Davis, *op. cit.*, p. 254.
86. Quoted by Cooley, *op. cit.*, pp. 152, 153.

Notes to Chapter 7: International Ambitions

1. Quoted by David Blundy and Andrew Lycett, *Qaddafi and the Libyan Revolution* (London: Weidenfeld and Nicolson, 1987) p. 69.
2. *Ibid.*, p. 70.
3. Tabitha Petran, *Syria: A Modern History* (London: Ernest Benn, 1972) p. 238; the Tripoli Federation is described in detail (pp. 254–6).
4. *Jaysh Al-Shab* (The People's Army), 25 November 1970.
5. Mohammed Hussein Heikal, *Autumn of Fury: The Assassination of Sadat* (London: Corgi, 1984) p. 50.
6. *Ibid.*, p. 54.
7. Jonathan Bearman, *Qadhafi's Libya* (London: Zed Books, 1986) p. 102.
8. *Ibid.*, p. 103.
9. Quoted by John K. Cooley, *Libyan Sandstorm* (New York: Holt, Rinehart and Winston, 1982) p. 108. The submarine incident is described by Hasseinine Haykal, *The Road to Ramadan* (London: Collins, 1975) pp. 192–4.
10. *Al-Amal* (Tunis), 16 January 1974.
11. Conversations (cited by Cooley, *op. cit.*, p. 77) with Tunisian Prime Minister Muhhamed M'Zali and Foreign Minister Hassan Belkhodja (Tunis), 4 November 1980.
12. Lillian Craig Harris, *Libya: Qadhafi's Revolution and the Modern State* (London: Croom Helm, 1986) p. 93.
13. *Libya*, Country Report, no. 4 (1991) The Economist Intelligence Unit, London, p. 5.
14. Donald Trelford interview in Tripoli with Muammar al-Gaddafi, *The Observer* (London), 26 January 1992, p. 11.
15. Patrick Seale, *Abu Nidal: A Gun for Hire* (London: Hutchinson, 1992).
16. Report given to David Blundy and Andrew Lycett in 1986, quoted in Blundy and Lycett, *op. cit.*, pp. 150–1. This report, manifestly 'evidence supporting interest', is cited without comment.
17. *Ibid.*, p. 150.
18. *Ibid.*, p. 151.
19. *Ibid.*, p. 151.
20. Wilhelm Dietl, *Holy War*, trans. Martha Humphreys (New York: Macmillan, 1984) p. 185.
21. *Libya under Gaddafi: A Pattern of Aggression* (US State Department, January 1986).

22. *International Terrorism in 1985* (Tel Aviv University, 1986).
23. Blundy and Lycett, *op. cit.*, p. 156.
24. *Ibid.*, pp. 146–8.
25. Peter Theroux, *The Strange Disappearance of Imam Moussa Sadr* (London: Weidenfeld and Nicolson, 1987); the Libyans disclaim all responsibility for Sadr's disappearance, claiming that he took a flight out of Tripoli.
26. Richard Adloff and Virginia Thompson, *Conflict in Chad* (California: Hurst, 1981) p. 4.
27. Cooley, *op. cit.*, pp. 98–9.
28. Adloff and Thompson, *op. cit.*, p. 55.
29. Blundy and Lycett, *op. cit.*, p. 187.
30. Cooley, *op. cit.*, p. 197.
31. Philippe Rochot, *La Grand Fièvre du Monde Musulman* (Paris: Sycomore, 1981) pp. 126–7.
32. Blundy and Lycett, *op. cit.*, p. 187.
33. Bearman, *op. cit.*, p. 217.
34. Patrick Brogan, *World Conflicts* (London: Bloomsbury, 1990) p. 24.
35. *Ibid.*, pp. 24–5.
36. Richard Dowden (Africa editor), *The Independent* (London), 4 January 1992.
37. Brogan, *op. cit.*, p. 103.
38. *Ibid.*, p.107.
39. Cooley, *op. cit.*, p. 224.
40. Blundy and Lycett, *op. cit.*, p. 23. Imelda told William Deedes, then editor of *The Daily Telegraph*, that Gaddafi had given her a romantic telegram and a signed copy of the *Koran*, and asked her to become a Muslim.
41. Cooley, *op. cit.*, p. 102.
42. Blundy and Lycett, *op. cit.*, p. 79.
43. Jack Holland, *The American Connection* (New York: Viking Penguin, 1987) p. 109.
44. Blundy and Lycett, *op. cit.*, p. 80.
45. *Ibid.*, p. 81.
46. Donald Trelford interview in Tripoli with Muammar al-Gaddafi, *The Observer* (London), 26 January 1992, p. 11.
47. *Libya*, Country Report (1991), *op. cit.*, pp. 16, 17.
48. Angus Hindley, *Middle East Economic Digest*, 28 June 1991, pp. 4–5.
49. *Ibid.*, p. 4.
50. *Ibid.*, p. 5.
51. This episode is described in Blundy and Lycett, *op. cit.*, pp. 160–79.
52. *The Independent on Sunday* (London), 23 June 1991.
53. *The Guardian* (London), 11 June 1991, observed that: 'It would have been more sensible to reserve judgement – and comment – while the strength of these overtures was being tested.

Notes to Chapter 8: United States versus Gaddafi

1. Howard Zinn, *A People's History of the United States* (London: Longman, 1980) pp. 291–2.
2. *Ibid.*, p. 292.

3. J. A. Hobson, *Imperialism* (London: Unwin Hyman, 1902).
4. Zinn, *op. cit.*, pp. 297–8.
5. J. William Fulbright, *The Arrogance of Power* (London: Jonathan Cape, 1967).
6. J. William Fulbright with Seth P. Tillman, *The Price of Empire* (London: Fourth Estate, 1989).
7. Steele Commager, *The New York Times Magazine*, 12 March 1967.
8. There is a massive literature covering these events. Accessible and well documented publications include: William Blum, *The CIA: A Forgotten History* (London: Zed Books, 1986); Thomas Bodenheimer and Robert Gould, *Rollback! Right-wing Power in US Foreign Policy* (Boston: South End Press, 1989); John Weeks and Phil Gunson, *Panama, Made in the USA* (London: Latin American Bureau, 1991).
9. John K. Cooley, *Libyan Sandstorm* (New York: Holt, Rinehart and Winston, 1982) p. 26.
10. Majid Khadduri, *Modern Libya: A Study in Political Development* (Baltimore, Md: John Hopkins University Press, 1963) p. 71.
11. Nathan Miller, *The US Navy: An Illustrated History* (New York: American Heritage Publishing, US Naval Institute Press, 1977) p. 45.
12. Cooley, *op. cit.*, p. 28.
13. Carter reply to Senator Birch Bayh, Chairman, Subcommittee of the Committee on the Judiciary, an Inquiry into the Matter of Billy Carter and Libya (the *'Billy Carter Hearings'*), 4 August 1980, hearings to investigate the activities of individuals representing foreign governments, Ninety-sixth Congress, 2nd session, vol. 3, appendix, p. 1479; quoted by Cooley, *op. cit.*, p. 82.
14. *Billy Carter Hearings*, US Senate, 2 October 1980.
15. 'The Most Dangerous Man in the World', *Newsweek*, 20 July 1981.
16. Emirates News, *UPI Report*, 10 July 1981.
17. *Newsweek*, 20 July 1981.
18. Jonathan Bearman, *Qadhafi's Libya* (London: Zed Books, 1986) p. 230.
19. *Ibid.*, pp. 230–1.
20. *Jamahiriya Review*, September 1981.
21. Third World Reports, *From El Salvador to the Libyan Jamahiriya: A Radical Review of American Policy under the Reagan Administration* (London: The Main Event Ltd, 1981) p. 63.
22. Cooley, *op. cit.*, p. 269.
23. *Ibid.*, p. 269.
24. *The Times* (London), 21 February 1983.
25. *Ibid.*
26. *The Guardian* (London), 4 August 1983.
27. *The Guardian* (London), 20 March 1984; *The Guardian* (London), 21 March 1984.
28. Patrick Seale, *The Observer* (London), 13 March 1984.
29. Bearman, *op. cit.*, p. 234.
30. Cooley, *op. cit.*, p. 83.
31. *Ibid.*, p. 83.
32. *Ibid.*, p. 84.
33. One such coup attempt is described, albeit with some proper names changed, in Patrick Seale and Maureen McConville, *The Hilton Assignment* (New

York and Washington: Praeger, 1973), Cooley, *ibid.*, (pp. 86–96) profiles these events and comments that the Seale/McConville narrative 'leads almost to certainty that the CIA, working with British and Italian services, thwarted an elaborate plot to assassinate Qaddafi'.

34. The Nugan Hand Bank crops up in many accounts of espionage, subversion and drug trafficking. See, for example, Alfred W. McCoy, *The Politics of Heroin: CIA Complicity in the Global Drug Trade* (New York: Harper and Row, 1991) pp. 461–78.

35. Jonathan Kwitny, *The Crimes of Patriots* (New York: Simon and Schuster, 1987) pp. 100–1.

36. McCoy, *op. cit.*, p. 471.

37. Kwitny, *op. cit.*, pp. 89–93, 122–3, 162–4.

38. Peter Maas, *Manhunt* (New York: Random House, 1986) pp. 6–9.

39. J Marshall *et al.*, *The Iran–Contra Connection* (Boston: South-End Press, 1987) p. 194; *The New York Times*, 14 July 1981.

40. *The Washington Post*, 22 May 1986.

41. S. Butler *et al.*, *Mandate for Leadership II* (Washington, DC: The Heritage Foundation, 1984) p. 285.

42. *The Miami Herald*, 5 June 1983.

43. Noam Chomsky, 'Libya in US Demonology', *Covert Action Information Bulletin* (Summer 1986) pp. 15–24.

44. *The New York Times*, 9 July 1985.

45. *Conservation Digest*, June 1986.

46. David Blundy and Andrew Lycett, *Qaddafi and the Libyan Revolution* (London: Weidenfeld and Nicolson, 1987) p. 211.

47. *Ibid.*, p. 211.

48. Jane Mayer and Doyle McManus, *Landslide: The Unmaking of the President, 1984–1988* (London: Fontana, 1989) p. 405.

49. *Ibid.*, p. 406.

50. Donald T Regan, *For the Record* (London: Hutchinson, 1988) p. 29.

51. Bob Woodward, *Veil: The Secret Wars of the CIA, 1981–1987* (London: Simon and Schuster, 1987).

52. Much of this is based on the account in Woodward, *ibid.*

53. Quoted in Woodward, *ibid.*, p.158.

54. Woodward, *ibid.*, p. 166, cites a secret memorandum of 17 August 1981 headed 'Libya: Covert Airline Operation'.

55. *Ibid.*, p. 166

56. *Ibid.*, p. 182.

57. Cooley, *op. cit.*, p. 269.

58. Woodward, *op. cit.*, p. 184.

59. *Ibid.*, pp. 184–5.

60. Quoted by Woodward, *ibid.*, p. 185.

61. *Ibid.*, p. 186.

62. *Ibid.*, p. 409.

63. *Ibid.*, p. 412.

64. Quoted by Ben Lowe, 'Libya and NATO's Out-of-Area Role', in *Mad Dogs: The US Raids on Libya* (London: Pluto Press, 1986) p. 87.

65. Lou Cannon and Bob Woodward, 'Raid Called Outcome of Long Debate', *International Herald Tribune*, 17 April 1986.

66. Marcelino Komba, 'Precarious Initiatives', *Africa: The International Business, Economic and Political Magazine* (June 1985), pp. 28–9.
67. Bearman, *op. cit.*, p. 291.
68. Bob Woodward, 'Cables Point to Gadaffi Link', *The Guardian* (London), 23 April 1986.
69. Mayer and McManus, *op. cit.*, p. 325.
70. *Ibid.*, p. 325.
71. Robert Fisk, *The Times* (London), 15–17 April 1986.
72. Fisk, *op. cit.*, 15 April 1986.
73. Bearman, *op. cit.*, p. 288.
74. George Wilson, 'Colonel "was the target"', *The Guardian* (London), 19 April 1986.
75. *Ibid.*
76. Christopher Thomas, 'Shultz Hoping for a Military Coup', *The Times* (London), 19 April 1986.
77. *The New York Times*, 11 January 1986.
78. Hugo Young, *One of Us* (London: Pan Books, 1990) p. 476.
79. *Hansard*, 15 April 1986.
80. He records these episodes in *Thatcher: Patterns of Deceit* (London: Cecil Woolf), 1986); and *Misrule* (London: New English Library, 1987).
81. Dalyell (1987), *ibid.*, pp. 105–27.
82. William Broyles Jr, 'The Politics of War', *US News and World Report*, 12 May 1986.
83. *Aviation Week*, 21 April 1986.
84. *Sanity*, April 1986.
85. Bob Woodward, *The Guardian* (London), 23 April 1986.
86. Quoted by Bearman, *op. cit.*, p. 295.
87. Bob Woodward, *The Guardian* (London), 23 April 1986.
88. Bearman, *op. cit.*, p. 295.
89. Reproduced in Dalyell (1987), *op. cit.*, pp. 113–18.
90. Michael Gordon, *The New York Times*, 31 January 1990.
91. Noam Chomsky, *Necessary Illusions: Thought Control in Democratic Societies* (London: Pluto Press, 1989) p. 272.
92. *Ibid.*, p. 272.
93. *Ibid.*, p. 273.
94. Regan, *op. cit.*, p. 329.
95. Mayer and McManus, *op. cit.*, p. 357.
96. Sheena Phillips, 'The European Response', in *Mad Dogs*, *op. cit.*, p. 41.
97. *Ibid.*, p. 43.
98. Woodward (1987), *op. cit.*, p. 471.
99. *Ibid.*, p. 472.
100. *Ibid.*, p. 474.
101. *Ibid.*, p. 475.

Bibliography

Adloff, Richard and Thompson, Virginia, *Conflict in Chad* (California: Hurst, 1981).

Allan, J. A., *Libya: The Experience of Oil* (London: Croom Helm, 1981).

Ambrose, Stephen E., *Rise to Globalism* (Harmondsworth: Penguin, 1988).

Anderson, Ewan W. and Rashidian, Khalil H., *Iraq and the Continuing Middle East Crisis* (London: Pinter, 1991).

Anderson, Lisa, 'Qaddafi's Islam', in *Voices of Resurgent Islam*, ed. John L. Esposito (London: Oxford University Press, 1983).

Askew, William, *Europe and Italy's Acquisition of Libya, 1911–1912* (Durham, N.C.: Duke University Press, 1942).

Ayoub, Mahmoud, *Islam and the Third Universal Theory: The Religious Thought of Mu'ammar al Qadhdhafi* (London: Kegan Paul, 1987).

Bearman, Jonathan, *Qadhafi's Libya* (London: Zed Books, 1986).

Bennett, Ernest N., *With the Turks in Tripoli* (London: Methuen, 1912).

Berque, Jacques, *The Arabs* (London: Faber and Faber, 1964).

Berque, Jacques, *French North Africa: The Maghreb between Two World Worlds* (London: Faber and Faber, 1967).

Birks, S. and Sinclair, C., *Arab Manpower: The Crisis of Development* (London: Croom Helm, 1980).

Blum, William, *The CIA: A Forgotten History* (London: Zed Books, 1986).

Blundy, David and Lycett, Andrew, *Qaddafi and the Libyan Revolution* (London: Weidenfeld and Nicolson, 1987).

Bodenheimer, Thomas and Gould, Robert, *Rollback! Right-wing Power in US Foreign Policy* (Boston: South-End Press, 1989).

Bresheeth, Haim and Yuval-Davis, Nira (eds), *The Gulf War and the New World Order* (London: Zed Books, 1991).

Briggs, Lloyd Cabot, *Tribes of the Sahara* (Cambridge, Mass.: Harvard University Press, 1960).

Brittain, Victoria (ed), *The Gulf between Us: The Gulf War and Beyond* (London: Virago, 1991).

Brogan, Patrick, *World Conflicts* (London: Bloomsbury, 1989).

Bromley, Simon, *American Hegemony and World Oil: The Industry, the State System and the World Economy* (Cambridge: Polity Press, 1991).

Bulloch, John, and Morris, Harvey, *Saddam's War: The Origins of the Kuwait Crisis and the International Response* (London: Faber and Faber, 1991).

Cachia, Anthony J., *Libya under the Second Ottoman Occupation (1835–1911)* (Tripoli: Government Press, 1945).

Carrington, Richard, *East from Tunis: A Record of Travels on the Northern Coast of Africa* (London: Chatto and Windus, 1957).

Chomsky, Noam, *Necessary Illusions: Thought Control in Democratic Societies* (London: Pluto Press, 1989).

Chomsky, Noam, *Deterring Democracy* (London: Verso, 1991).

Cooley, John K., *Baal, Christ and Mohammed: Religion and Revolution in North Africa* (New York: Holt, Rinehart and Winston, 1965).

Cooley, John K., *Libyan Sandstorm* (New York: Holt, Rinehart and Winston, 1982).

Corm, Georges, *Fragmentation of the Middle East* (London: Hutchinson, 1988).

Dalyell, Tam, *Thatcher: Patterns of Deceit* (London: Cecil Woolf, 1986).

Dalyell, Tam, *Misrule* (London: New English Library, 1987).

Daniels, Charles, *The Garamantes of Southern Libya* (Harrow, England: Oleander Press, 1970).

Darwish, Adel and Alexander, Gregory, *Unholy Babylon: The Secret History of Saddam's War* (London: Victor Gollancz, 1991).

Davis, Brian, *Qaddafi, Terrorism and the Origins of the US Attack on Libya* (New York: Praeger, 1990).

Davis, John, *Libyan Politics, Tribe and Revolution* (London: I. B. Tauris, 1987).

Deeb, Marius K. and Deeb, Mary-Jane, *Libya since the Revolution: Aspects of Social and Political Development* (New York: Praeger, 1982).

Denti di Pirajno, Alberto, *A Cure for Serpents: A Doctor in Africa* (London: André Deutsch, 1955).

Dietl, Wilhelm, *Holy War*, trans. Martha Humphreys (New York: Macmillan, 1984).

Evans-Pritchard, E. E., *The Sanusi of Cyrenaica* (Oxford: Oxford University Press, 1949).

Eveland, Wilbur, *Ropes of Sand: America's Failure in the Middle East* (New York: Norton, 1980).

Falk, Richard A. (ed.), *The Vietnam War and International Law* (Princeton, N.J.: Princeton University Press, 1968).

al-Falhali, Omar and Palmer, Monte, *Political Development and Social Change in Libya* (Washington D.C.: Lexington Books, 1981).

el-Fathaly, Omar, Palmer, Monte and Chackerian, Richard, *Political Development and Bureaucracy in Libya* (Lexington, Mass: D. C. Heath, 1980).

Fergiani, Mohammed B. (compiler), *The Libyan Jamahiriya* (London: Darf Publishers, 1983).

First, Ruth, *Libya: The Elusive Revolution* (New York: Africa Publishing Co., 1975).

Furlonge, Geoffrey, *The Lands of Barbary* (London: John Murray, 1966).

Glubb, John Bagot, *A Short History of the Arab Peoples* (London: Quartet, 1978).

Gunther, John, *Inside Africa* (London: Hamish Hamilton, 1955).

Habib, Henri, *Politics and Government of Revolutionary Libya* (Montreal: Le Cercle du Livre de France, 1975).

Hajjaji, S. A., *The New Libya* (Tripoli, 1967).

Haley, Edward P., *Qaddafi and the US since 1969* (New York: Praeger, 1984).

Hammer, Armand with Lyndon, Neil, *Hammer, Witness to History* (London: Coronel, Hodder and Stoughton, 1987).

Harris, Lillian Craig, *Libya, Qadhafi's Revolution and the Modern State* (London: Croom Helm, 1986).

Haykal, Muhammed Hasseinine, *The Road to Ramadan* (London: Collins, 1975).

Haykal, Muhammed Hasseinine, *Autumn of Fury: The Assassination of Sadat* (London: Corgi, 1984).

Herodotus, *The Histories*, trans. Aubrey de Sélincourt (Harmondsworth: Penguin, 1954).

Hinnebusch, Raymond A., 'Libya: Personalistic Leadership of a Populist Revolution', in *Political Elites in Arab North Africa: Morocco, Algeria, Tunisia, Libya and Egypt*, ed. I William Zartman *et al.*, (New York: Longman, 1982).

Hiro, Dilip, *Islamic Fundamentalism* (London: Paladin, 1988).

Hiro, Dilip, *The Longest War: The Iran–Iraq Military Conflict* (London: Paladin, 1990).

Hiro, Dilip, *Desert Shield to Desert Storm: The Second Gulf War* (London: Paladin, 1992).

Hollis, Christopher, *Italy in Africa* (London: Hamish Hamilton, 1941).

Holmboe, Knud, *Desert Encounter: An Adventurous Journey through Italian Africa* (London: Harrap, 1936).

Howe, Russell Warren, *Weapons* (London: Abacus, 1981).

Joffe, E. G. H. and McLachlan, K. S. (eds), *Social and Economic Development of Libya* (Cambridgeshire, England: North Africa Studies Press, 1982).

Kaldor, Mary and Anderson, Paul (eds), *Mad Dogs: The US Raids on Libya* (London: Pluto Press, 1986).

Khadduri, Majid, *Modern Libya: A Study in Political Development* (Baltimore, Md: John Hopkins University Press, 1963).

Kubbah, Abdul, *Libya, its Oil Industry and Economic System* (Baghdad: Arab Petro-Economic Research Centre, 1964).

Lawless, Richard and Findlay, Allan, *North Africa: Contemporary Politics and Economic Development* (London: Croom Helm, 1984).

Leppard, David, *On the Trail of Terror* (London: Jonathan Cape, 1991).

Mansfield, Peter, *Nasser's Egypt* (Harmondsworth: Penguin, 1965).

Ma'oz, Moshe, *Assad: The Sphinx of Damascus* (London: Weidenfeld and Nicolson, 1988).

Mayer, Jane and McManus, Doyle, *Landslide: The Unmaking of President Reagan* (London: Fontana, 1989).

McCoy, Alfred W., *The Politics of Heroin: CIA Complicity in the Global Drug Trade* (New York: Lawrence Hill Books, 1991).

McDermott, Anthony, *Egypt from Nasser to Mubarak: A Flawed Revolution* (London: Croom Helm, 1988).

Miller, Nathan, *The US Navy: An Illustrated History* (Annapolis: American Heritage Publishing, US Naval Institute Press, 1977).

Moore, Martin, *Fourth Shore: Italy's Mass Colonisation of Libya* (London: Routledge, 1940).

Odell, Peter R., *Oil and World Power: Background to the Oil Crisis* (Harmondsworth, Penguin, 1970).

Owen, Roger, *Libya: A Brief Political and Economic Survey* (London: Chatham House, 1961).

Parker, Richard, *North Africa: Regional Tensions and Strategic Concerns* (New York: Praeger, 1984).

Pelt, Adrian, *Libyan Independence and the United Nations: A Case of Planned Decolonisation* (New Haven: Yale University Press, Carnegie Endowment for International Peace, 1970).

Porath, Yehoshua, *In Search of Arab Unity, 1930–1945* (London: Cass, 1986).

Rand, Christopher, *Making Democracy Safe for Oil: Oilmen and the Islamic East* (Boston, Mass.: Little, Brown, 1975).

Regan, Donald T., *For the Record: From Wall Street to Washington* (London: Hutchinson, 1988).

Ridgeway, James (ed), *The March to War* (New York: Four Walls, Eight Windows, 1991).

Rodinson, Maxime, *Israel and the Arabs* (Harmondsworth: Penguin, 1968).

al-Sadat, Anwar, *In Search of Identity: An Autobiography* (New York: Harper and Row, 1977).

Salinger, Pierre with Laurent, Eric, *Secret Dossier: The Hidden Agenda behind the Gulf War* (Harmondsworth: Penguin, 1991).

Sampson, Anthony, *The Arms Bazaar* (London: Coronel, Hodder and Stoughton, 1977).

Sampson, Anthony, *The Seven Sisters: The Great Oil Companies and the World They Made* (London: Hodder and Stoughton, 1975).

Santarelli, Enzo; Rochat, Giorgio; Rainero, Romain and Goglia, Luigi, *Omar al-Mukhtar: The Italian Reconquest of Libya* (London: Darf Publishers, 1986).

Sanders, J. J., *A History of Medieval Islam* (London: Routledge and Kegan Paul, 1965).

Seale, Patrick and McConville, Maureen, *The Hilton Assignment* (New York: Praeger, 1973).

Seale, Patrick, Abu Nidal, *A Gun for Hire*, London: Hutchinson, 1992.

Segal, Ronald (ed.), *African Profiles* (Harmondsworth: Penguin, 1962).

Sifry, Micah L. and Carf, Christopher (eds), *The Gulf War: History, Documents, Opinions* (New York: Random House, 1991).

Soames, Jane, *The Coast of Barbary* (London: Jonathan Cape, 1938).

Sterling, Claire, *The Terror Network: The Secret War of International Terrorism* (New York: Holt, Rinehart and Winston, 1981).

Stookey, Robert W., *America and the Arab States: An Uneasy Encounter* (London: John Wiley, 1975).

Taheri, Amir, *The Cauldron: The Middle East behind the Headlines* (London: Hutchinson, 1988).

Theroux, Peter, *The Strange Disappearance of Imam Moussa Sadr* (London: Weidenfeld and Nicolson, 1987).

Tibi, Bassam, *Arab Nationalism* (London: Macmillan, 1981).

Tugendhat, Christopher, *Oil: The Biggest Business* (London: Eyre and Spottiswoode, 1968).

Villard, Henry Serrano, *Libya: The New Arab Kingdom of North Africa* (New York: Cornell University Press, 1954).

Waddams, Frank C., *The Libyan Oil Industry* (Baltimore: John Hopkins University Press, 1980).

Woodward, Bob, *Veil: The Secret Wars of the CIA, 1981–1987* (London: Simon and Schuster, 1987).

Woodward, Bob, *The Commanders* (London: Simon and Schuster, 1991).

Wright, John, *Libya* (London: Ernest Benn, 1969).

Wright, John, *Libya: A Modern History* (Baltimore: John Hopkins University Press, 1982).

Yergin, Daniel, *Prize: The Epic Quest for Oil, Money and Power* (London: Simon and Schuster, 1991).

Young, Hugo, *One of Us* (London: Pan, 1990).

Ziadeh, Nicola A., *Sanusiyah: A Study of a Revivalist Movement in Islam* (Leiden: E. J. Brill, 1958).

Zinn, Howard, *A People's History of the United States* (London: Longman, 1980).

Index